ST MARTIN'S
TRUE CRIME
CLASSICS

Acclaim for Gary M. Lavergne's *BAD BOY* . . .

"Texas still feels the pain inflicted by Kenneth Allen McDuff, despite the relentless efforts of law enforcement officials to solve his crimes and bind up its wounds. *BAD BOY* . . . is an impeccably researched, compellingly detailed account of the crimes and the long search for justice. Gary Lavergne takes us directly to the scenes of the crimes, deep inside the mind of a killer, and in the process learns not only whom McDuff killed and how—but why."   —Dan Rather, CBS News

"Gary Lavergne succeeds in giving us an inside look at one of the most savage killers in our history, and at the same time exposes the failure of our criminal justice system."
          —Gary Cartwright, Senior Editor, *Texas Monthly*

"Gary Lavergne's portrait of unalloyed evil—and of the criminal justice system's failure to protect us from it—is a sobering reminder of any free society's vulnerability to the bad seeds scattered amongst the good. A fine, dismaying work."   —Robert Draper, Writer-at-Large, *GQ* magazine

"Gary Lavergne provides a fascinating account of McDuff's killing sprees and how a dysfunctional criminal justice system released him to kill again. Anyone who questions the wisdom of the death penalty or why we need tough criminal laws, needs only to read this book."
          —Ken Anderson, author of *Crime in Texas*

"Part Ted Bundy, part legendary small-town ogre Ken Rex McElroy. Lavergne's descriptions of McDuff, his crimes, and the trouble the minions of justice had in putting him away are the stuff of a book in which many a chapter ends with a cliff-hanger that impels the reader into the next. McDuff's monumentally cruel, breathtakingly brutal antics may make even the most hardened true-crime fans sweat. A must for aficionados of the grisly and a thrill ride to hell for more casual crime fans."   —*Booklist*

BAD BOY

The Murderous Life of Kenneth Allen McDuff

(published in hardcover as *Bad Boy from Rosebud*)

GARY M. LAVERGNE

St. Martin's Paperbacks

Bad Boy was published in hardcover under the title *Bad Boy from Rosebud*.

Published by arrangement with University of North Texas Press.

BAD BOY

Copyright © 1999 by Gary M. Lavergne.

Cover photograph courtesy of Texas Department of Criminal Justice.

Library of Congress Catalog Number: 99-22050
ISBN: 0-312-98125-2
EAN: 9780312-98125-9

Printed in the United States of America

St. Martin's Paperbacks edition/November 2001

10 9 8 7 6 5 4 3

For Charlie, Mark, Amy, and Anna

Contents

Contents

Author's Notes and Acknowledgments

Because of the utterly bizarre stories and characters in this book, I am concerned that some episodes will be misread as insensitive or irreverent attempts at dark humor. With the exception of occasional playful banter between police officers, this book is *incredible*—not funny.

I firmly believe in the necessity of historians keeping their personal passion out of their writing, but that was very difficult to do with this book. I cannot imagine how anyone could report this story and not be outraged. For me, this was an intensely powerful personal journey, but my documentation is exhaustive, and it speaks for itself. I also freely admit to having a great admiration for the remarkable men and women who brought McDuff to justice.

This is a work of non-fiction; all of the characters are/were real people and all of the episodes are documented through interviews, official records, sworn statements, or eyewitness testimony. I have tried to make clear those few instances where I have drawn conclusions or made assumptions.

Some of Kenneth Allen McDuff's victims were prostitutes who lived tragic lives in a degraded subculture. Because some of them have surviving family members, I agonized over how to strike a balance between sensitivity and brutal honesty about the destructive power of prostitution and drugs. I made up my mind after watching the television network premiere of the movie *Pretty Woman.* I could not help but wonder how many young girls throughout America were left with the impression, even for a moment, that whores look like Julia Roberts, are picked up by handsome Richard Geres in $200,000 cars, and taken to five-star hotels for a week of champagne and strawberries, spending sprees, opera, and polo matches. The truth is that there is no such thing as "safe sex" for prostitutes. Prostitution is a tool for those who hate, not love, women. It makes beautiful women ugly—and it kills them. *In my treatment of this tragic topic, I want to make clear that this book does not suggest that these women deserved the treatment inflicted on them by Kenneth McDuff.* I sincerely ask for the understanding of those who may be hurt by uncomfortable truths, but I am determined this book will not add to the dangerous notion that drugs and prostitution are safe—much less glamorous.

In producing *Bad Boy*, I collected many thousands of pages of official and unofficial documents. Quite often, I was allowed to view reports that are not yet public record. On other occasions, during interviews, sources gave me information on the condition that they not be identified. Since this is an account of relatively recent crimes, and since most of the major characters are still alive, I accepted those conditions. Information from confidential documents will hereafter be cited as "Confidential Document." Confidential information secured through an interview will be hereafter cited as "Confidential Source."

In some instances I used only first names, slightly-altered first names, or nicknames of some individuals who deserve privacy or a chance to reform themselves. In the footnotes, these names are bracketed.

Finally, social graces do not always accompany history. The world of Kenneth Allen McDuff can neither be described nor understood without the profoundly disturbing use of its "native language" and graphic descriptions of its inhabitants and what they do.

It must be difficult living with someone writing a book about a monstrous serial killer. And yet, my wife and soul mate, Laura, patiently allowed me to work on this very large project for over a year, sapping nearly all of our vacation days, weekends, and spare time. On those few occasions when we went out, friends inevitably asked us about McDuff. She could have reasonably put an end to such an immense distraction to our lives. Instead, when she could, she helped. She is an expert writer and editor, who helped to craft a first-rate book. (At least those parts she could bear to read.)

Our two sons, Charlie and Mark, accompanied me on trips to trailer parks, long drives from Austin through the Blackland Prairie, and hikes through woods and across the infamous abandoned road in Bell County. They helped me with pictures and notes. Our two daughters, Amy and Anna, saved me a great deal of time by locating rolls of microfilm in libraries and carrying them to my study desk. All four of them are neat people to be around. In my home I am surrounded by beauty; they are what is beautiful about Central Texas.

My very good friend and colleague, Scott Kampmeier, a master history teacher and a gifted writer, read every chapter as I wrote it, asked very good questions, and provided valuable suggestions on how to improve the manuscript. Other colleagues, Martha Salmon and Frances Brown, on their own time looked over portions of this work with the eyes of experienced English teachers. I am very lucky to be surrounded by such talent on a daily basis at my real job.

I am truly indebted to each of the persons I interviewed (listed in Notes on Sources). Beyond sacrificing their valuable time for an interview, some of them helped me secure other forms of information. My very good friend J. W. Thompson of the Austin Police Department, who would rather not see his name in print—anywhere—patiently accepted my frequent calls to his office and home. His dear wife Julie graciously endured my year-long disruption of their lives. Our mutual friend, Charles Meyer, has an astonishing eye for detail and a first-rate memory.

Travis County Assistant District Attorney Buddy Meyer helped to expedite my securing the statement of facts of the Reed Trial at a time when he was a lead prosecutor of some of the most high-profile crimes in Travis County. In Bell County, Tim Steglich took the time to show me the area where McDuff hung around. Tim would have made a great teacher; he taught me a lot about the subculture I have written so much about.

It was a joy to meet and become friends with Charles Butts of San Antonio. Charlie read each chapter and provided written, very insightful suggestions and observations. I shamelessly exploited his brilliant legal mind. Crawford Long and Mike Freeman of the McLennan County District Attorney's Office met with me on a Saturday for a lengthy interview. They also lent me their copy of the statement of facts of the Northrup Trial. Crawford also kept me informed throughout the course of McDuff's appeals process.

On June 15, 1998, I had a telephone conversation with Chief John Butler of the United States Marshal's Service office in San Antonio. After explaining my project to him, he assured me that the Marshal's Service would cooperate with me in any way. They could not have been more generous. Chief Butler made my interview with Mike and Parnell McNamara possible. Additionally, on their own time, Mike and Parnell, along with Bill Johnston, took me to many of the locations described in this book—places I could never have found and would never have ventured into alone. If this book has imagery and power, it is due in large part to my good friends: The Boys from Waco.

Texas Department of Criminal Justice Investigator John Moriarty has a vast knowledge of ex-cons like Kenneth McDuff. His observations were very valuable.

That I am an author would never have happened had it not been for the courage of Frances Vick, the Director of the University of North Texas Press. All writing successes I enjoy come from her sponsorship. Charlotte Wright, the Associate Director and Editorial Manager of UNT Press, crafts outstanding literature—even books about murders. It was easier for me to work on this manuscript through many sleepless nights knowing that a truly artistic book would result.

My friend, Robert Draper, a writer at large for *GQ* magazine, could not have been more helpful and generous in helping me refine a book of which I am very proud. And this was the second time he has helped me make a manuscript better. I am also indebted to Gary Cartwright of *Texas Monthly*, for the time he took looking over portions of this book, and for his words of advice. Jim Hornfischer of the Literary Group International, my agent, has endured my impatience through two books now.

Last, but certainly not least, I wish to thank Brenda and Richard Solomon, Lori Bible, and Jack Brand. They are the survivors. They are the ones with courage. My interviews with them included painful, and at times tearful recollections. All Robert Brand did was go out on a date with a good and decent girlfriend; all Melissa Northrup did was go to work; and all Colleen Reed did was wash her car. Kenneth McDuff devastated their families, and yet, these remarkable people greeted me with kindness and respect. I am a better person for having met them.

No doubt there are others. For those whose names I forgot, be assured it was due to a fatigued mind, and not my heart.

Gary M. Lavergne
Cedar Park, Texas

Prologue

ROSEBUD

"He was the bad boy from Rosebud—always has been."
—Ellen Roberts, Former Justice of the Peace, Falls County

The rolling hills of central Texas cradle a hamlet called Rosebud. It lies in the Blackland Prairie. With the luck of ample rain, the dark, rich soil supports a diversity of crops. But the land can be unforgiving as well. During periods of drought the waves of brown grain, chest-high dead cornstalks, or emaciated cotton plants prove that nature rules and serve as witnesses to the death that can overshadow the otherwise lush and living countryside.

The inhabitants of the Blackland Prairie are as diverse as their homes. Sprawling ranch-style houses exist alongside crumbling trailers—some with elaborate steps, porches, and roofs that cost as much as the trailers. In some cases, almost within arm's length, expensive satellite dishes bring the world, good and bad, to televisions in small living rooms with rotted particle-board floors.

Once, the hamlets of the Blackland Prairie catered to small family-owned farms. Today, the hamlets evidence the merger of those farms into fewer, larger, self-sufficient agricultural giants. Numerous old, dried-out, useless barns and sheds lean dangerously, ghosts of a simpler and perhaps better time.

When those barns and sheds stood erect during the post–World War II agricultural boom, Rosebud's Main Street bustled with business activity. A sign greeted visitors entering the small town: "Rosebud—We call it home." It betrays a simple lifestyle. According to a local brochure, visitors on their way into town drove by stately "homes that made Rosebud beautiful." The Tarver Home, the Nich-

olson Home on South First Street, the palatial "Rosebud
Castle," the Reichert House on Second Street and several
others nestled in quiet neighborhoods among mature, mag-
nificent trees.[1] Rosebud was "a town of good people working together for the betterment of their community" extolled
the Chamber of Commerce. In an effort to encourage residents to plant a rose bush in every yard, the *Rosebud News*,
and later the Chamber of Commerce, gave away cuttings
to anyone who did not have a bush. "The City of Rosebud
has a lot to be proud of, but Rosebud is not remembered
instantly for its excellent hospital, rest home, businesses,
library, schools and friendly people. The name and the reputation for having a rose bush in every yard is its main
claim to fame." On the other hand, lore said there was also
a saloon on every street, and as a result, women never went
into town on Saturdays.[2] On Sundays everyone went to
church and some worshippers, like those attending services
at the Rosebud Church of Christ, were greeted by signs
offering homespun wisdom: "Don't pray for rain if you
plan on complaining about the mud."

Rosebud, now a bedroom community populated by
workers commuting to Temple, Marlin, and Waco, is one
of the few remaining places where markets close on Saturdays. Empty, dusty store fronts line Main Street.

The first indication to travelers that they are near Rosebud is a huge gleaming water storage tank, large enough to
meet the needs of a far larger city. The water system and
tank—with "Rosebud" painted on the north side above a
huge stemmed red rose—and the accompanying sewer system, are a result of the tenacity of Ms. Wanda Fischer, who
lives in the Reichert House, one of the homes that made
Rosebud beautiful. After serving on the City Council and
then as City Manager for ten years, Ms. Fischer retired from
public service in May 1996. She has lived in Rosebud most
of her life.

One of Ms. Fischer's friends said that "every little town
needs a benevolent despot." And Rosebud had Ms. Fischer.
Residents were known to knock on her doors or windows

at all hours of the night with their problems—ranging from
serious city-related issues to family arguments only Ms.
Fischer could mediate. She is a graceful and dignified
woman who remembers an earlier Rosebud. She watched
sadly as some of the "homes that made Rosebud beautiful"
were torn down and the Blackland Prairie farms grew larger
and fewer while Main Street grew quieter—and more store-
fronts covered polished glass with ugly knotted plywood.

Ms. Fischer is the symbol of a nice little town populated
by decent people. But her eyes narrow at the mention of
Rosebud's most infamous son: Kenneth Allen McDuff. "He
was just a vicious killer," she said venomously.[3]

To many Rosebud oldtimers, the name Kenneth Allen
McDuff brings to mind a rowdy, downright mean, bully on
a loud motorcycle. He liked to fight and he liked to scare
the small and the weak. Sometimes he hurt people, but the
only time he ever fought someone with a reasonable chance
of fighting back, he got kicked around a ravine traversed
by a bridge where school children crowded in order to relish the long-overdue administration of "justice for Mc-
Duff." But the name McDuff conjures up more than just a
school yard fight between two ninth graders. People remember the horror of the 1966 "Broomstick Murders" of
three teenagers for which McDuff was arrested, tried, convicted, and sentenced to death by electrocution.

"Only a few people from Rosebud ever went to prison,
and one of them was for stealing two turkeys," lamented
the former editor of the *Rosebud News*.[4]

"He was the bad boy of Rosebud—always has been,"
confessed Ms. Ellen Roberts, a former Justice of the Peace
and one of Kenneth's teachers. She remembers him coming
from a hard-working family headed by a stern mother and
a father who worked so much it seemed that was all he did.
Other neighbors said that the McDuffs were hard to figure.
They were not overly loud and obnoxious—but they were
not warm people either.[5]

In October of 1989, in a twist of history that many in
Rosebud, indeed, in all of Texas and throughout the nation,

still cannot believe, the State of Texas set Kenneth Allen McDuff, the Broomstick Murderer, free. It was not just some incredible ruling by an activist bleeding-heart judge. No trial error dismissed his case. No suspicious California or New York conspiracy set him free. He was *paroled*—by Texans!

All of a sudden the fear returned. "A lot of people around here are scared, and they have a right to be," said Texas State Trooper Richard Starnes. Rumors ravaged an already tremulous little town. In nearby McLennan County, Detective Richard Stroup reported that his office had been getting calls from housewives afraid to leave their kids by themselves during broad daylight. Schools took precautions, and bus drivers were warned by school administrators to be alert for the bad boy from Rosebud. The very sad irony was that, thirty years after he had dropped out of school, Kenneth McDuff was still scaring school children and giving principals trouble. Rosebud, and the world, would soon discover that he had never grown up; he had only gotten frightfully larger and much more dangerous.[6]

Kenneth Allen McDuff eventually became the architect of an extraordinarily intolerant atmosphere in Texas. He helped bring about the restructuring of the third largest criminal justice system in the United States. The first sentence of Ken Anderson's excellent book, *Crime in Texas: Your Complete Guide to the Criminal Justice System*, consists of two words: "Kenneth McDuff" followed by, "More than any other person, McDuff has come to represent everything that was wrong with the Texas criminal justice system. He convinced everyone—citizens, politicians, the news media—just how broken the Texas system was."[7]

Indeed, McDuff managed to forge a coalition—one that could never have been formed under a normal political discourse—to do one thing: build prisons. In the May 1996 issue of *Texas Monthly*, Robert Draper described "the biggest prison system ever concocted by any free society in history." Draper's article, which does not mention McDuff, clearly shows that the great Texas buildup had its roots even before the McDuff story hit the stands. Federal law-suits involving prison overcrowding and media coverage of gang violence put Texas on the path of a building binge. From 1990 to 1995 the Texas Department of Criminal Justice's budget more than tripled (from $700 million to $2.2 billion). By 1996 the prison system had more than 146,000 beds. In a two-year period (1994–1996) the number of units (prisons) went from 65 to 102, and the number of inmates grew from 72,000 to 129,000.[8] But the bulk of the funding, a huge new Texas Department of Criminal Justice budget and a billion-dollar bond issue passed in 1993 which made possible such a penal explosion, resulted in part from emotion-ridden "debates" laden with references to McDuff. At the very least, Kenneth McDuff validated an urge for a prison buildup. Today, only Russia and China (and possibly California, depending on how you measure) have larger prison systems than Texas.

The spasm of prison construction and parole reforms collectively called the "McDuff Rules," resulted from an enormous display of anger vented towards a system that had broken down. "This guy beat the system," said Austin Police Department Detective Sonya Urubek. "If I have to spend every day at the Capitol, if I have to scream, [I'll do] whatever I have to do," promised Lori Bible, the sister of one of McDuff's victims.[9] They were typical comments in a flood of outrage. It turns out that from 1965 to 1992, McDuff had been arrested for burglary, sent to prison, paroled, arrested for three brutal murders while on parole, sent back to prison and placed on death row, taken off death row, convicted of a felony while in prison, paroled, arrested for making terroristic threats while on parole, sent back to prison, paroled again, arrested for driving while intoxicated while on parole, put in jail, released from jail, placed on probation, arrested for public intoxication while on parole and probation, arrested for murder while on parole and probation again, and finally, put back on death row. Texans will no longer take such chances.

The case of Karla Faye Tucker removed all doubt about

Texans' commitment to capital punishment. She was a born-again Christian whom few doubted had truly rehabilitated herself, but she was executed by lethal injection in February, 1998. Texas state officials received thousands of appeals for clemency, including those from the Pope, Jerry Falwell, Pat Robertson, Amnesty International, and the United Nations. Significantly, even after such an outpouring of support, she would not receive a single favorable vote from the eighteen-member Board of Pardons and Paroles. Governor George W. Bush, hardly a rabid advocate of capital punishment, refused to intervene. Tucker's execution re-ignited the debate for a few days, but it did virtually nothing to move the state away from its historic commitment or its new-found allegiance to the death penalty. Some even took perverse comfort in knowing justice is indeed "blind" in Texas. A capital murderer will be executed, even if she is a good-looking, white, Christian woman. David Botsford, Tucker's lawyer, would lament after her execution that "Texas has no mercy."[10] When it comes to capital murder, he is absolutely right—the result of the long-term effect of historical support for capital punishment by Texans compounded by the short-term effect of Kenneth Allen McDuff. For many, McDuff removed the doubts and discomforts good and thoughtful people have of supporting the death penalty, even in a case like that of Karla Faye Tucker. Indeed, he has become the poster boy of capital punishment.

How did he gain such notoriety? Because in *his* case, the advocates of the death penalty are right: Had Kenneth McDuff been executed after the Broomstick Murders of 1966, the young women he murdered from 1989 to 1992 would be alive today. McDuff tragically illustrated that even a death sentence is not a certainty. As long as pardons and clemency exist, and as long as there is a possibility that one day the Supreme Court can rule that capital punishment, whether *de facto* or in its application, is cruel and unusual, there is no such thing as a guaranteed execution, much less a true "life without parole" sentence.

McDuff managed to outrage more than just the kooks who party in Huntsville during executions. The massive Texas prison buildup came about during the administration of liberal Democratic Governor Ann Richards, who readily admitted that she would much rather have spent such a vast sum of money on other things. Her career championing liberal causes took a back seat to what "had to be done." Conservative Republicans did an about face as well; at a time when their doctrine was to reduce spending and the size of government, they encouraged and supported one of the largest expansions of state government in the history of the United States, as well as its necessary revenue enhancements. Only Kenneth McDuff could inspire ultra-conservatives to see big government as a solution. It had to be done—such was the effect of the bad boy from Rosebud.

Investigators in dozens of law enforcement jurisdictions, hardened by years of dealing with brutality of all types and the evil they see, were aghast at what they learned about McDuff. A descendant of a legendary law enforcement family, United States Marshal Mike Earp, said that McDuff was "basically an animal who had to be taken off the streets."

"A sadistic bastard is what he is," said McLennan County Deputy Richard Stroup, as he straightened his stance and gritted his teeth.

Fred Labowitz, a renowned Dallas psychologist, summed up the mystery and the frustration, and our unsettling helplessness: "This guy goes beyond the study of human behavior." No matter how much we contemplate the Ted Bundys and Charles Mansons of the world, "none of this can prepare us for an encounter with Kenneth McDuff."[11]

Other mass murderers have caught our attention. Charles Manson exposed a fascination we have with the bizarre, but he had virtually no effect on our behavior or our laws. Ted Bundy, John Wayne Gacy, Henry Lee Lucas, and Jeffrey Dahmer horrified us with what they did. But in those cases we were caught by surprise—we could not have predicted that they would do what they did.

Kenneth McDuff set himself apart from the others. What he did from 1989 to 1992 was utterly predictable because he had done it before. That he was paroled to kill and paroled to kill again galled every civilian public official who knew of him. Some of his own family members could not believe he had been set free. How on earth could this happen? Who did this? After finding out that Kenneth had been freed through a perfectly legal process, Charlie Butts, a former assistant district attorney from Tarrant County, and a truly refined country gentleman, bristled at the suggestion that anyone could possibly consider McDuff rehabilitated. "I don't give a damn what he did in prison; he is a killer and he will always be a killer."[12]

On a personal level, Kenneth McDuff brought out atypical behavior in people. J. W. Thompson of the Austin Police Department, a person of faith and a kind and gentle father of two young daughters, as well as an easy-going and unassuming homicide detective, gets angered when reminded of assertions once made by McDuff's former lawyer and former parole board members who claimed to genuinely believe that the convicted murderer could have contributed to society. "Well, he did!" J. W. said uncharacteristically in a voice dripping with anger and sarcasm. "He gave me a lot of damn overtime I did not want!"[13]

Noted defense attorney F. Lee Bailey is probably right when he asserts that we are often caught off-guard at the discovery of mass murderers because we have not done what he calls "our homework." The frustration of not knowing what to do caused Bailey to ask rhetorically: "What should be done about such creatures?" Truman Capote, the author of *In Cold Blood*, suggested that we cannot begin to understand mass murderers and thus cannot pretend to treat them.

Others are like Charlie Butts, who, seasoned by more than four decades of prosecuting and defending the accused, says that people like McDuff have "no conscience and it doesn't make him crazy; it just makes him mean." Another prosecutor of Kenneth McDuff, Crawford Long of the McLennan County District Attorney's Office, stated simply, "He was not driven to this; he chose it."[14]

Truman Capote may be right. Maybe we cannot treat mass murderers because we cannot understand them. But then, maybe there is nothing to treat. Maybe some people, like McDuff, are mean because they want to be and kill because they like it. In the case of Kenneth Allen McDuff, a serious search for an answer begins with his first victim— Rosebud.

1

They Was Just Pranks

*"I got sent to prison because I was an asshole.
They should have been able to overlook that."*
—Kenneth Allen McDuff

I

On the eastern edge of Rosebud, Linden Street heads south
from Main Street toward a baseball field carved out of surrounding farmland. Small wooden houses, old but well
kept, and shaded by large pecan trees, line the streets. On
the east side of Linden, only the second building from
Main, stands what once was the Rosebud Laundromat. A
small living area connects to the rear of the laundromat
where the family of John Allen "J. A." McDuff lived. At
least some of the McDuff children, including two boys
named Lonzo ("Lonnie") and Kenneth, were born in far-
off Paris, Texas, and no one seems to know why the
McDuffs, who lived in the Blackland Prairie before moving
to Rosebud, ended up in the area.

J. A. did farm work. His wife was a hefty, domineering
woman named Addie. Addie ruled. She controlled everything, including the money, the children, and J. A. "The
only opinions J. A. had were Addie's," a long-time Rosebud resident would say.[1] At least one of Kenneth's teachers,
however, knew of some who thought that at one point
J. A. had made some effort to bring discipline into the lives
of his two sons. In reality no one knew for sure. The family
was a mystery to those around them. In *Texas Monthly*,
Gary Cartwright wrote that the McDuffs were not the
friendliest people, in fact, they were downright weird—"but
they weren't white trash either."

In addition to farming, J. A. McDuff did masonry and

concrete work, and soon he left farm work to run his own successful concrete business during the Texas construction boom of the sixties and seventies. After moving to Linden Street, Addie started her own business. She opened and maintained the Rosebud Laundromat. J. A. and Addie McDuff worked very hard for everything they had. Neither has ever had a criminal record—"not even a parking ticket," Addie said years later.[2]

But, for the next four decades Addie McDuff's volatile and unpredictable behavior scared people, even some seasoned police officers accustomed to breaking down the doors of crack houses. Many in Rosebud considered her unstable. Neighbors, both in Rosebud and out in the Blackland Prairie, had no way to prove it, but they looked toward Addie with suspicion when pets or hogs were found dead of gunshot wounds. "She was just that type of person," said a Rosebud resident.[3]

In 1992, when Kenneth made the cover of *Texas Monthly*, Addie became upset about the article, although she also claimed never to have read it. She particularly resented references to her as a "Pistol-Packing Mama." "I didn't do any of that," she insisted to a Bell County investigator.[4] But Rosebud teachers did refer to her as "Pistol-Packing Mama McDuff" after she allegedly accosted a school bus driver and warned that there had better not be any more disturbances involving her children on his bus. She also had a reputation for refusing to believe that any of her children, especially her boys, could possibly misbehave or do any wrong.

Another Addie McDuff legend involved the Rural Electrification Association and her displeasure at the amount of time it was taking for a line to be connected to her house. On that occasion, Addie was rumored to have gone to the REA office and said something to the effect that she was not called "Pistol-Packing Mama McDuff" for nothing. Even if untrue, the townspeople believed it and most steered clear of her.[5]

When it came to her boys, Addie was a conspiracist.

Complaints about Lonnie and Kenneth from neighbors, school officials, and especially law enforcement officers brought about protests of cabals against her boys. In the process, she reinforced a notion in the boys' minds that they could do no wrong and that whatever they said, no matter how outlandish, was *per se*, the truth. Kenneth's prison record later included a quote from Rosebud High School's principal:

> Did not get along with students, teachers or anyone. He would lie, steal, and destroy the property of others. Was in some form of trouble every few days. He had trouble in the community for reckless driving and stealing. His family would seldom believe he did anything wrong and were always angry with school officials and local police for punishing him. His family is very unpopular in the community. This young man has been angry with the world ever since he was in the fourth or fifth grade. His mother was neurotic and unreasonable. His father not neurotic, but often unreasonable. However, the father and mother did work to provide Kenneth with all the necessities. Kenneth had the ordinary comforts as much as the average boy in this community.[6]

Addie's harsher critics believe firmly that she knew what her boys did and did nothing about it. She lavished praise on and protected Kenneth, and would attempt to do so for the rest of her life. More charitable observers wondered how she could not have seen what was going on, but most concluded that she genuinely wanted what was best for all of her children.[7]

The atmosphere in the living quarters behind the Rosebud Laundromat was described as very depressing. Minimal light barely illuminated a neat, but not clean, dwelling. The walls were dark and the ceilings were low. Even their house seemed to reinforce what people thought about the McDuffs.

Addie's Rosebud Laundromat was the only one in town.

Most of the people who did business there were unaware
of the strange people who ran it. One such unsuspecting
customer was Essie Trubee. While doing her laundry, Essie
noticed a young boy playing around the washers. Apparently, while Essie made a quick trip to her car, Kenneth
stole her purse. It had $100 hidden in a secret compartment.
After searching in vain at the laundromat and at home, Essie concluded it had to be Kenneth; he was the only other
person around at that time. Naturally hesitant to accuse a
little boy of thievery, and not knowing the McDuffs, Essie
continued to search, even in places where she knew her
purse could not be. As time went by she became more
convinced that Kenneth had stolen it. Her anger built up,
culminating in a confrontation with Addie, who of course,
defended Kenneth as a little boy who would never do such
a thing. But Essie, who could be brusque herself, went nose
to nose with Addie, not knowing she had taken on "Pistol-
Packing Mama McDuff." When Addie backed down and
promised to find Essie's purse, Essie replied, "You damn
sure better, and the money better be there!" Essie got her
purse back, and the money was there.

Several days later Essie Trubee would relate what had
happened to a number of astonished women in a Rosebud
beauty parlor. Only then would she find out about the
McDuff family, and it "scared her to death."[8]

As J. A. and Addie's separate businesses became more
successful, the family could afford to move into a much
nicer two-story house on Linden Street almost directly
across the street from the laundromat. Addie became an
active member of a somewhat raucous Assembly of God
Church.[9] Neighbors around the building where the congregation worshipped often watched as the celebrants shouted
and carried on. Reportedly, there was little evidence of a
traditional church service like Bible study, teaching, or
preaching. Some of the neighbors could see Addie, a leader
of sorts, standing before a group, completely possessed by
the Spirit and speaking in tongues, only to stop, fix her
dress, get re-possessed, and continue. After services, some

of the inhabitants of nearby homes were convinced that she
threw items she picked off the street at their houses.[10]

The people of Rosebud had no such suspicion of J. A.
McDuff. He was a quiet man who worked so much that
most people wondered if he did anything else. No one questioned his devotion to Addie and his family. He seemed
different, and he had a reputation for quality work. Kenneth
and Lonnie worked with their father and years later Kenneth would talk about what an overseer J. A. could be.[11]
Apparently, J. A. was the master of the workplace—and
nowhere else.

Both Kenneth and Addie would later speak of Kenneth
mowing lawns for elderly Rosebud women, who reportedly
developed a liking towards him. The story may be credible
because they related it on separate occasions. The elderly
women, Addie said in a *48 Hours* broadcast, loved Kenneth. Kenneth maintained that his success in mowing lawns,
in which he claimed to have made more money than many
adult males in Rosebud, combined with the business success earned by Addie and J. A., caused most Rosebud
adults to resent the McDuff family as a symbol of upward
social mobility. It was then, according to Kenneth, that jeal-
ousy birthed a conspiracy to keep the McDuffs down.[12]

II

There was a sense in the school system that Kenneth was
just hopeless. He was not considered retarded, just dull.
Addie's assertions of his perfection led to a denial of his
academic problems, and frustrated the attempts teachers
made to help him. Martha Royal, Kenneth's fifth-grade
teacher, remembers him as a regular fifth-grade boy. Once
when he had been running down a hallway, he ran into Ms.
Royal who saw him coming soon enough to put out her
hands and knock him to the floor.

"Did you like being knocked down?"

"No," Kenneth replied.

"Well, I don't like being run over."

Kenneth walked away with an angered look, and Martha Royal wondered if she was in for a visit from Addie. Otherwise, during the fifth grade, "Kenneth blended in." Ms. Royal believes that had he not become so infamous as an adult he might have been one of those kids that "you just forget."[13]

He was large for his age, and soon he learned that his size alone could intimidate others. His disciplinary problems appear to have begun during his sixth-grade year. That year, and on through the ninth grade when he would drop out of school, he would become a memorable discipline problem. His IQ was estimated at 92, barely within the average range, but he courted failure and seemed to think it was funny. School children in the 1950s remembered his maniacal laughter at things no one else thought were funny; so would writers and law enforcement officers in the 1990s.

During the sixth grade, Kenneth's teacher referred him to Ellen Roberts, a special education teacher and speech therapist, who also functioned as a counselor for Rosebud High School's sixth through twelfth grades. Her class was next door to Kenneth's and so it was easy for him to spend thirty to forty minutes each day with Ms. Roberts. Back then, however, meeting the needs of special students carried a stigma it does not carry today. In some ways Ms. Roberts's class became a dumping ground for students other teachers had given up on.

Ms. Roberts tried for three consecutive days to get Kenneth to respond to her. He said nothing the entire time. He entered the class with hostility, probably because of the dumping ground mentality at the time. Ms. Roberts could do little more than send Kenneth back to his teacher.

Ellen Roberts also had the occasion to work with Addie, who appeared to be far more concerned with Lonnie. Lonnie's problem was far more apparent than Kenneth's; he had multiple speech impediments. Later, much would be made of Lonnie's attachment to the nickname "Rough, Tough, Lonnie McDuff." When he said it, however, it came out as "Wuff, Tuff, Wonnie McDuff." Ms. Roberts, who had a therapist background, got along well with Addie, and Addie seemed genuinely grateful for the attention Roberts paid to her boys. Later when Ellen Roberts was elected Justice of the Peace in Falls County, she made other, very different attempts to help Addie.[14]

The principal of Rosebud High School was the legendary D. L. Mayo. He was a typical post–World War II high school principal, a veteran hardened by military training and toughened by war. He was strictly business. The teachers were terrified of him, and the only way to communicate effectively with him was through curt, military-style memos. The pep squad of Rosebud High School, for example, was trained in military fashion because that was what Mr. Mayo wanted. He had a "thump" on his forehead that astute teachers used as a barometer; if the "thump" got red it was best to get out—fast. Post–World War II principals like D. L. Mayo were above question. They never smiled. They ran schools as they saw fit, and school boards and lawyers left them alone. Students behaved and learned because men like Mr. Mayo had taken care of the Nazis; discipline at Rosebud High was not a problem. Even the McDuffs found that out.

D. L. Mayo's discipline policy never took the form of an elaborate handbook. It was really quite simple: Students were not to lie or steal or show disrespect to teachers or anyone else. They were to respect property. If something had been stolen, Mr. Mayo found out who did it. Once a student with a nice new baseball glove sadly entered Mr. Mayo's office to report he had laid it down only long enough for it to have been stolen. Apparently, the boy and his parents had saved for quite some time to purchase the glove and were quite proud of it. Whether for the love of baseball, or an admiration for the virtue of a young man saving money for something special, or because stealing was wrong and he would not have it at Rosebud High, Mr. Mayo decided he would find the glove—and the thief. He put the pressure on. Shortly after the search began, Kenneth entered the front office with the glove, now smeared with black shoe polish, and announced, "Look what I found in a ditch!"[15]

No one remembers exactly what Mr. Mayo did to Kenneth that day. What everyone does remember was the reaction of Lonnie, who apparently was outraged at the thought of his brother being accused of thievery and being disciplined. In *Texas Monthly*, Gary Cartwright wrote that Lonnie pulled a knife on Mr. Mayo. At the very least Lonnie made some attempt to protest directly. At that point, D. L. Mayo lifted Lonnie off the floor and threw him down a flight of stairs. No one remembers Addie contacting Mr. Mayo about the incident.[16] Years later, Kenneth would boast to police officers that he had once knocked around a principal. When told that, Ellen Roberts laughed out loud, "Nobody knocked around D. L. Mayo. He was the Iron Man."

The incident with the baseball glove did, however, illustrate one significant fact about the life of Kenneth Allen McDuff. The only person he seemed to respect, or even like, was his brother Lonnie. They had a true relationship. Kenneth said that they were very close as brothers because they were friends as well. Otherwise, he added, "I don't have any friends."[17]

Lonnie never earned the reputation Kenneth did. He was not a killer, but many thought he could become one. In the fall of 1964, Kenneth allegedly told Lonnie that he had raped a girl, cut her throat, and left her for dead. Lonnie reportedly replied that Kenneth should forget about it and go to bed.[18] Judging by their behavior, and the testimony of those who knew them, the brothers seemed to share a common sense of invulnerability. Something in their value system taught them that what they did could not be wrong, because *they* did it; what they said was the truth, because *they* said it; and whatever they believed was right, because *they* believed it. Like Lonnie, Kenneth existed in an extraordinarily self-centered world. Kenneth had his things, but what everyone else had could be stolen; Kenneth spoke, while others existed to listen—and believe; and tragically, when he grew to be nearly 6'4" tall, weighing over 250 pounds, Kenneth would see other people as things to be "used up." As a result, he took pleasure in "performing" before an audience. This, of course, led to his downfall. To a lesser extent it would lead to Lonnie's downfall as well. Charles Meyer, an ATF Special Agent who came to know Kenneth as well as anyone, summed up his egocentric personality: "He loves the sound of his own voice."[19]

And so, Kenneth Allen McDuff, a big, mean, loud bully, continued to torment the students of Rosebud High School. Every once in a while residents out in the Blackland Prairie could hear a loud motorcycle and gunshots. The next day someone would find holes in a mailbox.

His size intimidated nearly all of the students and even some of the adults. Moreover, Kenneth took joy in harassing smaller boys and watching their fear. Presumptions of his invincibility and daring, however, would soon be shattered by a smaller, truly courageous Rosebud freshman named Tommy Sammons.

"Tommy Sammons was one of the sweetest boys I ever knew," said Martha Royal. He was a good, quiet kid with an inner strength Kenneth could not see. On the day Kenneth called Tommy "chickenshit" in front of his friends, he finally encountered a young man who would not back down. "He just got tired of Kenneth's foolishness and he did something about it," Ms. Royal recalled. One of the most popular boys in his class, Tommy was athletic, reserved, and unpretentious. Kenneth challenged him to a fight in a ravine traversed by a bridge near the school. Soon, every student knew of the scheduled event, and nearly everyone showed up to watch. Some fully expected Tommy to get slaughtered; he was not a fighter—he was a good kid.

At the appointed hour the boys showed up and the fight began. Tommy might have been smaller, but it was readily apparent that his athletic ability and strength would carry the day. Kenneth was big and loud, but he was neither strong nor fast. Tommy got Kenneth in a headlock; Kenneth bit Tommy's arm. That was about all Kenneth could do. Students lined up along the ravine and leaned over the bridge to cheer for Tommy.

For the kids it was a shallow display of suppressed resentment, but it felt so good. They whooped and hollered and clapped louder and louder with every punch. One of the boys at the site, Bud Malcik, was so elated that he ran home to his mother to tell her, "Old Tommy just whipped the snot out of him."[20] Soon, the word spread throughout Rosebud that, at last, there was "justice for McDuff." The unknown, however, was what Addie or Lonnie would do. Many in the community worried about what could happen to Tommy, but nothing did.

The bubble had burst. Kenneth McDuff was no longer invincible. After walking out of the ditch where he had the "snot whipped out of him," he no longer bothered Tommy Sammons or anyone else at Rosebud High School. Shortly thereafter, he quit school and began working full time pouring concrete with his father.[21]

III

Kenneth hated farm work and pouring concrete. With his father he worked hard and behaved himself. Unlike most other boys, very little of his adolescence was spent in school engaging in activities with other kids his age. Instead, he labored at construction sites. But after work he had access to cars and motorcycles with which to roam the countryside and hamlets of the Blackland Prairie. During this period his energy, by his own admission, seemed to be directed at fast driving and the destruction of cars. Years later he loved telling torturously long stories about how well he drove. The stories, though, included vivid accounts of his many accidents. When asked to reconcile how someone who drove so well could manage to wreck so many cars, he smiled, and with the self-assurance of someone whose words were the "truth," replied, "Yea, but I had a touch."[22]

The Rosebud area had no real drug problem at the time because young people did not have access to drugs. As Merle Haggard would soon sing, "White lightning [was] the biggest thrill of all." Like many teenagers, Kenneth started drinking at the age of fifteen. He maintained that Rosebud's "parents knew it and it didn't seem to matter."[23]

What did matter was a string of burglaries he and some other boys began committing in the spring of 1964. His prison record contains his own, though incomplete, account of his activities. In March, he and an accomplice burglarized Lotts Store in Falls County by cutting a bolt off the front door. They took about $500 and some checks from a safe. The next month, in Milam County, he did the same thing in three stores, taking assorted shotgun ammunition and two bars of ice cream. With yet another accomplice he burglarized a coin changer and took about $20. Later that same month he broke into a machine shop in Bell County and took a skill saw and tools. That same night he broke into a 7-Eleven store, but he could not open the safe and just took some .22 caliber bullets. They tried a boat house near Temple, but could not get in and left. Moving north to the little town of Troy, they broke into three more businesses.

On April 17, 1964, Temple Police rounded them up. When asked by prison officials what rationalization he had for those offenses, Kenneth replied, in a rare moment of complete honesty, "Stupid."[24] Years later when asked directly about why he did it and how he could possibly think that he could get away with so many break-ins, he would grin, laugh and say, "Aw, they was just pranks." He followed with a more serious protestation of how law enforcement officers and the courts should have been "mature" enough to recognize that he was just an immature kid.[25]

In August of 1966 the *Temple Daily Telegram* reported that in January of 1965 Kenneth was convicted of stealing and stripping his own car. By January and February of 1965 the criminal justice system finally caught up with him. The best sources indicate that on January 22 he was convicted of eight counts of theft or burglary in Bell County, of two counts on January 29 in Falls County, and of four counts on February 3 in Milam County for a total of fourteen counts.[26] He was sentenced to a total of fifty-two years in prison (four years each for thirteen offenses) but each of the four-year sentences ran concurrently, meaning that for all practical purposes he was really sentenced to only four years in prison. On March 10, 1965, Kenneth was delivered to the Ferguson Unit of the Texas Department of Criminal Justice.

In nine months and two weeks, on December 29, 1965, Kenneth Allen McDuff was paroled for the first time.[27] Exactly twenty-six years later, he committed one of his most heinous crimes—at least as far as we know.

IV

Roy Dale Green lived with his mother in Marlin, Texas, the seat of Falls County. Charlie Butts remembered him as "just a skinny kid." Larry Pamplin, the son of Falls County Sheriff Brady Pamplin, went to school with Roy Dale and remembers him as a quiet boy who had never been in trouble. Roy Dale was easily impressed with people and things because he was not very bright. He appeared to want to hang around with exciting people. In July of 1966, like many hundreds of others, Roy Dale went to the Bremond Street Dances, where he met Kenneth McDuff.[28]

The Bremond Street Dances were not teen events. They were family events similar to festivals, attracting people from all over Central Texas. By that time Kenneth was twenty and Roy Dale was eighteen. They had a mutual friend named Richard Boyd. According to Kenneth, he hung around Richard because he had a new Impala and an "in" with the girls.[29] Shortly after they met, Roy Dale worked with Kenneth for J. A.'s concrete business. They were made for each other. Kenneth needed a weak-willed, easily impressed audience for his immaturity; Roy Dale wanted to run with the "big boys."

Both Richard and Roy Dale knew Kenneth kept a .38 caliber pistol in his car. It did not seem to bother either of them. Kenneth often talked to them about killing. Roy Dale later testified to horrified courtrooms that Kenneth boasted that "killing a woman is like killing a chicken; they both squawk." Roy once asked Kenneth if he had ever killed before and he answered that yes he had, and that he had buried them in shallow graves. Roy Dale never believed any of it. When Kenneth talked about going out and killing people, Roy thought it was another of Kenneth's tall tales. Had he been a little smarter he would have known better. Roy later admitted to federal agents that Kenneth enjoyed pinning a girl against a floor and squeezing a tube of Deep Heat or Ben Gay into her vagina.[30]

They were acquainted with a girl named Jo Ann, and on one trip to Hearne, Texas, they were walking back to Kenneth's car when Richard caught sight of a broken broomstick. Without thinking he picked it up, played around with it and threw it into the back seat. The broomstick with the jagged edge would stay in Kenneth's car for nearly three weeks.

On Friday, August 5, 1966, Kenneth got on a motorcycle and visited his brother Lonnie. Later that night Roy spent the night with Kenneth in Rosebud. That evening they picked up Richard and went to Hearne where Roy got very drunk. As usual, Kenneth spoke of killing. "I know where people park and we can kill 'em," he said.[31] The next morning Kenneth and Roy Dale woke up early and helped to pour concrete at a construction site in Temple. At about noon they hurried back to Rosebud to wash up. Kenneth had decided to go out that night to Fort Worth. It was all very exciting for Roy Dale Green; he had never seen Fort Worth before.

2

The Broomstick Murders

"It was like taking a bird that was taught to love and respect people out of its cage and blowing its head off."
—Jack Brand

I

The summer of 1966 was hideously hot even by Texas standards. It was also a period of great sadness. August began with the largest mass murder in American history—the University of Texas Tower shootings in Austin by Charles Whitman. After murdering his wife and mother during the night and spending the next morning preparing, Whitman began a ninety-minute killing spree in which he fired over 150 rounds at innocent and unsuspecting people, killing fourteen and wounding at least thirty-one. The Texas Tower tragedy came at a time when Texans were just starting to live down the assassination of John Kennedy in 1963. The irony of both crimes was that neither Whitman nor Oswald were native Texans, yet both will forever be associated with Texas.[1]

Five days after the Tower tragedy, on August 6, 1966, Roy Dale Green and Kenneth Allen McDuff began their day by pouring concrete with J. A. and Lonnie McDuff. They were anxious to go out and have fun when their Saturday workday ended sometime between noon and 1 P.M. Years later, Texas Ranger John Aycock discovered that Roy Dale had been Kenneth's second choice to go out to Fort Worth. He had asked another friend named Nicholas to go with him. It probably did not matter to Kenneth, at least not for what he had planned. On that night Kenneth wanted to perform before an audience, and he settled for Roy Dale.[2]

During the previous two days, as usual, Kenneth had regaled and enticed young Roy Dale with tales of killing and sex—"sexcapades" he called them. Roy Dale was only eighteen years old—and easily impressed. He had not graduated from high school yet. It was the summer between his junior and senior year. Roy Dale either chose to delude himself, or he was not bright enough to get it; he did not appreciate what were obvious signs of Kenneth's plans. "I thought it was all a joke. I didn't think he meant it," Roy Dale said.[3]

Kenneth and Roy Dale finished their job in Temple, rushed to Rosebud to wash up, and left for Fort Worth. On the way, they stopped in Waco and bought beer at a 7-Eleven convenience store. They drank the brew on the way to Fort Worth and arrived there a couple of hours later. According to a statement Roy Dale made only two days later, Kenneth "showed him the town."

While in Fort Worth, Kenneth bought another two six-packs of Schlitz and spotted a friend named Danny at a place called Helen's Bar. Kenneth had dated Danny's sister, a young girl named Edith. After talking to Danny and finding out that Edith was home, he dumped Danny and dropped Roy Dale off at the Hamburger Hut in a suburb called Everman. Roy Dale waited there until Kenneth returned with Edith. While Roy Dale drove, Kenneth sat in the back seat with his "date." They rode around Everman for about an hour until they brought Edith to a relative's house in nearby Forrest Hill. She and Kenneth talked on the front porch of the house and took a short walk together. It was about 9:30 P.M. Afterwards, Kenneth and Roy Dale cruised the streets of Everman. Apparently, Kenneth knew the area, and more significantly, the rural area to the south.[4]

When roaming small town streets, young people are often drawn to the local high school. If Kenneth and Roy Dale were to find girls, that was a good place to look. Located on the southern edge of town, the Everman High School campus was bordered by farmlands. Gravel covered the unpaved streets. Baseball fields lined the western edge

of the campus, and even though the school was within the
Everman city limits, the area was nonetheless isolated. The
school building itself hid much of the baseball field from
the busier streets.

As Kenneth steered his Dodge Coronet around the campus, he found what he sought. Near a baseball field he could
see a large, parked, 1955 Ford. At that time of night he
probably assumed that inside the Ford he could find a
young couple "parking." After carefully surveying the area,
Kenneth decided to prey upon the occupants.

He placed his car in a field about 150 yards away, and
from a console between the two front seats of his Dodge,
he removed a Colt Special revolver that belonged to Lonnie. Roy Dale knew of the gun, having looked at it on the
way to Fort Worth. Kenneth then exited the car and told
Roy Dale to "get the stick and follow me." Roy Dale
grabbed the three-foot, faded red stick from the back seat
and did as he was told. In the dark, still night, he followed
Kenneth slowly toward the Ford. Incredibly, Roy Dale still
thought it was all a joke. About halfway to the car Kenneth
told Roy Dale to stop; again, Roy Dale did as he was told.
"I'll handle this," Kenneth said.[5]

When he reached the Ford, he did not find two necking
teenagers. Instead, he discovered three high school students
talking leisurely: two were cousins named Robert Brand
and Marcus Dunnam. The third was a girl named Edna
Louise Sullivan.

II

A popular girl, Edna Louise Sullivan was to begin her junior year at Everman High School at the end of August 1966.
Her friends and family called her Louise. She liked bas-
ketball and played on Everman's team, but participated in
"little else because she had to work extra hard to keep up
some of her grades." At 5'2" tall and weighing 110 pounds,
she was a small girl. Her shoulder-length hair resembled

the style of the time: parted to the side and curled inward
at the end. With her family, she attended the First Baptist
Church in Everman. There, Louise volunteered to help in
the nursery. Sometime in late June or early July of 1966,
she began dating a young boy from Alvarado named Robert
Brand.[6]

Robert Brand was a handsome young man who loved
music. He had worked at various odd jobs to buy the guitar
he played with a group of friends at teenage clubs. His
younger cousin from California, Marcus Dunnam, was staying with the Brand family that summer in Alvarado. Marcus
and Robert were more like brothers than cousins; they both
liked the outdoors and sometimes hunted together.

Marcus liked to play the drums and he, too, played in
informal teenage groups. He wanted to be a machinist in
the Navy. On August 6, 1966, Marcus had been visiting
his grandmother in Fort Worth. At about 4 P.M. he decided
to hitchhike to Alvarado. Marcus made it safely to the
Brand house and the boys left for Everman late that afternoon.

Apparently, the boys had planned a double date involving a friend of Louise named Rhonda. In 1996, writer Bob
Stewart revealed that Rhonda, when hearing of Marcus's
plans to hitch to Alvarado, considered it a premonition to
tragedy and refused to go out on the date. (The elder Mr.
Brand does not remember Marcus doing any hitchhiking,
and he does not believe Marcus did that.) Instead, she faked
ill health and Robert, Louise, and Marcus went on without
her.[7]

Louise was to have spent the night with Rhonda. They
lived only a few houses from one another on Marlene Street
in Everman. The neighborhood, indeed all of Everman, was
a quiet and safe area. Marcus had with him an extra shirt,
a blue and white striped one he intended to wear after
spending the night with Robert.[8]

Louise's mother later testified that Louise left home with
Robert and Marcus at about 7 P.M. Mrs. Hughes "imagined
they would go to a movie." Sometime during the evening,

probably while parked at the secluded baseball park, staring thoughtlessly at the sky through the back windshield of Robert's 1955 Ford, one of the three teenagers removed mascara from Louise's purse and wrote "Louise" on the glass.[9] In a few hours, hardened police officers would discover the haunting signature.

III

Roy Dale stood about seventy-five yards from the 1955 Ford and watched Kenneth creep closer to the unsuspecting teenagers. Roy went over to the car in time to hear Kenneth tell Louise and the boys to get out or he would shoot them. After taking the boys' wallets, he put all three teenagers into the trunk of the Ford. Kenneth wryly observed, "These boys don't have much money." He then told Roy Dale to get into the Ford. Kenneth drove Roy Dale back to the Dodge and instructed him to follow. Throughout the evening, Roy Dale did as he was told, never thinking to drive away in Kenneth's Dodge.[10]

Kenneth led Roy Dale south into the countryside near the Tarrant and Johnson County line near Burleson. They crossed a highway, probably US 81, and proceeded down gravel roads to a cow pasture. Kenneth stopped, looked around, then pronounced: "This isn't a good place." They backed out and drove to another, presumably more isolated, field.[11]

The sloppiness that put him in prison after his burglaries only a year earlier had taught Kenneth a "valuable" lesson. On this night and for the rest of his criminal career, he was as sophisticated and evidence-conscious as any criminal could be. During the evening of August 6, 1966, he took extraordinary care in deciding where he would commit his crimes. He brought Roy Dale and his teenage captives to a tiny farm-to-market road numbered FM 1017. Mr. and Mrs. Raymond McAlister lived only 400 yards away. Mrs. McAlister later testified that she saw two vehicles pull off the road and into a field at about 10:35 P.M. When another car passed by, the lights of the first two cars were turned off. Although kids used the area to park and neck, on that Saturday Mrs. McAlister was too tired to bother checking it out.[12]

According to Roy Dale's statement, Kenneth opened the trunk of the Ford and pulled Louise out by her arm. Without saying a word, Louise slowly exited the Ford as Kenneth ordered Roy Dale to place her in the trunk of the Dodge. Roy Dale did as he was told. Kenneth then looked at Roy Dale and said: "They got a look at me. I'm gonna have to kill them. We can't have any witnesses. I'm gonna have to knock them off." Even then, Roy Dale did not think Kenneth was serious: "I didn't believe him—[then] he started shooting."

Robert and Marcus begged to be spared. In vain, they had assured Kenneth that they would say nothing. Each shot seemed to bring Kenneth more pleasure.[13] Roy Dale Green shook with the blast of each round. "He kept shooting and shooting and every time he shot, I jumped," Roy Dale said. He remembered seeing the fire spurt out of the barrel as Kenneth shot Robert in the ear and the forehead. Roy Dale covered his ears and looked away as the killing continued. Then, Kenneth pointed the gun at Marcus and shot him three times, once through the arm as Marcus tried to wave off the volleys. As if to retaliate, Kenneth then grabbed Marcus by the hair, placed the gun against his head and fired the last round.[14]

"Good God, Kenneth, what'd you do that for?" Roy Dale asked after the firing finally stopped.

"I had to," Kenneth replied as he looked coolly into Roy Dale's eyes. He seemed calm and collected like he had done nothing wrong. Incredibly, Kenneth got more upset at not being able to close the trunk, even after Roy placed one of the boys' legs back inside. Instead of reaching in and repositioning the bodies, Kenneth started the car and backed it up to a fence so that the open trunk would not be easily visible from the road. At Kenneth's instructions,

Roy Dale used Marcus's extra shirt to wipe fingerprints off
the Ford and flatten out tire tracks left by Kenneth's car.
During this crime scene cleansing, Louise Sullivan lay
helplessly trapped in the trunk of the Dodge.[15]

In the Dodge, Kenneth and Roy Dale traveled farther
south into Johnson County. Before reaching the little town
of Egan, Kenneth turned from FM 917 onto an isolated
gravel road. The path cut through a hay field of tall grass.
Clearly distracted by the trouble into which he had gotten
himself, Roy first stated that he and Kenneth drove only
about one mile from where the boys were murdered; it was
actually eleven. After stopping, Kenneth walked over to the
trunk and ordered Louise out. She got out of the trunk and
Kenneth directed her to the back seat of his car. She sat on
the driver's side. Kenneth went back there with her as Roy
sat outside on the trunk and, at times, watched. He saw
Louise take off her clothes; then saw Kenneth rape her.[16]

After he raped her, Kenneth ordered Roy Dale to get
into the car. As Roy Dale sat behind the wheel, Kenneth
asked him if he wanted to have a turn with her. Roy said
he did not, and when Kenneth leaned forward and asked
why, Roy thought about Lonnie's gun and decided that he
had better. He then climbed into the back seat, and, at least
according to Roy Dale, had trouble getting aroused enough
to rape Louise—eventually he did. He also claims to have
kept his eye on Kenneth the entire time. After that, Kenneth
returned to the back seat and raped her again, and this time
he violated her with the jagged end of the broomstick lying
on the floorboard. Roy Dale remembers the agonizing
screams, but during the entire assault, he remembers Louise
saying only one thing: "Stop! I think you ripped something."[17]

Finally, Kenneth told Louise to put her clothes back on.
Her horror, though, had not yet ended.

Kenneth drove Louise and Roy Dale a short distance to
yet another lonely road covered with white crushed stone.
He stopped the car and ordered Louise to get out and sit
on the road near the front of the car. She had no choice but

to do what he wanted. When she asked what was going to happen to her, Kenneth replied that he was going to tie her up. She said: "Why? I'm not going anywhere." Kenneth then turned to Roy Dale and asked if he had a belt. Hoping that Kenneth was going to tie her up and leave her alone, Roy happily gave his belt to Kenneth, who promptly threw it back into the car. He then grabbed the broomstick and walked towards Louise, telling Roy Dale to get the belt. As Roy Dale turned to go back to the car he heard an odd sound. Kenneth had gone over to Louise, sat on her chest, and placed the broomstick across her throat. As he pressed her against the white crushed stone, "it sounded like air escaping out of a balloon or air hose," Roy Dale remembered.

"No, no, leave her alone," Roy Dale said in a rare moment of assertion.

"It's got to be done," Kenneth replied.[18]

Kenneth pressed hard enough to break bones in Louise's neck. As she gasped for air and struggled for life, her arms and legs flapped in a *danse macabre*. Kenneth ordered Roy Dale to hold her legs. When he let go, Kenneth told him to grab her legs again—and he did. Roy Dale did as he was told. The second time he grabbed her legs, however, he did not have to struggle to keep her still. By that time Louise could no longer feel the pain inflicted by her captors. Kenneth was reported to have said, "It was like you kill a possum."

Kenneth ordered Roy Dale to turn the car around. Roy did as he was told, and Kenneth continued to press the broomstick across Louise's neck long after she could possibly have held on to her life. Kenneth grabbed her arms and Roy Dale grabbed her legs; they heaved her over a barbed wire fence into a field with long grass. Kenneth crossed the fence and choked her again. Asked by Kenneth to check her heart to make sure she was dead, Roy Dale moved her bra over to feel her chest for a beat. Kenneth then decided that he had better check her body himself after having to tell Roy Dale that her heart was on the left side.

That was when he noticed a German Cross necklace around Louise's neck. He ripped it off and put it in his pocket. Kenneth then looked at the gun and noticed that he had fired all of his rounds into Robert and Marcus; he had wanted to shoot Louise—just in case. Then they dragged her to a clump of oak trees with ground covered by dense brush.[19]

And finally, they left her alone.

IV

On the way back to Roy Dale's house in Marlin, Kenneth and Roy Dale stopped in Hillsboro at a filling station for soft drinks. Kenneth lectured Roy Dale: "Keep your mouth shut. If the police beat on you, it's better than what'll happen if you tell them. They'll put you in the electric chair."[20]

As they motored south towards Marlin, they tossed out empty shells from Lonnie's pistol. They also threw out the broomstick—it would never be found. Later, they stopped near a road sign and buried Robert and Marcus's wallets. After reaching Marlin, they tried unsuccessfully to flush their bloody underwear down a gas station toilet. Frustrated, Kenneth threw the garments on the roof of the station. After reaching Roy Dale's house, they spent the night together in the same bed.[21]

The next morning Roy Dale and Kenneth washed up and went outside. After finding a shovel and a cigar box, Kenneth tried to place the Colt revolver into the box but it did not fit. He ripped out one side of the box, wrapped it in rags and buried it and the gun in a two-foot hole he dug near Roy's garage. In an effort to conceal the burial, he carefully placed leaves over the fresh dirt. Then they went to a car wash and thoroughly washed the inside and outside of the Dodge. While cleaning out the inside Kenneth held up one of Louise's long brown hairs, told Roy Dale that it could "get you convicted" and threw it to the ground.

Later that day, Sunday, August 7, 1966, Roy Dale ac-

companied Kenneth to Robertson County to pick up a girl
named Jo Ann. She and Kenneth had a date that night.
Kenneth then took Roy Dale to Richard Boyd's house and
went on his date.[22]

In Alvarado, Jack Brand returned home from work at
Bell Helicopter at 2:15 A.M. to find his wife pacing the floor
in a frantic state. Their son, Robert, and his cousin, Marcus,
had not yet returned. Immediately, Mr. Brand began searching for the boys. "I drove all night," he said, only to return
home to lie down and get some well-deserved rest. For a
while, Mr. Brand thought that the boys might have taken
off to Little Rock.

Louise's mother did not know to be concerned; she
thought all along that Louise was at Rhonda's house only
a few homes down Marlene Street. She assured police officers that Louise was "a good girl and always comes home
on time."[23] Early Sunday morning, at about the time Kenneth and Roy Dale awakened and the parents' of Louise
Sullivan and Robert Brand began to get seriously concerned
for the safety of their children, Bill Sanders of Burleson,
Texas, was driving west on FM 1017. He intended to go
fishing when he spotted a 1955 Ford parked against a fence.
Thinking it unusual to see an unattended, parked car with
the trunk opened, he stopped to check it out. He was the
first to see the grisly scene. Tarrant County Sheriff Lon
Evans later said that "it looked like an execution."

Immediately, Sanders went to the McAlister home to call
the authorities. In a matter of hours, Rhonda's parents informed the Brands of the senseless tragedy. Before the day
was out 250 volunteers and police officers were searching
for Louise. The next day, Monday, August 8, over 2,000
people assisted in a search using helicopters, horses and
motorcycles.[24] The search, however, did not conclude until
a guide arrived—Roy Dale Green.

Kenneth had dropped Roy Dale off at Richard Boyd's
house at about 11:30 A.M. on Sunday. Early that afternoon
Richard and Roy Dale drove to Richard's girlfriend's house
and picked her up for a Sunday afternoon drive. Her name

was Shirley, and she and Richard could see that something was clearly wrong with Roy Dale.

While seated in the back seat, he began to cry. When a radio news report broke the story of the discovery of two murdered boys in Tarrant County, Roy Dale broke down completely. Richard remembered that Roy Dale "fell over in the seat and started crying again."[25] Clearly, Richard had to do something; he stopped the car and took a walk with Roy Dale. At that time, Roy Dale confessed to what he and Kenneth had done the night before. Richard, Shirley, and Roy Dale went to Shirley's parents' in Bremond. After that they went to the Boyds' home where they called the Sheriff of Robertson County, E. Paul "Sonny" Elliot. Roy Dale was taken to the nearest Justice of the Peace and placed under arrest. Roy Dale and Sheriff Elliot then went to Marlin and picked up the Sheriff of Falls County, Brady Pamplin. The two sheriffs and the hapless youth went directly to Roy Dale's house in Marlin. There, Roy Dale took them to the spot where Kenneth had buried the Colt revolver. It had been removed. Before the day was out, Roy Dale was placed in jail in Robertson County and taken back to Fort Worth. It was only his second trip to the city.[26]

V

As the news broke that a Falls County teenager named Roy Dale Green had confessed to his participation in the murders of Robert Brand, Marcus Dunnam, and Louise Sullivan, a massive search was already underway for Louise's body. The brutality of the murders became public knowledge before much of the law enforcement family, and the general public, learned about the true nature of the relationship between Kenneth McDuff and Roy Dale Green. Consequently, for a short time Roy Dale had a brief reputation for viciousness and brutality. It became readily apparent, however, to the sheriffs, deputies, and newsmen covering the story (including a young *Fort Worth Star-*

Telegram reporter named Bob Schieffer), that this stupid
and cowardly boy could not have committed those murders.
Roy Dale signed his sworn statement in front of several
newsmen who quoted him as saying, "I just had to tell it.
I kept seeing it. I kept hearing those boys moan."[27] Kenneth's criminal record, and information from Sheriff Brady
Pamplin in Falls County, quickly discounted Roy Dale as
a primary villain. And so, two massive searches took place
simultaneously—one for Louise in Johnson County and another for Kenneth in Falls and Robertson Counties.

For a while, it appeared as if 2,000 searchers were
stumped. The area the parties combed was vast and sparsely
populated. Woods, tall grass, and thick brush carpeted
much of the landscape. Roy Dale's complete ignorance of
the area compounded the problem. "I don't know much
about the country up there, but I kept seeing a sign that
read Burleson," Roy told the search parties.[28]

Hundreds of volunteers formed skirmish lines and covered the area in successive waves. Skin-divers searched
stock tanks and ponds. Officers with binoculars flew low
in helicopters in an effort to cover as much area as possible.
As dusk drew near that Sunday, Roy Dale had been brought
to the area twice to try to remember where he and Kenneth
had been. Finally, someone handed Roy Dale a napkin and
asked him to draw a map based on his recollection of the
events of that evening. When he handed back the napkin,
the searchers shifted their efforts to northern Johnson
County in an area near Egan. At one point, Roy Dale excitedly hopped over a fence and said, "This looks like it."
But the sun was setting and the grass was tall. "I know
she's here somewhere," he whispered in frustration, as he
was taken back to the Tarrant County Jail. A local Chief
of Police, Homer Barnes of Burleson, and several other
men decided to stay behind and not give up on the area.
They found Louise lying face down beneath the thicket of
oak trees, barely visible in the thick grass. Later, two of
her uncles arrived at the scene and positively identified
her.[29]

Finding Kenneth was not as difficult. Roy Dale knew that Kenneth had had a date with a girl from Bremond named Jo Ann. That afternoon, Kenneth and Jo Ann went to Lonnie's house northeast of Rosebud. Jo Ann later stated that Kenneth and Lonnie took something behind a barn. After leaving Lonnie's house, she and Kenneth went to a movie in Temple. Meanwhile, Sheriff Brady Pamplin of Kenneth's native Falls County, and Sheriff Sonny Elliot of Robertson County, where Jo Ann's Bremond home was located, went to Jo Ann's mother, explained the situation, and asked to stay and wait for Kenneth to return.

The two sheriffs lay in wait behind shrubbery when Kenneth drove up with Jo Ann at 10:50 P.M. Apparently, his headlights shined through the shrubbery and illuminated Pamplin and Elliot. Kenneth immediately put his car in reverse and floored the accelerator. Just as immediate was the response by the sheriffs. Brady Pamplin fired two rounds of buckshot from a 12-gauge shotgun at Kenneth's radiator and tires. Elliot fired his pistol at the same targets. Jo Ann quickly hit the floorboard of the car and, incredibly, Kenneth managed to get out of the driveway. He did not get far.

Near the M&M Café on Bremond's Main Street, Kenneth spotted Jo Ann's brother in a vehicle. Kenneth jumped in and told the boy that someone was shooting at him and demanded to be taken to the constable. Brady Pamplin had instructed his son, Larry, to stay a safe distance away from where he and Sheriff Elliot waited for McDuff. Larry parked two and one half blocks away from the scene. After the shooting, Larry picked up the two sheriffs, gave chase and caught up to the boys. "I hollered for them to stop and get out of the car with their hands up. They got out of the car and stuck up their hands," the elder Pamplin later testified.[30]

After the gun battle, the cause for which Kenneth was surely aware, the only question he had for officers was whether his insurance would repair the bullet holes in his car.[31]

It was the only time in Kenneth's long and infamous criminal career that law enforcement officers actually fired their weapons at him. That singular experience, however, apparently had a lasting impression, and was enough to give Kenneth an exaggerated and lifelong animosity towards Sheriff Brady Pamplin and his son, Larry Pamplin, his successor in the Falls County Sheriff's Office. With the exception of two of the fourteen counts of burglary that sent him to prison in 1965, there is no record of Kenneth ever being arrested or jailed in Falls County or ever having another direct encounter with the Pamplins. Today, Kenneth Allen McDuff's name is not even in the index of cases in the Falls County Sheriff's Office. Many other jurisdictions, however, would come to deal with Kenneth Allen McDuff.[32]

3

A Prisoner of the State

*"People in prison are vicious and crazy;
this is worse than hell."*
—Kenneth Allen McDuff

I

On August 9, 1966, after Kenneth McDuff had committed
the Broomstick Murders and was back in jail, the State of
Texas revoked his parole.[1]

Sheriff Brady Pamplin established, at least to his own
satisfaction, that Kenneth and his brother Lonnie had actively engaged in the destruction of evidence. Jo Ann, Kenneth's date, told Pamplin that the brothers had taken
something behind a barn at Lonnie's home. Pamplin
quickly secured a search warrant for Lonnie's residence
northeast of Rosebud.

The nighttime search did not yield any incriminating evidence, but Lonnie was arrested anyway for "fraudulently
and illegally concealing a weapon used for murder." Jo
Ann's statement apparently served as the probable cause
for his arrest. Pending a hearing, the Justice of the Peace
set his bond at $10,000. Shortly after daylight, Constable
R. J. Brannon and Rosebud City Marshal Terry Fletcher
returned to the residence and found charred remains of
clothing in Lonnie's driveway. Metal studs, common to
western-style shirts, were mixed with the ashes of burnt
cloth.[2]

The Falls County Justice of the Peace for the precinct
including Rosebud held a preliminary hearing at the Rosebud City Hall to determine if Lonnie should be held for
willingly aiding his brother's escape and destroying evidence. He set Lonnie's bond at $10,000. City Marshal

Fletcher testified that the burned clothes were not in the driveway of Lonnie's house when he first was there at 2:30 A.M., but they were there when he returned at 5:50 A.M. He also established that kerosene was used to ignite the clothes.

A Waco attorney named Godfrey Sullivan represented Lonnie at the hearing. Sullivan, a spectacled, distinguished-looking attorney with "salt and pepper hair" had a reputation for "talking a juror's language." It is likely, though, that no lawyer could have overcome the image the McDuff boys (and their mother) had in Falls County, especially in Rosebud.

While the brutality of the Broomstick Murders shocked most Rosebud residents, most were not surprised that Kenneth was involved in something so hideous. In hindsight, many saw that Kenneth had been building up to more serious "adult" crimes. He was capable of anything, thought Ellen Roberts. Others thought that if Lonnie had known Kenneth to be a murderer and assisted him in the destruction of evidence, it was yet another example of a pattern of behavior both men had exhibited all their lives: Kenneth could do no wrong.[3] It did not take long for Addie to demonstrate "predictable" behavior as well. J. A., as usual, said little. During Lonnie's hearing before the Justice of the Peace, he sat on a folding chair and leaned against a wall.

The entire McDuff family gathered around Lonnie and Godfrey Sullivan at a cafeteria-style folding table for the hearing. The only surprise came when Lonnie's twelve-year-old sister took the stand. The terrified little girl contradicted statements given by Kenneth's date—that they had visited Lonnie's house before going to a movie in Temple. The little sister testified that she had been at Lonnie's house on Saturday and Sunday and had not seen a gun at any time. When asked directly if she saw Kenneth at the home at all, she cried out that she had not and that "Kenneth had not done all those things."[4]

Near the end of the hearing, Brady Pamplin and an investigator for the Tarrant County D.A. named Harry Beason approached the Justice of the Peace and quoted Lonnie as saying, "If my feet ever hit the ground again, I'll leave this country." The J.P. doubled the bond at $20,000.[5]

Had the Texas Tower tragedy not dominated the news in August 1966, the Broomstick Murders would have gained even more national attention. The first news reports focused on Roy Dale Green. Newspaper photos showed him pointing to a hole in the ground near his garage in Marlin where Kenneth buried, then retrieved, Lonnie's pistol. The media had been given unusual access to Roy Dale. He signed his statement, which amounted to a full confession, in the presence of newsmen. Before the throng, Roy Dale blurted out, "My God, I've got to tell somebody about it. I can't sleep. I can't think. I can't do nothing. I don't think people will ever understand. You've got to understand the circumstances. But I don't think anybody ever will." When informed that the body of Louise Sullivan had been located, Roy Dale collapsed in the arms of Tarrant County Chief Deputy Earl Brown.[6]

In contrast, in the Tarrant County Jail, Kenneth behaved the same way he had acted in Ellen Roberts's special education class at Rosebud High. He said very little. Sheriff Lon Evans observed, "He won't say anything. I said good morning to him today and he answered with profanity."[7] The first published pictures of him show a tall, slender man with inordinately long arms and huge hands. His extremities, like his hands and head, looked like they had been taken from an even larger person and put on his frame. His shiny, greased hair was long, but neatly trimmed. Each day in court he wore a dark suit and tie. No pictures of Kenneth taken at the time of the trial show a smile or any other emotion. "His eyes were just so cold. He had the coldest, deadest eyes I have ever seen or ever want to see," said one of his prosecutors, who also observed that McDuff's ominous manner seemed to intimidate his own lawyer. But less than a week after being apprehended, Kenneth was visited by an Assembly of God preacher who later revealed that Kenneth "gave his heart to the Lord." The cleric added that he left Kenneth reading the white Bible he had left behind.[8]

II

In some ways, Tarrant County District Attorney Doug Crouch was like Rosebud High School Principal D. L. Mayo: toughened by military training and hardened by war. Crouch, a veteran of World War II, had been stationed in the South Pacific. Almost immediately after reading Roy Dale's statement, he announced plans for quick trials. He also made clear that he would seek the death penalty—for both boys.

Crouch decided to lead the team himself and was an excellent "field marshal." From his staff he chose two extraordinarily talented attorneys to assist him in the prosecution of Kenneth Allen McDuff. The two provided a contrast in courtroom presence. Grady Hight, who filed the original rape charges based on the statement of Roy Dale Green, had an aggressive and bombastic reputation. Crouch assigned him the task of marshaling the witnesses and handling law enforcement officers. Charles "Charlie" Butts had a quiet, dignified, and deliberate courtroom manner. The results of their work, however, were similar; they put criminals in jail. Both men had brilliant legal minds and were up to the task of prosecuting Kenneth. The charge of working up the case, however, largely fell on the lap of "a quiet man who almost never raises his voice"—Charlie Butts.[9]

Judge Byron Matthews presided over the McDuff trial. Before becoming a judge, Matthews was considered one of the best lawyers in all of northern Texas. He would be one of the first lawyers inducted into the Texas Criminal Defense Lawyers Association Hall of Fame. "He was tougher than a boot," Charlie Butts would say. In the McDuff trial, as in all of his trials, Matthews maintained control of his courtroom.[10]

During the proceedings a number of reports of planned

assassination attempts reached Sheriff Lon Evans's office. As a result, security in and around the courthouse was extraordinarily tight. Evans posted four armed deputies and three bailiffs around McDuff. At one point, even a District Judge was prevented from entering the courtroom.[11]

The McDuff family attended the trial *en force*. "The mama was very much the matriarch," Charlie Butts remembered. "I just can't bring myself to believe Kenneth could do such a thing," Addie said. "I can only hope they are wrong about my boy," added J. A.[12] Throughout the trial, Addie, her daughters (including the twelve-year-old), Lonnie (charges against him had been dropped) and his wife, and a girl named Maryane, who claimed to be Kenneth's girlfriend, attended the trial. (Maryane apparently did not care that Kenneth had been arrested while on a date with another girl.) The family announced that J. A. suffered from a heart condition and would stay in Rosebud. (It is more likely that he stayed home to work; he lived for almost thirty more years.)

It did not take long for Addie to draw attention to herself. She whined that Brady Pamplin had finally succeeded in getting Kenneth into serious trouble. She maintained Kenneth's innocence by claiming that he was with a young girl at the time of the murders. (This, too, did not seem to matter to Maryane.) According to Addie, Kenneth refused to divulge her identity because the girl was from his church. "He won't say anything about it. He thinks she should be the one to say." Addie concluded, "He's too good for his own good."[13]

III

Kenneth Allen McDuff was tried for the murder of Marcus Dunnam in November 1966. His defense amounted to a simple proposition: Roy Dale Green had committed the Broomstick Murders and framed him. Godfrey Sullivan publicly announced the defense strategy only a few days after Kenneth's arrest. It was the only real defense he could possibly argue. Kenneth could not deny being in Everman on the night of August 6, 1966, and Roy Dale had already admitted to being present during all of the murders. Hence, through his counsel, he argued that Roy Dale was the predator, because he was angry and frustrated at not being able to get a date. Simply put, Roy Dale was trying to avoid the electric chair.[14]

The jury consisted of nine men and three women. Kenneth was reported to have been personally involved in the selection. The prosecutors did notice that at times Kenneth "bent Sullivan's ear." Butts suspected that such a shameless display of arrogance would catch up with the defendant— sooner or later.[15]

The emotion-ridden trial included testimony of Mrs. Jack Brand, Robert's mother, and Louise's mother. Mrs. Brand testified that she did not see her son alive after he drove away from her home in Alvarado. The true value of her testimony, however, came when Charlie Butts held a blue and white striped shirt and asked her if she had ever seen it. In a slow, quiet voice, Mrs. Brand answered, "Yes, Mark carried it with him when he left." The shirt established a number of key prosecution points: Brady Pamplin found it in Kenneth's car on the night of the shootout in Bremond; Roy Dale testified that the same shirt was used to wipe fingerprints off the 1955 Ford; it would also be used to wipe off the broomstick, and tire tracks from remote roads in Tarrant and Johnson counties.

Louise's mother testified that Louise had left home at about 7 P.M. with Robert and Marcus. She assumed the three teenagers were going to a movie. Shortly into her testimony, she broke down so completely that the judge excused her. She had to be helped from the courtroom. Immediately, Godfrey Sullivan moved for a mistrial, arguing that the incident was a demonstration and, thus, prejudicial. Just as quickly, Byron Matthews denied the motion.[16]

The trial also featured heartbreaking testimony about the

condition of the victims' bodies and the causes of their deaths. Louise's horrifying sexual assault and murder was established in excruciating detail.

In preparing for their case, Grady Hight, Chief Deputy Brown, and Charlie Butts replicated the route Green and McDuff had taken on the night of the murders. It was important for the men to establish the time frame and the sequence of events as provided by Roy Dale's statement. It all fit. While at the McAlisters' farmhouse, Butts stood in one position and took a series of pictures. When placed side-by-side, they showed a panoramic view of the area. The collage of pictures would come in very handy when it came to establishing what the McAlister family could see from their porch.

Raymond McAlister, it turns out, remembered seeing Kenneth earlier that summer in the area where the boys were discovered. The only hitch was that he remembered seeing Kenneth in a Mustang, not a Dodge. Edith, Kenneth's Everman girlfriend, confirmed that Kenneth had once owned (and totaled) a blue Ford Mustang.[17]

The most anticipated event of the trial was the five-hour testimony of Roy Dale Green, which riveted the courtroom and the press corps assembled from throughout the nation. Spectators must have been shocked and surprised at the difference between preconceived notions made about Roy Dale, based only on news accounts, and the young man who took the stand on November 9, 1966. He shook as if he had been locked in a refrigerator. He constantly shifted in his chair and was unable to control his arms. Under comfortable circumstances, Roy Dale's speech was inarticulate; in the courtroom he could barely communicate. "He was scared out of his gourd of McDuff," said Butts. At times he groped for words, and towards the ends of sentences his voice faltered to an inaudible level. Oddly, however, it strengthened his credibility. "Anybody could look at him and tell he was telling the truth," Butts said of his star witness.[18]

Under cross-examination, Godfrey Sullivan further demonstrated Roy Dale's cognitive shortcomings, his utter lack of courage, and thus the stunning contrast between the pitiful youth on the stand and the emotionless predator behind the defendant's table. When Sullivan asked the obvious question, why didn't Roy Dale just drive away and escape the horror and make some attempt to help Robert, Marcus, and Louise, Roy Dale could only stutter a painfully inadequate response: "I . . . I . . . I just don't know."[19] Had Roy Dale said anything else he might have given jurors some reason to suspect deception.

On November 13, 1966, just when the spectators of the courtroom thought that the trial could not get any more dramatic, Godfrey Sullivan announced, "If the court please, the defendant would like to take the stand in his own behalf."[20] What Charlie Butts had suspected came to fruition; Kenneth's arrogance was beginning to lead to his downfall.

According to Kenneth, during the Broomstick Murders, he was asleep at a burned-out shopping center in Everman. In direct contradiction to what the jurors had seen for themselves only a day or two before, Kenneth described Roy Dale as angry, frustrated, and determined to look for girls. "Roy was very mad because he hadn't got a date. He wanted me to wait someplace while he used the car. We argued. He was real mad. I was just tired and wanted to go home and go to bed. I just sat down beside a wall and went to sleep," Kenneth testified. He added that it was Roy Dale who kept the broomstick because he had trouble with "some boys." The contrast between the assertive, determined Roy Dale Green Kenneth described, and the one the jurors had seen whimpering and shaking in the witness chair, was dramatic.[21]

Kenneth had never grown up. He still believed that whatever he said was the truth and others had to believe it—because *he* said it. He was still entering the principal's office with a baseball glove covered with black shoe polish announcing, "look what I found in a ditch." He made no mention of protecting the reputation of a church-going girl, and thus, he had either lied to Addie or Addie created the story she told to newsmen. To compound the debacle, Godfrey Sullivan asked Kenneth under direct examination, about being in a "little bit of trouble" in the past. In doing so, he made it possible for the prosecution to introduce Kenneth's past extraneous offenses.

In order to emphasize Kenneth's icy presence, Doug Crouch selected Charlie Butts, with his deliberate, gentlemanly manner, to cross-examine Kenneth. On the night before his cross-examination, Butts spoke by phone to a number of sheriffs and police chiefs throughout the Blackland Prairie.

Years later, Charlie Butts remembered the next day. Shortly into his cross-examination, Butts calmly said something like: "Now, Kenneth, let's talk about the 'little bit of trouble' you've been in."

As Butts slowly dismantled Kenneth, he began to squirm. Each time he was caught in a lie or tripped up, he nervously grabbed a knuckle on his left hand and twisted it. Since the open end of the witness stand faced the jurors, they could observe all of a seated witness during testimony. The astute observation by some of the jurors that, at times, Kenneth "looked like he would rip his knuckle off of his hand," became part of the deliberation when the jury retired.[22]

As the trial came to a close, Butts and Crouch presented final arguments for the state. "I have a deep-rooted feeling of the dignity of the courtroom, and I feel very strongly that the prosecution should see that the rules are followed," Charlie Butts was quoted as saying before the trial began. Indeed, true to his reputation as a gentleman, Butts deliberately used the law to bring about justice. That is probably why it made the newspapers when, during his closing argument, he uncharacteristically raised his voice and betrayed his outrage: "He choked the life's blood out of her!"[23]

Doug Crouch made the final argument for the state. Butts assisted by surreptitiously handing him strips of paper

containing elements of the argument in an order that gave
the presentation continuity.

On November 15, 1966, the jury received its instructions
and deliberated between three and four hours. The short
deliberation could have meant anything. The prosecutors
had failed to produce either the murder weapon used
against the boys—a .38 caliber Colt pistol—or the pink
broomstick used to violate and strangle Louise Sullivan.
But then, there was the credible testimony of Roy Dale
Green compared to the utterly incredible performance of
Kenneth McDuff. As soon as the jury returned to the courtroom, Godfrey Sullivan noticed that the three women jurors
had tears in their eyes. He knew what the verdict would
be.

Judge Matthews had warned the spectators that any out-
burst would bring a contempt of court citation. The McDuff
family sat together on the second row. Everyone reacted to
the guilty verdict and the death sentence in silence. Kenneth
"didn't show any more emotion than if he had squashed a
cockroach," Butts remembered. Almost immediately, a
wave of deputies surrounded Kenneth and quickly escorted
him from the courtroom.[24]

IV

Most people in Rosebud quietly voiced a sense of relief.
Kenneth was going to be put to death. It was just as well.
No one seriously thought he was going to get any better.
The older and bigger he got, the more dangerous he became. Along with the details of the Broomstick Murders
there came a deep sense of satisfaction that the death penalty would take care of Kenneth McDuff.

The only hitch during the trial came when a bailiff provided the sequestered jury with a bottle of booze for a quick
snort. The issue made it to Judge Matthews's bench in the
form of a motion for a new trial. Doug Crouch asked Charlie Butts to handle the motion. Butts argued that the statute

prohibited intoxication, not an innocent snort by tired and lonely jurors. Judge Matthews denied the motion for a new trial once he was thoroughly convinced that none of the jurors had gotten intoxicated. More than thirty years later, with some measure of glee, Butts would recount the appeals court referring to the booze as a bottle of "needful."[25]

After McDuff's conviction, Roy Dale Green pled guilty to murder without malice in the death of Marcus Dunnam. He received a five-year prison sentence. For the death of Louise Sullivan, however, his attorney, Brantley Pringle, convinced Roy Dale to plead guilty to murder with malice. It was clearly his best option. A jury, after hearing details of the gruesome murder of Louise Sullivan, could very well have returned a death sentence for Roy Dale. Instead, he was sentenced to twenty-five years.

While in prison, Roy Dale was despised by other prisoners for having snitched on McDuff. During the McDuff Trial, and while awaiting his hearing, the other inmates in the Tarrant County Jail unmercifully tormented him. "The boys upstairs [other prisoners] have told him that if he testified against McDuff he would not last out the first year in prison, that the other cons would get him. He believes them," said Pringle. Pringle added that Roy Dale was resigned to death in the electric chair or at the hands of other prisoners.[26]

In 1976, after hearing voices and seeing visions that kept him awake at night, Roy Dale was transferred to Rusk State Hospital. He spent three years there until he was paroled in 1979, after serving thirteen years for his part in the Broomstick Murders.[27]

McDuff stayed locked up in the Tarrant County Jail pending an automatic appeal to the Texas Court of Criminal Appeals. On October 8, 1968, the Court affirmed his conviction. His first date with the electric chair was set for December 3, 1968. The higher court ruling cleared the way for his relocation to state prison, and he arrived at the Texas Department of Corrections on October 9, 1968.[28]

McDuff probably did not experience the trauma of

prison life in the way Roy Dale did. Although there were
rumors that he was not the "bad" inmate he later claimed
to be—at least at first—after a while he did develop a reputation for being a tough guy. Until a federal court ruled
the practice to be illegal, McDuff served as a "Building"
or "Block Tender." Such inmates, who had earned the respect or fear of the other inmates, were given special privileges to keep order in their section of the prison.[29]

For the rest of his life, McDuff turned his prison experience into an expression of his toughness. He regaled in
long, excruciating stories of how he flourished in the "old"
system. His long descriptions of how guards beat him unmercifully and his fights with prisoners inevitably concluded with, "I quickly whipped his butt."[30]

While in prison, Kenneth tested at about a seventh-grade
achievement level. Two IQ tests measured him at 92 and
84. Relatively speaking, he appeared to be an average prisoner. He did manage to earn his Graduate Equivalency Diploma (GED) through the Windham School System (the
prison school system) with the class of 1973. He also completed forty-five hours of college credit through extension
courses from a local community college.[31]

His prison record, however, was less than pristine. He
was almost certainly involved in smuggling and using drugs
while an inmate. Years later, in an interview with federal
agents, someone who claimed to be a close, live-in female
acquaintance with Lonnie, charged that Lonnie smuggled
drugs into prison for Kenneth by bribing a guard.[32]

Kenneth's good luck first surfaced with a simple, albeit
careless, clerical error. In the charges of the capital murder
and rape of Edna Louise Sullivan, Kenneth, through his
attorney, filed a *Writ for a Quick and Speedy Trial*. The
writ had been received by the court in Johnson County on
June 15, 1970, and was incorrectly treated as a *Writ of
Habeas Corpus* and denied. Over seven years later, on September 15, 1977, McDuff's new attorney, Gary Jackson of
Dallas, Texas, correctly argued that the *Writ for a Quick*

and Speedy Trial should have been granted at the time. Thus, Kenneth had been denied a constitutional right. Jackson's motion included arguments assuming McDuff's innocence of the Dunnam conviction. Judge Byron Crosier's ruling accepted Jackson's argument of the denial of a speedy trial, but clearly rejected the notion of Kenneth's innocence. The murder and rape charges against Kenneth were dismissed on March 8, 1978.[33] To the revulsion of those who knew the facts, for the rest of his life, Kenneth correctly asserted that he had never been tried or convicted of doing anything to Louise Sullivan. In retrospect, the simple clerical error was but the beginning of an extraordinary string of luck for Kenneth Allen McDuff.

A seemingly unconnected crime being committed over one thousand miles away in Georgia would bring even more luck to McDuff and many others. A burglar named William Henry Furman was breaking into a home when the owners arrived and surprised him. While attempting to escape, Furman tripped and fell. The gun he was carrying fired a round through a closed kitchen door from the outside, killing a resident inside the home. At the trial, he testified: "They got me charged with murder and I admit, I admit going to these folks' home and they did caught [sic] me in there and I was coming back out. . . . I was coming out backwards and fell back and I didn't intend to kill nobody. I didn't know they was behind the door." The jury thought otherwise. After deliberating only one hour and thirty-five minutes, they delivered a guilty verdict and a sentence of death.[34]

The appeal of William Henry Furman was later combined with those of Lucious Jackson, Jr., and Elmer Branch, the latter two convicted of rape and sentenced to death in Georgia and Texas, respectively. Furman, a twenty-six-year-old laborer at an upholstery shop, and Jackson and Branch, through their appeals to the United States Supreme Court, saved the life of Kenneth Allen McDuff.

V

The Constitution of the United States, as amended by the Bill of Rights, specifically Amendment Five, reads in part, ". . . nor [shall an accused person] be deprived of life, liberty, or property, without due process of law . . ." Few things in our Constitution are as clear as the recognition of the power of the state to deprive a person of life as punishment for a crime against the state—as long as the accused has had the benefit of due process. The phrase is repeated in Amendment Fourteen in the same section as the Equal Protection Clause. The Constitution, however, also prohibits "cruel and unusual punishments" in Amendment Eight and requires "equal protection of the laws" in Amendment Fourteen. Our Constitution tells us, in theory, when we can execute people. But, while capital punishment is recognized, it is not required, and the Constitution does not prohibit us, as a people, from concluding that executions are morally impermissible.

Thus, our Founding Fathers left us with state-sanctioned power to inflict capital punishment and a huge debate over how to do it—if we should do it at all. The debate is almost as old as the Constitution itself.

In 1972, that debate reached a climax with a Supreme Court ruling in the case *Furman v Georgia*. The five-to-four decision pretty much reflected contemporaneous American divisions over the issue. The majority (Justices Douglas, Brennan, Marshall, Stewart, and White) ruled that in the cases of Furman, et al., the imposition and carrying out of the death penalty constituted cruel and unusual punishment and unequal protection in violation of the Eighth and Fourteenth Amendments.

However, only Brennan and Marshall, both lifelong opponents of the death penalty, argued that the death penalty was, *per se*, cruel and unusual punishment. Brennan asserted that it did "not comport with human dignity." Marshall argued that it was impermissible because it was "morally unacceptable" and "excessive." Douglas, Stewart, and White essentially argued, for different reasons, that the *infrequency* of executions evidenced unequal application. Byron White, in his concurring opinion wrote: "I begin with what I consider a near truism: That the death penalty could so seldom be imposed that it would cease to be a credible deterrent or measurable to contribute to any other end of punishment in the criminal justice system. . . . [W]hen the imposition of the death penalty reaches a certain degree of infrequency, it would be very doubtful that any existing general need for retribution would be measurably satisfied."

Potter Stewart wrote: "These death sentences are cruel and unusual in the same way that being struck by lightning is cruel and unusual. They are capricious."

Justice Brennan, the most eloquent and outspoken opponent of capital punishment, wrote: "When a country of over 200 million people inflicts an unusually severe punishment no more than fifty times a year, the inference is strong that the punishment is not being regularly and fairly applied."

Finally, William O. Douglas argued that imbalances in executions amounted to an incompatibility with the Equal Protection Clause.[35] Each of the arguments suggested that the death penalty could be made more equitable by *increasing* its use.

So, the Court ruled that the death penalty, as it was administered—i.e., giving juries near-unlimited discretion over sentences—was unconstitutional. The victory for anti–death penalty advocates was shallow and short lived and their celebrations premature. Through *Furman*, the Supreme Court "taught" states how to make death penalty laws constitutional, and almost every state would rush to pass laws assuring a more "equal" application—making executions far more, not less, common in the United States.

At the time, however, the nearly 600 men and women on death rows throughout the country, including 127 in

Texas, magically had their sentences commuted to life in prison. Many of them would be eligible for parole in a surprisingly short time; one of them was Kenneth Allen McDuff.[36]

4

Freed to Kill Again

*"You know, when you're on parole and you been on death
row, it's hard to find a date."*
—Kenneth Allen McDuff

I

Furman v Georgia was not the only significant development affecting the prison life of Kenneth McDuff in 1972.
That year, a disgruntled Texas prison inmate named David
Ruiz, who was serving a twenty-five-year sentence for
armed robbery, initiated a handwritten lawsuit alleging a
variety of violations of his civil rights in the prison system.
His complaint alleged overcrowding, poor medical care,
and the use of Building Tenders as guards of other inmates.
The Building Tenders kept control of their area, and in turn,
received preferred treatment by guards and prison officials.
Ruiz alleged that Building Tenders beat other prisoners to
keep them in line.[1] The Ruiz case went before United States
District Judge William Wayne Justice of Tyler. Thus began
the longest and most expensive trial in the history of Texas.

Years later, during the early to mid 1980s, Judge Justice,
in effect, seized the prison system from the people of Texas.
His ruling concluded that the system violated inmate rights
through crowding, poor medical care, using inmates as
guards, brutality by professional guards, and unconstitutional grievance and discipline procedures. He ordered a
complete overhaul of the prison system and set up federal
monitors and "masters" to assure compliance. The Ruiz
controversy lasted over twenty years; Judge Justice's reign
over Texas prisons lasted over nine.[2]

Before the prison construction boom that resulted from
the Ruiz lawsuit, the immediate problem of overcrowding

had to be addressed. The state scrambled to comply with
Justice's order, which did not even allow for full occupancy
of a facility. In 1987, Justice ruled that occupancy above
ninety-five percent capacity, or about 48,400 inmates, was
a violation of prisoners' rights. As a result, county jails
became filled with backlogged state prisoners awaiting
transfer to prisons that had no space. In some areas, county
jails became so crowded that "tent cities" of prisoners were
seriously discussed. In frustration, Bob Ozer, an assistant
attorney general, lamented, "Federal court orders control.
[If] we go over the cap [we] risk $800,000-a-day in fines."[3]

The enormous cost of satisfying Judge Justice's order
caused even the Texas State Legislature to halt its traditional tough-guy attitudes toward crime and criminals. During the 1991 legislative session, fewer than sixty bills were
filed creating new crimes and felonies, and of those, less
than a dozen passed. Chairman of the House Corrections
Committee Allen Hightower suggested that, "Maybe we finally realize that if we only have 50,000 prison beds, that
we need to keep only the worst 50,000 criminals there and
not keep trying to lock everybody up."[4]

During a time of reduced spending and a war against
big government, Texas prisons overflowed and resistance
to raising taxes or passing bonds continued. As the backlog
of felons clogged county jails and the populace reacted in
horror to the notion of criminal "tent cities" surrounded by
chain-linked fences near their neighborhoods, public officials had only one tool left to ease overcrowding—parole.

Parole seemed like the answer. Prisoners who had served
some time could be released quietly into a society mostly
unaware of the parolee's past. Parolees had no identifying
scarlet letters or tattoos, and parole hearings seldom, if ever,
generated public interest. Very few Texans knew anyone
on the parole board, and thus, there was little oversight or
public accountability. Without much fuss and with near an-
onymity, a few board members could release prisoners and
relieve the governor and legislators of the burden of raising
taxes or increasing bond indebtedness.

The Texas Department of Corrections instructed the parole board to release 150 prisoners a day—750 prisoners a week—3,000 per month—36,000 per year—or nearly seventy-five percent of the population Judge Justice allowed to be housed in Texas prisons in 1987.[5] The desperation to expedite the exodus from incarceration birthed a novel concept: Parole in Absentia, or PIA. PIA meant that an inmate, while housed in a county jail, could get a parole from state prison, without ever having spent a day in the prison.[6]

And so, an unelected federal judge seized a prison system and placed the rights of prisoners above the safety of the public. The state responded with an utter lack of political courage. In effect, the people of Texas slept, to awaken later to find that felons who might have been housed in the dreaded tent cities surrounded by chain-link fences were now in their neighborhoods—without tents or fences.

II

By 1976, less than ten years after his conviction for the murder of Marcus Dunnam, Kenneth McDuff had accumulated enough good time credits to be eligible for parole. At the time, however, a request for parole for a capital murderer was not reviewed by all of the eighteen-member board. Three members reviewed each case. The majority ruled.[7]

The Texas Board of Pardons and Paroles was an independent agency charged by law with the authority to make decisions regarding granting and revoking paroles. Its eighteen members were appointed by the Governor to staggered, six-year terms. A Governor could remove any member at any time for any reason unless another Governor had appointed that member. Kenneth's first three parole reviews, on April 4, 1976, and on February 18 and November 16, 1977, were conducted as the Ruiz case slowly progressed through the federal court. During those deliberations, there was no urgency to release prisoners. On January 11, 1979, Edward Johnson cast the first favorable vote for Kenneth's parole. The other two members, however, voted no. The second board member to vote for approval was Helen Copitka on January 2, 1980. Again, this was a lone yes vote, and Kenneth was forced to stay in prison—for the time being.[8]

By March 1981, McDuff had been denied parole five times. On two of those occasions, he had received single favorable votes from two different individuals. The sense of invulnerability he and Lonnie shared as boys must have been reinforced by this bizarre turn of events. On March 23, 1981, his arrogance returned and it would get him back into trouble.

Glenn Heckmann had been hired as a parole commissioner by the parole board. His job was to conduct face-to-face interviews of inmates and then cast a vote on their parole request. Afterwards, two members of the board voted on the recommendation. At the time, McDuff was an inmate at the Retrieve Unit near Angleton. Heckmann and McDuff met in the Chaplain's office. As Heckmann went through routine questions about McDuff's prison career and about the Broomstick Murders, McDuff interrupted with, "I don't know how to put this, but if you get me out on parole, I'll guarantee you you'll find $10,000 in the glove compartment of your car." Stunned, Heckmann made no response. He proceeded with the interview, but McDuff could not help himself; he tried again. "What I said earlier I meant. You'll have $10,000 in the glove compartment of your car before I leave. You can get me out. You're the vote I need."[9]

A few minutes later Heckmann left the room and the next morning went directly to local prosecutors to report the bribery attempt. Over a year and a half later, on August 6, 1982, McDuff was convicted of bribery, another felony, and sentenced to two years. He returned to the Retrieve Unit on September 3, 1982, unfazed by the incident. The sentence amounted to nothing, as it ran concurrently with

his life sentence. At best, this latest felony conviction de-
layed his parole, even though it took less than two years
for him to begin getting more favorable votes. In 1982 and
1983 his parole attempts were denied unanimously. On
March 19, 1984, board member Sue Cunningham cast a
favorable vote. Kenneth was back on the road to parole.[10]

In 1984 and 1985, Sue Cunningham cast two more favorable votes, but in both requests she was outvoted. In
1986, Kenneth appeared to have lost ground when the
three-member panel unanimously denied his request.[11] That
year was a particularly bad one for Kenneth McDuff. It
started with the only incident in which he would ever show
emotion.

III

As J. A. McDuff aged, Lonnie took on more responsibilities
in his father's concrete finishing business. Some of Lonnie's employees were decent, hard-working men. Others
were like a young man named Alva Hank Worley, from
nearby Belton, Texas. Hank really liked beer. Years later,
during an interview with psychologist Dr. Matt Ferrara,
Hank talked about routinely drinking a six-pack of beer at
a single sitting, and a total of about a case a day. According
to Hank, he did this while employed as a truck driver. He
quit truck driving "cause it was dangerous" and returned to
construction. Hank was also a petty thief. He had prior
arrests and convictions for larceny and evading arrest.[12]

Another of Lonnie's employees was a man named Larry.
At the age of eighteen, he had been arrested on a charge
of murder with malice, but the count was later reduced to
aggravated assault. He received a sentence of two years in
the Bell County Jail. He worked for Lonnie for four or five
years until he quit over conflicts with him.[13]

Lonnie never had the reputation Kenneth had in criminal
circles; some law enforcement officers say it was because
he had a better criminal mind. No record exists of his ever

engaging in a violent crime, but investigators did suspect him of gun running and drug trafficking. However, his criminal activity caught up to him on November 22, 1985, when he was arrested and charged with theft of more than $750 (a felony) and released on a $2,500 bond two days later. The next month, on December 14, he was charged with possession of methamphetamines and released on a $10,000 bond on December 16. Legally or illegally, Lonnie had access to big money. Posting bonds did not seem to be problematic, and when he was arrested on December 14, he had $975 in cash on his person.[14]

At about 8:30 P.M., on January 5, 1986, Lonnie and a girlfriend named Michelle arrived at the home of Larry's estranged wife, Doris. The home, a duplex in a poor section of Rogers, Texas, was owned by the Belton Housing Authority. It was a small, three bedroom, one bath, single-family dwelling inhabited by Doris and four children. Lonnie immediately poured everyone a drink from a bottle of Jack Daniel's whiskey he brought along. Michelle sat on a sofa in the living room and polished the fingernails of one of the little girls in the apartment. As Doris washed dishes in the kitchen sink, Lonnie walked up to her and made an inappropriate pass. According to statements, Michelle got angry and slammed the kitchen door as she left the house. Lonnie followed her out to his truck and they argued over whether he would immediately take her back to Temple.

About that time, Doris's cousin Tim arrived and agreed to bring Michelle back to Temple in Lonnie's truck. According to Doris's statement, as she was asking Tim to take Michelle back to Temple, she was really shaking her head to indicate that she did not want to be left alone with Lonnie. But Lonnie handed him the keys and Tim left with Michelle in Lonnie's truck. This left Lonnie and Doris alone in the home (along with the children).[15]

Shortly after Tim and Michelle left the duplex, Doris went into the back bedroom to change the diaper of one of the children. When Larry arrived at 10:15 P.M., he took a

Ruger 6 shot .22 magnum revolver out of his truck and placed it in his waistband. In his statement, Larry indicated that he did not know Lonnie was there and that it was routine for him to carry the gun into the house and place it on top of the refrigerator. When Lonnie answered the door Larry became enraged.

Immediately, Larry and Lonnie argued. Larry went down the hallway to his wife and shouted directly, "Are you fucking him?" She insisted that nothing happened. The enraged husband then returned to the kitchen and argued with Lonnie again. Doris remembered hearing Lonnie say, "No! No!" before hearing shots. Larry's statement read:

> I went back down the hall and he said something smart to me again and I told him I didn't want to hear any of his bullshit. I walked to get a drink of water and he got off of the couch and came in the kitchen after me like he was going to whoop my ass. I don't remember what I said but I told him something when I pulled out the pistol I had and shot him. He was standing near the kitchen table and I shot him in the head. He grabbed his head and stumbled back and I shot him again, which I think also hit him in the head. He fell on the floor across the hallway.[16]

Immediately, Larry's wife put her baby down and entered the hallway in time to see the other children hop over Lonnie's body, running towards her in a panic. Larry followed with the gun in his hand. She screamed and cried, "See, I knew it was going to happen." Larry told her he loved her and was tired of Lonnie making passes at her. Then he told her he was going to call the law.[17]

The duplex had no phone so Larry had to drive to the Rogers Inn to call the police. An employee witnessed the call and remembers Larry saying: "My name is [Larry] and I have just shot a man in my wife's apartment. Send an ambulance. I know he's dead. I will be waiting in the road when you get here." The Bell County dispatcher who received the call also recalled that Larry identified Lonnie and advised them that they should know Lonnie, as he had been in jail there recently. Larry assured the dispatcher that he had "no where to go" and would be waiting for the deputies to arrive.[18]

The first to arrive at the scene was patrolman Mike Brackman. Larry met him outside the duplex and said, "Mike, I shot a man." Without being instructed to do so, Larry turned around and placed his hands on a wall to be frisked. Brackman then handcuffed Larry and they re-entered the house.

Shortly afterwards, Bill Miller of the Bell County Sheriff's Office arrived. By 11:15 P.M., Texas Ranger John Aycock had been contacted as well. They found Lonnie lying on his back in a narrow hallway leading to the small bedrooms of the home. Nearby, on top of a television set that was still playing, right where Larry had put it, was the gun he had used to kill Lonnie. Lonnie's head lay in a large pool of blood, and some of his teeth were on the floor next to his body.[19]

Four Smurf glasses filled with coke and Jack Daniel's whiskey sat on the kitchen table as the officers processed the crime scene and arranged for Larry to be taken to the Rogers Police Department. Doris removed the children from the home through a window, placed them in a patrol car, and went to the Rogers Police Department as well. When Officer W. J. Bryan advised Larry of his rights, Larry responded, "I killed the man; what else do you want?" He added to Mike Brackman that he had done something he would probably always regret, "but that man was a sorry son-of-a-bitch, and deserved it." Larry was placed in the Bell County Jail under a bond of $15,000. He posted it and was released less than twenty-four hours after he had killed Lonnie.[20]

On the floor of a low-income project, in a pool of blood, lay the only person Kenneth Allen McDuff might have ever cared about. After finishing their work at the crime scene, the officers wrapped Lonnie in a bed sheet and placed him in a garbage bag.[21]

The autopsy revealed that the first shot entered Lonnie's head through his upper lip. The .22 round exploded in his mouth, destroying his upper teeth on the left side. The second shot entered his left temple and moved through his brain in a left-to-right direction. Lonnie had died almost instantly.[22]

IV

In October 1976, not long after Kenneth became eligible for parole, Addie retained an attorney from Dallas named Gary Jackson. Jackson and his wife Gloria, also an attorney, steadfastly believed in Kenneth's innocence. In an interview with federal agents, the couple insisted that there was no way Kenneth could have committed the crimes for which he had been accused and convicted. According to a confidential report, the Jacksons believed in a rather large conspiracy between the judiciary and several law enforcement agencies to wrongly convict Kenneth of murder. Gary Jackson appears to be among very few people who believed Kenneth's testimony during the Broomstick Murders Trial. Jackson maintained that Kenneth lent his car to Roy Dale to commit robbery and murder while he slept in a burntout shopping center in Everman, just as Kenneth had testified.[23]

To bolster the argument of Kenneth's innocence, Jackson commissioned the firm of Leavelle-Hilliard and Johnston, a polygraph service, to administer him a polygraph. During the session on September 6, 1977, Kenneth showed no deception on any of the questions asked of him.[24]

While polygraph results are not admissible in a court of law, they are, nonetheless, used often in investigations as a tool to filter out questionable sources of information. Jackson apparently accepted the results as definitive. One week later, he successfully filed a motion to dismiss pending charges against Kenneth for the rape and murder of Louise Sullivan. The granting of the motion, however, was based on the denial of a speedy trial and not on the arguments connected to the polygraph results. Still, the victory must have bolstered the hopes the Jacksons and the McDuffs had for getting Kenneth out of prison.

So convinced were the lawyers of Kenneth's innocence, that, as Gary Cartwright in *Texas Monthly* chronicled, they started a long and expensive campaign to expose the "true" Broomstick Murderer—Roy Dale Green. In his motion to dismiss, Jackson correctly argued that Roy Dale was the only person who had ever admitted to being present when the murders took place.[25]

Gary Jackson's allegiance to Kenneth McDuff went beyond a traditional attorney-client relationship into a business venture. Kenneth was marketed as a victim, unjustly convicted of murder, and wrongly sentenced to death and sent to prison. Talk of a book and movie deal led in 1989 to the incorporation of a business called "Justice for McDuff, Inc."[26]

But the first priority was to get Kenneth out.

V

On January 7, 1988, board members Ken Casner and Chris Mealy voted in favor of Kenneth's parole. He appeared to be headed for freedom until additional information was presented to the board, reportedly including letters of protest from a host of local officials from Falls County. The approval was almost immediately rescinded. Only four months later, the board reviewed the case again. Ken Casner voted again for approval, but his was the only affirmative vote. In July and September 1988, Kenneth's case received separate administrative reviews. So in one year—1988—four actions on a petition for the parole of Kenneth McDuff were taken.[27]

Political pressure from Judge Justice's rulings began to build and a crisis came to fruition. In 1988, 28,090 of

49,126 requests (fifty-seven percent) for paroles were approved; in 1989, 34,536 of 61,221 requests (fifty-six percent) were approved; in 1990, 56,442 of 71,074 requests (seventy-nine percent) were approved.[28]

During the late eighties and early nineties almost everyone was being released after only an initial review. Through good time credits, an inmate could serve less than six percent of his sentence. A prisoner who behaved himself could conceivably get credit for serving a full year in just twenty-two days. It was not uncommon to see petitioners with twenty-year sentences being released after serving only fourteen months.[29]

Addie McDuff added to efforts to secure Kenneth's release by contacting the office of an attorney named Bill Habern, who at the time employed a parole consultant named Helen Copitka. Copitka was a former member of the parole board and had voted on McDuff's parole requests on at least four occasions during the late 1970s and early 1980s. On at least one of those occasions, she voted for his release. In 1992, when McDuff's successful efforts to secure parole came under an intense review, Habern released a statement: "We did an initial evaluation. And we gave them [McDuff's family] the report and that was the termination of the relationship." But during an exhaustive series of investigative reports by television station WFAA-TV in Dallas, a gifted journalist named Robert Riggs reported that Helen Copitka had gone beyond providing a report to the McDuff family. She contacted and made attempts to influence the board. Citing phone messages in McDuff's confidential file, Riggs reported that Copitka talked to at least two parole board members. A phone log written by Cora Mosely, who voted on McDuff's release later the same year, stated: "Ms. Copitka pointed out some of the improprieties which occurred during the trial concerning the trial officials. She also referred to the continued instability of the inmate's co-defendant [Roy Dale Green] who was the prosecution's key witness."[30]

On September 1, 1989, Kenneth McDuff made a fif-

teenth request for parole. The three-member panel reviewing the case consisted of Cora Mosely, Dr. James
Granberry, and Chris Mealy. It is not likely that Copitka's
call to Mosely had an influence on her vote; incredibly,
Mosely later admitted that she probably did not look at
McDuff's file before voting. At the time, Granberry served
as the chairman of the parole board. Governor Bill Clem-
ents had appointed him to the influential position, for which
he had no apparent formal training. Granberry was an or-
thodontist who had also served as mayor of Lubbock and
was very active in political campaigns. When reporter Robert Riggs of WFAA-TV News in Dallas interviewed him,
Granberry asserted that he had looked very carefully at
McDuff's file and noticed the name of an old high school
buddy—McDuff's lawyer, Gary Jackson.[31]

James Granberry and Gary Jackson grew up together in
the little town of Lindale, near Tyler, Texas. By his own
admission, Granberry called Jackson to inquire about the
McDuff case. According to Granberry, Jackson spoke to
him for about two hours about McDuff, asserting McDuff's
innocence. Within a day or so, Granberry wrote an internal
memo which read, in part, "I wish to abstain from voting
due to a long-standing friendship with the attorney representing Mr. McDuff's parole procedure." Another board
member named Henry Keene took Granberry's place on the
panel.[32]

Officially, on September 1, 1989, Cora Mosely and
Chris Mealy voted to approve the parole; Henry Keene
voted to deny. The approval had been complicated, however, by protests from the Tarrant County District Attorney,
Tim Curry, and the Brazoria County District Attorney, Jim
Mapel. This led to a re-examination of the McDuff application.[33]

The new three-member panel consisted of Chris Mealy
and Henry Keene, neither of whom changed his vote, and
Dr. James Granberry, who only two weeks earlier had ab-
stained from voting on the same request. Granberry cast the
deciding vote. On September 14, 1989, slightly less than

twenty-three years after being convicted of the Broomstick
Murders, Kenneth Allen McDuff had been granted parole.
On September 24, he was transferred to the Michael Unit
for processing out of the prison system. By October 5,
McDuff's parole certificate had been issued, and on Octo-
ber 11, 1989, he walked out.[34]

VI

McDuff's release from prison appeared to provide a boost
in activities related to Justice for McDuff, Inc. According
to its president, Albert C. Shore, a former executive with
Fox Television, and someone who convincingly maintained
he had no other ties to McDuff or his family, the corporation was formed in order to protect the McDuff Project
from copyright infringement. The Jacksons had recruited
Shore because of his expertise in the marketing field.[35]

In a letter from Gloria Jackson to Shore, dated January
28, 1991, Jackson attached a letter that was a response to
Joseph D. Tarwater, the marketing director of the United
Screenwriters Production Partners (USPP) of Euless, Texas.
It was a counterproposal to USPP for the development of
a screenplay about the McDuff story. In the letter, Jackson
indicated that the goal of Justice for McDuff, Inc. was to
rectify a miscarriage of justice. Towards that end, the principals of the corporation (which apparently amounted to
Gary and Gloria Jackson) had already expended a great deal
of time and energy documenting the McDuff saga and securing the copyright to a preliminary treatment of the story.
Jackson proposed a 60/40 split with USPP.[36] Gloria Jackson's counterproposal also insisted on an extraordinary artistic control over the project, including the retention of
music rights and the selection of music for the soundtrack,
the selection of creative talent, and a veto to assure "fidelity
to the objective."[37]

Kenneth himself served the corporation as its vice president. Gary Jackson also recruited two other officers named

Joe and Ellen Ellard. Joe served as another vice president; Ellen served as the secretary-treasurer. According to a report filed by federal investigators of an interview with the Ellards, the couple appeared to be utterly convinced of a conspiracy against Kenneth, as described by the Jacksons. Mr. Ellard indicated that he and Gary Jackson had visited Kenneth in prison in early 1989. The Ellards described Kenneth as intelligent, well-mannered, and an individual who was a lady's man. Moreover, they asserted, Kenneth only dated nice girls and never did drugs.[38]

Justice for McDuff, Inc. was the business equivalent of Addie McDuff. The business people involved in the project accepted Kenneth's account of his criminal past, and attributed his troubles to conspiracies. On January 28, 1991, Gloria Jackson wrote a letter to Kenneth stating, in part: "My impression is that Mr. Jackson is truly interested in your success. . . . He expects your native ability, perseverance, and determination to give you an advantage many ex-convicts lack."[39]

5

Parole

"I don't know why people got so excited; I was just standing there with my knife."
—Kenneth Allen McDuff

I

At the time of the Broomstick Murders, Bill Miller was a law enforcement officer in the Fort Worth area. He remembers vividly the horrible deaths of Robert, Marcus, and Louise at the hands of Kenneth McDuff. Later, he had first-hand experience with the McDuffs when he assisted in the investigation of Lonnie's murder. One day in October 1989, while at his office at the Bell County Sheriff's Department, he took a call from a friend who owned a convenience store:

"Guess who just came in my store? Kenneth McDuff," said the caller.

"Well, there's going to be problems," Bill said.[1]

On October 14, 1989, only three days after Kenneth McDuff walked out of prison, a pedestrian strolling the 1500 block of East Avenue N in Temple came upon the body of a black female lying in a field of tall grass. She was in her twenties, about 5'6" and weighed about 115–120 pounds. She had been beaten and strangled, no more than twenty-four hours before her body was found. Within days, she was identified as a suspected prostitute named Sarafia Parker. Texas Ranger John Aycock later located and interviewed a witness who could allegedly place Parker in a pickup truck driven by McDuff on or about October 12, 1989. On that day, Kenneth McDuff had reported to his parole officer—in Temple. No other connection between the murder of Sarafia Parker and McDuff has ever been established or made public. Although the case is still open, at least officially, and McDuff was never accused of any crime involving Sarafia Parker, informed confidential sources are convinced that Kenneth Allen McDuff resumed his murderous life with her death.[2]

On the day Kenneth was released from prison, a woman named Angela claims to have met him. In her statement, she said that she witnessed one of his nephews trying to set him up with a woman named Kim who had "a reputation for being agreeable with sex"—sort of a present for Kenneth, who had not had sex with a woman for twenty-three years. Angela described McDuff as not being able to talk about anything but prison life. She quoted him as saying that, "Once you've done the first one [kill a person], it's easy." She also remembered that his speech and references toward women were crude, rude, and abrasive.[3]

The first few months of his newfound freedom can only be described as aimless and tumultuous. Paroled to Milam County, McDuff was supposed to live with his sister in Rockdale. Officially, he was to work for one of his nephews who owned an air conditioning business. On October 17, 1989, he applied for a driver's license, using a car belonging to his sister's family to take the driving test.

That his sister in Rockdale helped to make his parole possible made no difference to him; he showed no gratitude and managed to severely disrupt her household, causing the accommodating family considerable tension. In an interview with federal investigators, his Rockdale sister readily admitted that Kenneth took advantage of her entire family. For example, because of a grudge Kenneth had against her son, he took the son's pickup truck, which had only 25,000 miles on it, and "tore it up." Kenneth apparently did not like her husband either. When asked by investigators if he had any friends, his sister said, "Ain't nobody close to Kenneth." Less than a month after his parole, he requested a transfer out of Rockdale to another sister's home in the Waco District in McLennan County.[4]

By December 5, 1989, Kenneth had successfully transferred his parole to the Waco District and was living with the other sister. This sister, too, had a son. He admitted to running around with his ex-con uncle, but soon backed away after witnessing McDuff beating up a black kid in Rosebud. Only four days after moving to Waco, McDuff's parole officer reported an unverified meeting between Kenneth and "producers" in Dallas. In an interview in 1996, McDuff asserted that his "lawyers" had told him that within two months, movies and other "Justice for McDuff" projects would make him a millionaire. As a result, McDuff insisted, he had no ambition to find a job or otherwise exert any effort to earn a living.[5]

Indeed, Kenneth McDuff had no visible means of support. In a confidential report, a member of the McDuff family maintained that Addie supported him by giving him money and cars. In a conversation with a Bell County Investigator, and later in testimony, Addie admitted that she got Kenneth a credit card "cause we didn't want him to carry any money. I just paid the bill when I got it."[6]

He seemed utterly unconcerned about instructions from his parole officer. On December 19, 1989, only twelve days after transferring to his sister's home in Waco, Kenneth asked to have his parole transferred back to Temple. Almost immediately, he was told not to move to Temple, yet only five days after that admonition his parole officer's own records established that Kenneth had moved anyway—in violation of direct instructions. By January 4, 1990, Addie confirmed that he was living with her. His insolence carried with it no sanction. Quite the opposite; less than two weeks later, on January 17, 1990, Kenneth Allen McDuff was removed from sex offender supervision.[7]

In February 1990, McDuff's youngest sister was involved in a serious automobile accident. He reportedly stayed in her Tyler home with other family members during much of February through May to assist in her recovery. While there, he stayed in contact with his parole officer by phone.

By the end of May, he indicated that he might like yet

another transfer, this time to Lewisville, just north of Dallas. On May 29, 1990, he reported having a job at a construction company and living nearby in The Colony, Texas. This job did not last any longer than the others had. Two weeks later, he canceled his request to transfer to Lewisville and moved back in with Addie.

On July 5, 1990, he reported that he was working with his father; four days later he requested assistance to attend a technical college or a truck driving school. Three days after that he violated the conditions of his parole again—in Rosebud.[8]

II

It did not take long for the people of Rosebud to hear the news—Kenneth was out. The "tormentors" of his past—Tommy, Richard, Roy Dale, the former Justice of the Peace—all went about their business a lot more carefully. A "cloud of intimidation" descended over Rosebud and the surrounding communities of the Blackland Prairie. Now, McDuff—more than a bully on a motorcycle—was a convicted murderer hardened by twenty-three years of prison. He no longer needed Addie to protect him. At nearly 6'4" and weighing well over 200 pounds, he was bigger than ever. Only 1,035 parole officers—each averaging seventy-three cases—watched over him and 70,000 other offenders.[9]

He was supposed to stay out of Falls County, but on July 11, 1990, Kenneth and his nephew went to Rosebud. Outside a storefront at 301 Main Street, he sat on the sidewalk to listen to a band practice. One of the band members, Robert McBee, stepped outside during a break. He recognized Kenneth because he had introduced himself to the band during a practice the night before. As the two men sat on the curb on Rosebud's Main Street, four young black males walked by. Kenneth greeted them with, "Hey, nigger,

I bet you don't like white boys any more than white boys like you."

"No, I don't," replied the young man.

After a heated exchange, Kenneth retrieved a switch-blade knife from his car and approached the most vocal of the young men, a sixteen-year-old high school student. The young black man ran into an alley that bordered the building on 301 Main and grabbed two bricks to defend himself. Clutching his knife, Kenneth chased him, but backed off and returned to his car when he realized that he would soon be outnumbered.[10]

Kenneth McDuff thought that blacks were inferior to whites and he thought of himself as one of very few whites who had the courage to confront them, a skill he perfected in prison. In his car, he carried what most people called a "tire-thumper," which is a long piece of round wood with a metal cap on one end and a leather wrist-strap on the other. McDuff, however, called it his "nigger-thumper." He also carried a "hunting knife" under the seat of his car; it was probably the knife he had used during the incident in Rosebud.[11]

McDuff was a virulent racist, and yet he chose to spend a great deal of his time with blacks. His relations with African-Americans were inconsistent, at best. He routinely bought "dates" with black prostitutes. His hateful mind and his egotistic, childish need to impress others drew him to anyone he considered inferior to himself—blacks, slow-witted whites, and smaller people, especially women.

Later during the evening of the racial confrontation in Rosebud, the black teenagers who had been accosted by McDuff, accompanied by one of their fathers, contacted the Justice of the Peace, Judge Ellen Roberts. The father was concerned for the safety of the boys, but they drew up a complaint against McDuff anyway. Interestingly, the next day, Sheriff Larry Pamplin called Judge Roberts and asked that she drop her complaint in favor of a County Court Complaint and Warrant. Judge Roberts agreed to the request and noted it on her original complaint on July 12,

1990. The parole office issued an emergency warrant the next day.[12]

There is no indication that the Falls County Sheriff's Department took action or made a significant effort to arrest McDuff. TDCJ records suggest that he was arrested as a parole violator for making a terroristic threat on July 18. On that day, he was arrested by Bell County Sheriff's deputies during a visit to the parole office in Temple and taken directly to the Bell County Jail. Falls County Sheriff Larry Pamplin apparently preferred to have Bell County house McDuff. The Falls County Jail was secure enough, but it had only sixteen cells. According to a Bell County Sheriff's Office memo, Pamplin agreed to have McDuff held there for the parole hearing. While McDuff was in the Bell County Jail, Thomas Sehon, Falls County District Attorney, wrote a letter to TDCJ in which he stated that, "The above [McDuff] is probably the most extraordinarily violent criminal to set foot in Falls County, Texas."[13]

McDuff was a seventeen-year-old child in a forty-four-year-old body. His silliness and immaturity knew no bounds. Only two days before his arrest in Temple, he had wrecked yet another car, causing injuries to his sixteen-year-old nephew.[14]

On September 11, 1990, at 9:35 A.M., an Administrative Release Revocation Hearing on Kenneth's parole took place at the Bell County Jail. Listed as participants were McDuff, Gary Jackson—identified as Kenneth's *pro bono* attorney—Michael Hull, the Hearing Officer, Robert McBee (the Rosebud band member), two observers, and three parole officers. Even though the offense had occurred in Rosebud, in Falls County, and only one month earlier the Falls County District Attorney described him as a "most extraordinarily violent criminal," the record does not indicate attendance by Larry Pamplin or anyone else from the Falls County Sheriff's Office. Additionally, Michael Pressley, a supervising parole officer, who started the proceedings with a statement of the status of the charges, reported that the charge of terroristic threat had been referred to the

Falls County Court of Law at Marlin. However, at the time of the hearing, no court documents were available, and no court date had been set, even though it had been two months since Sheriff Pamplin had asked Ellen Roberts to drop her complaint in favor of a county complaint. (Today, Larry Pamplin argues that the issue was between TDCJ and McDuff and it did not require his presence.) The four young men who had been threatened by Kenneth had not shown up either. The mother of the primary witness refused to allow him to testify; she feared for his safety. Thus, the only witness against Kenneth was Robert McBee.[15]

Robert made it clear that he was fearful of testifying. Gary Jackson added to the tension with his constant objections to nearly every question asked of Robert. The record described one Jackson objection as, "OBJECTION entered to any further testimony relative to the knife as the knife itself is the only testimony as to what it was. OVERRULED." At least twenty-nine Gary Jackson objections were noted in the Hearing Report.[16]

As in his trial in Fort Worth, Kenneth insisted on testifying in his own behalf. The official record of his testimony read:

RELEASEE [McDuff] essentially testified to being in Rosebud, Texas on the night of the alleged incident. RELEASEE was at the building where the band practices listening. RELEASEE walked out of the building and bumped into a black male. The black male stated to the RELEASEE "Watch where your [sic] going peckerwood." RELEASEE said the same thing back to the black male. RELEASEE went to his car and returned to the building where he listened to the band some more. RELEASEE walked out of the building at the intermission. A black male with a white woman came by and spoke to the RELEASEE. There were no threats exchanged. While outside [a black kid] came jitter bugging by speaking in slang. After passing by RELEASEE [the black kid] was some distance away when he turned and

assumed a fighting stance. RELEASEE walked to the
edge of the building where two black males were waiting with large pieces of debris in their hand. RE-
LEASEE turned and went to the car where RELEASEE
retrieved a knife. With the knife at his side RELEASEE
asked the two males what did they have in mind.[17]

Had he stopped there, McDuff's testimony might have
had some credibility. He admitted to an exchange with the
young boys and that he had held his knife in the altercation.
But Kenneth McDuff could not help himself; he had to
pontificate, and in the process revealed the depths of his
racism. The record continues:

Everywhere people go blacks intimidate whites. . . . At
this point in the testimony RELEASEE's attorney had
to shout at RELEASEE in order to stop him from testifying. RELEASEE had begun to make assertions as to
how different racial groups react in social situations and
how RELEASEE was intimidated by blacks.

Under cross-examination, Kenneth's joy at being a
tough, old-time ex-con came back to undercut his testimony. He readily admitted that he would never have complained to the police because he was raised to take care of
his own business. Further, he grew up in prison and had
learned to take care of himself. Essentially, he admitted that
at almost 6'4" tall, and weighing 245 pounds, he had no
real fear of a few high school boys.[18]

The hearing ended at 1:10 P.M. Based on the testimony
of Robert McBee, the officer concluded that Kenneth had
violated Rule #2 of the conditions of his parole, making a
terroristic threat, placing a high school student from Rosebud in fear of imminent serious bodily injury. The hearing
officer and the field officer agreed to a recommendation for
the revocation of Kenneth's parole.[19]

On October 11, 1990, Kenneth McDuff returned to the
state prison system, exactly one year after he had been re-

leased. At the same time, however, several forces were already working toward the reinstatement of his parole. According to an undated paper in the Austin Police Department case file on McDuff, on October 23 Gary Jackson submitted a motion to reopen Kenneth's parole revocation hearing and wrote a letter to Parole Board Chairman James Granberry requesting that the revocation be set aside. In an interview with Robert Riggs, Granberry claimed never to have seen the letter, which began with "Dear Jim" and reportedly asserted that McDuff's continued imprisonment was not benefiting the prison system, the parole system, McDuff, or anyone else. When handed a copy of the letter, Granberry stated that it looked like the letter was forwarded to Bettie Wells, a parole division staff attorney.[20]

On December 6, 1990, Bettie Wells made an administrative decision to reinstate Kenneth McDuff's parole. As Gary Cartwright pointed out in *Texas Monthly*, there was no hearing, no testimony, and no advocacy of any kind. Almost two years later, Bettie Wells testified before a Senate Committee investigating the entire McDuff saga: "In reviewing the information that was presented to me, based upon the criteria, the rules and procedures and operating procedures that we were operating under at the time, he fit the category for the person who would be qualified to be reinstated [on parole], and that's what I went by." She added that McDuff had been accused of making a terroristic threat, but his accusers never showed up at the hearing. Moreover, after Judge Ellen Roberts withdrew her complaint, if any charges were ever filed against Kenneth through the Falls County Sheriff's Office, they were dropped after witnesses refused to testify.[21]

At the time of the Wells decision, the impact of federal Judge William Wayne Justice's seizure of Texas prisons had reached its zenith. So had the unwillingness of Texans to address prison overcrowding through capital outlays. In 1990, McDuff was but one of 56,442 convicts set free while the parole rate reached an all-time high of seventy-nine percent. State government continued to act in a way that sup-

ported a belief that parole was a painless way to meet Judge
Justice's demands and avoid his fines.

On December 18, 1990, Kenneth Allen McDuff walked
out of prison—again.[22]

6

An Absence of Beauty

*"You look out the window and wonder and say, 'Somebody
ought to neuter all these people.' "*
—J. W. Thompson, Austin Police Department

I

Interstate Highway 35, the major artery for Central Texas,
connects San Antonio, Austin, Belton, Temple, and Waco.
Around Austin, the highway runs along the Balcones Fault,
separating alluvial bottoms and agricultural lands to the
east, from the rocky sediments of the Hill Country ranches
to the west. In his biography of Lyndon Johnson, Robert
Caro called the Hill Country "The Trap," which accurately
contrasts its mesmerizing beauty with the hardiness it took
to tame the area.

San Antonio and Austin are splendid examples of the
power of multiculturalism, and monuments to cooperation
among diverse populations. Further north, the hamlets of
the Blackland Prairie surround the larger cities of Belton,
Temple, and Waco. Baylor University in Waco, the University of Mary Hardin-Baylor in Belton, Southwestern
University in nearby Georgetown, and other colleges and
technical schools in the area provide splendid educational
opportunities to the people who live here. The hard-
working, conservative, largely religious people help contribute to and take pride in their neighborhoods and schools.
Throughout the area, man-made lakes provide water, rec-
reation, and breathtaking scenery. Central Texas is a beautiful place to live.

Central Texas also holds beauty in the quality of its people. Families dressed in their Sunday best visit places of
worship in the belief that their faith in God makes them

better people. Proud homeowners mow their lawns and wipe their brows in the unrelenting Texas heat. Mothers and fathers walk with children they love more than life itself. These parents ease the pain of a bruised knee, cheer their children at concerts and football games, encourage them, and instill in them an appreciation for the beauty in their lives. Friendly strangers smile and welcome one another. In Temple, Belton, and Waco, indeed, in all of Central Texas, the prevalent culture is one of honor, morality, and scholarship. In all such things, there is beauty.

For visitors and for many residents, it is hard to imagine the existence of anything in Central Texas but this beauty. But there is another side to the region—a subculture with an absence of beauty—the side of Central Texas in which Kenneth Allen McDuff chose to spend his time.

Those who populate this subculture live in a world of their own—largely unknown to the rest of Central Texans. At first glance, the major difference between the two cultures appears to be monetary; a closer look reveals more than poverty. It reveals an absence of pride of any type and the complete lack of social graces and any moral base upon which to gauge appropriate behavior. Hope, requiring an investment in deferred gratification, cannot be found. For some, beauty is a twelve-pack of beer and a carton of cigarettes. Others find fleeting satisfaction in harder, more dangerous highs.

Some of the inhabitants of this beauty-less culture live in trailer homes like those found in the S&S Mobile Home Park outside of Belton. The S&S trailer park shows no evidence of a lawn mower. Many of the "homes" straddle rough gravel pathways. Some trailers are empty shells, abandoned by former inhabitants fleeing a bill collector, parole officer, or creditor/drug dealer. Other rotted single- or doublewides only *look* empty; in time, dwellers emerge with children following because they have nowhere else to go—and nothing else to do. Too many of these children are growing up believing that what they see is normal. Parked outside some of these dreary shacks are Harley-

Davidson motorcycles or shiny, spotless pickup trucks—
worth a block of those mobile homes.

Sometimes, members of this subculture become
"friends" for years without ever knowing each other's
names. During the early nineties, Alva Hank Worley knew
Kenneth McDuff for well over a year without ever knowing
that his name was either Kenneth or McDuff. He was "Big
Mac." Area prostitutes lose their real names, and with them
any sense of humanity. Diana was "Little Bit," Jean was
"Duckie," and Donice was "Little Run." There was a
"Black Jennifer" and a "White Jennifer," and not even the
police ever knew White Jennifer's real name. Two men
named Harrison and Frankie, and maybe a few others, were
called "Indian."[1]

Buddy, a resident of the S&S Mobile Home Park in
1992 and a sad example of its subculture there, astounded
local, state and federal investigators with the totality of his
alcoholism. "He is drunk when he is awake," marveled Bell
County Investigator Tim Steglich. "How he is still alive I
have no idea. He drinks anything with alcohol in it." When
he finished whatever beverage he was able to buy, Buddy
was known to resort to drinking Aqua Velva and other toi-
letries. During very short periods of sobriety, he was dry-
mouthed and nervous. He shook, chain-smoked, and cursed
constantly. Detectives later concluded, however, that while
he may have been a brain-damaged old drunk, at least he
was harmless.[2]

Living outside of the trailer park, another product of the
subculture, Billy, had watched his father brutally murder
his carousing mother by shooting her in the face with a
shotgun. Before being arrested, Billy's father "tiretooled"
Billy as well. Incredibly, after the father had been released
from prison, Billy chose to live with his father. He explained to investigators that after the beating, he and his
dad got along pretty well. When reminded that his father
had murdered his mother by blowing her face off, Billy
replied, "Well, my uncles live next door and they seem to
like him, so maybe she needed it."[3]

This subculture that McDuff joined after his release from prison in 1989 extended well beyond the S&S Mobile Home Park and some of its residents. Its symbols included drugs in cheap motels, whorehouses, whore rows, and crack houses inhabited by ex-cons, perverts, degenerates, and people living in a world with an utter absence of beauty. To them, truth was whatever got you out of trouble, sex was a way to make a living, relationships lasted minutes, the reward for work was drugs, and there was no such thing as stealing.

In Waco, the subculture centered around a stretch of Faulkner Lane McDuff called "The Corner." It was better known as "The Cut." At night, drug dealers and prostitutes lined Faulkner Lane at Miller Street and at the corner of South Loop, also called the Old Dallas Highway, to service customers. With few houses and no businesses on Faulkner, such activities generated few, if any, complaints to the Waco Police Department. Customers drove down Faulkner and slowed down so that prostitutes and drug dealers could come to the vehicle proposing services and offering products.

Michael, a frequent visitor to the Cut, first met McDuff there. He remembers that McDuff was into "rock" or crack cocaine, and occasionally, other illicit drugs. "Rock is the most terrible thing in the whole world," Kenneth would say. "It makes you get on edge after the first time you smoke it." His rock habit fueled an already vicious personality. One evening, McDuff drove through and said that he had a prime "lick," which meant that he intended to go to a crack house and rob it. If someone could just lend him a gun, he promised, he would return from the lick with $50 for the gun owner. According to Michael's statement, McDuff spoke constantly of robbing drug dealers and killing people. Specifically, McDuff used to say he could kill a person in a heartbeat; it "wasn't nothing" to him.

After McDuff asked for a gun, an onlooker named Chester reached into some bushes along Faulkner and handed McDuff a 12-gauge, single-shot shotgun, and asked for

$40.[4] McDuff called him "Chester the Molester." He
thought Chester was a likable guy, but he was a shyster,
too.[5] Law enforcement officers thought he was a "little
scumbag opportunist." At the Cut, Chester was ubiquitous,
to say the least. The only job officers ever knew Chester
to have held was at a barbeque shack in Waco.

The gun Chester pulled out of the bushes for McDuff
had been placed there the night before. According to Michael's statement to McLennan County deputies, Chester
had used the gun to attempt to rob the trick of a prostitute
named Jennifer. Jennifer, apparently in an attempt to defend
a paying customer, kicked Chester in the face. As Chester
hastily retreated towards some bushes, the gun went off.
Everyone at the Cut laughed at his clumsiness. No one
seemed concerned about an attempted aggravated armed
robbery. McDuff soon discovered that the cheap gun did
not work because the shell fired by Chester was stuck in
the barrel.[6] Such was a night on the Cut. (No evidence
exists that McDuff ever actually used the gun to rob a crack
dealer.)

For some time, Chester hung around McDuff. He fit the
profile of the kind of person McDuff felt superior to: a
small, black man. In an interview in 1996, McDuff described himself as an ambassador of sorts. He went down
to the black sections of Waco to get drugs from blacks for
whites who were afraid to get attacked. According to
McDuff, dealing with black drug dealers at night was particularly frightening especially when "all you can see are
their eyes and teeth."[7] According to a statement by an acquaintance of both Chester and McDuff, Chester claimed
to be McDuff's "main man." Like McDuff he spent time
talking about ripping off dope dealers, although like his
mentor, he probably spent far more time talking about it
than doing it. Chester could be particularly irritating to
other members of the subculture because he "bummed" cigarettes from everyone. Often, Chester, McDuff, and any one
of a number of prostitutes, like Little Run or someone else
from the Cut, could be seen riding in a red pickup truck

with McDuff. After returning from an over-indulgence of sex and drugs, Chester would be driving.[8]

McDuff soon discovered that Chester was not very trust-worthy. In February of 1992, at the Bar X Hotel on South Loop, McDuff was in the company of Michael and a prostitute named Bonnie. McDuff gave Michael his car keys and $70 and told him to go out and get three rocks (crack cocaine). He warned Michael that "he had better come back." When Michael got to the dope house, Chester emerged and said that McDuff was looking for him. Michael replied that that could not be true as he had just left McDuff at the Bar X Hotel. While in the dope house, Michael left McDuff's car unattended and running. Chester hopped into the car and drove away. After that, Michael hid in dope houses and never saw McDuff again.[9]

On February 12, 1992, McDuff reported the theft of his car to the Waco Police Department. It did not take the detective long to determine that drugs and prostitution were involved. The Texas State Technical Institute (TSTI) Police recovered the car, but not before what must have seemed like a bizarre demonstration. Late that night, Chester showed up at McDuff's, and according to a Waco Police Department report, McDuff immediately became suspicious of Chester's attempts to get him out of the apartment. Chester suggested that McDuff's car had been impounded and that they should go and get it right away. McDuff reportedly told Chester that he had no money and would have to get the car in a few days. Chester then admitted that McDuff's car was in the parking lot. McDuff looked outside and saw his car; he also saw Chester run back to the car and begin driving around the parking lot. McDuff, on foot, chased Chester and his car in the parking lot as Chester drove in circles, refusing to return McDuff's car. A short time later the TSTI police arrived and told Chester to get out and put his hands up. Chester got out of the car, put up his hands, and ran away. The campus police never caught up to him.[10]

When McDuff said that he was in a hurry, and that all

he wanted was his car back, the officers of the Waco Police Department concluded that he had engaged in soliciting prostitution, had lent his car to someone he did not know, and attempted to use the Waco Police Department to find it. WPD concluded: "Therefore, this case is unfounded."[11]

McDuff often bragged to his associates on the Cut that he could easily outsmart the Waco cops. But then, McDuff felt superior to all of the people of the Cut as well. "I was operating at a level higher than them, but these people are so loaded that they'll kill your ass," McDuff said. ATF Agent Charles Meyer agrees with the second half of that quote: "The Cut is kind of like the hyenas you see on the Discovery Channel; once they get something they turn on each other."[12]

Chester introduced McDuff to a woman named Linda. Shortly before the incident with McDuff's car, Chester and McDuff showed up at Linda's house. She remembers that they met on January 6, 1992, because on that day she got into an argument with her husband about whether she was having an affair with the mailman. During the argument, her husband ended up being arrested by the Bellmead Police for an outstanding warrant. Chester and Kenneth were interested in meeting Linda's husband. "I told them [my husband] was in jail and I could sure use a beer."

"We can fix that," said Chester, as McDuff removed a twelve-pack from the trunk of the car. Linda was uncomfortable around Chester. She knew that he spoke to McDuff about raping her. "He would always look at me like he was undressing me with his eyes," she said in a statement to the Austin Police Department. On the day she met McDuff, she alleges that Chester intentionally moved curtains in her trailer in order to see her undressed.[13]

Linda remembers that McDuff was constantly interested in getting a gun. But he did not want to get it himself. He wanted someone else to get it for him.[14] Since he had no problem securing illicit drugs, knew all sorts of ex-cons and felons, and had money, he could have gotten one easily if he had spent as much energy getting a gun as talking about it. In any case, some of his acquaintances saw that he carried a gun while continuing to talk about getting one to rob drug dealers.

Soon, even the inhabitants of the subculture began to tire of his lies. He claimed to have been sent to prison for having beaten a man to death with a baseball bat. He bragged that he was the "big guy" in the pen and "ran" things wherever he was. Some, every bit as tough as he was, had no use for him and did not want him around. McDuff was careful around some of the street people. "They'd kill me for the money I have in my wallet," he asserted. When Linda took McDuff to a biker bar called Runts, the owner made it clear to her that he did not want to see Kenneth around his club. They never returned. McDuff was so volatile, especially after smoking crack, that no one ever stayed with him for very long. Every time he drank he got "louder and louder and had a goofy laugh." Yet some did continue to run around with him when he had money. Such was life in the subculture.[15]

"At first he was just full of shit. The more I got to know him, he was just scary," said someone who knew McDuff. But while he spoke often about getting guns, he was not a lover of firearms. Moreover, while he very often hired prostitutes, no one who knew him ever stated that he had an interest in pornography, and sexually explicit materials have never been inventoried among his possessions.[16]

McDuff never tired of talking about getting guns and robbing drug dealers. His friend Linda claimed that they did "rip off" a crack dealer from Waco after an unsuccessful attempt to locate another pusher in Fort Worth. McDuff drove up to crack dealers and handed them rolled-up one-dollar bills. He would slap the pusher's hand so that the crack spilled into the car, then drive off quickly. He also suggested to Linda that she could pose as a prostitute to lure johns for him to rob. At that idea, she told McDuff to "go to hell."[17]

Once, while riding with McDuff, Linda asked for a cigarette and McDuff told her that she could find some in his glove compartment. She opened it and noticed the driver's license of a white female with blonde, curly hair. When she asked him who that was he answered, "Just a dope whore and a good fuck." At the time, she thought nothing of the remark.[18]

McDuff did not limit his talk of robbery and murder to dope dealers and johns. He spoke of robbing legitimate businesses and his thievery included shoplifting in grocery stores. He stole food, even perishables like meat, by placing them in his boots and walking out. After he and Linda visited her husband's grandparents in Bellmead, the elderly couple made clear to her that they "did not like his looks" and that he was "bad news." They were right; that day McDuff suggested to Linda that they could rob and murder the grandparents because they had money and guns. Linda replied that "it wasn't no fucking way he was going to do that."[19]

To characterize his sexual behavior as bizarre is a gross understatement. He took a childish pride in his private parts: "Have you ever seen a set of balls like this on anybody?" he would say as he grabbed his crotch. He "dated" a number of prostitutes on the Cut. Their dates often included highs from crack cocaine. He seldom got violent with prostitutes who got assertive with him or showed no fear of his grandiose lies. For example, he never assaulted Black Jennifer, who stated, "I was not afraid of him and I told him so." His own descriptions of his sexual behavior before going to prison, and of course, what he did to Louise Sullivan, powerfully evidences that he had always been perverse. Twenty-three years of prison could only have pushed his urges further into an already depraved state. His sex was beneath the animalistic; mammals do not intend to inflict pain during procreation. It excluded any trace of emotion. None of the statements of the women who admitted to having sex with him includes the slightest hint of tenderness, much less love. "Duckie," a prostitute from the Cut, told others of a date she had with McDuff in which he forced her to have every conceivable type of sex with him for three hours. (He called it "going around the world.") When offered a chance to file sexual assault charges against McDuff, she declined—she was a prostitute. While McDuff lived in a dorm, other residents remembered a steady stream of prostitutes in and out of his room.[20]

In July of 1992, Linda gave a description of Kenneth McDuff's dysfunctional sex life in a statement to the Austin Police Department. The disturbing statement gives keen insights into the behavioral elements of a sexual predator. She indicated that McDuff never got completely naked for sex and often kept his boots on during the sex act. There was very little touching. He enjoyed her pain, and assured her that "it won't hurt very long and it will feel better in a little bit." He knew nothing or cared less about what his partner might enjoy. She suspected that he often faked orgasms, and that maybe he could not have one unless he was having anal sex.[21]

Oddly, the worst thing a partner could do while having sex with McDuff was to appear to enjoy it; he did not want that. Linda's vivid descriptions of Kenneth McDuff supported a consistent theory among all law enforcement officers involved in the Kenneth McDuff murder cases: He was a predator first. He did not enjoy sex; it was an occasion to inflict pain, and that was what he enjoyed.

Eventually, Linda returned to her husband. Reports were that they were long-haul truck drivers. But before going back to her marriage, she did experience McDuff's violence, and is lucky to be alive. After making a court appearance with McDuff, she and a friend named Jimmy were riding in McDuff's car with him. Jimmy was a thug with a long list of prior arrests for violent crimes and felony convictions. He was considered one of the most dangerous ex-cons in all of Bell County. Jimmy sat in the back seat on the passenger side. The threesome drove to Waco and approached a crack dealer. As the man placed three rocks into Linda's hand McDuff sped away, hitting a curb, causing beer to spill all over himself. When he asked Linda to hold on to the beer, she said it was his beer spilling all over. McDuff went into a rage over being "disrespected and dishonored." While still driving the car McDuff began slapping and beating her by slamming her head into the passenger-side window. "What the fuck you did that for?" she asked.

"Don't ever disrespect me in front of my friends again," he screamed. His anger and ferocity terrified her. In her statement, Linda indicated that she tried to get out of the car, but from the back seat, almost as if it had been choreographed, Jimmy reached over and locked the door to keep her trapped. Almost as quickly, and most uncharacteristically, McDuff apologized. A few minutes later Jimmy assured Linda that McDuff was sincere. He said that he had never seen McDuff treat a woman that way. "He must love you," Jimmy said.[22]

The occasion of the end of the relationship between Linda and McDuff came while smoking crack at the home of someone named Jewel. Another of the drug abusers was a prostitute named Natalie. When McDuff admitted that he had "fucked" Natalie, Linda came to a decision: "I knew [Natalie] to be a *whore of bad reputation* so I cut McDuff off from having sex with me. When I told him it seemed like he didn't care."[23][Emphasis added.]

Indeed, Kenneth McDuff did not care, because he did not like women—or sex.

II

The Austin Police Department case file on Kenneth McDuff contains a white paper entitled *Investigations of Sexually Sadistic Offenses* by Robert R. Hazelwood, Park E. Dietz, and Janet Warren. Without meaning to, the paper magnificently illustrates a quandary over a basic question now facing criminal justice: Does evil exist? In the first paragraph, the authors assert that "Human cruelty reveals itself in many kinds of offenses, but rarely more starkly than in the crimes of sexual sadists."[24] In their paper, the authors define sexual sadism as "a condition in which an individual is sexually excited by the suffering of others." A distinction is drawn between normal discomforts commonly felt by a sexual partner, and a consistent and enduring pattern of sexual response to the suffering of others. The paper tends to discount free will. "Antisocial personality disorder is the current name for what in the past has been known as sociopathy, psychopathy, moral insanity, *or in pre-psychiatric days, evil*."[25] [Emphasis added.] The suggestion, however subtle, that evil may not exist, can only lead to the transformation of criminals into patients, and crimes into disorders. Conversely, to what extent are we, as humans, thinking individuals with a free will to do good or evil?

Kenneth McDuff provides a case in point and far more questions than answers. Was what he did to Louise Sullivan an evil act, or was it the result of a sexually sadistic, antisocial personality disorder? The American system of criminal justice has never really defined the difference in a clear and consistent manner. Furthermore, if Kenneth McDuff suffers from such a disorder, should the diagnosis be an absolute: Is he *completely* controlled by his urges, or does he have some measure of control over himself, rendering him at least partially responsible for what he did? If Kenneth McDuff suffers from a psychiatric malady, where did this condition come from? His upbringing? His genetic makeup? If it is genetic, what should be done with people carrying those genes? As F. Lee Bailey asks: "What should be done about such creatures?"

There is no reasonable doubt that Kenneth Allen McDuff was a sexual predator. He prowled as long as he did because he lived in a subculture where the normative behavior made him only slightly deviant. As an ATF agent asserted, the people of the Cut, and the subculture in general, lived in a world where survival methods consisted of dope and prostitution. Each member was a depraved rugged individualist in an extraordinarily self-centered setting. Dozens of people mingled within inches of one another, but there was no sense of community. There, Kenneth McDuff felt he belonged. He was totally self-centered. He had no allegiance to anyone or any group—not even the subculture. McDuff even approached the Waco Police Department and offered himself as a snitch to identify drug connections.[26] Had WPD been foolish enough to take him up on his proposal, he would likely have gone to the Cut and demanded "protection" money from the dealers. After a thorough search of official and unofficial records, and testimony of dozens who knew him, only his mother, Addie, and Kenneth himself, ever alleged a single episode or moment in which McDuff showed kindness or selflessness—even as a child.

Does that make him mean, or crazy? In that debate Kenneth McDuff is extraordinarily resilient. Surely, someone so void of virtue has to be crazy? Maybe that is what insanity is? On the other hand, shouldn't conscious acts of wrongdoing demand justice? Is it not true that creatures like McDuff think before they act? Isn't it enough that he knew what he was doing was wrong? Just recently, in a television special about Ted Bundy, his former defense attorney wondered aloud how someone who brutally murdered at least seventeen women could *not* be crazy. Is that an acceptable defense? The more people murdered, the stronger evidence of insanity? If McDuff had killed only Louise he would have been sane, but since he would kill many others he has to be crazy—right?

"They think I'm a civil citizen now. . . . I'm going to give them time to get off my back and then I'm going to show them the real McDuff," he said to a prostitute. Society, he added, owed him for the time he spent in prison.[27]

And who was the "real" McDuff? After admitting to his parole officer that he had smoked marijuana, McDuff was ordered to attend individual and group sessions at the Mental Health and Mental Retardation Heart of Texas Center in Waco. In yet another dismissal of direct instructions from his parole officer, he announced at the center that he would not attend the group sessions. His counselor believed that McDuff had no remorse for what he had done. McDuff also seemed concerned about whether women would be at the group sessions, but his counselor did not note whether or not he wanted to attend with the women. In these sessions, as in most of his other interviews, his lies were oxymoronic. During a session about AIDS, he proudly asserted that he did not use condoms and that after the session, he would chase down a prostitute. But he also claimed to want to buy a house, join a church, meet a decent woman, marry her and then quit going to church.[28]

7

Going to College

"This guy is sitting by somebody's wife and somebody's daughter in class!"
—Parnell McNamara, Deputy United States Marshal

I

At the beginning of 1991, McDuff reported to his Temple parole officer that he was working in a warehouse in the Dallas area as a forklift operator. Six days later he asked to transfer his parole supervision to the Dallas District. But less than two weeks after that he reported to his Temple parole officer that he was back in Temple living with J. A. and Addie. Kenneth's aging parents apparently had little energy for raising a forty-five-year-old teenager; McDuff moved into the Jean Motel in Temple during much of March. Only six weeks earlier McDuff had discovered a way that he could have access to a private room, eat three meals a day in a cafeteria, receive money for subsistence—even during holidays—and receive an education. All he had to do was go to class. Kenneth Allen McDuff was going to college.[1]

Project RIO (Re-Integration of Offenders) was an outgrowth of the Job Training Partnership Act. It started in 1985 as a joint project between the Texas Employment Commission (TEC) and the Pardons and Paroles Division of TDCJ. TEC administered the project, and on January 21, 1991, McDuff's parole officer referred him there. The project provided assistance in the form of grants to ex-convicts to attend colleges or trade schools. The goal of Project RIO was to turn untrained, uneducated ex-convicts into employable workers.[2] The program was voluntary, which logically assumed that its clients genuinely wished to be trained for gainful employment.

Texas State Technical Institute (TSTI) was a two-year technical college located in Waco. It provided training in thirty-four technical fields with forty-one different programs. On the campus, men outnumbered women by nearly four to one. Located north of Waco on the remains of an old Air Force Base, to this day the area looks more like a military installation than a school. Some of the dorms, like Neches and Sabine Halls, are old barracks: drab, dreary buildings bisected on the interior by narrow hallways. During the early nineties, the residents of these dorms lived very close to one another. Students usually were seventeen- to twenty-year-olds looking for a marketable trade to allow them to get a good, steady job. Sprinkled into a population of young boys fresh out of high school, were ex-cons. Some of the parolees were genuinely trying to go straight, and others, like Kenneth McDuff, saw an ideal setup: a nearly maintenance-free room; someone else to cook for him; access to smaller, younger men, some of whom were mightily impressed with and/or afraid of his 250-pound frame; and ready access to remote, wooded areas surrounding the campus.

On February 8, 1991, Mac applied for housing on the TSTI campus. Less than one month later, on March 5, he was placed in room 118 in Sabine Hall, a single men's dorm. On March 7, he started his first day of classes.[3] He had been exempt from Texas's mandatory state placement exam because he had already earned credits from Alvin Junior College while in the Retrieve Unit in Angleton, and because he was enrolled in a certificate, not a degree, program. Technically, he was a transfer student who "majored" in CNC (Computer Numerically Controlled) Machine Shop Operations. When asked to develop a résumé, he listed rough and finish carpentry, concrete form builder, concrete finisher, and front-end loader operations.[4]

In 1991, Texas State Technical Institute was what most people would call a "trade school." It granted certificates as well as degrees. Many classes were competency-based, requiring the completion of a series of tasks or the attendance at a series of events. This made it possible for students to learn skills at their own pace. For those who went into class already having mastered certain skills, and for others who learned quickly, it was possible to earn credit for or otherwise complete some courses without attending class regularly or consistently throughout the year. Such classes are not uncommon in a trade school. But in some other courses, mostly requiring classroom rather than shop work, TSTI did, as a matter of policy, require attendance. "An absence is assessed each time a student is not in attendance. . . . Please pay close attention to the definition of excessively absent, and the consequences of excessively absent," instructed one of McDuff's handbooks.[5]

Because of his CNC Machine Shop Operations major, Kenneth McDuff had many competency-based classes requiring the demonstration of skills, and thus, regular attendance was not as crucial as in a more traditional liberal arts or science education degree program. The classes included basic shop machines, precision tools and measurement, basic lathe and mill operations, blueprints, and other shop classes.

Even so, given his known activities and statements from those who knew him, McDuff's absences from classes must have been frequent and excessive. Slightly more than one year after his enrollment, frustrated law officers determined that the attendance records of the school were wholly unreliable and that they could not determine exactly what class sessions he had attended. McDuff's friend, Linda, in a statement to the Austin Police Department, confidently asserted that he had to have missed many classes, because he spent so much time at her house. On Mondays, Wednesdays and Thursdays he was supposed to spend eight hours in class; on Tuesday he was scheduled to attend five hours of class; and on Fridays he had nothing scheduled. Linda asserted in her statement that he often arrived at her house at noon with a twelve-pack of beer and would not leave until he drank it all, or ran out of money and could not get more. On several occasions he arrived at 7 A.M. and spent the entire day with her.[6]

But he did attend some classes and even engaged in some school-related activities. TSTI's grading policy was based on a 10-point system: 100–90 was an "A," 89–80 was a "B," 79–70 was a "C," etc. By the end of his program he had attempted 44 credits and successfully completed all of them. Incredibly, on a 4-point scale, he earned a grade point average (GPA) of 3.786 during the fall semester of 1991 and was listed on the "Dean for Instruction's Honor Roll." His transcript shows that by the end of 1991 he made As and Bs in everything except a course entitled "Indus Spec and Safety." By the end of his matriculation in April 1992, Kenneth McDuff graduated from TSTI with a 3.364 GPA.[7]

During the semester in which he earned a spot on the Dean's Honor Roll, McDuff had taken a course entitled "Human Relations." The syllabus of the course outlined an introduction to human relations which engaged students in exercises in learning about themselves, behaviors in relationships, developing careers in the world of work, and stress and stress management. His work in the course provided a gold mine of information on an intensely self-centered individual.

In an answer to a question about how he intended to benefit from taking a human relations course, McDuff answered: "Yes, I feel that I can benefit from the Human Relations Course. To better get along with people in my personal life. And also in my professional life. In my professional life it'll help me with the people I'll work with. Also with the manager. Hopefully, to get a better salary and befits [sic]."[8] When asked to best describe his personal characteristics he wrote: "The four traits that best describe my characteristics are reliable, respectful, perceptive, and open minded. I feel that I acquired these traits through life experiences."

McDuff's own writings provide a hint into what goes

through the mind of a predator and serial killer (the following is as McDuff wrote it):

1. Reliable

I choose reliable as number one, as some of the most important things in life depend's on a person being reliable. Such as your job. Without a job one's life becomes very difficult at once. With along line of problems associated with the fact you've lost your job. And by failing to keep appointments one loses reliability with friends, family, and associates.

The trait of being reliable was influenced upon me by family and people I've known attitude toward being reliable.

2. Respectful

Respectful was chosen as number two of importances. This trait is also needed to maintain good relation's on the job, and in one's social life. I must admitt that I have one major problem in showing respect when it is not shown in return! I tend to do the opposite, that is to show the most disrespect as possible! Being disrespectful is something one learns through the people he meets in life.

3. Perceptive

I chose perceptive as number three, but at some points in my life I would have placed it number one. As my life, body, and limb had depended on it! (Smile) Being perceptive in everyday life is important in understanding others and their intent. Understanding what a person is really saying, isn't always what they are saying. Also, understanding body language is an important part of being perceptive.

I feel being perceptive comes naturally, and through life experiences.

4. Open Minded

I feel that I am open minded. And I feel that it important for people to be open minded. The world would be a much better place to live if we were all open minded. I try to look at both sides of every issue. As the saying goes, walk a mile in my shoes. Being open minded, is experiencing life.[9]

Of course, his writings were a combination of what he thought his instructors and classmates wanted to read and what he wanted others to believe. His statements were self-contradicting: having someone else walk in his shoes made him open-minded.

In another series of exercises McDuff was asked to rate himself according to a list of proverbs. Using a scale of 5 for "very typical of the way I act in a conflict" to 1 for "never typical of the way I act in a conflict" out of a possible score of 35, his results were: 34 for Confronting, 30 for Withdrawing, 23 for Forcing, 21 for Compromising, and 16 for Smoothing. In the exercise the "5s" included:

- You scratch my back, I'll scratch yours.
- Come now and let us reason together.
- A fair exchange brings no quarrel.
- Stay away from people who disagree with you.
- Tit for tat is fair play.
- Avoid quarrelsome people as they will only make your life miserable.
- A gift for one another makes good friends.
- Bring your conflicts in the open and face them.
- When both people give in halfway, a fair settlement is achieved.[10]

In yet another exercise, students had to choose five traits that seem to best fit the impressions they had of themselves. McDuff chose: Aware, Considerate, Loyal, Productive, and Trusting. Years later, Tim Steglich looked at the word "trusting" and said in disgust, "Yea, he trusted them until he strangled them." When asked to list two negative traits about himself, McDuff wrote "not good at meeting people" and, in a phrase that would have made Addie proud, "Too trusting sometime."

The Human Relations course McDuff took at TSTI was divided into units that were, in turn, sub-divided into lessons. He did particularly well in Unit V. Specifically, Lesson 13 dealt with sexual harassment; he made a perfect score on that quiz. Lesson 14 was about Drugs and Drug Testing; he made a perfect score on that one, too.[11]

"He was just a supercharged teenager," said U.S. Attorney Bill Johnston. Some of McDuff's younger "friends," like a boy named Bobby, agreed. He was a "nineteen-year-old in a forty-year-old body." Bobby was not quite right; McDuff was nearly forty-five.[12]

"I don't have any friends," McDuff said, and he was right. A confidential source for federal investigators indicated that McDuff spent so much time talking about killing and robbing people that it became intolerable to be around him. Allegedly, he asserted that he did not like to kill more than three people at one time because he could not dig that many graves in one day. And he liked to talk about graves. He engaged in vivid descriptions about disposing of his victims. He indicated that it was better to put brush over the fresh graves so that the bodies could not be easily discovered.[13]

Very few of those who knew him knew his name was Kenneth McDuff, and even fewer knew he was a kid-killer. He was known as "Mac," "Big Mac," or behind his back, "Crack Mac." The other residents of Sabine Hall called him "Big Mac." They all knew he was weird and dangerous, and yet, some of the younger residents "admired" his utter lack of caution when it came to drugs and prostitutes. About one year after McDuff moved to TSTI, Richard Stroup of the McLennan County Sheriff's Office interviewed about fifty students who had come to know "Big Mac." Every single one of them was afraid of him.[14]

The residents also noticed that when Mac showered, he always entered the shower alone, carrying his clothes with him, and emerged fully clothed.[15]

Louis lived in Sabine Hall in room 124, across the hallway from Mac's room. He remembers that Mac provided

several others in the dorm with a variety of drugs ranging
from marijuana to LSD. Louis was one of the other ex-cons
living in Sabine Hall, but his convictions were for non-
violent crimes. Even though he was about half Mac's age,
for a while they appeared to have a fairly good relationship.

As usual, Mac spoke often of robbing and killing, but
his boasts now expanded from crack and other drug dealers
to stores, namely convenience stores. According to Louis,
Mac actively, albeit unsuccessfully, recruited fellow TSTI
students to rob convenience stores. In one conversation,
Mac referred to a convenience store on the corner of Interstate Highway 35 and New Road. He claimed to know the
layout and the times during which preoccupied employees
would make a robbery easy. In sworn statements and testimony under oath, Louis graphically described Mac's procedure for "properly" disposing of a body: wrap the feet in
chains, slice the stomach, and throw it in a river, and, since
it would not float, the body would never be found.[16]

Another dorm resident named Mark, who claimed to be
a former Navy SEAL, testified that Mac knew that another
student named Richard was due to get a federal loan check
the next day. While walking to the cafeteria, Mac suggested
to Mark that they just kill Richard and take his money. Mac
didn't kill Richard, but Richard did find out that it was not
safe to be around Mac, especially with money in your
pocket. When Richard picked up his check, he foolishly
decided to use his federal loan to go out with Mac to get
a whore. The girl they picked up, Black Jennifer, was a
prostitute at the Cut. The trio rented a room at the Motel 6
where they began smoking rocks of crack cocaine.

According to Jennifer's statement, all of a sudden, Mac
flew into a rage and accused Richard of disrespecting him.
He pushed Richard into a chair and knocked the chair over
backwards and onto the floor. Mac got on top of Richard
and beat his face unmercifully. Both of Richard's eyes were
blackened and damaged severely when Mac stuck his
thumbs into the sockets and asserted that he was going to
"put his eyes out." Horrified, Jennifer cried out, "Leave him

alone. Stop." Mac paid no attention and continued to beat Richard.

When she noticed the manager of the motel heading towards the scene, Jennifer "grabbed her pipe and left the room." She told Mac that "y'all better stop fighting" and that the manager was going to call the police. Somehow, Richard got away from Mac, met up with Jennifer, and the two walked back to the Cut.[17]

Those who saw him during the three days after his beating at the hands of Kenneth McDuff remember that his entire head was swollen and his eyes were horribly discolored. Richard told Mark that had the whore not been there, Mac would have killed him. Three days later Richard left TSTI and was never seen again on the campus.[18]

Over a year later, ATF Agent Chuck Meyer and Austin Police Department Detective J. W. Thompson located Richard in Lubbock. In his report, Thompson noted that Richard's mental state was noticeably confused. Because of his instability, the investigators decided not to take a statement from him.[19]

Another Sabine Hall resident was Frankie, one of few students nearly as old as Mac. Frankie was a recovering alcoholic when Mac asked him to go out for a six-pack. It was only after they left that Frankie found out that he would have to buy the brew because Mac had no money. According to Frankie's statement, Mac knew, however, how to get quick cash; he could steal from his father.

Frankie and Mac drove to an area north of Belton where, years earlier, J. A. and Addie McDuff had relocated. Their home was several hundred yards off Cedar Creek Road, near the junction of Highway 317. Directly across the driveway from the McDuff home was an abandoned gravel road cutting a path through a wildlife preserve. Mac parked the pickup truck loaned to him by J. A. on the path and told Frankie that he was going to get a compressor in a shed to sell for drug money. He instructed Frankie to wait in the truck because there were dogs on the property that could "tear him up." Ten minutes later Mac returned and said that J. A. had locked the shed and he could not get into it.

Frankie calmed him down when he said, "That's alright Kenneth, I got $50, we'll go get some more beer." Mac smiled and drove away like nothing had happened.[20]

As Frankie and Mac drove around the Cedar Creek Road area near the McDuff home, Mac pointed to an area and stated that it would be a great place to dump a body.

Like everyone else who knew him, Frankie came to fear Mac and began avoiding him. While smoking crack outside of a motel room, Frankie announced that he was not going to buy any more rocks. Angrily, McDuff snapped back, "You're not going to get me started then cut me off while you still got money in your pocket—I'll kill you with my bare hands." Frankie gave Mac all the money he had.[21]

Other students told of Mac's attempts to recruit accomplices for robbery and murder. Mac was also interested in burglarizing a chemical company so that they could set up a drug-producing area in the dorm. On another occasion he wanted to run down to Austin to "roll some fags." Mac seemed willing to do anything to get money. He let the entire dorm know that he would steal anything if they would pay him for it. He treated the boys in the dorm the same way he treated his family; he shamelessly exploited whatever kindness he could get. He once borrowed the motorcycle of another resident on a Friday night, only to return it the following Sunday after having driven it over 1,000 miles.[22]

As time passed, none of the residents wanted anything to do with him, and some actually hid while he was around—he was dangerous and crazy. And no one in the dorm had the courage to alert authorities to the madman in room 118.

II

On May 7, 1991, Mac applied for a cashier's position. He probably thought that all cashiers had to do in a conven-

ience store was stand behind a register and collect money.
He found out that they did much more after applying for
and accepting a job with Quik Pak Stores, a chain of convenience stores based out of and located in and around the
Waco area. On his application he put the Sabine Hall address on Campus Drive as his current address and Addie's
address as his permanent address. He also put Alvin Junior
College as prior school experience and Machine Shop Management major at TSTI as a current educational endeavor.
When asked if he had ever been convicted of a felony, he
checked "no."[23]

Leonard Bradbury, a supervisor for the Quik Pak Stores,
interviewed McDuff for about one and a half hours and
decided to offer him the job. The first step was to train him
for his new position. That task belonged to a more experienced employee named Aaron Northrup, who later testified that "the training of another employee for a Quik Pak
Store is basically you stick the trainee with another employee." Mac and another novice named Carl "stuck" to
Aaron.[24]

Aaron trained Mac at the Quik Pak #11 near the main
entrance to the TSTI campus. Mac learned about the cash
registers, the safe drop, where money was located, store
procedures, the lack of security, and work schedules and
routines. He learned that there were only three ways to open
the drawer of the register: hit no sale, register a sale, and
a third method requiring a code used by supervisors only.
While training Mac, Aaron introduced him to his petite,
very attractive young wife, Melissa Ann Northrup.[25]

Of course, this job, like all of the others, lasted about
three weeks. Mac worked nearly all of the graveyard shifts
at the Quik Pak #11. On May 22, 1991, he was transferred
to the Quik Pak #8 in an unincorporated area between
Waco and Robinson on an access road along Interstate 35.[26]
There were businesses in the immediate area, but none of
them were open twenty-four hours a day. Even though the
store is only a few feet from the Interstate, it is surprisingly

hard to see. During graveyard shifts, the area could be considered isolated.

Several hundred yards north of the Quik Pak #8 is the New Road Inn, named for the road intersecting the Interstate at that location. The inn is hidden from the Quik Pak by a thatch of trees which borders the store on the north and east sides. From May 22 to June 2, 1991, Kenneth McDuff had ample time to learn everything there was to know about Quik Pak #8, and its opportunities for robbery. On or near June 2, Louis visited Mac at the store to tell him that a few guys were going to the lake to drink beer. According to Louis's testimony, Mac called in and quit his job right then and there. Officially, Mac was terminated for not returning to work when scheduled without giving notice. It did not matter to him. He probably thought he could steal or extort much more than the $686 he earned in the three weeks he worked at the Quik Pak.[27]

Kenneth McDuff could not get the idea of robbing the Quik Pak out of his mind. He first talked about doing so while in Louis's room in Sabine Hall. He talked about how easy it would be to rob it because there was no security there—no cameras—nothing like that, Mac said. He talked more about it while the men were at the lake, and on one occasion they drove past the Quik Pak in Mac's pickup truck. As they looked at the store, Mac talked about how the robbery could take place while the attendant was emptying the trash at about 3 A.M. Mac talked about how he could open the cash register after hitting the attendant with a pipe.[28]

He had the same conversations with Mark, but this time he added the detail that he could cut the sleeves off a sweater and place it over his head to look like a ski mask. Mark testified that he got scared and left the room. In yet another conversation about the same store, this time with Hank Worley, Mac saw another weakness in the store's security; the attendant was a girl—a "little short and damn good-looking girl, too." She was Melissa Ann Northrup— Aaron's wife.[29]

Kenneth Allen McDuff was convinced he knew exactly how to rob the Quik Pak #8 and get away with it.

III

Kenneth McDuff drank only beer. He liked cheap beer like Budweiser and Milwaukee's Best and was concerned more about whether the brew was cold. He liked grabbing cans out of barrels of ice. He drank a lot of beer, but he claimed not to like it because, "it is hard on you." He preferred to smoke marijuana because it mellowed him out. And in yet another oxymoronic set of lies, he denied being violent, but blamed his violence on his parole officer, who would not let him smoke his pot. So, he resorted to crack cocaine that brought about the violence he denied in the first place. In Kenneth's mind, he was a victim of a "stupid bastard" parole officer who could prevent him from smoking pot, but not crack. It also began to dawn on him that "Justice for McDuff, Inc." was a complete failure. "If only the movie had come through. I could have started my own business," he said in 1996.[30] In other words, he had to resort to crime because he was not a millionaire.

Since his parole, he had held many menial jobs, none for longer than a few weeks. For a very short time, he worked with his father, and undoubtedly, had he shown initiative, he could have taken over that business. But in truth, McDuff did not want to work; he wanted to roam as predators do. He "covered a lot of concrete" as he said, and was not interested in any responsibilities preventing him from his hunts.

As time passed, he descended deeper and deeper into the subculture. During the summer of 1991, Mac renewed an acquaintance with another parolee named Billy (see Chapter 6). They had first met between April and September of 1987 at the Ramsey II Unit of the Texas Prison system where both were serving time. Billy was paroled two or three months later, and about two years after that Mac walked out. Their paths crossed again in Temple at a place called Poor Boy's Lounge.

As Billy got drunk, McDuff asked another barfly named Morris if he knew where to score an "8-Ball." Mac said he had $300 to spend for the speed. Mightily impressed by McDuff, and his beer money, Morris wanted to stick around with him. Morris told him that they could score at his cousin Beverly's house in Del Valle, a suburb south of Austin.

Minutes later, Morris, Billy and Mac got into Mac's truck and headed for Del Valle. By that time, Billy was so drunk that he crawled into the back of the truck and passed out. He slept until they reached Del Valle. On the way there, Mac and Morris talked. Later, in sworn testimony Morris admitted that he was illiterate, and as usual, Mac reveled in another opportunity to impress a younger man lacking in cognition. He spoke of "stabbing three niggers" once he got out of prison, picking up whores, and getting guns.[31]

The trio went directly to Beverly's trailer in Del Valle and arrived at about 8:15 P.M. Beverly took them to the home of a man named Ron, but his gate was closed, which meant he had no speed. Then they went to a pink house in Webberville, where Beverly scored two grams of speed. They all returned to the trailer and shot up. A short while later Morris asked to speak to Beverly in the back room; he asked her if she would have sex with McDuff. She hit Morris on the head—that meant "no."[32]

While Mac and Beverly talked alone, Mac asked her if she could score any more speed. She said that he would have to come back later. When he answered that he did not know how to get to her trailer, she said that he should bring Morris back. Mac then replied that he did not know how to get in touch with Morris, so Beverly drew a map on a sheet of notebook paper. Her work schedule, along with her mother's, was on the other side of the map she drew.

Soon things got out of hand and Beverly became concerned. Two men with no shirts, who smelled, arrived and began to make more noise than Beverly wanted. She told Morris to tell everyone to leave. On the way back to Temple, Mac turned on Morris. He got angry after concluding that he should have gotten much more speed for the $300 he spent. Mac chased Morris around the truck until he calmed down enough to get back into the vehicle. Billy had sobered up enough to sit in the front of the truck between Mac and Morris. Mac pulled out a pistol and threatened to "whip Morris' butt."[33] Neither Beverly nor Morris ever wanted to see Mac again.

8

Every Woman's Nightmare

*"He knew where there was a good-looking girl in a
convenience store that he was going to take."*
—Alva Hank Worley

I

Unlike other Louisiana parishes, Evangeline Parish reflects
the cultural and geographic diversity of the entire state. On
the southern end, Cajun Catholics and other Louisiana
French descendants inhabit a fertile prairie. Farmers take
advantage of the high water table to flood fields for the
planting and harvesting of rice. The recent craze for Cajun
food transformed the flooded rice fields into aquafarms,
supplying crawfish to customers around the world. On the
northern end of Evangeline Parish, Anglo-Saxon Protes-
tants dominate piney woods, red dirt, and rolling hills. Louisiana's geo-demographic, political, religious, and cultural
dichotomy, "north" and "south" Louisiana, meet in Evangeline Parish. This cultural fault line between north and
south Louisiana is where Allen and Pat Reed raised their
family. They had two daughters, Lorraine ("Lori") and Colleen. Two older daughters named Anita and Mae, from
Pat's previous marriage, completed the family of six.[1]

Colleen Reed was born in the Evangeline Parish seat of
Ville Platte in April, 1963. She was the youngest of the
Reed family, but Lori was only eighteen months older; in
many ways they grew up as "twins." Colleen attended kindergarten in a Ville Platte public school, then attended the
Evangeline Academy from the first through the sixth
grades. Her half-sister, Mae, remembers the week Colleen graduated from kindergarten. It was the same week
Mae graduated from high school and began packing to go

off to college. The ever-observant Colleen packed as well, insisting, "I'm going to college with Mazie," as she clutched her own diploma and put on her hat.[2]

After Colleen's sixth-grade year, the Reed family moved farther into the piney woods into a picturesque area near a hamlet called Bayou Chicot. She attended Bayou Chicot High School until the end of her sophomore year. Afterwards, she went to a parochial high school called Sacred Heart High in Ville Platte, then finished requirements for a Louisiana High School Diploma through a dual enrollment program with Louisiana State University at Eunice.[3]

Her sisters remember Colleen as a real tomboy. "She'd go riding through the trees on her Shetland pony, and the trees would rake her off. She'd . . . sock him and get back on and ride some more. She was always energetic and curious and into things," remembered Mae. The sisters had three special trees in the woods. They spent hours playing there, swinging from ropes and having races to determine who would get to the top limb first. But, as Lori remembers, Colleen "could be a little 'chit' " as well. She enjoyed skinning frogs because she knew it grossed out her sisters, and she could be annoying. Her one-liners were particularly good, and she had a gift for planning practical jokes and hiding as they developed. On one occasion she went too far; she threw a snake around Lori's neck. Shortly afterwards, the sisters agreed to explain away their fight and Colleen's bruises by claiming an accident. Her laughter was high-pitched and irritating, and she could be an annoying little kid—but they all loved her.[4]

Lori remembered that when Colleen decided she wanted to sleep, she did not care where she was—she slept. That was probably why she was a morning person; "She woke up happy." Years later, Lori could look at photos of Colleen and tell whether the picture had been taken in the morning or the afternoon.[5]

Lori admits to being the more rebellious of the two sisters. As soon as she graduated from high school, she headed for Austin, Texas. Her father, Allen Reed, a veteran once

stationed in nearby San Antonio, had spoken often of the
beauty of the central Texas area, especially Austin. In December 1978, only seventeen years old, but determined to
"get the hell out of Ville Platte," Lori drove her truck to
what O. Henry had called the "City of the Violet Crown."[6]

While still in high school, Colleen visited Lori in Austin,
and she, too, fell in love with the capital city. The two
young women did "tourist things," visiting the Hill Country, Barton Springs, the highland lakes, and enjoying panoramic views from places like Mount Bonnell. Their
sisterly bond, however, was severely strained when Colleen
announced, at the age of seventeen, that she would marry
Keith, her high school sweetheart from Pine Prairie, Louisiana. Lori had married at a very young age and considered
herself in a position to impart some wisdom relative to Colleen's decision. Colleen married anyway; the union lasted
about two years and ended in divorce.[7]

Colleen finished her degree requirements in Accounting
at LSU in Baton Rouge. Shortly afterwards, she passed the
exam to become a certified public accountant and took her
first job in New Orleans. She did not like it there, and after
only one year she accompanied her boyfriend Jamil to Austin, where his employer, the Marriott hotel chain, transferred him. It worked out well for Colleen; Lori lived in
Austin and Colleen knew and loved the area. Colleen and
Jamil lived together for about two years and then split up.
The breakup was a bitter one, both emotionally and finan-
cially, because during their two-year relationship the couple
had commingled much of their assets. After the breakup,
Colleen moved in with Lori until she could get her life back
together.[8]

Lori and Colleen were extraordinarily close, even for
sisters. Their friends often marveled when, even as adults,
the sisters sat in the same chair. Through rough times, Lori
often rubbed Colleen's back as Colleen cried. Lori needed
support as well. Her first marriage had ended in divorce
and she had two small sons to raise. The fact that both lived
together after divorces brought them closer together.[9] Lori

was the organizer, the one who paid the bills. Colleen was
the player, which came in handy in a house with two small
boys. Her neighbors remember Colleen as a friendly, down-
home woman who never bothered anybody. She never took
drugs and rarely drank. She and Lori often treated their
neighbors to authentic Cajun cooking. Lori admits that Colleen made a better gumbo, but both sisters entertained with
delicacies like tasso and crawfish etouffeé.[10]   •

"Colleen was brilliant but she was a ditz," remembered
Lori. She would run out of gas, lose her keys, or discover
she had nothing to wear to work because she had forgotten
to pick up her dry cleaning. Quite often, Lori had to stop
cooking dinner, put her kids in a car, and bring Colleen a
gallon of gas or an extra set of keys along some highway
or at work. But at work, Colleen was a professional. While
her personal matters were uncharacteristic of what was expected of an accountant, her career was important to her
and she had specific, long-term goals. She intended to continue her education in order to advance. She had a vision
for her personal life as well. She wanted to get married and
have children, and she seemed anxious not to let the "bi-
ological clock" catch up to her.[11]

Colleen's first Austin job was as an accountant for the
city, but during the summer of 1989, she applied for and
accepted a position as an accountant with the Lower Colorado River Authority (LCRA). At the time, LCRA was
implementing a reorganization plan and new positions in
the audit department opened. (Employees joked, among
themselves, that LCRA really means "Let's Consider Re-
organizing Again.") She started her new job on September
1, 1989. Her friend at LCRA, Heather Bailey, remembered
her as "very professionally motivated."[12]

While still a city employee, Colleen had met and developed a relationship with Oliver Guerra. A native of Killeen,
Texas, he was one of her supervisors. At the time they met,
Colleen was engaged and he was separated. After she broke
off her engagement, they went out on a few dates to Austin
nightspots like the South Point Restaurant and Esther's Fol-

lies, Austin's legendary comedy theater. They jogged,
hiked, biked, and golfed together. Oliver remembers Colleen's habit of picking up wildflowers and placing them on
their golf cart, and how her Cajun accent surfaced when
she spoke to family and friends in Louisiana. The couple
worshipped together in the Catholic Church. In May, 1991,
after her engagement was broken off for good, and his divorce was final, they began to live together, but in October,
it became apparent that Oliver was not yet ready for another
marriage, so she decided to move out. Even after their separation, however, their relationship continued to be loving
and intimate.[13]

After leaving Oliver, Colleen moved into an apartment
on the 1800 block of Westlake Drive in an Austin suburb.
The apartments were simple, but Colleen was attracted to
the view of a wooded area near Bee Creek. It probably
reminded her of romps through the piney woods of Evangeline Parish. After moving into the apartment, she noticed
a small, emaciated stray cat shivering during the first cold
spell of 1991. Immediately, she adopted the cat and called
it "Menou" (pronounced MEE noo—Cajun French slang
for "cat"). Colleen's spontaneous adoption and her extreme
patience when the cat made a mess of her apartment surprised none of her neighbors.[14]

Colleen earned two promotions in two years, and at age
twenty-eight she supervised older and more experienced
people. As in all offices, relations with colleagues varied
and could get tense, but Colleen enjoyed working at LCRA.
Her professional life was in order.

Colleen had large, dark brown eyes and dark brown,
shoulder-length hair. She had an infectious smile, and was
a very attractive young lady. But she was never quite satisfied with how she looked. She wore gold, wire-rimmed
glasses "whenever she wanted to see," said Lori. But more
importantly, she considered herself clumsy and pudgy, especially when compared to her very skinny sister. "If Colleen passed by a buffet you could see it on her hips," said
Lori, who asserted that her sister was never fat. And so,

shortly after moving to Austin, Colleen joined the Army Reserves. She wanted to get whipped into shape at someone else's expense and get paid for it. She also figured that basic training would give her the coordination she believed she lacked, and a figure she wanted. It did. "She came out looking wonderful," Lori remembered. Colleen took care not to lose her new-found physique. For the rest of her life she jogged, played golf, worked out at Future Firm Fitness Center in Austin, and otherwise led a healthy lifestyle.[15]

Her Army Reserve Unit was the 363rd Support Group stationed in nearby San Marcos, Texas. By late 1991, she had attained the enlisted rank of Specialist, E-4. For the most part she enjoyed her enlistment, but after about two years she apparently decided to take advantage of the military downsizing that came with the end of the Cold War. After summer drills in August 1991, Colleen quit going to her regular monthly meetings. Many of her fellow soldiers never knew why she stopped going. She was never charged with any inappropriate absences. Few knew that she was being processed out.[16]

As Lori's children grew older and Colleen's career began to take off, the sisters spent less time together. They saw each other about once every two weeks and tried to talk every few days. By the fall of 1991, Lori remarried and Colleen seemed to be doing very well for herself. Each sister had been through hurtful times with husbands and boyfriends, and each, in her own way, came through for the other.

II

In a rural area south of Waco, just off Interstate 35, a picture of Melissa Ann Northrup hangs in the hallway of the home of her mother and stepfather, Brenda and Richard Solomon. Melissa is in a baseball uniform and her smile and image project a picture of a beautiful little girl growing up amidst the beauty of Central Texas. Melissa and her brother, Clay, were the children of a Frenchman named Clebert Leger, from Rayne, a small town in the heart of Cajun Country, and about forty miles from Ville Platte, where Lori and Colleen Reed grew up. The Leger marriage broke up and Melissa's mother, Brenda, later married Richard Solomon when Melissa was fourteen. Richard Solomon treated Clay and Melissa as if they were his own children.[17]

Melissa grew to be a small young woman. She wore a size 6-1/2 shoe, was less than five feet tall, and weighed around 100 pounds. Her eyes squinted during a full smile, and in spite of her beauty, she hated to have her picture taken. Her room was always a mess, and like Colleen Reed, she often had trouble finding things. To make things easier, she simply put everything that was important to her in her purse.

At age sixteen, Melissa became infatuated with an older boy who, according to Brenda and Richard, convinced her to run away from home. The young couple ended up in Kansas. Soon, they were married, but the union lasted only long enough for them to have two children—a boy and a girl. After the breakup of her marriage, Melissa and her children moved back to the Solomon home.[18]

The extended family had an understanding: Brenda and Richard provided for Melissa and her children, but Melissa worked to provide what she could and was wholly responsible for paying for the day care required for her children. She had a healthy work ethic and genuinely wanted to provide well for her son and daughter, but since she had no high school diploma, and no other employment training to speak of, she had to accept low-paying menial jobs. She worked at taco and hamburger places. While working as a cashier at a Whataburger, a well-known fast food chain, during the summer of 1990, she met another employee, a young man named Aaron Northrup. Their courtship was very brief; Aaron and Melissa were married on June 17, 1990.[19]

Like Melissa, Aaron was a high school dropout and had to settle for low-paying jobs. Shortly after their marriage, both Melissa and Aaron left fast food for jobs in convenience stores. Melissa became a cashier at a Circle K store while Aaron went to the Quik Pak Stores. On his job application, Aaron indicated that he wanted a management position with the company. By the late summer of 1991, Melissa left Circle K and joined Aaron as a Quik Pak employee.[20]

The young couple lived in a small residence in Hewitt, a small town outside of Waco. Quik Pak had hired Melissa as a $4.50 per hour cashier. Her duties, however, were not limited to working the cash register. Attendants like Melissa were expected to clean inside the store, sweep or hose down the driveway around the pumps, and perform other janitorial duties, like take trash to an outside bin. Quik Pak Stores required their $4.50-per-hour employees to buy their own smocks. She paid for hers through two payroll deductions of $12.60. Company rules also called for the smock to be worn zipped at all times.[21]

From the beginning, Melissa had concerns about the security of the Quik Pak she had been assigned to. While she was completely responsible for the cash register and the contents of the store, she had to go outside to go to the bathroom and had no key to lock the front door. Years later, Brenda Solomon shared an incident Melissa talked to her about involving a meeting of Quik Pak employees. At the meeting, she voiced a concern about stocking what was called the "vault," which referred to the upright refrigerators in the store. "When I'm in the vault stocking, if someone comes into the store I can't hear them."

Melissa indicated to her mother that the response to her concern was, "Well maybe you need a hearing aid."[22]

After a little more than a year, Aaron and Melissa's marriage ran into hard times. Their problems were many and complicated. According to Aaron, they separated in late August 1991 because Melissa felt he was ignoring her. On Labor Day, Melissa and her two children moved back into the Solomon home, and the extended family was reunited.[23]

At that point in her life, it occurred to Melissa that being a cashier at a Quik Pak was about all she was qualified to do. She hated that job, and only a few days after her hiring, she received a reprimand from the Quik Pak Stores for unsatisfactory performance. On July 27, 1991, her receipts were $41.23 short. "Melissa was verbally reprimanded and understands that this type of problem will not be tolerated," the Quik Pak report stated. She accepted the disciplinary action, signed the report, and court records never indicated evidence of any other similar reprimands.

Because she worked the graveyard shift, Melissa's shift ended at 7 A.M. Routinely, on her way to work, Brenda brought Melissa's daughter to the store. Melissa then brought the baby to day care and would go home to sleep. Normally she slept until about 2:30 P.M. or until Brenda called from work to wake her. Brenda's calls were Melissa's alarm clock. Late afternoon and early evening were quality times for Melissa and her children. They played until about 8:30 or 9 P.M. Each evening she lay with the children in bed until they fell asleep. Sometimes she dozed off as well, and Brenda would wake her up to be at the Quik Pak by 11 P.M., wearing her red smock with blue trimming and a badge that said "Quik Pak."[24]

III

Kenneth McDuff continued to take advantage of a laudable program designed to help parolees. And yet, he wanted more. On February 7, 1991, he applied for and got food stamps. Later in the year, he reported to the JTPA office that he had only twenty-five cents left, but on the same day he made purchases at a Wal-Mart in Belmead. On May 27, he failed to show up for work, but two days later he reported to his parole officer that he was working six days a week. On June 10, he reported that he quit his job because work and school were just too much for him to handle, when in fact he quit to drink beer with friends at a lake. On July 22, he requested more financial aid from the JTPA office, and on August 19, he requested funds for food during the semester break. Most of those requests were denied. He continued to live in Sabine Hall, and as each day passed the other residents saw more and more of his dangerous and bizarre behavior. He seemed to get more immature. TSTI students, and some of McDuff's own family saw him, while in his mid-forties, taking the cars they gave him and doing "donuts" in vacant lots and parking areas. One of his own family members described his behavior as "asinine."

TSTI dorms apparently had little or no supervision, or if they did, it was totally ineffective. In tens of thousands of pages of investigative reports, court documents, and primary sources only one document pertains to supervision or an inspection of any type during his matriculation at TSTI. On February 11, 1992, someone inspected his room; the word "fair" had been handwritten above the word "great," which had been scratched out.[25]

He made hundreds, perhaps thousands, of excursions from his Sabine Hall home base. On some of those occasions, weak-willed, slow-witted followers tagged along, and of course, Kenneth regaled them with stories of his brutality and murder. Even if only a small portion of his many stories were true, he preyed upon hundreds and murdered dozens of people in Central Texas. But with Kenneth McDuff, truth was always a mystery, and in his mind, it consisted of whatever he wanted to say at a given moment.

One excursion was a trip to Austin, which included a man named Harrison. Harrison lived in Temple with his grandmother, who had allegedly snatched him, while still an infant, from a day-care center. Others in the subculture called him "Indian." (There were a number of "Indians"; it was one of the more popular names.) In any case, Harrison met Mac during the summer of 1990 in the Bell County Jail while Mac awaited his parole revocation hearing for making a terroristic threat in Rosebud.

During the spring of 1991, Harrison, Mac, and Alva Hank Worley left Temple for Austin to look for drugs. The trio traversed the northern sections of Austin and its adjoining suburbs. After several unsuccessful stops, they decided to go back to Temple. In statements and testimony, Harrison indicated that Mac started the trip with a vivid description of a young woman. Harrison thought, at first, that Mac was describing a girlfriend. Near the Bruceville–Eddy exit on I-35, Mac admitted that he did not know the girl, and that he was just going to "take" her. He said that she worked in a convenience store during the graveyard shift. Harrison eventually concluded that Mac was really talking about kidnapping and murder. He told Mac that he wanted no part of such a scheme.[26]

Only weeks later Mac learned that Larry, the man who had murdered his brother Lonnie, had been released from prison. Larry was the only person that Mac ever admitted he wanted to kill; all his other threats were general in nature. Mac was incensed that his brother's murderer had been paroled—quite an irony. He made sure all of his acquaintances knew that he intended to kill Larry, and his search for a firearm appears to have intensified. That search took him to the home of one of his sisters, where he violated federal law by taking a revolver. Mac probably thought that Larry would become frightened, as had all others he sought to intimidate. Precisely the opposite happened. Larry, though a much smaller man than either Kenneth or Lonnie McDuff, refused to run. He let it be known that, not only was he not afraid of Kenneth McDuff, but that killing another McDuff would be no big deal to him. "If they were going to cross one another [Larry] was going to win that gun battle—no question about that," said Bell County Investigator Tim Steglich. And so, Kenneth McDuff was the one who backed off.[27]

Years later, McDuff claimed that he searched for Larry but could not locate him because no one was willing to help.[28] The assertion is patently ludicrous; Larry had been paroled to the little town of Holland. Holland was even smaller than Rosebud, and with the criminal network McDuff was familiar with to assist his search, and given the amount of time he spent traveling throughout the Blackland Prairie, if he'd really wanted to find Larry he could have done so easily. McDuff had no intention of facing Larry. The incident supports the conclusion that Kenneth McDuff was, in fact, cowardly. When Tommy Sammons "beat the snot" out of him in high school, Kenneth dropped out; when Brady Pamplin fired a shotgun at him, McDuff forever feared not only Brady, but his son Larry Pamplin, who never arrested or confronted him. He boasted of planning to kill his brother's murderer, only to claim that he was unable to find him—in Holland, Texas.

IV

Kenneth McDuff seemed to be getting away with everything. His life-long tendency to feel invulnerable must have been reinforced by his ability to cavort with ex-convicts, to rent whores, to abuse hard drugs, to fight, and to carry weapons, while subsisting on food stamps and living in a dorm supplied by the state and paid for with federal funds. The audacity of his behavior was matched only by the inability of the criminal justice system to recognize the danger he was to the public.

On the night of September 1, 1991, at 10:55 P.M., Temple Police Officer Bruce Smith observed a pickup truck run a red light and swerve across traffic lanes in a reckless manner on 43rd Street. Smith stopped the truck and discovered Mac and Hank Worley. Mac got out of the truck and walked unsteadily towards the officer. His eyes were glassy, and his speech was slurred. He also smelled like a rundown beer joint. When the officer asked him how much he'd had to drink, Mac answered that he'd had one beer about three hours earlier. At the site, Mac failed a number of sobriety tests and was immediately arrested for driving while intoxicated. Worley was not found to be drunk, and so the truck, its floorboard covered with empty Old Milwaukee cans, was left in his custody.

According to Officer Smith's report, on the way to the

jail, Mac begged not to be charged and to be set free. At the jail, however, he became belligerent and refused to take a breath test or cooperate in any way.[29]

Two days later, on September 3, Mac reported the DWI arrest to his parole officer. He also admitted to smoking marijuana. Each of the offenses was a violation of his parole, which could have sent him back to prison. But at the time, the combination of federal Judge Justice's rulings and the dependence of the state on parole to meet those demands, made it unlikely that McDuff would be sent back to prison, and indeed, he was not.[30]

Even more farcical was his court appearance. On January 3, 1992, he pleaded guilty to Operating a Motor Vehicle in a Public Place While Intoxicated. Allegedly, his attorney was able to successfully negotiate an astonishingly light sentence. Punishment was assessed as a $500 fine plus court costs of $202, and ninety days' confinement in the county jail. The court order continued: "However, it appeared to the Court that the Defendant has made a sworn motion for probation and that the ends of Justice and the best interest of the public as well as the Defendant will be served if the imposition of the sentence in this case is suspended and the Defendant is placed on probation under the supervision of the Court."[31]

His probation was for twenty-four months, and the conditions of his probation included:

- Committing no criminal offense
- Avoiding injurious or vicious habits like taking drugs or drinking alcohol
- Avoiding persons and places of disreputable character
- Reporting to probation officer and obeying the rules of probation
- Permitting the probation officer to visit him at home or elsewhere
- Finding a job

Of course, he honored none of the above-listed conditions.[32]

V

Alva Hank Worley does not remember if he dropped out of Belton High School during the ninth or tenth grade. At age eighteen, he was convicted of larceny for breaking into a car and given probation, only to have it revoked after getting caught during the unauthorized use of another vehicle. He received a two-year sentence. His record indicated that when he went to jail he was only 5'6" tall and weighed 130 pounds.[33]

Hank believed his parents had done a good job of raising him and his siblings. His father worked for the Texas Highway Department and was a firm disciplinarian; he never shied away from using a belt to punish his children. His mother worked at a garment factory. Neither of the parents drank to excess or had other vices, but they were not particularly close either. Hank was close to his older brother, who was a foreman of one of the construction crews Hank worked on.[34]

Hank's first marriage lasted only one year. He attributed the failure to two reasons. First, "We just ran off and we thought we was in love. It was just a heat stroke, I guess," he said. And second, he was only sixteen years old.

He worked at menial jobs on construction sites, and one of his early employers was Lonnie McDuff. At the time, Kenneth was in prison and Hank did not get to know him until years later. He was a splendid example of a weak-willed member of Mac's audiences. It was Roy Dale Green all over again. Hank Worley was "a big time loser in a small time place" said Tim Steglich, about a man who delighted in drinking beer and smoking weed with friends while engaging in horrid conversations. While living at Bloom's Motel in Belton, Hank and a few other residents pondered, "Can you imagine being in a room with body parts?"[35]

As Hank grew older, he became pudgier, mostly because of his eating habits and love for beer. "He carries a twelve-pack everywhere he goes," his sister said in sworn testimony. He could drink a six-pack in minutes. But Hank Worley was content with himself. He worked, drank beer, took drugs, and ate. In 1992, a psychologist asked him if he had ever tried to hurt himself. "Oh, no," Hank laughed. "I love myself too much."[36]

Hank's second marriage lasted longer than his first. He wed an attractive woman named Janice, and their union lasted seven years and produced two children, an older daughter and a younger son. After divorcing Hank, Janice married again, divorced again, and then married Billy, the ex-con and acquaintance of Kenneth McDuff. During the summer of 1991, at his former brother-in-law's trailer at the S&S Mobile Home Park, Billy introduced Hank to Mac. Frequently, the threesome met at Buddy's trailer and partied.[37]

Directly across the road from Buddy's trailer in the S&S Mobile Home Park lived Hank's sister, Diane. She had been living there for over ten years in one of the nicer, better-kept mobile homes. The inside of her home was spotless; she cared for herself, her family, and even her brother Hank. She and her husband let Hank move in with them after his divorce from Janice. But the arrangement got complicated when Hank's daughter and his ex-wife, Janice, found it impossible to live with one another. That, plus other complicated reasons, motivated Hank to look for another place to stay. He had no choice; Diane's trailer could not accommodate another Worley.

Diane remembers her first encounter with Big Mac. "He came by the house one day, several times, and the only time I met him is [when] he came up on the porch one day. I had the door open and I was mopping the floor. He came up and knocked on the door and asked if Hank was there and I told him 'No,' Hank was not there. Hank was at work.

And he turned around and walked off, and I told him, I said if you leave your name, I'll tell Hank you stopped by. And he said just tell him Big Mac stopped by." Most other times, however, Mac just drove up, stuck his head out of the car, and asked if Hank was there.[38]

Hank described his conversations with Mac as "talking shit." Mac spoke of the tire-tool beatings he inflicted on others and leaving them for dead. And, of course, he also spoke of getting guns and taking and using up women, including very specific references to a good-looking girl in a convenience store in Waco, where Mac used to work. They drank a lot of beer, and when not riding around the Belton and Temple area, they usually stopped in smelly beer joints like Poor Boys, The He Ain't Here, and Dundee's Club. Sometimes they went to Waco, to the Cut, to score dope from the whores.

Psychologist Matt Ferrara, in an interview with Hank, later suggested that Mac was really planting a seed—he wanted to see how Hank would react to such bizarre conversations and even more bizarre behavior. Hank's other sister, Bess, saw clearly that Big Mac had an overpowering effect on Hank. In reality, Mac was preparing his next accomplice. He was setting up Hank Worley to be a 1990s version of Roy Dale Green, and Hank was not smart enough to see it until it had become a *fait accompli*.[39]

On November 24, 1991, during one of their trips to Waco, Mac's car broke down near a convenience store south of Waco. It was not the convenience store where the good-looking girl Mac wanted to "take" worked, though. Stranded, Mac and Hank called Billy and Janice to come by and pick them up. Janice noticed that Mac was no longer driving a pickup. Mac had returned the pickup to his father and was now driving another vehicle, a cream-colored, 1985 Ford Thunderbird. The next day, Janice secured a new water pump for Billy to fix the car. The incident was significant only because there was no doubt that on November 25, 1991, the day Janice bought the water pump, Kenneth was in possession of a light-colored 1985 Thunderbird.[40]

VI

Kenneth McDuff began the day on which he appeared in court for the pronouncement of his two-year suspended sentence for driving while intoxicated by going to his friend, Linda, and asking her to go to court with him. They drove to Addie and J. A.'s house to kill time. On the way, Mac told Linda that he would steal Valium and Darvoset from his mother. When they arrived at the McDuff home, according to Linda's statement, Mac took a shower while Addie made coffee, toast, and hamburgers. While sitting at the table eating, Mac talked openly about the Justice for McDuff, Inc. movie proposal. Linda noticed a strange look on Addie's face and concluded that Addie would have much preferred that Mac stop talking about movie deals to a stranger. Once Addie left the kitchen, Mac jumped up and walked over to a cupboard, and asked Linda to be on the lookout for Addie's return. He searched in vain for his mother's medicine, only to look at Linda and say, "Damn, the bitch done caught onto me and hid 'em somewhere else where I can't find 'em."[41]

While Linda sat in the living room, J. A. McDuff, now a frail old man, entered. At first, he did not even notice her. When he did see her, he looked surprised, waved, and kept moving out of the room. Linda and Mac left the McDuff home and went to a nearby dam where Mac said there was a scenic overlook. Mac decided that since he needed to be in court that day he would not have anything to drink. Linda, though, had a beer as she and Mac looked over the area. "This would be a good place to dump a body, because the water's so high, the body would just wash away," she remembered him saying. He just sat there looking over the water.[42]

After McDuff's court appearance, he and Linda went to a house to buy and smoke crack, violating both his parole and probation only minutes after his appearance. Several old men sat outside the house when they arrived. McDuff pointed to Linda and asked, "Don't she have a nice ass?"

"Yeah, I'll give you a screwdriver, a pair of pliers and something else if I can take her in the house for a while," one of the old men said.

"Not in this lifetime," replied Linda.

Mac and Linda joined Jimmy and Billy and all four smoked rocks of crack. After they left the house, they headed back to Addie's place and smoked more crack on the way. Mac entered the home, and according to Linda, returned to the car with money in three pockets; it looked like several hundred dollars. When she asked him where he got all that money, he laughed and told her not to worry about it.[43]

They left Addie's house and went to Waco to get more dope. Then they went back to Temple and rejoined Billy and the others. They smoked so much crack that "McDuff got so fucked up that he insisted that [Linda] drive." She did not want to drive because she was pretty high herself and, as she said, "it was raining like a son-of-a-bitch." Finally, they made it to her trailer. Incredibly, Mac pulled out two more rocks he had been saving and they smoked those as well.

The saturation of drugs in Mac's system probably produced what Linda described as a fit of paranoia. He accused her of setting him up, grabbed her by the hair, and walked her out to his car. While standing next to the passenger side door, Linda watched Mac get into his car and take off, spraying mud in all directions.[44] It was the end of an extraordinary day in the life of Kenneth Allen McDuff.

On that day, January 3, 1992, McDuff thoroughly beat the system. He walked into court having violated his parole in several ways only to walk out having to pay a few hundred dollars in fines and court costs, which in all probability, he did not pay himself. He returned to the streets of Central Texas on parole and on probation, and within *minutes*, shamelessly violated the conditions of both. His complete lack of a moral compass on January 3, 1992, was more remarkable when placed in the context of what he had done less than one week earlier. On December 29, 1991, Kenneth McDuff had reached a level of cruelty and depravity seldom seen in the annals of crime, and on that day he was not drunk or high on speed or crack. He knew precisely what he was doing when he became what J. W. Thompson said was "every woman's nightmare."

9

The Cut

"There's an awful lot of weirdos out there, and you never know when you are going to meet one."
—Richard Stroup, McLennan County Sheriff's Deputy

I

Living her adult life in a culture with an absence of beauty took its toll on Brenda Kay Thompson. She looked much older than her age—thirty-seven. At 5'5" tall and weighing only 115 pounds, she was a small woman. Her drawn and hollow-looking face made her look emaciated, almost skeletal. What were once beautiful brown eyes were instead sunken into bony sockets surrounded by a rough complexion. She looked tired. Her tragic life gave her a "worn" look common among the "older" (both in terms of age and arrests) girls at the Cut. She had several aliases, including Debbie Johnson and Debbie Ward. A criminal background check reveals a long history of a dozen or so petty crimes ranging from small thefts settled by paying fines to more serious charges of possessions of controlled substances carrying with them five- and six-year sentences. Additionally, she had a history of DWI and moving traffic violations, trespassing charges, and numerous counts of forgery.[1]

Brenda lived in a house on Delano Street in Waco and prostituted herself on the Cut and the Strip (Highway 77 or the "Old Dallas Highway"). Others there remembered her as quiet and "to herself." Even for the Cut, where impersonality was the rule, no one knew much about Brenda. She had been paroled to Waco after getting into trouble in Fort Worth, where she had been placed on parole in Tarrant County. On May 24, 1991, the Waco Police Department arrested her for violation of her Tarrant County parole. On that day, she wore a floral, white dress. Her straight, shoulder-length hair had no body and had apparently been cut without the benefit of a mirror. The arresting officer indicated in his report that she spoke fast but was polite. The specific violation of her parole was not spelled out in the report, but it could not have been very serious—very shortly she was back out on Faulkner Lane with the other girls at the Cut.[2]

On September 6, Brenda Thompson was arrested again. This time the charge was prostitution. At 11:10 P.M., she had offered sex and described her services for money to an undercover officer who promptly took her from the Strip to the McLennan County Jail. The arresting officer noted that she had missing teeth and a birthmark on the back of her neck. This time, her speech was soft, but rude. Apparently, Brenda was tiring of her frequent arrests. This prostitution charge, like her earlier parole violation, brought with it no serious sentence. According to the arrest report, since the charge was not a felony, she was released.[3] Within hours, Brenda was back on the Cut and the Strip plying her trade, but within five weeks her luck would run out and this time her fate would not be determined by law enforcement officials.

Regenia DeAnn Moore was a much younger and far more reckless prostitute on the Cut. According to police reports, she lived on Dutton Street, but often rented cheap motel rooms to accommodate her dates. At 5'4" tall and weighing only 110 pounds, she was even smaller than Brenda Thompson. Police officers characterized her speech as soft. At age twenty-one, she had already had three children who had been adopted by a relative. Like Brenda, Regenia—called "Gina" by McDuff and other members of the subculture—began to look worn. Her teeth were perfect, and her blonde hair had hints of red. Even her mug shots show her to be lively. Her blue eyes sparkled, but like Brenda Thompson's, were sunken into sockets surrounded by bags and a rough, ruddy complexion that seems to be a mark of living a nightlife on the streets. Poorly tattooed letters on the fingers of her right hand spelled either "RAT!" "RAIL" or "RATE." Had she lived a healthier, more wholesome life, she would have been extraordinarily beautiful. But she lived in an atmosphere with an absence of beauty—and it took its toll on her, too.

Regenia and Brenda were pictures of the destructive power of places like the Strip and the Cut. They, and the other women of the Cut, were far removed from glamorous movie characters. None of these women dated billionaires in luxury hotels, rode around in expensive cars, or got married to handsome men in business suits. The women of the Cut did not have the matching panties and bras that Sidney Biddle Barrows, the Mayflower Madam, required of her escorts. They never saw Heidi Fleiss celebrities. They were more likely to provide their services on the ground in fields of tall grass. Their lives were and still are dominated by drugs, sex, disease, beatings—and the threat of violent death.

Regenia had a "bad rock habit" which led to reckless behavior, even for someone who worked the Cut. McDuff himself marveled at her fearlessness; he spoke of her spending an inordinate amount of time in the "black projects." Black Jennifer, herself a prostitute, said Regenia was young and reckless and more so when smoking crack and drinking liquor. Her behavior, of course, centered on getting money to support her dangerous habit. Her first arrests in Waco were for charges of credit card abuse. On September 25, 1991, Waco Police arrested her near the Strip on the corner of Sealy Street and South Loop Drive. She was almost immediately released because the offense was not a felony. Only two days later, on September 27, Waco Police stopped a vehicle she was riding in and arrested her again for another credit card abuse offense. Again, she was released.[4]

Gina's desperation to sustain her drug habit included the extraordinarily dangerous practice of "clipping" her dates, or stealing from their wallets. Other prostitutes, and a self-appointed missionary who befriended Regenia, candidly admitted to Waco Police that Gina's angry johns often re-

turned to look for her and their money. According to an
unidentified prostitute, one john in a red and white Thunderbird with a machine gun in the front seat hunted for Gina
after she had stolen his money. Another prostitute identified
yet another one of those johns as McDuff, who asserted,
"When I find her I'm going to kill that bitch. She ripped
me off and I'm going to kill her." The informant told Mike
Nicoletti of the WPD that "if anyone should not be ripped
off it was McDuff." Black Jennifer, in a sworn statement,
said, "I knew that of all the customers to clip, McDuff was
not the one she should have done that to."[5]

Gina's last arrest was for possession of controlled substances and drug paraphernalia. On October 9, 1991, Waco
Police set up a driver's license check stop near the intersection of Miller Street and Faulkner Lane. The checkpoint
served the purpose of discouraging traffic through the heart
of the Cut. At 9:30 P.M. the officers stopped the car Gina
was in and as she stepped out, one of them noticed she
clutched a handful of crack cocaine rocks in her left hand.
Apparently, she had already been smoking rocks; her
speech was slurred and she was clearly under the influence
of narcotics. She was immediately arrested and taken to the
McLennan County Jail. (The facility serves as the jail for
the City of Waco as well.) By 12:32 A.M., Gina had been
booked, and only eight minutes later, at 12:40 A.M. on October 10, 1991, she was able to post bond through a bail-
bond service and was released.[6]

While Gina was booked at the McLennan County Jail,
Waco police officers continued to man their checkpoint on
Faulkner Lane. It had been set up by the Special Operations
Team to check verification of insurance as well. At some
other location Brenda Thompson had gotten into a red
pickup truck with Kenneth McDuff. Most likely, she was
by herself in an isolated spot when he picked her up. After
their date, he drove south on Miller Street and encountered
the WPD roadblock on Faulkner. He stopped about fifty
feet from the checkpoint. One of the officers walked toward
McDuff's truck, and as he did so, he shined his flashlight

on himself so that the driver could see who he was. McDuff could clearly see the officer.

All of a sudden, Brenda began screaming and kicking. Her arms appeared to the officer to have been bound behind her back. "This is my belief because I never could see her hands, and it did appear that she did not have such control in the vehicle as she was sitting in the passenger seat," wrote the officer in his report. Clearly, she desperately tried to get out of the truck; she lay back and began kicking the windshield with such a force that it shattered it on the passenger side. She continued to kick viciously as she lay on her back while her legs, clothed in a pair of red polyester pants, cracked the windshield more and more with each kick.

Immediately, McDuff floored the accelerator and made a run for the officers. According to the same WPD report, filed that day, three officers had to move quickly to avoid being hit. As he sped by, the officers shouted as they identified themselves, and scrambled to their cars to give chase. McDuff raced south on Miller Street toward Waco Drive, turned off his lights, and disappeared into the darkness, taking Brenda Thompson with him. McDuff eluded police by going the wrong way on one-way streets. Eventually, he turned west on US 84, and then north on Gholson Road for about eight miles to a wooded area.[7]

Other members of the usual crowd on the Cut had watched the spectacle with surprising indifference. Michael saw Brenda kicking and screaming and could see, as everyone else could, that she was in trouble. No one did anything. Little Run, another prostitute, said, referring to McDuff, "Ah, man, that's just that fool."[8]

Given his fondness for vehicles, McDuff must have been incensed at what Brenda had done to his windshield. If his behavior that night was consistent with what he had done in the past, and what he would do in the coming months, Brenda Thompson endured a slow, excruciatingly torturous death.

II

Since McDuff ran the roadblock at Faulkner and Miller almost at the moment Gina was being released from the McLennan County Jail, she could not have been on the Cut to witness the abduction of Brenda Thompson. (Even today, many law enforcement officers and news reports continue to incorrectly identify Regenia Moore as the woman seen kicking and screaming in McDuff's truck on October 10, 1991.) She might not have heard about the incident from the others on the Cut, who universally concluded that, indeed, McDuff was weird and crazy. Even so, the people of this subculture, for one reason or another, were drawn to money, and on occasion, McDuff had some.

Only a few days after the roadblock incident, Gina was seen in McDuff's pickup truck on the corner of Faulkner and the Strip. During an interview with federal investigators, the consistently unreliable "scumbag opportunist" Chester asserted that McDuff drove up to him while Gina was in the truck and asked if Chester had any cocaine. When Chester indicated he had none, McDuff drove away. Chester claims to have been the last person, other than McDuff, to see Gina alive.

Chester's account was at least partially supported by a more reliable friend of Gina's (hereafter referred to as William), who became intrigued with the culture of the Cut. Although reportedly not a customer, William came to know a lot of the people of the Cut and became sort of a counselor/advisor to many of them. William was convinced that she was last seen alive between 11 P.M. and midnight on October 15, 1991, in Kenneth McDuff's pickup truck. Most accounts place the truck at the corner of Faulkner and US 77, within sight of a fast food restaurant called the Chicken Shack.[9]

McDuff took Gina to a remote area along Highway 6 north and east of Waco. At the site of a bridge traversing the Tehuacana Creek, McDuff could have pulled off the road onto a very steep embankment down to the banks of the creek where he drove under the bridge. Passing motorists could not have seen his car. The road there is a freeway, and cars rushing over the bridge easily made enough noise to drown out any screams Gina may have made.

Within a day or so William contacted Gina's mother, a remarkable and courageous woman named Barbara Carpenter. Barbara immediately went to the Cut and was the first outsider to determine that indeed Gina and Brenda were missing. On October 19, while asking questions on the Cut, Barbara noticed a Waco Policeman, an Officer Barrington, patrolling the area. She stopped the officer and voiced a concern for Gina's safety.[10]

For the next several months Barbara Carpenter believed that she was not taken seriously by the Waco Police Department. "I think they looked down on her, just another prostitute and dope user," she said.

For the Waco Police Department, the unfortunate truth, as insensitive as it might sound, was that prostitutes on the Cut frequently and willingly got into the vehicles of strangers and rode off. "She could possibly be anywhere. She is a street person. She is a prostitute. She could be from here to Kalamazoo. We don't have any information otherwise," said WPD Captain Everett January. Most of the time they returned, but sometimes they moved on to another city. The fact that Gina was missing could have meant anything—at the time. But the erroneous connection between Gina and the roadblock sent Barbara Carpenter, William, and the Waco Police Department looking for Kenneth Allen McDuff.

William had spent enough time on the Cut to know its people. He also knew of Kenneth McDuff and was able to tell Barbara Carpenter that McDuff was a student at TSTI. Shortly after Regenia's disappearance, Barbara, her husband, and William went to the Cut to talk to many of the girls there. They told her that Regenia was last seen with a regular customer named McDuff. The trio then went to

Sabine Hall where they encountered Frankie, who told them of his rides with McDuff and McDuff's unsuccessful attempt to steal J. A.'s air compressor.

They then confronted McDuff in his room at Sabine Hall. When asked where Regenia was, McDuff reacted violently, threw up his hands, and said, "Don't try to pin that on me." Months later, in an interview with federal investigators, Barbara indicated that at the time McDuff protested his innocence, no mention had been made that anything had happened to Regenia. She added that McDuff insisted that he had taken Regenia back to the Inn 7 Motel around 9 P.M. After letting her out of his car, he claimed she almost immediately went to another car, talked to the driver and left with him. McDuff only remembered that the car was tan.

As Barbara left Sabine Hall, she believed that she would never see her daughter again. "I just got this instinct. . . . I hope, I wish, I pray I am wrong, but I don't think I am."[11]

On the Cut, it was common knowledge that McDuff had taken and done something to both Regenia and Brenda. When one of the prostitutes asked him what he had done to Regenia, McDuff shot back, "I dropped the bitch off; I didn't even fuck her." Only a few months later, ATF Special Agent Charles Meyer became so sickened by the gross indifference of the inhabitants of the Cut, he lamented, "It was like, 'Okay, Regenia's gone—big deal.'" When asked by another Sabine Hall resident what happened to the windshield of his truck, McDuff replied that he had parked it in the wrong neighborhood.[12]

In the middle of the whole tragic affair was Chester. All of the investigators of the McDuff case eventually concluded that Chester was a monumental waste of time. But, at the very least, he witnessed some of Regenia's last hours. At least one Cut prostitute believes she saw Chester in the red pickup truck with McDuff and Regenia the last time she saw Regenia there. This same prostitute also stated that a few days later Chester asked her if the police questioned her about Regenia's disappearance.[13]

The day after Barbara Carpenter accosted McDuff in Sabine Hall, five officers from the Waco Police Department, some of whom wrote that they had to dash from McDuff's truck so that he would not run over them, visited McDuff. One of the officers positively identified McDuff's red truck as the truck that ran the roadblock on October 10. They noticed that the windshield had been kicked out and shattered on the passenger side, but the inside was very clean and had been washed out. The owner of the auto glass shop that later changed the windshield also remembered that it was so badly damaged that it looked like it had been broken with a chain; he also confirmed the cleanliness of the inside of the truck. The back of the truck, however, had a lounge chair and a lot of empty beer cans. Incredibly, the same officer positively identified McDuff as the driver.

Two of the Waco police officers then interviewed McDuff for a short time in his room. In a report of the interview, McDuff was said to have admitted that he knew Gina and that on the date in question, he picked her up on the corner of Faulkner and the Loop. He said that he dated a number of girls at the Cut regularly, and that after he finished his "business" with her, he dropped her off. Throughout the interview, McDuff was very calm. The WPD report has no reference to any action taken against McDuff—not even a ticket. Eight days later, on October 28, a separate WPD report asserted that the officers, who on October 10 reported that they had to run from McDuff's speeding truck, did not write an offense report for aggravated assault against an officer because they were not placed in fear of their lives.[14] The roadblock incident is steeped in controversy to this day.

Kenneth McDuff's childhood sense of invulnerability had to have been reinforced by what he was able to get away with in Waco in mid-October of 1991. He had assaulted police officers with a vehicle and had been positively identified by the same officers who also witnessed a woman passenger, who appeared to be bound, in panic and distress—and nothing happened. He considered skipping town, but after he called Addie and asked if the police were looking for him, and she said they had not contacted her, he concluded that "everything was o.k."[15]

And life and death on the Cut went on. Within a five-day period, Kenneth McDuff had abducted Brenda and Regenia within an area of one hundred yards. On other occasions, he even brutalized the prostitutes he did not murder. Duckie's three-hour ordeal, sex "in every hole in her body" with McDuff, meant nothing to the girls who kept getting into his truck. And *every* woman on the Cut interviewed by officers stated that McDuff was weird, crazy, and dangerous. These women behaved in a way that toyed with and almost invited death, through either violence or virus. One tragic example, Little Bit—who before entering the subculture with an absence of beauty, was named Diana—contracted AIDS and died.[16] Undoubtedly, there were many others. And life and death on the Cut went on.

III

In early November, Kenneth McDuff returned the red pickup truck with the broken windshield to his father, J. A., who did not bother to ask what had happened. According to J. A., if Kenneth had given him an explanation he would not have believed him anyway. At that time, according to a cousin, McDuff had taken possession of a 1985 Ford Thunderbird. The original owner of the car was one of his sisters, whose family put well over 100,000 miles on the vehicle. Without question, on November 24, McDuff was driving the Thunderbird.

The tan, 1985 Ford Thunderbird was a powerful mid-sized car. In some ways, it was perfect for what McDuff had in mind. Even though Thunderbirds have only two doors, the inside is somewhat spacious, and passengers seated in the rear cannot exit without the consent of those in front. On December 2, 1991, McDuff applied for a title for the vehicle, which was issued on December 30, the day after he would use it for kidnapping, torture and murder.[17]

As the Christmas holidays approached, McDuff continued to roam the highways and back roads of Central Texas. He had no visible means of support, but he had money. He spent much of Christmas Eve of 1991 with a Bastrop woman named Angela. According to her statement, they spent some time at the home of one of his sisters. The sister appeared to be very close to him; she suggested to Angela that her brother would do well and that he had not committed the Broomstick Murders. On that day, McDuff complained to Angela that his nephew (the son of that same sister) "disrespected" him because he would not let him in on dope deals. The nephew was a major Central Texas distributor of methamphetamines, reportedly grossing over $500,000 per year. According to Angela's statement, the young drug dealer feared that his uncle would try to take over the "business."

Angela and McDuff then went to the County Line Bar for beers and a few games of pool. McDuff began to get very upset when Angela started beating him at the game. Afterwards, she stated, all he wanted to do was sit down. He got even more upset when he "hit" on her and she did not respond. He called her a lesbian and suggested that he was going out to "get some pussy." Later that evening, however, McDuff had asked Angela if she wanted to go with him to Killeen to score dope. Angela declined, saying that she wanted to spend Christmas with her family. Almost a year later, she reflected that the seemingly insignificant decision might have saved her life.[18]

IV

Christmas time at Lori Bible's home was much more familial and traditional. Her sister, Colleen Reed, drove up to Lori's Round Rock residence in a new car she had purchased only a few months earlier. It was a 1991 white Mazda Miata. She loved her new car and had paid for it in full by mortgaging land she owned in Louisiana. It was a fun Christmas Day for the sisters, who enjoyed watching Lori's boys "wash" Aunt Colleen's car with the "super soakers" she had given them as presents. They also planned parties for the boys, who both had birthdays in January, and agreed to go to a Neville Brothers concert in Austin in February. It would have been a fun night out for the sisters.

At the end of Christmas Day, 1991, Lori and Colleen bade farewell to one another; Lori would never see her sister alive again.

Even though her engagement with Oliver had been broken off, Colleen continued to see him, and as Lori said years later, "She loved him—big time." But at the time she also dated others. During October or November she had placed a personal ad in the *Austin American-Statesman*, and as a result, dated a man named Francois. During the holidays she spent time with a co-worker from LCRA, and while their relationship was never intimate, they enjoyed each other's company at movies and dinners, and on sailing trips. They also enjoyed cooking for each other. Oliver believed that during their separation they tried to get over each other, but could not. He believed that 1992 was going to be their year.[19]

Kenneth McDuff did not celebrate Christmas like most other people. The holiday season did nothing to temper his lust for robbing dope dealers, purchasing the services of prostitutes, and getting a gun. On December 23, 1991, McDuff drove to the Harker Heights home of a female speed dealer named Sandy. Their mutual friend, Billy, had introduced them. While at her home, McDuff met a most unique character named Jackie. Also known as the "One-eyed Jack" (because he had one good eye), Jackie was better known for the tattoos that nearly covered his body. Austin detective J. W. Thompson remembers that the first time he met Jackie he wondered why this enormous man was wearing a heavy, long-sleeved shirt during the heat of a Central Texas summer. As Jackie got closer, J. W. realized that what he mistook for the long sleeves were really two massive arms covered with tacky, dark blue ink.[20]

His criminal record described him as 5'9" tall and weigh-ing 190 pounds, but as he got older he put on much more weight. By 1991, he must have weighed at least 250 pounds. The forty-nine-year-old ex-con had matured into an utterly hideous-looking physical specimen. His long, scraggly, brown hair, thinning on the top, rested on thick shoulders covered with multi-colored, carnival art. Each shoulder was so completely covered with permanent ink that elements of the collage could barely be discerned; above his right breast a bosomy cat-woman-like female pre-sented her nipples; around his neck a blue chain, never to be removed, held a medallion that looked like a stop watch; up and down each arm other cartoon women duplicated Jackie's frightful, icy stare. His green eyes were small for his massive skull. No transition existed between his neck and head. His complexion was "street-person ruddy" and covered with growth somewhere between an Arafat stubble and a full beard. His torso was shaped like an hourglass and covered with an even coating of short, pubic-like hair. Hanging breasts protruded over the tops and sides of his ribs. Below the ribs, in all directions, exploded a massive stomach, so large that its front came to an apex at the belly button, leading him as a bow leads a ship.[21]

Jackie was an old-time con. He played the game and was an "honest crook," readily admitting to anything—if he got caught. This perverse honesty actually endeared him to most officers who dealt with him; Jackie understood the rules—take your punishment like a man. His record in-cluded burglary, larceny, escape, and aggravated assault of a police officer. The assault must not have been very seri-ous; Jackie paid a fine and was released. It probably hap-pened while police were trying to break up one of his many fights. He loved to fight, and delighted in saying he was "the meanest son-of-a-bitch in the jungle." Nobody scared Jackie—until Christmas Day of 1991.

And so, on December 23, at Sandy's house in Harker Heights, McDuff became acquainted with Jackie. As usual,

McDuff was interested in robbing drug dealers and he wanted to know if Jackie knew of any dealers to clip. Jackie thought McDuff was full of hot air and quickly tired of the conversation. He told McDuff of a prostitute in Austin known as Sylvia. At the time, Jackie rented a room with a family in Austin, and after McDuff left, Jackie told Sandy not to let McDuff know where he lived.

In fact, Jackie lived with a family in north Austin in a neighborhood where crack houses had begun to spring up. Jackie and his landlord entertained an idea that McDuff could rob the drug producers and maybe run them out of the neighborhood. On Christmas Day, Jackie and the family intended to celebrate with a fine meal and an exchange of presents. McDuff disrupted their plans. Sandy had given him directions to the north Austin home. When the man of the house answered the knock on the door, McDuff walked in uninvited and asked, "Where's Jack?"

Again, McDuff spoke of killing and robbing drug dealers. He vividly described how he could get crack dealers into his car and shoot them in the head as they were getting out so that blood would not get in his car. The homeowner told McDuff to quit talking that way in front of his family; McDuff cared not that the homeowner's wife and children were in the same room and could hear everything. Eventually, the man had to tell his wife to bring their kids into another room until Jackie agreed to accompany McDuff on a search for Sylvia.[22]

Before he could rob anyone, McDuff had to get a gun. He insisted on cruising Austin in search of a big gun, not just the .357 magnum he had been offered. He and Jackie looked for a pawnshop—on Christmas Day—to buy a gun; none were open. 7-Eleven convenience stores, however, were open and McDuff stopped at one on North Lamar Street to steal gas by filling up and placing the nozzle on the ground. He told Jackie he learned how to do that by working at a convenience store. Jackie also noticed that McDuff often intentionally drove the wrong way on one-way streets.

Most disturbing to Jackie, though, was McDuff's reaction to seeing two young girls on rollerskates. McDuff drove up to them and had Jackie ask them if they knew where Sylvia could be found. When one of the young girls said "no" and skated away, McDuff turned to Jackie and said, "Let's get them, throw them in here, and go." Jackie reacted emphatically; he wanted nothing to do with that. He told McDuff that he had girlfriends and did not have to do that sort of thing. Moments later, at a convenience store, the two men saw two more young girls using a pay phone. Jackie watched McDuff, in a near hypnotic state, leering at the two girls. When McDuff stated, "Look at that . . . that sure looks good, doesn't it? . . . Let's get 'em," Jackie repeated his refusal with a more emphatic, "Hell, no!"

Sometime between 3 and 4 P.M., after hours of trying to convince Jackie to go with him to Temple to get a gun, McDuff brought Jackie back home to north Austin. As McDuff drove away in his tan 1985 Ford Thunderbird, Jackie thought, and later told federal investigators, that McDuff was a lunatic, weird, crazy, and the scariest person he had ever been around. He had never encountered anyone so totally unpredictable and obsessed with robbing and killing. "All I wanted to do was get away from him," Jackie said. Given Jackie's own background and experiences, that was quite a statement.[23]

10

The Car Wash

"Nobody should be put through that type of torture."
—Alva Hank Worley

I

Every Christmas season miles of multi-colored lights illuminate Congress Avenue in downtown Austin. From the Colorado River, which Austinites insist on calling Town Lake, to the State Capitol, the bulbs form a colorful tunnel, and at times motorists have trouble seeing traffic signals. But it does not matter; Austin drivers have little respect for traffic lights anyway. Mild weather usually greets Christmas time; hardy Austinites do not bother with winterwear like sweaters or coats. At best, light windbreakers suffice, especially during the Christmas season of 1991 when the average minimum temperature was about forty-six degrees.

The tragic murder of four teenage girls in a Yogurt Shop dominated Austin news in December of 1991. The "Yogurt Shop Murders" broke the city's heart. Billboards with pictures of the four beautiful high school girls begged for information about what had happened. Not since Charles Whitman went on his shooting spree at the University of Texas Tower in 1966 had Austin been through such a collective traumatic event. The Austin Police Department became a hub for a multi-jurisdictional effort to solve the murders; and within the department all available resources were marshalled. A conviction for that case would not be realized for nearly a decade.

In a city still reeling from the Yogurt Shop tragedy, Colleen's boyfriend, Oliver, had warned her to be careful. He represented a prevalent mood in Austin. Statistically, Aus-

tin is a safe city in which to live, but occasionally, high
profile crimes like the Charles Whitman Murders, the James
Cross Murders and the Yogurt Shop Murders remind Austinites, like Oliver and Colleen, that no city or town is completely safe and it is best to be prudent and watchful.[1]

Colleen Reed spent Christmas Day of 1991 at the home
of her sister, Lori Bible, who had remarried the previous
October. Throughout the Christmas Holidays, Colleen had
a tenuous relationship with Oliver, but as 1991 came to a
close, Oliver, and probably Colleen as well, had reason to
believe that 1992 would be their year.

On Saturday, December 28, Colleen spent some time at
her LCRA office and afterwards rented a movie to take to
Oliver's house. They ate dinner, watched the video, and
spent the night together.[2] Early the next morning, December
29, Colleen left to return to LCRA. She had volunteered to
assist the emergency hotlines used by flood victims. While
there, she sat next to her good friend Jo Ellen, who remembered that Colleen wore a white windbreaker. Before leaving the phone banks, Colleen called Oliver at about 10:00
A.M. and they agreed to attend the 12:15 P.M. mass at St.
Catherine of Siena Catholic Church. Since the church was
in Oak Hill, they drove their own cars and met there.[3]

After mass, Oliver and Colleen had lunch at a popular
Oak Hill restaurant called Trudy's. Both went to their
homes to take naps after leaving the restaurant at 2:30 P.M.
Colleen felt tired because she had a cold. When Oliver
asked if she wanted to nap at his place, she declined. She
wanted to check on Menou. She felt guilty about not spending enough time with her adopted cat. Colleen also indicated that she was behind on a number of chores and
errands. She needed to do laundry, go to the grocery store,
deposit her father's Christmas present into her checking account, and wash her new Mazda Miata.[4]

Colleen's sister, Lori, always marveled at how Colleen
could fall asleep at will. On the afternoon of December 29,
Colleen took a major nap. She did not wake up until shortly
before Oliver called at about 7:00 P.M. She had to ask him

what time it was, and when he told her, she got pretty upset
with herself because she had not done any of her chores or
errands. Oliver assured her that the chores could wait. By
the end of their conversation, Oliver thought he had convinced her to put off those things until Monday.[5]

Well-rested from her long nap, Colleen decided to do
her chores and run her errands. She probably felt pressed
to go to the bank to deposit a $200 Christmas gift she
received from her father. Allen Reed had established a family tradition of giving money to his children for a present;
then he insisted that they call him to let him know what
they had purchased for themselves. Allen wanted them to
get fun things. (Lori fondly remembered that she once used
her present to buy a new washing machine for her home.
When she told her father about it, he sent her another $200
check.) Colleen, though, probably rushed to the automatic
teller machines at Texas Commerce Bank on the corner of
Eighth and Lavaca to deposit her check because her checking account there was close to being overdrawn. Wearing
her gold-rimmed glasses, and dressed in a white and black
windbreaker, slightly stone-washed Zena jeans, and tennis
shoes, Colleen got into her Mazda Miata and headed for
downtown Austin.[6]

II

On Sunday, December 29, 1991, Hank Worley spent the
day doing dry wall work at a hospital in Killeen. His day
started at 7:00 A.M. and ended shortly after 6:00 that evening. His older brother picked him up at the end of the day
and took him to their sister's house in the S&S Mobile
Home Park in Belton. Hank had been living with his sister
Diane for a few months. His personal life was complicated
by a sometimes-nasty custody battle with his ex-wife, Janice (Billy's wife), over the guardianship of their daughter.
According to Hank's own statements, he drank a six-pack
of beer between 6:00 and 7:00 P.M.[7]

At about 7:00 P.M. Kenneth McDuff drove up to Diane's trailer in his Thunderbird. Diane believes that it was McDuff's fourth trip to her house. On two previous occasions Hank had been at work, and McDuff left with, "Just tell him Big Mac came by." On another occasion, Hank was bedridden after an accident with a grinder sent debris into his eyes. McDuff never actually entered her home; Diane had a strict rule about not letting strangers into her house. During the early evening of December 29, Hank and Diane were alone; Diane's husband was out deer hunting on his lease. The brother and sister sat and watched television as Hank drank more beer.[8]

Sitting on a chair near a front window of her trailer, Diane was the first to see Big Mac drive up. It was almost dark, but she recognized him and his car. Her six dogs barked as she went to the door and told Hank, "Big Mac is here." Hank rose from the couch and went outside to talk to McDuff. She heard someone say, "Let's go have a couple of beers." Almost immediately, Hank returned, went to the refrigerator, grabbed a twelve-pack of beer and told Diane, "I'm going to go with Big Mac and have a couple of drinks. I won't be long."[9]

Hank lied to Diane; in his own statement, he admitted that it was understood that he and Big Mac were going to Austin to score speed, or cocaine, or whatever they could find. He also admitted to suggesting that they go to Austin, which Big Mac considered the "Speed Capital of the World." Hank assumed that they would cruise the University of Texas campus to score dope. They headed to Austin after a short excursion north of Belton to the little town of Troy. While there, Big Mac stopped at a Love's Truck Stop to fill up his car. Doug, the attendant on duty, later remembered an "ugly Thunderbird" driving up and running off without paying. While Doug was busy doing paperwork on a diesel truck transaction, McDuff filled up his car and drove off. Doug found the pump's hose lying on the ground. Back on the interstate, like his conversation with Jackie four days earlier, McDuff reveled in telling Worley about how he learned to steal gas from convenience stores.[10]

As Big Mac and Hank drove south towards Austin, they ran out of beer and stopped at a Conoco truck stop near the little town of Jarrell. Hank bought another six-pack of Budweiser long necks. He was going to get a twelve-pack, but Mac insisted on a six-pack only. "That struck me as odd," Hank said later.

Their conversation was worthy of their intellects; they spoke of drinking beer, taking dope and dating whores. Mac also talked about shooting tires on cars driven by women. By the time they reached Round Rock, McDuff talked of kidnapping a girl and "using her up." Worley claims not to have understood what McDuff meant by that. "I thought he was talking shit," Hank said later. Austin Police Detective Sonya Urubek never believed Hank's plea of ignorance: "Worley knew what McDuff was capable of." Other detectives learned that Hank was once outraged to learn that his ex-wife had allowed his daughter to get into a car with Big Mac. Indeed, he surely knew of McDuff's violent history. For his part, McDuff later asserted, "The only reason I went to Austin was to rob the big-time drug dealers. Worley wanted to abduct a woman off the street. I told him, 'No.' "[11] It was a Roy Dale Green defense; Hank Worley pushed Big Mac around and forced him to do his will!

As they spoke of beer, drugs, whores and murder, Big Mac and Hank motored closer and closer to the capital city—Austin.

III

As Big Mac and Hank roamed the streets of Austin in the tan Thunderbird, another two men, as opposite of Mac and Hank as two men could be, riding in a silver BMW, entered the city from the south. Bill and Mike Goins were handsome, intelligent and accomplished young men. They drove in from Houston, where Mike was employed as an engineer for a lawn chemical company called Fina Oil and Chemical.

At the time, he did applications development research for plastics. On December 29, 1991, however, Mike could not drive his BMW because he was still sore from an abdominal operation; he had been advised by his doctor not to work the manual transmission of his car. His brother, Bill, visiting from his adopted hometown of New York City, drove his younger brother from Houston to Austin. Bill had his own business called Tall Tales Productions; he directed and produced films.[12]

Bill and Mike set out for Austin to visit their sister, Denise, who was married to an electrician named Stephen Marks. Bill intended to stay with Denise and Stephen, but Mike planned on staying with his girlfriend, Kari, a photographer for an engineering firm. She had just returned from a trip to Oklahoma and had not seen any of the Goins family during the holidays. Mike and Kari had dinner plans at a favorite restaurant. As soon as the Goins brothers arrived, Stephen called Kari and told her they were headed for her house. Kari lived in the northern third of an old house converted to a triplex near downtown Austin at 505 Powell Street. Shaded by aged, twisted trees with weathered bark, older homes lined Powell Street. Bill and Stephen were to deliver Mike and his car and return so that Bill could visit his sister.[13]

Stephen tried to lead the way to Powell Street, but a red traffic light caught the brothers at the corner of Sixth Street and Lamar and pretty soon Stephen was out of sight. It did not matter, because Mike knew how to get to Kari's house. At Sixth and Lamar, Stephen turned right and headed west on Sixth street towards Powell. When he reached Powell Street, a one-way going south, he had to stop; in front of him was a tan, 1985 Thunderbird. Stephen, feeling awkward with his 45-degree position across the street corner, flashed his bright headlights to alert the driver in front of him to move on. Formerly an automotive manager for a Foley's Department Store, Stephen remembered that the car had three distinct taillights on both sides; he also remembered that the car was a Ford product. He could only see two figures in the car. The tan Ford moved southward on Powell as Stephen reached Kari's house. As he parked his car, he noticed that the Ford made a U-turn into a ground-level garage situated below a small office building. At that point, Stephen noticed that the car was a two-door. He thought nothing of it and walked over to the front porch of the triplex. While on the porch, Stephen and Kari talked about Christmas and waited for Bill and Mike to arrive.[14]

Inside the Thunderbird, Big Mac and Hank Worley waited in the office building garage on the corner of Powell and Fifth Street for Stephen Marks to walk away from his car and move towards Kari's front porch. From the office Mac drove north, going the wrong way on a one-way street, on Powell back towards Sixth Street. At the corner of Powell and Sixth, they encountered Bill and Mike.

Bill made a complete stop and looked at Mike. He said something like, "Where are these boneheads going?" Both brothers remember being within thirty yards of the tan Thunderbird. Mike remembered that McDuff and Worley "were leaning forward in the front seat looking out of the front windshield, basically trying to determine which way to go because they looked a little bit lost." Big Mac and Hank's preoccupation with where to go was why the four men never made straight eye contact. But because of their position, the Goinses' BMW illuminated Big Mac and Hank, as the Thunderbird turned left on Sixth and drove away. Mike got a better look at Big Mac than at Hank. After the Thunderbird cleared the way, Mike and Bill turned left on Powell and headed for Kari's house.[15] Stephen and Kari were on the front porch waiting for them.

IV

On Christmas Day, Colleen joked with Lori that she would have to use her $200 gift from her father to "cover her checks." At 8:45 P.M. on December 29, she drove up to an ATM and deposited her gift; at the time her available bal-

ance was only $128.33. A security camera took two pic-
tures of Colleen as she did her bank business. On the film,
and in bank records, she was transaction number 7967. The
black and white pictures gave police officers, and her
friends, a last look at Colleen Reed. She had her gold-
rimmed glasses on and was wearing a white windbreaker.
Her earrings sparkled in the fluorescent lighting of the
bank's floodlights. In the first picture, she is looking down
at her purse, probably readying the deposit envelope. In the
second, she is looking ahead, having completed her deposit.
Then she put her Miata in gear and headed for a popular
Austin grocery store—Whole Foods.[16]

At Whole Foods Colleen bought a gallon of milk and a
bottle of vitamins. Protective of her checking account, she
paid the $31.12 bill in cash and left the store at 8:59 P.M.
At the time, Whole Foods was located at 914 North Lamar.
She missed being at the corner of Sixth and Lamar at the
same time as Stephen, Bill, and Mike by only a few
minutes. After leaving Whole Foods, Colleen had one more
errand—to wash her car.[17] She knew of a self-serve car
wash on West Fifth Street. The stalls were of various
shades of brown brick, blue metal, and cinderblock white
walls. It appeared to be made of every kind of building
material. The concrete driveway was of different shades,
and on the periphery stood large, majestic oak trees. The
stalls there had brushes to scrub the car and high-powered
wands spewing soapy or clear water. She wanted to scrub
down her car with the brush, so from Whole Foods she
turned right on Sixth, then left on West Lynn, and left on
Fifth. She entered the third stall from the west. As she sat
in her car in the stall of the car wash, directly ahead of her
to the north was a blue wooden building with white trim.
It housed the offices of the Travis County Democratic
Party. To the west, across the street from West Lynn was
Don's Depot, a piano bar and saloon with an outside porch
and two railroad cars in the back. Nearby was El Arroyo,
the restaurant where Mike and Kari planned to eat. And
less than one hundred yards to her right, across a vacant
lot, was Powell Street.[18]

When Colleen stepped out of her car to wash it, she caught the attention of Kenneth Allen McDuff. He and Hank had been cruising Austin long enough to have traversed Congress Avenue, where they stopped for a hamburger at a Dairy Queen, and Sixth Street, the center of Austin's entertainment district. Sixth Street is a congested one-way street going west. As Mac and Worley drove down it, they reached an area where older houses had been remodeled into small offices. Just behind those offices were homes, certainly not an area where Mac thought he could find any whores or drugs. Suddenly, he parked his Thunderbird and walked towards a well-known restaurant called the Z-Tejas Grill. Hank later remembered the grill because it had a patio with large umbrellas hovering over the tables. McDuff asked someone where the whores were and the man answered, "South Congress."

McDuff and Hank then returned to the Thunderbird and headed farther west on Sixth. McDuff probably turned south on West Lynn (the wrong way) and then turned east on Fifth. That was when he noticed Colleen washing her car. Somehow, he got back to Sixth Street and turned south on Powell; that was when Stephen Marks had to "move" him along. After making the U-turn at the office building parking garage and heading north on Powell (the wrong way), he reached Sixth again, where he encountered Mike and Bill Goins. The brothers remembered that the Thunderbird turned west on Sixth. Big Mac and Hank turned south again on West Lynn (the wrong way) and entered the car wash from the north.[19]

McDuff navigated the Thunderbird into the stall farthest east of Colleen's location. In his numerous statements, Hank insists he did not know why Mac got out of the car. According to Hank, Mac just got out, did not say anything, walked around the front of the car and over to another stall. Maybe, Hank claims to have thought, Mac was interested in getting change from the woman he saw when they drove into the car wash. Hank steadfastly asserted that when they stopped, he began to gather the many beer bottles and cans that littered the Thunderbird to throw them in garbage cans. "The next thing I know he comes back with a woman." She was kicking and screaming. McDuff had walked over to Colleen's stall, grabbed her by the throat with one of his massive hands and lifted her off her feet. He held her arms still with his other hand.[20]

Alva Hank Worley is almost certainly telling the truth about Kenneth McDuff; and he is almost certainly lying about himself. The many inconsistencies in his numerous statements and courtroom testimony nearly all involve his own actions, but his account of what *McDuff* did throughout the evening never significantly wavered. But Worley's assertion that he was caught by surprise by what McDuff did at the car wash is simply not credible. By his own admission, they spent most of the evening talking about violent crimes; and they had circled the car wash twice.[21] Stephen Marks saw McDuff and Worley make a U-turn for the specific purpose of going the wrong way down a narrow one-way street; and the Goins brothers remember that Mac and Hank *both* looked as if they were lost. They could only have been trying to figure out how to get back to the car wash. If Hank did not know McDuff was stalking Colleen, what did he think McDuff was determined to do? Wash his car?

The major investigators of the case, including Chuck Meyer and J. W. Thompson, are convinced, however, that Kenneth McDuff alone carried out the actual abduction. "This wasn't his first rodeo," Chuck Meyer said. McDuff knew exactly what he was doing and how to do it. He might have been able to walk right up to her and take her. Hank's problem, they believe, was a combination of cowardice and stupidity. "This was Hank's first opportunity to do something other than what he did. He could have just ran from there," J. W. said in utter disgust.[22]

While still in her stall, Colleen let out a loud, sustained scream, and began "kicking like hell," according to Hank. She gurgled and struggled to get words out of her mouth as McDuff clutched her neck. Within seconds McDuff had her over to his car.

"Not me, not me," Colleen cried.

"You're going with me," McDuff replied.

"Please let me go, please don't let this happen to me."

"Get your ass in the car," McDuff barked at Hank.

Hank, in a tragedy chillingly identical to what Roy Dale Green had enacted a little over twenty-five years earlier, did as he was told. After having some trouble forcing Colleen into the back seat, McDuff ordered Hank to hold her down. Hank climbed into the back seat and held her wrists against the back driver's side window as McDuff got into the driver's seat. In testimony, Hank candidly asserts that as he held her down she quit screaming because no one was holding her by the throat; he remembered that at that point she began to cry. And yet, on another occasion, Hank spews the unbelievable: "I am not sure if I helped him put her into the back seat, but I might have."[23]

Standing on the front porch of 505 Powell Street, Mike and Bill Goins, Stephen Marks, and Kari engaged in small talk. Stephen remembered that Mike and Bill might have mentioned being slowed down by a couple of idiots going the wrong way on Powell. Stephen and Kari talked about the Christmas holidays, and Stephen offered to serve everyone dinner at his home. His wife, Denise, was cooking spaghetti and there was plenty for everyone. Mike and Kari gracefully declined; they were looking forward to eating alone at El Arroyo. That was when they all heard Colleen's long, loud scream. It lasted long enough for the four of them to look towards the car wash and then at one another. Because of their position, they could not see what was happening inside the stalls, but they could see the area directly in front adjoining Fifth Street.

Stephen remembered what he heard as "an all-out serious scream." Bill, who thought life in his adopted hometown somehow uniquely qualified him to better evaluate screams, later stated, "I'm from New York; I know what a real scream sounds like."[24]

The screams were followed by the sounds of slamming doors. Mike remembers two slamming doors, which means that Hank was almost certainly standing outside of the car when McDuff abducted Colleen. As the foursome on the porch watched the car wash, they saw a light colored Ford Thunderbird head out of the stalls towards Fifth Street. The car then headed west (the wrong way). Immediately, the three men recognized the car. The tan Thunderbird moved in the same slow, indecisive manner as when they saw it on Powell only minutes earlier. McDuff had to drive in such an erratic way that the witnesses on the porch noticed how often the brake lights kept going on and off. It went down the right lane with cars coming at it in the opposite direction. It came dangerously close to running into at least two other vehicles going the right way on Fifth.

Bill asked if that happened in Austin all the time; he knew something was seriously wrong. He made the comment that it was the same car he and Mike had seen going the wrong way on Powell. Stephen immediately realized that it was the same car he saw make the U-turn to go the wrong way. Bill and Stephen agreed to rush to the car wash. They took Stephen's car and headed there.[25]

Stephen drove through an alley across the block connecting West Lynn and Powell and reached the car wash in seconds. Colleen's car had thick suds all over it; she had been using the brush to scrub down her Mazda. Mike and Stephen could not see inside the car without wiping the suds off the windows. They could see Colleen's purse and keys on the front seat, and her small bag of groceries on the floor. It was pretty clear to them that the owner of the car had not left the scene voluntarily. Bill decided to stay with the car and told Stephen to race back to Kari's and tell her to call the police. Kari and Mike were already inside her apartment when Stephen stuck his head inside and told her to dial 911.[26]

V[27]

Inside the tan Thunderbird Alva Hank Worley pressed Colleen's wrists against the side of the back seating area to keep her still as Kenneth McDuff dodged cars on Fifth Street. In the midst of the horror, Colleen probably noticed that McDuff was driving the wrong way. She blurted out that he should go on to the Mopac Expressway. Hank thought that was unusual because no one had asked her where to go. Eventually, McDuff crossed a median separating Fifth and Sixth streets near Mopac and headed south on the freeway. Only slightly more than three miles from the car wash, McDuff exited Mopac near the Capitol of Texas Highway. At the exit, he ordered Worley to drive, but he did not let Worley out of the car. He ordered him to crawl over the seat to get to the driver's seat. Then, McDuff went to the back seat with Colleen. McDuff placed a fairly large stereo on the back dashboard to get it out of his way. It also provided some cover from other drivers who might look at what was about to happen in the back seat. According to Worley, McDuff told her, "If you'll just fuck you'll be all right." She had no choice but to say she would cooperate. Then he instructed her to take off her clothes. After she placed her clothes on the back floor, McDuff began to rape her.

Worley made a U-turn around some tall, rocky cliffs (which he mistook for large piles of dirt) and headed north on Mopac. By the time he reached the Fifth Street exit where they had first entered Mopac, McDuff had ordered Colleen to have anal sex. Worley remembers Colleen's cries of pain and pleas for mercy as McDuff made jokes, taunted, and humiliated her.

As Worley continued north on Mopac he could feel the car rock as McDuff continued to sexually assault Colleen. He turned north on US Highway 183 intending to go to Round Rock, and from there, on to Belton. In his statements, he claims that by this time, all he wanted to do was get back to his sister's trailer. A little more than twenty-three miles from the car wash, Worley turned right on to Ranch Road 620.

On Ranch Road 620 Colleen's horror continued. Mc-Duff sat back and ordered her to give him oral sex. Worley remembers him grabbing her head and forcing her down, making her gag. The area is sparsely populated and domi-nated by remnants of ranches slowly being consumed by deed-restricted, master-planned neighborhoods. By the time they reached the site of the historic Chisholm Trail in Round Rock, Colleen might have thought that she could attract attention and thus get help for herself. At or near the corner of Ranch Road 620 and Interstate 35, a dense busi-ness area, she scratched McDuff near his eyes. Enraged, McDuff shouted, "She tried to hurt me real bad." He began to beat her until she finally surrendered with pleas of "Okay, okay."

McDuff decided he needed to immobilize Colleen. Most likely, he grabbed her tennis shoes from the floorboard and removed the white shoe strings. He tied her hands at the wrists behind her back. Afterwards, she and McDuff both knew she was completely helpless. It seemed to give him immense pleasure.

Once he had established total control and dominance over Colleen, McDuff asked Hank for one of his cigarettes. Hank could see McDuff puff it to an orange glow. It be-came a weapon. Colleen let out a horrifying shriek as McDuff tortured her with the lit cigarette. Worley testified that McDuff admonished her to "act right" as he burned her vagina. This, too, seemed to give him immense plea-sure.

As Worley drove farther north along Interstate 35, McDuff's treatment of Colleen became more heartless and sadistic. Through Georgetown and Salado, Colleen endured nightmarish torture. Finally, McDuff stopped long enough to ask where they were. Just north of Salado, sixty-six miles from the car wash in Austin, McDuff ordered Worley to pull off at the Amity Road exit. As Worley did as he was told, he apparently spent too much time looking towards the back seat. He nearly hopped curbs surrounding medians near the intersection. "Watch where the hell you're going," McDuff commanded as Hank swerved wildly.

The Amity Road exit made for an ideal place to switch drivers. Whether he had intended to or not, McDuff could not have chosen a better-hidden place to stop. Amity Road has an overpass over the interstate creating groins along its sides. Even though it is only a few yards away, passing motorists on the interstate cannot see the service road where McDuff ordered Worley to stop. Moreover, there are no streetlights; at night the area is completely dark.

By now, McDuff had already put his clothes back on. He ordered Worley to get into the back seat with Colleen. In an instance hauntingly similar to the 1966 Broomstick Murders, McDuff asked Worley if he wanted to have sex with Colleen. Unlike Roy Dale Green, however, Worley shamelessly claimed that he went to Colleen and raped her in order to protect her. He claimed to have reasoned that by keeping her busy McDuff would not come back to her. He also claimed to have had a conversation with her in which she told him that she was an accountant who "worked for the city or something," was twenty-eight or twenty-nine years old, and had an apartment. During one of his statements, Hank later said, "I got to where I was liking the girl pretty good by that time." He never understood how grossly inappropriate that statement was.

Colleen complained to Hank that her hands hurt because they were tied too tightly together. Hank claimed that he tried to untie her but could not. He insisted that he could not take out his knife and cut the ligatures because he was afraid that McDuff would use the knife against him. Through all of his statements, Worley claims that Colleen begged him to protect her. If she did, it could only have added to her horror; she was a bright young woman who had to have realized that her only hope for rescue was a 1991 version of Roy Dale Green.

McDuff drove out of the Amity exit back on to Interstate 35. He continued northward. According to Worley, he intended to go to an area very near J. A. and Addie's home in a rural area north of Belton. To get there, they would have to go on State Highway 317. McDuff avoided driving by the Bell County Sheriff's Office and County Jail by taking Sixth Avenue to 317.

At the time, J. A. and Addie McDuff lived several miles north of Belton just a few hundred yards from the corner of 317 and Cedar Creek Road. Cutting the southeast corner of 317 and Cedar Creek Road was an old abandoned road that once led to the McDuff driveway. It formed a quarter circle on the southeast quadrant in the intersection created by Cedar Creek and 317. McDuff turned right onto the old road from 317. Overgrown bushes, tall grass and small trees bordering both sides of the road made it look like a tunnel. It was excellent cover for a crime. The nearest home was the elder McDuff's home, and even then it was several hundred yards away.

When he reached the point in the road equidistant from 317 and Cedar Creek, McDuff turned the car around so that it faced west. He got out of the car and took off his shirt. Then he turned towards the back seat, reached in and grabbed Colleen by the hair and dragged her out. Utterly helpless, she was naked and her hands were still tied behind her back.

McDuff lifted her up on the hood of the Thunderbird, lowered his pants, and raped her again. Then he grabbed her by the hair and jerked her off the car. As she knelt before him he said, "I want another head job."

The lead investigators of the Colleen Reed murder case are convinced that at that moment Colleen could "see the handwriting on the wall and she drew the line." Something happened; she had had enough. Since her hands were tied behind her back, she most likely bit him or did something else to hurt him.

"I'll kill you, bitch," McDuff screamed. Worley remembered: "He pulled his hand all the way behind himself, and

he hit her so hard I heard a loud pop or crack. I started
backing away from him. It sounded like a big tree breaking.
I was sure he broke her neck. She fell backwards toward
the weeds, and her head bounced off of the ground. She
did not move at all."

McDuff pulled up his pants and went to the car and got
another cigarette. He lit it and again puffed it to a bright
orange glow. He burned her again, but this time, Hank
heard no agonizing moans. Colleen was lifeless.

"Man, you got to stop this shit," Hank claims to have
said, before McDuff picked up Colleen by her hair and
lifted her into the trunk of the Thunderbird. After he put
her there, he reached in and grabbed a tiretool and walked
towards Hank.

"You should have let her go," Hank said as he backed
up.

"I can't. She can cause more shit than you can imagine,"
replied McDuff.

Holding the tiretool, McDuff growled at Hank that he
had better keep his goddamn mouth shut. "I didn't see shit,"
replied a sheepish Hank. McDuff asked to borrow Hank's
pocketknife; Hank lied about the knife he had in his pocket
and said he had none.

Worley claims that after McDuff's pointed warning,
they closed the trunk, got back into the car, and McDuff
drove him straight back to the S&S Trailer Park. On the
way McDuff asked to borrow a shovel; Hank said he did
not have one. During the entire trip back to Diane's trailer,
Hank never heard any noise coming from the trunk.

Diane was in bed when Hank returned, but she had not
been sleeping. She was reading a book when she heard
someone at the door. She got up, checked to make sure it
was Hank, and let him in. She only remembers that he
smelled like he had been drinking all night long. They said
little or nothing to one another and went to bed.

Without a doubt, Hank now knew what McDuff meant
when he said he would "use up" a woman.

11

Cowboy

"Something is wrong with that man."
—[Bruce] a.k.a. "One-Arm"

I

Before December of 1991, the people of Austin, Texas, did not consider going to a yogurt shop, or washing their car, a dangerous activity—and for good reason. The overall crime rate for Austin had fallen by two percent from 1990 to 1991, and although the murder rate rose by seven percent, the actual number of victims rose from only forty-six to forty-nine. Additionally, the Austin Police Department's Homicide Detail was particularly good at solving its cases. Nationally, about sixty-six percent of homicide cases were solved; in cities with more than 250,000 people the "clearance rate" was slightly over half; in Austin, the rate was an impressive eighty-six percent. The Yogurt Shop Murders and the abduction of Colleen Reed, however, spread fear throughout the Austin metro area. "I guess the public's attitude is developed by high visibility crimes, and certainly during the latter part of the year [1991] we had those high visibility crimes," said Assistant Police Chief George Phifer.

Austin's rapid, nearly uncontrolled growth contributed to crimes consistent with "growing pains." Residents in the northwest part of town learned of a serial rapist, crack houses cropped up in once-quiet neighborhoods on the north side (one of which was a crack house Jackie and his landlord thought they could use McDuff to rob, and thus, remove). There was a sense in Austin that if the price of prosperity and growth included crime and traffic jams, and if being in a big city included getting used to the horror of things like the Yogurt Shop Murders and the disappearance of Colleen Reed, affluence was not worth it.

Colleen's abduction was not the only high-profile case in Austin on December 29, 1991. On that day, a man entered an adult entertainment establishment called "Studio M" and shot and killed a twenty-two-year-old woman named Brenda Lee Anderson. Only a couple of days after the murder, Detective Scott Cary announced that a pickup truck was seen leaving the scene. A suspect was described as a "white or Hispanic" male, six feet or taller with a large build "and a big face." He also wore a cowboy hat. But this man had black hair, graying on the edges, and a thick black mustache. It was not Kenneth McDuff.

At one time, McDuff was considered a serious suspect in the Yogurt Shop Murders, but as more evidence was collected, both on the McDuff cases and on the Yogurt Shop case, he became less a central suspect. As time passed, the Yogurt Shop Task Force dwindled down to a single detective.[1]

II

With so many wrenching, high-profile cases coming down on the Austin Police Department at once, Lori Bible and others close to Colleen questioned whether the police had the necessary personnel to locate Colleen (who was, of course, still listed as a missing person).

The investigation into Colleen's disappearance began immediately after the abduction itself. Patrolling the Baker sector, in central and western Austin, Officer Robert Bohannan received a call at 9:25 P.M. to go to the car wash; he arrived three minutes later to find Stephen Marks and Bill Goins waiting for him. Mike Goins and Kari were walking up from her house. According to Bohannan's testimony, all four talked at the same time and he ended up listening primarily to Stephen. He noticed the smell of the

beer Stephen had had earlier in the day, but it was clear
that Stephen was not intoxicated. When the officer looked
into Colleen's car, he saw her keys lying on the center
console near the gear shift, her purse on the passenger seat
on top of some books, and her milk and vitamins in a bag
on the front floorboard. "Nothing had been tampered with,"
Bohannan said later.

When describing dark-complected suspects, but not
African-Americans, it is not uncommon for officers to use
the phrase "white, or possibly Hispanic." The phrase had
been used earlier in the day for the Studio M case, and it
was used again from the car wash. The first information on
the suspect's vehicle was that it was a Thunderbird or Cou-
gar, model year 87–89.[2] At 9:30 P.M., he immediately requested that investigators be sent to the scene. They arrived
while suds were still dripping from the Mazda.

The contents of Colleen's purse provided officers with
the first leads for their investigation. Various documents
had the addresses of her past boyfriends. Her driver's license still had her first boyfriend's address on it, and her
car registration still had Oliver's address. In cases involving
the abduction of young women, it is common to check out
boyfriends and former spouses first. As ATF Special Agent
Charles Meyer put it, it is a "statistically competent" thing
to do. APD dispatched police units to the addresses and an
APD Sergeant called Oliver at about 10:30 P.M. Officer
Bohannan also discovered the Whole Foods receipt and the
ATM slip. This sent APD looking for a way to retrieve the
film from the Pulse machine.[3]

When APD established that Colleen lived in Westlake,
a Westlake police officer went to her apartment to see if
she was there, and of course, she was not. After an agonizing night of waiting and repeatedly calling Colleen's
number, Oliver attempted call Lori at home at about 8:00
A.M., but she had already gone to work. When he reached
her at work, he immediately started to cry, alerting Lori
that something was terribly wrong. They spoke for only

three or four minutes and agreed to meet at the police department.[4]

At police headquarters, Lori and Oliver waited in a hallway outside of the Assault Unit. Lori had the impression that no one at the department knew much about Colleen's disappearance. While waiting, Lori sat on black plastic chairs near a second-floor reception desk by the elevators. Policemen walked by the desk leisurely talking to one another about a girl who was missing from a car wash. "Did you hear about our floater? She's missing from the car wash. We haven't found her body yet," said one of the officers. "Hey, wait a minute, you're talking about my sister," Lori thought, struggling to control what she admits is a very hot temper. After waiting with growing impatience for over an hour, feeling as if she could not get anyone to talk to her, she was finally invited into the office of Detective Don Martin of the Assault Unit.[5]

Don Martin had been with the Austin Police Department for over twenty-five years and was one of the most experienced officers on the force. He had graduated from the Police Academy in June of 1966. (A little over a month later, Don was trying desperately to secure the English Building as Charles Whitman went on his rampage atop the University of Texas Tower.) After reading the reports, Don immediately felt like Colleen had been kidnapped and killed. "I have a bad feeling about this," he said to his sergeant. His experience told him, and he related to Lori, that in cases such as these, persons like Colleen were most likely to have been abducted to be sexually assaulted. From the beginning, Don thought it best to be straight with the Reed family. He hoped to be proven wrong, but he thought Colleen had been killed.[6]

In trial testimony, Lori stated that her family had been told that the first twenty-four hours would be critical if Colleen were to be found alive. When the time came and went, the Reed family felt crushed. It was a nightmare complicated, according to Lori, by the astonishing and unfounded suggestion by APD Detective Robert Feuerbacher that Colleen was a drug-using prostitute who had run away and would return. Lori angrily protested that her sister had no record of any type.[7] (Note: None of Robert Feuerbacher's *Incident Reports* currently in the Reed Case Jacket make such references to Colleen Reed.) Eventually, Lori appealed to the Austin City Manager's Office; she felt that the APD was not doing enough to find her sister. Such appeals by the families of victims are common.

After seeing Don Martin at APD, Lori and Oliver went to Colleen's apartment to check for any clues as to where she might be. When they got there, the door was unlocked. They did not find that unusual, since Colleen often did that when she intended to leave for very short periods of time. They also assumed that the police had already been there. The floor mats of her car were sitting in the entryway near the front door. Her Christmas decorations were still up and Menou had turned over a potted plant and spilled dirt everywhere. The cat had also gotten into a stack of paper napkins and shredded them. Otherwise, the apartment was clean. Her bed had been slept in and her favorite flannel shirt lay on it. In planning for the next day, Colleen had hung a suit on a doorknob and set out a pair of shoes. It was clear to Oliver that Colleen had intended to be out of her apartment for no more than ten or twenty minutes.[8]

Very quickly, the leads in Colleen's kidnapping case dried up. No one ever seriously considered Oliver a suspect. A problem Colleen had experienced with a disagreeable employee at LCRA led nowhere. The fact that Lori was the beneficiary of Colleen's LCRA life insurance policy was easily explained—she was next of kin and Lori described an informal agreement between she and Colleen that the insurance money would go to Lori's boys. (Colleen knew that if anything ever happened to Lori, the responsibility of raising her nephews would be hers.) Colleen's family and friends, especially those at LCRA, racked their brains to come up with the name of anyone who could have remotely had a reason to do this to Colleen. No one could think of anyone with such a motive.

Within two or three days, it became clear that all APD had was the limited eyewitness testimony of Stephen Marks, the Goins Brothers, and Kari. The department knew to look for a two-door, tan Thunderbird or other Ford product with round taillights, driven by a "bonehead" who liked to drive the wrong way on one-way streets, and who had an unshaven accomplice. The kidnappers left absolutely no physical evidence at the scene. Solving the mystery of the disappearance of Colleen Reed would require a break. Immediately, Lori and a multitude of Colleen's friends mobilized to "beat the bushes" for just such a break.[9]

III

On the morning of December 30, 1991, Hank Worley's sister, Diane, was making coffee in her kitchen when she heard squealing noises coming from Hank's bedroom. He appeared to be having nightmares. "What's the matter with you?" she asked.

"Just having bad dreams," Hank said.

He could not get what McDuff had done to Colleen out of his mind. "I have had a hard time with this since it happened, and I have wanted to tell someone about it," Hank said later. The first hint that Hank would not be able to live with what he saw McDuff do, and indeed, what he himself had done, surfaced during a New Year's Eve party at the home of his other sister, Bess.[10]

Bess described her party as "a family gathering on New Year's Eve [of] every year. It keeps people off the road, and we're all together. We may have a drink or two. Most of us don't drink, but . . . we have alcohol there and we bring in the New Year in prayer." Hank had been drinking heavily (even for Hank), and he drank even more when he and Diane got to Bess's house. Jerry, his brother-in-law, noticed that he had arrived with a twelve-pack and was acting weird. "He, I guess, acted a little fidgety. He didn't stay in one place. He would get up and walk to the kitchen and come back to the table. We all sat around the dining room table normally when we were having a family gathering."

Apparently, Diane and Hank were the first to arrive for the party. Hank began to talk. He asked his sisters and brother-in-law what they would do if they saw a girl being beaten up or mistreated, but they could not help. When Bess asked him why he could not help, Hank answered that if he had tried he would have gotten killed. Bess told him that she would go to the police or someone else who could help. Bess could see her brother was bothered by whatever it was that he was talking about, but she could not figure out what was going on. The conversation abruptly ended when other guests arrived. Hank never brought up the subject again.[11]

And on, or about that day, Hank began to grow a beard.

IV

During the early afternoon of February 18, 1992, McDuff's parole officer visited him at his dorm room at TSTI. The officer later reported to the Austin Police Department that McDuff was in a very good mood and was very optimistic about his future.[12] On or about February 24, 1992, Keith, the occupant of room 117 in Sabine Hall, was awakened by a knock on his dorm window. When he looked outside, he saw a thin, black female, about 5'7" tall. "Oh, I'm sorry, I've got the wrong room," she said. She went to the next window and knocked on it. "Are you ready?" she asked the occupant of room 118—Kenneth Allen McDuff.[13]

The young black woman was Valencia Kay Joshua. She went by the name of Kay, and had a troubled juvenile and adult criminal record and was on probation. As early as 1985, she had been arrested for shoplifting. She attended but dropped out of Arlington Heights High School, and afterwards "worked truck stops." Her sister readily admitted that Kay was a prostitute and that no one in her family knew that she was in the Waco area towards the end of February.[14] Other than McDuff, Keith was the last person to see Valencia Kay Joshua alive. Later that night, McDuff went on a drug and drinking binge.

McDuff had been before a judge in Bell County only the month before on public intoxication charges. He got a two-year suspended sentence and was placed on probation. So, on February 24, 1992, he was on parole and probation at the same time when he killed Valencia Kay Joshua. It is hard to believe that he returned from burying her and went to school, because that evening he was back in his car and visiting bars with his friends, Billy and Buddy.

The evening did not start out well for McDuff. For the first, and probably the only time, Mac paid dearly for an attempt to rob a crack dealer. While on Eighth Street in Temple, Mac pulled up to a black male crack dealer who stuck his hand into McDuff's car. Like he had done a few weeks earlier when Linda was with him in Waco, McDuff slapped the dealer's hand and the rocks fell into the car. But this time, the dealer had a beer bottle in the other hand and used it to smack McDuff in the face, just under his left eye. Blood splashed everywhere from the gash under his eye and McDuff had to change his shirt. Surely, he was not in a very good mood when he, Billy and Buddy moved on to their next stop.

At the H&H Lounge in Temple, McDuff began to "hit up" on a woman named Debbie. He made other crude suggestions, and asked her if she wanted to go to El Paso with him. He became abusive towards her when she said "No." Debbie was with some of Billy's kinfolk, and when she moved away, McDuff got upset, grabbed her by the arm, and as Billy would later say, "started talking shit." Billy stepped in and told McDuff to shut up. "I told him that if he was pissed about the black male hitting him [with the beer bottle], I would go back with him [to fight the blacks]."[15]

Indeed, they returned to Eighth Street in Temple, where they caught the attention of Temple Police Officer David

Jarveis. McDuff had parked his Thunderbird near a garage. The owner of the garage had made numerous complaints that his lot was being used as a meeting place for drug dealers and trespassers. Before Officer Jarveis could get out of his car, McDuff got out of the Thunderbird and staggered towards the police unit. Jarveis pointed his flashlight at a "No Trespassing" sign; McDuff said he did not see it. Jarveis must have thought that in his condition McDuff could not see much of anything. When the patrolman asked him what they were doing there, McDuff answered that he, Billy, and Buddy were waiting for a black prostitute named Brenda to return with two more prostitutes. Then they could all have a "party." (They must have hoped for very cheap dates, because between the three of them they had a total of fifty-three cents.)

When Jarveis asked him about the cut under his left eye, McDuff answered that he had fallen down the day before. Very shortly, Officer William Llewellyn arrived as a backup. Interestingly, when Llewellyn asked McDuff about the cut under his eye, McDuff said he had been injured at work.

At about 11:30 P.M., the officers pulled Billy out of the front passenger seat, and Buddy was pulled out of the back driver's side. All three failed sobriety tests. On the way to the jail, McDuff again changed his story about the cut under his eye. This time he asserted that black males had robbed him. He also begged not to be arrested. By 1:00 A.M. on February 25, the three men were booked on charges of public intoxication and placed in jail. By 6:00 A.M. they were released.[16]

On February 28, McDuff drove his Thunderbird to the Goodyear Auto Service Center in Temple. With 110,422 miles on it, it needed work pretty badly. He had all four tires and the MacPherson strut assembly changed. At 4:34 P.M., he paid the $821.02 bill with a Visa card Addie had given him.[17] Having a dependable vehicle was important to McDuff. He liked to "cover a lot of concrete."

The next day McDuff drove over to Jim's Cycle Shop

in nearby Axtell, Texas. He needed cash and decided to use the credit card to get money. (Interestingly, she had given him the card so that he would *not* have cash.) While at the cycle shop, McDuff got into a conversation with the owner and one of his employees. The employee asked McDuff about the cut under his left eye. McDuff explained that he got it during a fight with a husband who caught him sleeping with his wife. McDuff offered to charge $110 on the card for $100 in cash. The owner agreed and once the card cleared at about 1:14 P.M., McDuff left with the money.[18]

Getting money from a cycle shop was not the only thing McDuff did with the credit card. During the early evening, he stopped by the Quik Pak #8 (where he had once worked) to get gas. The "good-looking woman" he so often spoke of, Melissa Northrup, was not yet at work; she would report for the graveyard shift at 11:00 P.M.[19] He moved on to Temple where he visited beer joints. The owners and customers of the beer joints like the H&H and Poor Boy's Lounge must have tired of McDuff's constant troublemaking. Only a few days earlier he had walked into Poor Boy's and had taken an old man's bottle of whiskey. McDuff's acquaintance, Jimmy, saw the incident. Taking an old, defenseless man's whiskey was too much, even for a hardened and dangerous criminal like Jimmy. The two men argued and McDuff asked Jimmy to "go outside." They did, but did not fight.[20]

Judging from his behavior, whether it was to taunt and scare Debbie, or steal a bottle of whiskey from a harmless old man, or just act like a silly teenage bully, McDuff wanted trouble because he liked it.

During the evening of February 29, McDuff ended up at the H&H Lounge in Temple. Across a parking lot from the H&H was the Ambassador Motel, where a man named Bruce had rented room #20. He had friends with him named Terry and Darrin, and they were all acquainted with a most unusual woman named Holly. (Holly called Darrin her cousin "because he's got several kids by my cousin.") As was life in the subculture, it was never clear whether any of the foursome knew each other's names. Terry was "T-Bone," Bruce was "One-Arm" because he had one arm in a sling. Darrin was, well, Darrin, but no one knew his last name. In turn, One-Arm called Holly "Speed Racer." In any case, late that night Holly walked across the parking lot from the Ambassador to the H&H for cigarettes and beer. After she entered the lounge, McDuff walked up to her and said, "I want some crack."

"Well, come on with me," Holly answered. Very quietly, Debbie warned her "not to talk to that man." But Holly thought McDuff had money. She admitted that she was able to smoke crack all night long by buying $20 rocks, cutting them in half, selling one piece and smoking the other. "You smoke all day like that," she once said. Then Holly did something she would regret; she invited McDuff to go with her to One-Arm's room at the Ambassador.[21]

Holly vividly remembers what McDuff wore that night. He had a dark, pullover short-sleeved shirt, blue jeans, a big belt, and black cowboy boots. He also wore a large, white cowboy hat. She called him "Cowboy" and made fun of his big, bulbous nose. When they arrived at One-Arm's room, One-Arm asked Holly why she had brought such a strange man to his room. Holly said it was all right—he had some money. T-Bone, One-Arm and Darrin were already smoking crack. Just to make sure McDuff was not a narcotics agent, she insisted that he take a hit of crack. Of course, "Cowboy" obliged.

He said he wanted $100 of crack and a girl, but he had no money. Instead, he had his father's credit card and it had a $10,000 limit. He suggested that they buy something and sell it for cash. What happened afterwards is not clear, but apparently Holly left with McDuff, who had insisted that Holly drive. (McDuff may not have wanted to risk another DWI or public intoxication charge.) They went out to look for a girl for McDuff, but he had no money—just the credit card. They soon returned and Holly asked One-Arm to drive Cowboy to a store to get cigarettes. Cigarettes seemed like a sellable commodity in the subculture, and so

McDuff and One-Arm got into the Thunderbird and left to buy some. They went to a 7-Eleven a short distance away on West Avenue H. By that time it was about 2:00 A.M. on March 1. McDuff entered the store and took eight cartons of cigarettes off the shelves. A cashier named Nancy tried to check out the purchase, but because it was for more than $30, she had to call in for a credit approval. McDuff let her know that the card had a $10,000 limit. Her problem was that she could not find the phone number to make the call. Other customers came in and she had to tend to them as well, and so McDuff had to wait almost twenty minutes for the approval. Nancy apologized a couple of times, but she never had a conversation with him. One-Arm wondered what was taking so long, but patiently waited outside in the Thunderbird. At one point he wondered if McDuff was robbing the place. Finally, the transaction went through and McDuff signed the credit slip. He also put the license plate number of the Thunderbird next to his signature.[22] He never thought about it, but in doing so he provided law officers extremely useful evidence establishing his whereabouts at that moment.

One-Arm and McDuff went back to the Ambassador Motel, met with Holly, Darrin and T-Bone, and drank more beer. They also discussed how and where to sell the cigarettes. Eventually they decided to go to a predominantly black section of Eighth Street in Temple. Holly drove, Darrin sat in the front seat, and McDuff and One-Arm sat in the back. Holly gave McDuff one more hit of crack and told him that he could have no more until he had money from selling the merchandise. When Holly suggested that all they could get for the cigarettes was about $20, McDuff said they could get more in Waco. And yet again, he talked about robbing and killing crack dealers for their money. Once they reached Eighth Street, Darrin got out of the car and tried to sell the cigarettes. All of a sudden, McDuff got out of the car and started yelling, "All I want is some fucking crack and a goddamn woman!"

"Get your crazy ass back into the car," pleaded Holly.

"I'll kill a motherfucker, too," McDuff said as he pulled out a switchblade. Holly told him to take a chill pill or he was going to get hurt. As Holly would later testify, "he was the only white person down there in a black neighborhood." McDuff said that he did not give a damn, but he got back into the car. In the midst of such a disruption, Darrin could not sell the cigarettes.[23]

Since McDuff was so unstable when they returned to the Ambassador Motel, Holly let him smoke some more crack. But while he went to the restroom, Holly ran out to the Thunderbird and, in her words, "took," not stole, the cigarettes. She felt that since she had been giving him crack all night long, the cigarettes were rightfully hers. She hid the eight cartons in One-Arm's hotel room closet. When McDuff emerged from the restroom, he flew into a rage when he discovered that his merchandise had been stolen. "Some son-of-a-bitch stole cigarettes out of my car," he screamed. Incredibly, he calmed down when Darrin said he knew where they could buy more stuff on credit. Shortly thereafter, Holly, Darrin, and McDuff got back into the Thunderbird; Holly drove.

They went back to Eighth Street, but this time both Darrin and Holly had decided to dump McDuff. He was crazy, cursing and getting more upset. She let Darrin off at a traffic light and drove on to a newly constructed bridge. She pulled the car over near the home of a friend of hers named Judy. Her plan was to run away to Judy's house, but when she started to get out of the Thunderbird McDuff grabbed her arm and insisted that she go to Waco with him. He said they could get a lot of crack out there. Holly said "no," and began to struggle to get loose of his grip.

"Yea, you're going. Bitch, you stay in this car," screamed McDuff, as Holly started blowing the horn and screaming. Earlier, she had taken off her shoes to drive, and instinctively, she grabbed one of them and hit him in the face with it. Stunned, McDuff took a half-step back and Holly was out of his grasp. By that time, Judy came out on her front porch. He got into his car and left, spinning his tires and driving away with Holly's other shoe.[24]

Holly would not realize how lucky she was for another two months.

McDuff sped away from Temple an angry man. He had tried extraordinarily hard to get money for crack, only to have his cigarettes stolen from him. And he did not get himself a woman either. Surely, his mood had to have been sour, and made even worse when his Thunderbird, which he (actually Addie) had spent over $800 having fixed, began to give him trouble.

V

On March 1, Melissa Northrup had some reasons to hope for her future. She and her husband, Aaron, had reconciled, but continued to live apart to save money for his education at TSTI. He intended to major in Information Management Technology. Aaron had secured a Pell Grant for his education, but he worked for a temporary services company to bring in extra money. (He no longer worked at the Quik Pak. He claims to have been fired for wearing a baseball cap while on the job. A representative for Quik Pak Stores, however, testified that Aaron had been terminated for not showing up for work.) On the next Monday, Aaron, Melissa, and her children were to move into married students' housing at TSTI.

In late February, Melissa had been to a temporary services firm, had taken a series of tests and scored well on data entry and keyboarding skills. She interviewed for a position in a bank and felt confident of her chances of getting out of her job at the Quik Pak. But her activities during their separation came back to haunt her. She had dated a very unpleasant ex-con who did not want her to reconcile with Aaron. Melissa and that boyfriend, at least initially, had had a good relationship; Brenda and Richard Solomon thought he seemed to be a nice guy. They had even invited him to spend Thanksgiving with their family. But according to sworn testimony, the boyfriend became abusive, and his harassment of Melissa included physical assaults. He harassed Aaron as well. On one occasion he jumped onto Quik Pak's counter as if to assault Melissa. After Aaron moved towards him he chased Aaron around the store. Melissa and Aaron filed charges against the young man and had him arrested, but according to Melissa, the stalking continued.[25]

During the graveyard shift of February 29/March 1, Melissa had been visited by two McLennan County Sheriff's Deputies named Bobby Hunt and Dean Priddy. The men remembered that her car was parked in the usual place, on the north side of the store pointing south. They stayed for nearly a half-hour and reported that nothing seemed to be out of order. During her conversation with the officers, however, Melissa stated that her ex-boyfriend continued to harass her. She told the officers that he frequently drove off without paying for his gas, or would walk into the store, take beer, and leave without paying.[26]

Only a few hours after the deputies visited Melissa, Kenneth's car trouble started on New Road, just south of Waco and due west of the Quik Pak. Exactly what happened during those early morning hours of March 1, 1992, may never be known. What is certain is that at one point, Kenneth Allen McDuff looked east towards the corner of New Road and Interstate 35—and saw the Quik Pak #8. It was still the graveyard shift.

12

The Convenience Store

"We had a feeling that this is bad; this can't wait."
—Bill Johnston, United States Attorney

I

Officially, Kenneth McDuff completed graduation requirements from TSTI in late February, 1992. The certificate he "earned" was mailed to J. A. and Addie. For most students, graduation means an opportunity to seek employment and build a future. For Kenneth McDuff, it probably meant an end to his state-supported lifestyle of sex and drugs. Reportedly, just a couple of days before his rendezvous with Holly, he had driven to Victoria, Texas, to interview for a job. According to Addie, he was excited at the prospect of gainful employment at the Victoria Machine Works, and then crushed to learn he was not hired. It was on February 29, 1992, according to Addie, that "Kenneth left [her home] so mad he didn't take his glasses or his clothes."[1]

And so, during the early morning hours of March 1, he might still have harbored anger over not getting a job he and his mother claimed he wanted very badly. More likely, however, his anger centered over the end of a very bad night. He had no money and could not get any because his cigarettes had been stolen from him; his Thunderbird had broken down the day after over $800 had been spent repairing it; he was coming down from an evening of smoking crack, and he had not had a woman. In a mood fashioned by such a bizarre evening, Kenneth McDuff headed towards the Quik Pak #8.

Aaron often stayed with Melissa at the store during her graveyard shift. "It was unsafe. It was in a bad neighborhood, not well lit, not any good police patrol [sic] around there, and I just knew it was an unsafe store, from experience," he said. Aaron was right. The store was located in a narrow, unincorporated strip of land between Waco and Robinson. "It is a no-man's land," said Detective Richard Stroup. Getting off and on the Interstate Highway was relatively easy, and wooded areas or businesses that were closed during graveyard shifts surrounded the store. For all practical purposes, the store had no security, and was normally manned by only one attendant. Kenneth McDuff knew all of that as he approached.[2]

Just after midnight on March 1, Aaron had visited Melissa at the store. He stayed until between 1:00 and 1:30 A.M., when she asked him to go on home to get some sleep because she wanted him to stay with her kids after she finished work. She needed sleep as well. Her parents planned to go with friends to the horse races at Bandera Downs. He called her as soon as he got back to his parents' home, but she was busy. She called him again at about 2:00 A.M. and they talked about how she disliked her Quik Pak job. They also talked about their future and her pregnancy—Melissa was two and one half months pregnant. Just after 3:00 A.M., Aaron called her again, but she was busy. He called her again at about 3:45 to tell her he was going to bed, but she asked him to hold on. He said "never mind" and hung up on her. Just before 4:00 A.M., Aaron's sister woke him up to tell him Melissa was on the phone. He reminded her that he needed to get some sleep if he was to watch her kids later that day. He wanted to go back to sleep but he felt badly about how curt he had been to Melissa, and a few minutes later, he called back to apologize. There was no answer.[3]

Only moments earlier, a young man named Richard Bannister and his wife, Ollie, had driven down New Road towards their temporary residence—The New Road Inn. They were living at the motel because he was doing temporary contract work for the Lockheed Aircraft Company. At the time, he was doing structural repair modifications to a Boeing 747. The couple resided in Piedmont, South Carolina. They had had quite an evening. They had been at a bar called Misty's until it closed at 2:00 A.M. Afterwards, they helped the owner restock his refrigerators. While heading east on New Road near the Veterans Hospital, Richard and Ollie passed McDuff, who was clumsily trying to push his Thunderbird with another car. Bannister could not positively identify the car McDuff used to do the pushing, but he remembered that it was a General Motors product. It was almost certainly Melissa's car, a heavily used, burnt orange Buick Regal even less reliable than McDuff's Thunderbird. Bannister remembers how McDuff would push, jump out and straighten the steering wheel of the Thunderbird, and run back into the Buick to push again. The task was made more difficult by the slight incline of New Road. During subsequent interviews, McDuff would later complain that he could not have done any murdering or kidnapping that night because he was so strung out that he almost hurt himself while pushing his car: he had even run over his cowboy hat.

Bannister drove by McDuff to the New Road Inn to put his intoxicated wife to bed. He also had a cocker spaniel that had been locked in the motel room for several hours; it needed a walk.[4] When Bannister walked his dog to a large, gravel-covered, truck parking lot located between the hotel and the Quik Pak, he noticed McDuff standing near the Thunderbird. From New Road, McDuff had pushed his car into the lot, and parked it in an odd position. Bannister remembers, "As he approached me I kind of yelled, 'Hey, you need some help?' and he said 'no, I got it.' And he got back in and pushed the car towards me. And he got out and kind of walked up to me and asked if he could get some wrecker service locally." Bannister said he would check at the office of the hotel. He vividly remembered McDuff wearing a short-sleeved shirt, and that one of those sleeves was dirty. McDuff also had a cut under his right eye.[5]

Most likely, McDuff had already abducted Melissa. Bannister never stated that he saw a female, but it is clear, as McLennan County Assistant District Attorney Crawford Long believes, that something "spooked" McDuff. After his encounter with Richard Bannister, he did something that was, for him, unusual—he fled. After throwing his wallet into his car and locking the doors, he got into Melissa's Buick, and drove away from Central Texas—never to return, at least voluntarily.

Right about that time, Louis Bailey, on his route delivering issues of the *Dallas Morning News*, drove by the Quik Pak, and noticed a car parked across the access road nearby. The driver's side door was opened and the interior light was on. He looked towards the Quik Pak but saw no one.[6]

Aaron called the store repeatedly until about 4:15–4:30 A.M. Then he decided something was wrong. He got into his father's Ford Taurus and raced fourteen miles to the store. He arrived at about 4:30–4:45 to find a bewildered customer waiting to be checked out. He asked the customer where the clerk was and the gentleman gestured as if to say he did not know. Immediately, Aaron jumped over the counter, hit the "no sale" button, and opened the register. All the money was gone. He saw Melissa's purse under the counter, where she always put it, and a notepad full of prospective names for the child in her womb. He took her purse and put it in his father's car. He threw the restroom keys to the customer and told him to look for the checker. Aaron ran throughout the store, searching through storage rooms, and the large, walk-in refrigerators Melissa called "vaults," looking for her. He looked around the area outside of the store. When he got to the south side, he saw that her car was gone. She was nowhere to be found. At precisely 4:47 A.M., he dialed 911.[7]

After calling 911, Aaron called and woke Brenda Solomon at her home. "Brenda, is Melissa at home?"

"No," replied Brenda.

"Is her car there?" asked Aaron.

"No."

"She is not here at work and her car is gone."

"Call the police," said Brenda.

"I already have."[8]

A few miles north of the Quik Pak, at an overpass at the intersection of Interstate Highway 35 and Waco Drive, a TSTI student named Jerry Meyers saw Kenneth McDuff driving Melissa's car in a northerly direction. He immediately recognized McDuff because he had seen him on campus on a number of occasions. He saw Melissa, too. He remembered that she had a terrified look on her face. He thought to himself—"frightened, scared. Something is up."[9]

McLennan County Sheriff's Deputies Bobby Ray Hunt and Dean Priddy were at the Sheriff's Office writing reports when Aaron's 911 call came in. The two men raced to the Quik Pak. Their conversation with Melissa, which had taken place only about five hours ago, was still fresh in their minds. She had complained about how her former boyfriend, well known to the deputies and considered by the department to be a major jerk, was still causing trouble and harassing her and Aaron. Hunt stayed and talked with Aaron in the store while Priddy remained outside talking to others gathered in the parking lot. Neither deputy saw any evidence of a struggle. Very soon a number of McLennan County Deputies were on the scene, including Ronnie Turnbough, who took pictures of the cash register area and found out that Aaron had removed Melissa's purse from the counter. There was some excitement when one of the officers thought he noticed Melissa's former boyfriend drive by. Two officers gave chase, but it was not him.

Soon to arrive were a couple of Quik Pak store officials, who were able to establish that since the drop safe had $350 in it, the money that was stolen was what Melissa had sold during her shift. $252.94 was missing. One of the employees observed that the officers seemed to be suspicious of Aaron, who showed no emotion or grief. There were also a number of people sleeping in a parked car on the Quik Pak lot, but that was not unusual. The detectives quickly established that those occupants had slept through the abduction and had seen nothing.[10]

Meanwhile, McDuff motored north on Interstate Highway 35 in Melissa's Buick Regal. Exactly where he exited the highway will never be known, but he took Melissa 100 miles away to an area of southeast Dallas County near a small community called Combine.[11] It is the most remote part of Dallas County. There, the country roads are narrow, and bordered on both sides by vast tracts of farmland. Occasionally, trailer parks or small neighborhoods dot the landscape. In other large areas, enormous piles of dirt line the roads where huge gravel pits have been dug out. Harvesting gravel and stone is a major industry in the area. The older pits are flooded, stocked with fish, and leased to fishermen. Barely noticeable dirt roads, some bordered by thick brush and small trees, wind between the flooded pits. At night, the area is completely dark; at some places the nearest street light is miles away.

On the morning of March 1, 1992, McDuff turned left from Bilingsday Road onto an unmarked dirt path called James Road. He did not get very far—only about two-tenths of a mile—before he bogged down in the sticky, thick, red mud of the area. McDuff managed to move the car near thick grass and was able to get out of the car on the passenger side without leaving footprints in the mud. He had about half an hour before sunrise. He had to have felt a need to put as much distance as possible between himself and Melissa, and her car. From her car, he marched her about 1.5 miles to an even more isolated area near a smaller, self-contained gravel pit just off Bois D'Arc Road. District Attorneys who prosecuted him later firmly believe that if McDuff was going to walk that far, he had to have decided to go to a specific point. Melissa's forced death march took her over open fields obstructed only by a loose barbed wire fence that they crossed easily.

Undoubtedly, during the long walk, she begged McDuff to let her live. Like his other victims, she could not have known that such pleas only fueled his lust for brutality and torture. He took her socks and the laces from her tennis shoes and made ligatures to tie her feet and her hands behind her back. Except for Robert Brand and Marcus Dunnam, his only known male victims, those McDuff are known to have murdered died slow, agonizing deaths. But unlike most of his other female victims, McDuff did not bury Melissa. After he "used her up," he threw her into a flooded gravel pit.

II

In 1992, every Saturday and Sunday morning, like clockwork, at 6:50 A.M. sharp, Pepper Cole left her home near Seagoville to head for work. Her route took her on Bilingsday Road past the intersections of Bois D'Arc and Malloy Bridge Roads. At about 6:55 A.M. on Sunday, March 1, she drove by what she described as a clean-cut, tall, man with dark brown hair walking northbound. She remembers seeing him because of the remoteness of the area, which is about seven miles from any community; and no one ever walks that area at that time of the morning. Also, she did not recognize him as being a local resident. It was pretty cold that morning and he was by himself. He was neither thin nor fat. He wore a blue jean jacket and had his hands in his pockets. He also wore a baseball cap and kept his face down, as if to protect it from cold winds. She does not remember much more because she passed him up from behind, and saw his front from her car's rear view mirror.[12]

Later that same day, Shari Robinson answered a knock on her door. She and her family lived in a trailer near the gravel pits. She remembers McDuff standing on her porch dressed in dirty clothes. She also remembers that he was on foot. He told her that he and his "old lady" had gotten into a fight and he wanted to know if he could have a sandwich. She said "no," but she had some leftover beans that he could have. Her husband, a tough-looking man, was clearly visible and seated near a shotgun. McDuff ate his beans and left.[13]

Richard Bannister and the abandoned Thunderbird

placed Kenneth McDuff near the scene of the abduction of
Melissa Northrup. Pepper Cole saw someone who fit
McDuff's description on Bilingsday Road, and Shari Robinson placed him on foot, and in dirty clothing near the
gravel pits where Melissa's body was found. That he abducted, transported, and killed Melissa near those gravel
pits is no mystery. What is *still* a mystery is how McDuff
got out of the area. Or more specifically, *who* helped him
get out of there.

On the night of February 29/March 1, 1992, Kenneth
Allen McDuff left a trail of evidence that led to his downfall. Coincidentally, on those same days, a gifted attorney
named Mike Freeman had begun a long journey from Nebraska to Waco, Texas. He was about to start a new career
as an Assistant District Attorney for McLennan County.
That, too, later contributed to McDuff's downfall.

III

Since Melissa had complained to deputies that she continued to be harassed by her former boyfriend, he was immediately the prime suspect. It did not take very long,
however, to clear him. At the time, the young man had a
relationship with a teacher in the small town of West. He
had spent the entire weekend with her, and she provided
an airtight alibi for him. Her statement was given even
more credibility when she readily agreed to take a polygraph test and passed it. The boyfriend, however, was arrested anyway. A "Blue Warrant" was issued for him for a
parole violation and he was brought to the McLennan
County Jail.[14]

The Northrup abduction case was assigned to Detective
Richard Stroup of the McLennan County Sheriff's Department. Originally from Pennsylvania, he was retired from
the Air Force. His military career included two years in
Vietnam. His first job with the sheriff's office had been in

the records section; he was hired because he could type. In 1991, he moved to the criminal section.

During a search of the area soon after the abduction, Stroup had seen the tan Thunderbird parked in an odd way near the New Road Inn, but he understandably concluded that it belonged to one of the guests.[15]

Aaron was never seriously considered a suspect, especially after he took and passed a polygraph test. During those first few hours, investigators considered the possibility, however remote, that Melissa had run off. For the first few days, there was no hard evidence that she had even been abducted.[16] Solving this case would require a break, or at least the discovery of something somewhere other than at the Quik Pak. The first real break came from a most unlikely source—Addie McDuff.

On March 3, 1992, Addie phoned the Bell County Sheriff's Office to report a missing person—her son, Kenneth. Following established procedure, a deputy was dispatched to take the statement, get the facts, and forward them to the Criminal Investigations Division (CID). Deputy Ralph Howell drove out to Addie McDuff's house where she insisted that the last time she saw her son was on February 29 at about 11:00 A.M. She told Howell that Kenneth was trying to get a machinist job in Victoria and that he went to a parcel mailing service located on Main Street in Temple. Howell took the information and returned to headquarters for it to be forwarded to CID.[17]

Of course, Addie could not have known it, and she certainly did not mean to do so, but when she reported McDuff missing, she contributed greatly to his eventual apprehension. Throughout Texas, virtually all law enforcement agencies had access to databases that now listed Kenneth Allen McDuff as a missing and possibly endangered person from Bell County. Virtually all inquiries would henceforth land on the desk of a Bell County Investigator, a central location. More significant was whose desk it would land on—Investigator Tim Steglich.

A native of Central Texas who had lived for some time

in Houston, Tim Steglich looked into the reputation of various police academies and chose to enroll in Houston's. Upon graduation, he worked as a Houston Police officer, a goal he set for himself as a young man. As he grew older, he wanted to raise his daughters in the more agrarian Central Texas, so in the mid-1980s, he moved to one of the Blackland Prairie's hamlets. He became heavily involved in the activities of its public schools. In truth, he'd always wished he could have been a football coach; and he would have made a good one. Tim Steglich never watched much television, and has little patience for reading. His gifts as an investigator lie in how he deals with people. He can find anyone, and when he does, he never burns bridges. Over the years, he has nearly perfected methods of effectively communicating with even the smallest of intellects; he gets information out of them. He is an astute observer of body language, and can analyze responses as well as many, more highly trained interrogators. And he never, ever, gives up. "Every once in a while, in some small towns and rural sheriffs' offices, you come across an investigator who is every bit as good as anyone, anywhere. Tim Steglich is one of them," said ATF Special Agent Charles Meyer.[18]

On the day Addie reported him as a missing person, McDuff was scheduled to report to his parole officer in Temple. Naturally, he failed to do so. The next day, one of McDuff's sisters went to Sabine Hall and cleaned out McDuff's room. Meanwhile, Tim Steglich, who had never heard of McDuff, did a criminal history on him to determine if he wanted "to make himself missing." As Tim stood and gazed at the printout near the only computer the department had to do such searches, immediately, and long before he had any idea of who Melissa Northrup or Colleen Reed were, he had a bad feeling about the entire case. Tim decided it was time to call Addie McDuff.[19]

From the beginning, Steglich believed Addie had been coached and told what to say about McDuff's disappearance. When he called her on March 5, the mind games began. She repeated her story about how Kenneth thought he had a job in Victoria and was upset at how it did not work out. She insisted that he had only one more test to take at TSTI and that he was looking forward to graduating. "He would never have missed that test. He loved that school," she said. According to Addie, Kenneth left her house to fax materials in a desperate attempt to land the job. She never saw him again. Moreover, she was convinced that someone had killed him—Kenneth was dead.

Addie never fooled Tim. "Most people do not immediately assume their child is dead. Particularly a grown man," Tim thought. And as he spoke to her further, he got her to admit that in the past Kenneth could be gone for days at a time. "Why is it that this time he is dead?" thought Tim.

Tim was in an odd situation; he was searching for Addie's missing boy, and at the same time he had grave reservations as to whether she really believed he was missing.[20] But why? At the time, Tim could not understand what purpose these mind games served.

On March 6, Larry Abner of the McLennan County Sheriff's Office responded to a complaint from the manager of the New Road Inn. One of the housekeepers, Janell Kinder, had noticed as early as March 1 that a tan Thunderbird had been parked in an odd position, making it difficult for truck-driving guests to park. Abner arrived to look at the vehicle, parked in the shadow of a large truck, and ran a license plate check. When the Waco Police Department reported that the vehicle belonged to a missing and endangered person, Larry Abner immediately impounded the car. Within minutes Richard Stroup had a complete criminal history of the car's owner. According to Lieutenant Truman Simons, after the criminal background check had been done, everyone knew they were on to something. McDuff's car being located that close to where Melissa had been abducted could not be a coincidence. Soon, police helicopters hovered above taking aerial pictures of the Quik Pak and the New Road Inn. Before the day was out, Tim Steglich and Richard Stroup, who had never met each other, were comparing notes on the cases of two missing persons—Melissa Northrup and Kenneth McDuff. They agreed that Tim should continue his communication with Addie—especially since she had requested it.[21]

After impounding McDuff's car, the McLennan County Sheriff's Department had it towed six miles to Big Boys Wrecker Service in Robinson. The trunk and doors of the Thunderbird were still locked and Abner ordered that they be opened. One of the smaller employees of the wrecker service had to crawl into the trunk to unlock it from the inside. Ronnie Turnbough and Larry Abner took an inventory of its contents. (No search warrant was necessary as this was routine and consistent with the Texas Uniform Traffic Code; after a vehicle has been abandoned for more than seventy-two hours, it is seized and towed away, and its contents inventoried.)

The owner of Big Boys knew the car must have been important; by the end of the afternoon, law enforcement officers crowded around the vehicle. Two FBI agents watched the inventory carefully. They found a number of items, including personal papers with the name of Kenneth Allen McDuff on them, a wallet with his driver's license, a Goodyear Tire Protection Plan, a crumpled-up, white cowboy hat, and a receipt for the purchase of gas—at the Quik Pak on February 29. The police officers and the employees of Big Boys Wrecker also determined that the car could be started; they hot-wired it and it ran.[22]

IV

On March 6, the same day that the McLennan County Sheriff's Department identified McDuff's car and discovered his criminal history, over 100 miles away, patrolwoman Aletha Jesttes of the Dallas County Sheriff's Office conducted her routine patrol of the southeast section of the county. She noticed a vehicle parked on James Road. She knew that the road had no outlet and that it was unusual for passenger vehicles to be down there. At the time, the road was in such poor condition that she parked her unit and waited for two other vehicles, pickup trucks located down James Road, to come to her. The drivers of the pickups were the owner of the property and his son. The son reported that the Buick had not been there on February 29, but was there on March 1. He was certain of that because on that day they had intended to grade the road. He apparently happened upon the car shortly after sunrise and remembered that the muddy water near the tires was still foamy and bubbly.

One of the trucks brought Officer Jesttes to the car, where she got information needed to do a check. In a very short time, Jesttes learned that the vehicle was reported stolen and had been involved in a robbery/abduction. Soon, several deputies arrived. They decided to force open the trunk to see if Melissa was there. They found only two large plastic bags of clothing Melissa had intended to give away to a Goodwill station in Waco.[23]

Later, Tim Parker of the Dallas Sheriff's Office arrived to process the scene. When he sat in the car, he immediately noticed that the driver's seat had been pushed as far back as possible. His first impression was that the driver had to be a very tall person. He also knew that the 4'11" Melissa Northrup could never have driven her car with the seat in that position.[24]

Indeed, March 6 had been a busy day in the efforts to bring Kenneth Allen McDuff to justice: McDuff's Thunderbird had been located and as a result the McLennan County Sheriff's Department had a prime suspect in the abduction of Melissa Northrup; Melissa Northrup's Buick had been discovered by the Dallas County Sheriff's Department, and a search for Melissa commenced there; Tim Steglich's initial hunch, that there was much more to the missing persons case filed by Addie, was confirmed, and he approached the case from a much different perspective. He headed to the elder McDuff's home for an interview with much more on his mind than a missing persons case.

Something else happened on March 6. At 11:45 A.M., just outside of the Federal Building in Waco, two Deputy United States Marshals leisurely walked towards their truck to drive over to the Waco office of their close friend, the Assistant United States Attorney. The three men looked forward to another of their many enjoyable lunches, but on that day it would be anything but that. Before the two marshals reached the parking lot, they encountered two FBI agents named Freddie Vela and Bobby Seale. In passing, Seale asked the marshals if they had ever heard of a fellow named Kenneth Allen McDuff. "Absolutely," replied one of the men. As Seale briefed the two men about the Melissa Northrup Case, and how Kenneth McDuff's car had been found only a couple of hundred yards away, "red lights" went off in their heads. As they listened intently, beneath their large cowboy hats, their brows furrowed and eyes narrowed. "You can quit looking. That's your man!" the elder of the two marshals said, with complete confidence.[25]

On March 6, many things happened to bring about the ultimate downfall of Kenneth Allen McDuff. Not the least of them was the outrage of those two marshals—Mike and Parnell McNamara.

They headed for the office of Assistant United States Attorney Bill Johnston with a new sense of urgency, and for more than just lunch.

13

The Boys

"These guys would fight the devil on the steps of hell!"
—Gary M. Lavergne

I

The three men sometimes call themselves "The Boys." Two of them are brothers and the third might as well be. Deputy United States Marshals Mike and Parnell McNamara are the sons of Thomas Parnell ("T. P.") McNamara. T. P. ran the United States Marshal's Office in Waco for thirty-seven years, a record that is now out of reach because of age requirements and mandatory retirement. So great was T. P.'s reputation as a lawman that he has been enshrined in the Texas Rangers Hall of Fame—quite a feat for a U.S. Marshal. From 1902 until his death in 1947, Mike and Parnell's great-uncle, Guy McNamara, was a McLennan County Constable, Chief of the Waco Police Department, a Deputy U.S. Marshal, and finally a full United States Marshal.[1] Law enforcement is as much a part of Mike and Parnell's genetic makeup as their blue eyes are.

William "Bill" Johnston, an Assistant United States Attorney, is the son of Wilson Johnston, an Assistant District Attorney of Dallas County during the heyday of District Attorney Henry Wade. Wilson Johnston was a pivotal figure in the prosecution and conviction of Jack Ruby, Lee Harvey Oswald's assassin. The elder Johnston handled about 40,000 cases before grand juries. Henry Wade grinned when Bill said publicly that, "If Henry Wade and Bill Decker (the Sheriff) cleaned up Dallas after the Bonnie and Clyde Era, it was Wilson Johnston who kept them straight while they did it." But what made Wilson Johnston unique was that he often accompanied police on raids and stakeouts. Within more stringent guidelines that exist today, Bill does the same; it is part of his makeup.

Mike, Parnell, and Bill: no novelist could have crafted such a unique trio. "[They] are the spiritual descendants of an unforgiving school of frontier lawmen," wrote Gary Cartwright.[2] Indeed, like Larry McMurtry characters, they have a well-defined sense of right and wrong; for The Boys, there is seldom a gray area. Those who know them wonder if they would not have been happier if they had been born 100 years ago, when the frontier—absent silly rules, regulations, and bureaucracy—meant real freedom to pursue criminals, and what was wrong did not have to be defined by statute.

Parnell is the older of the McNamara boys. He is equally comfortable showing a menacing face of stone, a piercing and terrifying glare, or a disarming, engaging smile. He tells stories with a deep, rich Central Texas drawl as well as any *raconteur*. Many of the tales are of himself and his younger brother, Mike. Every cell in his body is Texan. And he is fearless.

Mike says less than Parnell, and is more direct and selective with his words. His demeanor hides an inner strength but betrays an intensely thoughtful and analytical approach to challenges. When engaged in deep conversation, he narrows his mouth and eyes, and tilts his head forward. He watches and listens carefully to every microtremor of what he hears. He is patient—very patient. Every cell in his body is Texan. And he, too, is fearless.

The McNamara Boys both graduated from Baylor University as Marketing and Business Majors. Neither claims to be overly academic. "You don't catch a horse thief by pecking on a computer," Mike once said.[3] When asked to remember their Baylor matriculation, Parnell is likely to flash a face-wrinkling smile and launch into the story of Mike's initiation into the Taurus Society, a revealing tale

about how tough Mike McNamara really is, and the extent
to which he can take whatever is dished out—even from
Parnell. During the fall semester of 1966, Parnell served as
the pledge captain of the Taurus Society, a precursor to
fraternities. At that time, Mike was one of the pledges.
"Hazing was pretty bad in those days," said Parnell. First,
the pledges were taken on a "short walk" of about thirty
miles. After arriving at their destination, they were stripped
down and chained together. Then, they were taken to a
riverbank where "horns" made of sticks and branches were
duct-taped to their heads. As the pledges stood in various
stages of dress, resplendent with their horns, thick molasses
was poured over them. The molasses served as an adhesive
for an uneven coating of cornflakes. Whatever pride the
pledges might have had left vanished after they were "ral-
lied," which meant they were dragged about the area by
their horns. To be admitted to the Taurus Society, members
of a pledge class had to demonstrate their resourcefulness.

At about 3:00 A.M., Mike and fourteen other boys were
chained to a tree and left, with a small saw blade to get
themselves out.

One of the pledges managed to get loose. He grabbed a
sweatshirt, forced it over his legs like a pair of pants, and
headed to the nearest farmhouse. The startled occupants
nearly shot the poor boy before they called Sheriff Brady
Pamplin, who arrived to free the boys, wrap them in blan-
kets, and put them in the back of his pickup truck. In Marlin, the Sheriff stopped at a restaurant to get the boys donuts
and coffee. As Mike and his fellow pledges sat in the back
of the truck, throngs of Sunday worshippers walked and
drove by staring. Finally, the boys got to shower at Marlin
High School, where they called friends at Baylor to bring
clothes. When Sheriff Pamplin asked Mike and the other
boys if they knew who their tormentors were, Mike replied,
"Sure, one of them was my brother. He organized it." Mike
had demonstrated that he could "take it." Now, it was Parnell's turn.

The next day T. P. McNamara called Parnell over and

said, "You need to call the Sheriff. Last night he found some boys all beat up." The front page of the *Marlin Daily Democrat* carried a large article quoting Pamplin as saying, "I have never seen a nicer bunch of boys that looked so bad in all my life." The problem for Parnell was that a dean at Baylor saw the article, contacted Sheriff Pamplin, and indicated that the fraternity involved would be thrown off the campus. Parnell met with Brady Pamplin. "Sheriff, please don't tell him who it is," asked Parnell. Pamplin picked up the phone, called the dean, and quietly but firmly told him that the matter was closed.

The November 7, 1966, issue of the *Marlin Daily Democrat* ran a front page story entitled "Chained: Fifteen Baylor Students Rescued." In a haunting twist of history, on the same page, the article to the immediate left was entitled, "McDuff Goes on Trial, Death Penalty Sought."[4]

At 6' 5" Bill Johnston is as formidable as any lawman or criminal who ever walked into a courthouse. And yet, his physical features are almost boyish. He is a tough man with intellectual power, equally comfortable in a business suit arguing the law, or in western garb holding a shotgun tracking horse thieves. He is a deeply spiritual, excitable intellectual. He does not curse, and will doggedly avoid quoting someone else who does. Bill's view of prosecution is simple: "Prosecution is not a politically-correct business. It is a cold-blooded business." On another occasion he said: "Weak prosecution is the plague of law enforcement." Bill's good friend, Secret Service Agent Robert Blossman, said, "Bill believes in looking not just at the particular crime, but the individual—who he is, what he's capable of doing." Critics have hammered Bill for believing that it is important to look at what a suspect is *capable* of doing, and although it bothers him, he takes it, because Bill Johnston has no patience with the timid. From his office in Waco, where Theodore Roosevelt's "Man in the Arena" quote is framed and sits on a window ledge, Bill Johnston takes chances. And so, graphing his career produces a Rooseveltian, irregular line of spectacular wins—and losses. Bill Johnston will never "take his place with those cold and timid souls who know neither victory nor defeat." Every cell in his body is Texan. And he is fearless.

None of The Boys wears a watch. They have an infuriating irreverence for time. That they will be late is an accepted expectation of those who know and deal with them. Their families, extraordinary in their own right, long ago accepted the frequency and ease with which Mike and Parnell spend days and nights in vehicles tracking suspects and fugitives. That includes Bill, who feels that if he asks the McNamaras to spend nights on cases, he should be there too. And The Boys have spent many nights in cars, trucks, and especially a huge, white Suburban they call "Bigfoot."

On March 6, 1992, at the Miller Family Steakhouse, Mike and Parnell told Bill the story of Kenneth Allen McDuff. Bill remembered the Broomstick Murders; his father was an Assistant D.A. in the neighboring county, and he recalled hearing him talk about McDuff. As the lunch progressed, the three managed to work each other up. But there was little they could do; evidence that McDuff had violated a federal law was necessary before Bill or the United States Marshal's Service could get involved. Someone like Kenneth Allen McDuff, however, seldom decides to violate only state laws. Since McDuff was an ex-con who frequented places like the Cut, and they were all convinced he had something to do with Melissa's abduction, then establishing a drug connection, or the possession of a firearm would be enough to trigger federal involvement. Parnell had a discussion about the developments with his supervisor, Cliff Hoffman, who readily accepted the argument that McDuff needed to be tracked down immediately. Before the end of the afternoon, Bill had his warrant.[5]

II

Before the dust from towing McDuff's car from the truck parking lot of the New Road Inn could settle, McLennan

County deputies and investigators canvassed the New Road Inn's guests for any clues to what could have gone on in the parking lot the night Melissa was abducted. Richard Stroup came across Richard Bannister, who identified McDuff as the man he saw near the Thunderbird that night. But, when he was shown a picture of Melissa's Buick, he could not confirm that it was the car McDuff used to push the Thunderbird.[6]

The abduction of Melissa Northrup brought about a sense of urgency in the Waco area. Like Austin's reaction to the disappearance of Colleen Reed, friends and family spread out, handing out fliers and asking questions. McDuff's other victims had no such advocates, except for Regenia Moore, whose mother, Barbara Carpenter, courageously searched for her daughter—but she was alone in her determined search. Out in West Texas, Brenda Thompson's family wondered why she quit calling home, but no one from that family lived in the Waco area, and there is no record of her family reporting her missing. Valencia Joshua's family did not know she had been in the Waco area, much less that she was a missing person or a possible victim of a serial killer. The observation that law enforcement did not connect the string of murders until "good" girls became victims is correct. As a criticism, however, it is not entirely fair. It is not common for accountants and convenience store clerks with jobs and families to get into the cars of strangers. Melissa and Colleen left behind evidence of stable lives, like purses, drivers' licenses, cars, homes, and people who knew better than to believe that they just ran off. These victims' families organized themselves, and provided useful information to law enforcement officers. For example, Bethany Sneed, Melissa's sister-in-law, and her husband Kirk, grabbed a stack of fliers and visited Waco business establishments. Soon, thousands of the mint green posters with Melissa's picture papered Waco. At one convenience store on University Park Drive, Bethany and Kirk met a man who said, "I don't know that woman, but I know the store. A man asked me to rob it."

They had encountered Louis, a resident of Sabine Hall, and the young man McDuff had, on numerous occasions, invited to rob the Quik Pak.

Louis and all other Sabine Hall residents were afraid of McDuff. "He had seen McDuff beat the crap out of some people," remembered McLennan County District Attorney Mike Freeman, who later developed a close working relationship with Louis. Within days, the FBI had pictures of Kenneth McDuff to show Louis,[7] but FBI agents were not the only officers interested in him.

After lunch with the McNamaras, Bill arrived at the Sheriff's Office with FBI Agent Freddie Vela. From there, a deputy called the District Attorney's office to see if any movement had been made to indict McDuff. The answer was "no"; there just wasn't enough there. "I can't fault them for that," remembered Bill. At the time, the only thing linking McDuff to Melissa's abduction was the discovery of his Thunderbird near, not at, the scene. Bill asked around the office and came across a deputy who knew of a girl who worked at a bailbondsman office across the street. The deputy said she knew McDuff. She was brought over, and within two minutes she said that her boyfriend, Louis, "runs with Big Mac. He does dope with Big Mac." An adrenaline rush went through Bill: "Where is he? I'd really like to talk to him."[8]

At that moment, Louis was fishing down on the Brazos River. The Sheriff's Office sent a deputy to get him. Bill headed for his office, looking for a Drug Enforcement agent to assist in the interrogation. He found Jay Eubanks.

The McLennan County deputy brought Louis to Bill's office on the Baylor campus. Bill and Eubanks thoroughly questioned him about his and McDuff's involvement in drugs. Louis described an LSD tab he had purchased from McDuff. Eubanks was able to determine that Louis knew what he was talking about; he had described shapes and designs—blotter paper with a silver palm tree—matching known merchandise reaching Waco from Austin. He also accurately described the effects of the drug as "copping tracers" or catching hands. Within minutes, Eubanks drafted a complaint Bill took before a federal magistrate. Bill took out a pad and wrote out a warrant. "Kenneth Allen McDuff unlawfully, knowingly, and intentionally did distribute lysergic acid diethylamide (LSD), a Schedule I Controlled Substance, in violation of Title 21, United States Code, Section 841 (a) (1)." Bill had a federal warrant for the arrest of Kenneth Allen McDuff. McDuff was now a federal fugitive. Within days, the federal grand jury returned a sealed indictment.[9]

The investigators already involved in the case had reason to believe McDuff possessed guns—at least on some occasions. Bill Johnston alerted the ATF. The agent who initiated the investigation was a young, very energetic officer named Jeff Brzozowski. Jeff interviewed Louis, who stated that he saw McDuff with a small caliber pistol in the parking lot of Sabine Hall. To the best of his recollection, he had seen the weapon in August or September of the previous year. Two days later, Jeff presented an affidavit and secured a search warrant to look through McDuff's Thunderbird. Now, the ATF wanted McDuff.[10]

III

After Richard Stroup and Tim Steglich agreed that Tim should contact Addie McDuff in response to her filing a missing persons report on Kenneth, Tim drove over to Addie's house. Immediately, Addie reiterated her belief that someone killed her son. Tim convinced Addie to sign a Consent to Search Form, and she directed him to the bedroom Kenneth used when he stayed there. Inside the room, Tim found various papers, mostly related to McDuff's matriculation at TSTI. Only two days earlier, one of McDuff's sisters had cleaned out his dorm room and brought the items to Addie. McDuff had a briefcase with a broken latch that contained documents and other things like over-the-counter sinus medication, Preparation H, three cigarette lighters, a can opener, two El Chico Margarita Garters, and four cassette tapes. Steglich also found the title to the 1985 Thunderbird and a W-2 Tax Form showing employment at Quik Pak Stores, Inc. Tim was able to determine that Addie had purchased the Thunderbird for Kenneth after he had returned J. A.'s pickup truck with a badly broken windshield. The significance of the windshield meant nothing to Tim at the time. In a few days he would be told about the missing persons cases of Brenda Thompson and Regenia Moore; his first thoughts were "we are dealing with a serial killer." Tim now fully understood the enormity of his missing person case. In talking with Addie, Tim never detected any body language to indicate that Kenneth was there or nearby.[11]

Bill Miller picked up the phone and called Texas Ranger John Aycock and told him that McDuff's missing persons report was likely connected to the Melissa Northrup disappearance. Now, the Texas Rangers were involved. Aycock alerted officials in Milam County, where two of McDuff's sisters lived, to be on the lookout for McDuff and Melissa's Buick.[12]

Meanwhile, Mike, Parnell and Bill went to the Quik Pak for clues. They searched not only the Quik Pak, but the large fields and pastures surrounding the store and the New Road Inn. Bill came upon a number of abandoned mobile homes, and had the unsettling feeling that Melissa could be in one. The Boys had to contend with a vicious German Shepherd, but they looked inside each trailer and found nothing but trash. The next day they searched the fields on both sides of New Road, from the Quik Pak to the Veterans Hospital, where Bannister said he saw McDuff pushing his car. Then they went to an area behind TSTI and searched every brush, old shack, water well, pump house, gully, drainage ditch, pond, storm sewer, and any other place where a body could possibly be hidden. They even spent some Saturdays roaming the area. The heavily wooded, undeveloped tracts were littered with bones and the carcasses of dead animals, some of which were partially buried. The

Boys had a very anxious day. "Where is she? Where is she?" Bill could not get Melissa out of his mind.[13] Shortly, they would find out that they had come very close to one of McDuff's victims—but it was not Melissa.[14]

On March 8, Tim Steglich received a note from the Bell County Sheriff's Office dispatcher that Addie McDuff had called for him. Tim returned the call, and Addie told him she had received an anonymous call at about 10:00 A.M. that morning from a man who said he was calling from Victoria. According to Addie, the caller told her that McDuff was having trouble with his parole officer and that is why he left the Temple area. The caller told her that Kenneth's vehicle had been recovered in Waco, and that he was last seen getting into another car, which had been recovered in Dallas. The information meant little to Tim, who did not know that Melissa's car had been found in Dallas County. "Are you sure the po'lice hadn't picked up the car?" Addie asked. Tim found out the next day, March 9, during a phone conversation with Richard Stroup, that Melissa's car had, indeed, been recovered, but nothing in the car provided clues as to where she could be or what could have happened to her. Stroup stressed that no statement had been issued announcing the discovery of Melissa's car. How could Addie have known? Tim's belief that Addie was being told what to say was mightily reinforced.[15]

Later in the day, Parnell called Tim and told him that McDuff was a federal fugitive. Tim filled him in on his missing person investigation and his agreement with Richard Stroup that Tim should continue to contact Addie.[16]

Also on March 9, parole officers issued an Emergency Arrest Warrant for Kenneth McDuff. He was wanted for violating his parole.[17]

IV

"Someone has to crack sooner or later. Somebody's going to talk," insisted Lori Bible. She spearheaded a massive attempt to distribute English and Spanish versions of fliers within a 100-mile radius of Austin. Attached to many of the posters were pink ribbons, placed there because that was Colleen's favorite color. Different versions of the fliers showed different pictures. The hope was that someone might recognize her from one of the photos. Family and friends purchased advertisements in the Austin and San Antonio media outlets offering a $5,000 reward for information leading to Colleen's recovery. They also offered to pay APD overtime for extra work. LCRA contributed much to the effort. Its print shop cranked out thousands of the fliers, and employees posted notices asking for help. While working in Round Rock, Alva Hank Worley saw one of those fliers and recognized Colleen's picture. He later told a psychologist that he "figured McDuff must have killed that girl cause she never showed up."

One week after the abduction, the Austin Police Department assigned additional detectives to the case.

Lori spoke to hundreds of groups, stood out on the streets of Austin handing out information, and appeared on every television station as many times as she could. She was determined not to let others forget her sister. During sworn testimony, Lori described her relationship with the Austin Police Department: "Sometimes it was really good. They were nice and kind and, you know, truly, I believe, interested in finding her. And sometimes they were sick of me and I was sick of them, and I was frustrated with them and I was frustrated with the system. And it was a—very much a roller coaster kind of relationship due to the circumstances, I think."[18]

By the end of February, Lori had to clean out Colleen's apartment; it was a devastating process complicated by an inability to use Colleen's assets to pay bills. She was a missing person and at that time there was no hard evidence that she had been killed. As Lori said later, it was a legal nightmare.

But the efforts to find Colleen accelerated when nationally syndicated true crime shows aired reenactments of her abduction. *America's Most Wanted* and *Unsolved Mysteries* (which McDuff later referred to as "Mysterious Mysteries") aired segments filmed at the car wash.[19]

The break for the Austin Police Department came on March 10, 1992. Lieutenant Truman Simons of the McLennan County Sheriff's Department had made numerous attempts to alert APD about the discovery of Kenneth McDuff's Thunderbird. He noticed the description of the vehicle used in the Colleen Reed abduction in a flier sent to his office. He thought that APD might want to pursue McDuff as a lead. He spoke to Detective Sonya Urubek of the Assault Unit.

As the Colleen Reed Case "grew," APD Detective Don Martin had requested Sonya's assignment. She was new to the pool of detectives and approached her assignment with vigor and enthusiasm. One of few detectives who could claim Austin roots, she had grown up in a tough East Austin neighborhood and characterized herself as a "street kid" who never got into trouble but observed an awful lot. A graduate of Travis High School, she joined an insurance firm but quickly saw that she had gone about as far as she would go in the insurance business. At the time her brother was an Austin Police officer, and she had come to know many of his colleagues. She joined the force in the mid-1980s, and loved patrolling her old neighborhoods. In 1992, she dealt mostly with instances of domestic violence.[20]

Part of the reason Sonya was assigned to the case was to deal with Lori. They first met on Valentine's Day of 1992 and became fast friends. From the time they met to this day, the two young women have promised each other that they would go out for a margarita.[21] They never have; it is almost as if the promise bonded them. But Sonya did more than deal with Lori. On March 2, 1992, more than two months after Colleen's abduction, she was the first APD officer (at least according to the APD Case File) to canvass the businesses around the car wash.

Sonya was also the first at the Austin Police Department to hear of Kenneth Allen McDuff. "The more he [Simons] told me the more excited I got," she remembered. Simons immediately faxed information on McDuff, and as Sonya read it she became more convinced that it was a solid lead. Simons also told her that the ATF had a probable cause search warrant for McDuff's car, which was securely housed in a shed at Big Boys Wrecker Service in Robinson. The search was to take place on March 12, and Jeff Brzozowski was to execute it. He added that APD was welcomed to attend.

She immediately took the information to Don Martin and the head of the Assault Unit. Don readily admits that, initially, he did not share Sonya's enthusiasm. His experience taught him that "nothing is 100 percent sure or 100 percent false." He had many local leads at the time that he thought had to be followed, one of which was the owner of a tan Ford Thunderbird who lived in a trailer park in southeast Austin. The suspect had a criminal record. Eventually, Don conducted a two-hour interview with the suspect and was able to rule him out. After some discussion, Don and Sonya agreed to attend the ATF search.[22]

Two years later, one of McDuff's defense attorneys lamented: "Everybody and their mother was at that search."[23] He had a point, but each of the participants had a perfectly legal right to be there. The probable cause warrant allowed for the search for firearms and documents relating to the ownership of firearms. The Thunderbird's trunk had been locked, and someone from Big Boys crawled into the trunk from the back seat to try to open it up, but Jeff decided to pry it open. The trunk was "full of stuff." Jeff spread a tarp over the floor to take the items out of the trunk—one at a time. The trunk had an array of items: books, TSTI papers, a gray gym bag, clothing and grooming items, two maps, a Victoria newspaper, a light blue blanket, bed sheets, underwear, and assorted trash. The mat in the trunk showed evidence of stains. Sonya wanted to go through it all, but it was not her search and she would have to wait.

McLennan County Deputies Richard Stroup and Ronnie Turnbough were standing near the back bumper watching

as Jeff carefully removed each item. Turnbough saw hairs
fall out of the trunk onto the back bumper of the car. Immediately, he seized them, walked over to his car, and
placed them in evidence containers. When asked why he
never told the ATF about the evidence he had seized, he
answered that he did not pick up the hair as part of the
ATF search warrant. He felt that he had a right to take it
because he was there legally, they were in his view, and
thus he had the authority to take the evidence. His supervisor, Truman Simons, supported Turnbough's decision.
The alternative, Simons argued, was to ignore and possibly
lose the evidence.[24]

Texas Ranger John Aycock took McDuff's cowboy hat
and field-tested it for blood. The results were positive.
Sonya made note of that, and she watched carefully as Jeff
slowly and methodically removed every item from Mc-
Duff's trunk. She noticed that some of the items on the tarp
had hair on them and she wanted to be able to secure it at
a later date. She also noticed that the beige cloth on the
back seat had stains. In her report she indicated that she
thought they looked like stains made from secretions, not
spills.

When Jeff finished his search, Sonya asked that the car
be secured for a future evidentiary search. Jeff and other
officers took the tarp and placed the whole thing back into
the trunk. Immediately, the car was "taped." Don Martin
stood quietly. In an interview in 1998, he asserted that he
thought the car was a pretty good lead, and that McDuff
was, indeed, a suspect, but that since the occasion was an
ATF search involving guns only, it would be best to stay
out of the way. He was clearly not as enthusiastic as Sonya.
Nearly a week later, Martin was still skeptical. The April
7 issue of the *Austin American-Statesman* quoted him as
saying, "It is one of several cars we have been told to look
at." The newspaper further reported that Martin had discounted any connection between the Northrup and Reed
cases.[25]

The ATF search recovered no evidence of a gun. But

from the moment she saw it Sonya Urubek felt that the Thunderbird was used in the abduction of Colleen Reed. She felt something else that she admits she cannot explain. When she arrived, and as the garage door first opened, she felt as if Kenneth McDuff was there with his car. She and Don went to the McLennan County Sheriff's Office where they were allowed to look over items that had been removed from the car during the original inventory by Larry Abner. A piece of notebook paper caught their attention. It was a map with directions to a home in Del Valle, a suburb south of Austin. Kenneth McDuff had been in the Austin area, and it appeared that he had visited someone named Beverly. There was also a business card; it belonged to H. Copitka and Associates, parole consultants.[26] As they motored home, Don Martin and Sonya Urubek both knew they had things to do and people to find.

V

On March 8, Addie called Tim Steglich. "There's really no hope for me. He would have seen his parole officer and he would have taken his test," pleaded Addie McDuff over the phone as she continued to insist to Tim that Kenneth was dead. The mind games continued. Addie made clear that Gloria Jackson of Justice for McDuff, Inc. had contacted her, but she was never very clear as to why the contact was made. "Did you ever get in touch with Mrs. Jackson?" Addie asked. "She's been trying to crowd him out," she added. Addie seemed very concerned that Gloria Jackson's business card had been found in a car in Dallas. In fact, no such thing had happened. Addie continued: "You haven't heard nothing about Kenneth—his car or nothing?"[27] Tim hung up the phone and decided that it was time to revisit the McDuffs.

On March 11, Tim made his second visit. Addie still insisted that Kenneth was dead. She again allowed a search of her residence. Tim found it odd that there were two pairs of binoculars on the dining room table in the front of a bay window facing the main entrance of the property. Addie readily admitted that one of them belonged to Kenneth. In the garage, Tim saw the GMC pickup truck with a new windshield, and this time it meant something to him. Addie repeated to Tim that J. A. had lent Kenneth the truck, only to have Kenneth return it with a shattered windshield and without the camper that used to be on the back.

Tim asked her if Kenneth had ever had a girlfriend or if she had ever seen him with a woman. Addie stated that he had once brought a girl to her house. She was a short blonde who claimed to be a TSTI student taking computer classes. (Addie is almost certainly describing Linda, McDuff's sometime companion and a long-haul truck driver. On the same day Linda met Addie, she had described herself to someone else as a "titty dancer.") When Tim asked Addie if the woman's name could have been "Melissa," Addie showed no emotion and said it could not have been.

As he drove out of the long driveway connecting the McDuff residence to Cedar Creek Road, Tim had a feeling, however unscientific, that McDuff had been there. He knew enough about McDuff to know that "if he was there he'd kill me." During that visit Tim did his best to keep his back to the wall. After briefing his supervisor, Bill Miller—an experienced investigator who knew of the McDuffs and had predicted trouble the moment he heard McDuff had been paroled—Tim accepted Miller's clear instructions not to go back to that house alone.[28]

The bad boy from Rosebud: the first known mug shot of Kenneth Allen McDuff, after he was arrested on fourteen counts of burglary in 1965. He was nineteen. *TEXAS DEPARTMENT OF CRIMINAL JUSTICE.*

McDuff, age twenty-two. The first mug shot from Death Row.
TEXAS DEPARTMENT OF CRIMINAL JUSTICE.

Victims of the Broomstick Murders: Kenneth McDuff's first known victims were three teenagers he kidnapped from a baseball field near the Everman High School campus in Texas. He was sentenced to death in 1966 but was paroled in 1989. *COURTESY JACK BRAND.*

Charles Butts, circa 1966, the lone surviving member of the Tarrant County prosecution team that convicted Kenneth McDuff for the Broomstick Murders. Butts returned to court in 1993 and 1994 to testify during the punishment phases of the Northrup and Reed trials. *CHARLES BUTTS.*

McDuff walked free in 1989, but in 1990 he was returned to prison for making a terrorist threat. He was released two months later.

TEXAS DEPARTMENT OF CRIMINAL JUSTICE.

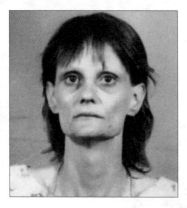

Brenda Thompson was abducted and murdered by McDuff on October 10, 1991. During her abduction, McDuff ran a Waco Police Department roadblock. An officer observed that Thompson appeared to be bound as she desperately tried to kick out the windshield of McDuff's truck.
WACO POLICE DEPARTMENT.

Regenia Moore was abducted and murdered less than a week after Thompson's murder.
WACO POLICE DEPARTMENT.

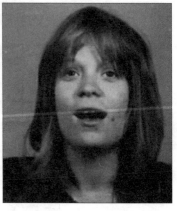

Valencia Kay Joshua was last seen knocking on the window of McDuff's dorm room on the Texas State Technical Institute campus. Her body was discovered partially buried in a heavily wooded area.
McCLENNAN COUNTY SHERIFF'S DEPARTMENT.

Only minutes before she was abducted, tortured and murdered by Kenneth McDuff, Colleen Reed stopped by a bank teller machine to deposit a Christmas present she had received from her father.

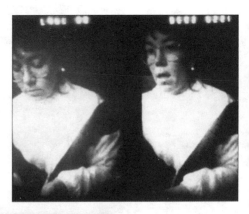

When bystanders arrived at the car wash after hearing Colleen's screams, they found her car had been abandoned. When police arrived, suds were still dripping off the car.

ROBBERY/KIDNAPPING
Victim

Melissa Ann Northrup

New Road Inn

McDuff's Car

New Road

Interstate 35

Quik Pak Store

Early during the morning of March 1, 1992, Kenneth McDuff's car broke down near the New Road Inn. McDuff pushed the car into the parking lot, abandoned it, and walked to the convenience store where Melissa Northrup was working the graveyard shift alone.

Left to right—Austin Police Detective J.W. Thompson, ATF Special Agent Chuck Meyer, and Texas Department of Criminal Justice Investigator John Moriarty played major roles in bringing McDuff to justice. *GARY LAVERGNE.*

Left to right—The McClennan County Prosecution Team. First Assistant D.A. Crawford Long, D.A. John Segrest, and Assistant D.A. Mike Freeman. *MIKE FREEMAN.*

The Travis County Prosecution Team. Assistant D.A. Buddy Meyer (*left*) and Assistant D.A. David Counts (*right*). *GARY LAVERGNE.*

McDuff listens quietly as a Waco judge pronounces the sentence of death for the murder of Melissa Northrup. Seated directly behind McDuff are Brenda and Richard Solomon, Northrup's mother and step-father. *CRAWFORD LONG*

14

"Don't Hurt Junior"

"Junior ain't never done anything wrong in all his life."
—Addie McDuff

I

Two years after Sonya Urubek became part of the Reed Case, she testified about the different methods used by investigators in approaching the abduction. Specifically, Don Martin methodically checked out the many leads received, placing no particular emphasis on any one. Sonya was so convinced that the McDuff lead was a good one that she thought it was important to begin gathering evidence from Colleen's possessions. Those possessions were in large plastic bags in Lori's attic. Lori took great care of Colleen's things, still hoping to one day return them to her younger sister. The plastic garbage bags had the effect of sealing and preserving the evidence, making it much easier to collect things like hair samples, and greatly reducing the chance of contamination. Sonya also asked Oliver (Colleen's boyfriend) to visit APD headquarters, where he volunteered personal evidence for comparison for what would be found on Colleen's clothes—and possibly her remains, if they should ever be found. Shortly after the abduction, Oliver went to the store where he bought the windbreaker he had given to Colleen—the one she was pictured wearing at the ATM. He tried to buy an identical suit, but could only find one that was nearly identical. The store insisted on giving it to him.[1]

II

Someone helped Kenneth Allen McDuff get out of the southeastern corner of Dallas County, and out of Texas altogether. He had to have help to get from the gravel pits to Dallas, and much more to get where he ended up. Whoever aided his flight has escaped justice—to this day.

What is known is that on March 10 McDuff stayed at a Salvation Army shelter in Tulsa, Oklahoma, under the name of Richard Dale Fowler. He had in his possession a tattered Social Security card with that name on it. How he got that is a mystery, too. The real Richard Dale Fowler was from Louisiana. In an interview with the ATF, Fowler remembered last seeing the card when he went to a pool hall and left the card with an attendant to check out a cue stick.[2]

On March 15, at about 6:00 P.M., McDuff walked into the Kansas City Rescue Mission in Kansas City, Missouri. The shelter had sixty bunks in a dorm for homeless men. The men there had to turn in their cigarettes, knives, and cassette players, and were required to take a breathalyzer test to be admitted. McDuff signed in as Richard Fowler. As if to tempt fate, he indicated that the next of kin was his father, Robert R. Fowler, of Belton, Texas. He stayed at the shelter from the 15th through the 18th free of charge. From the 19th through the 26th, he paid fees for his lodging and meals. At the mission the men were entitled to five free nights. Afterwards, they were charged $1.00 per night, or they could join a work detail for their sustenance. On March 19, McDuff purchased a pre-paid card, which was used in the shelter as cash. On that day, he started working for Dixie Temporaries and was assigned to the Longview Trash Disposal Systems, a garbage collection service. He worked as a garbage man for $190 a week. For the next few weeks, he never missed a day of work and was always on time. But he also applied the lessons he had learned on how to live off the public. Only one day after arriving at the shelter, he applied for food stamps.[3]

By March 25, McDuff acquired a flat at the Clyde Manor Apartments in Kansas City; he spent his first night there on March 27. In a few days, McDuff met a fellow sanitation worker named Francis. At 6'4" tall, weighing about 220 pounds, Francis was just as large as McDuff. The two men got along well enough to share McDuff's one-bedroom apartment and split the rent ($52 payable weekly) in order to save money.

McDuff lived in the apartment for three days before electricity was hooked up. The landlord remembered the day McDuff, using the name Richard Fowler, moved in. "He came up. He wasn't anxious. You know, a lot of times people come in and the hair goes up on the back of your neck and you think of some way to turn down their application. He wasn't that way." The manager continued, "When he moved in, he brought a couple of trash bags full of clothes. He didn't have much else because we furnished the apartment. And after that, we never really heard a peep out of the man. We had no complaints from neighbors. He went to work early, came home late and didn't socialize with any of the people in the building."[4]

But of course, McDuff could not bring himself to stay away from whatever subculture Kansas City had to offer. On April 10, he was arrested during a KCPD prostitution sting. He had solicited sex from an undercover policewoman and was brought down to police headquarters, printed, and booked under the name of Richard Fowler. The misdemeanor did not result in a criminal background check or fingerprint search. "Richard Fowler" was released. His juvenile sense of invulnerability must have resurfaced. The incident did not seem to faze McDuff, who made no effort to leave his apartment or Kansas City. The apartment manager described him as someone who came to the apartment every morning with a twelve-pack of beer and a mobile phone (which no one ever saw him use). A female tenant stated that once, while she was using a pay phone, McDuff approached her and that she became frightened, not by anything he said to her, but by the way he was acting. When interviewed by an ATF agent, she was never more specific.[5]

McDuff's conversations with Francis were similar to those of his discourses with Alva Hank Worley: They "talked shit." Francis stated that McDuff was into crack, but he said he never actually saw McDuff smoking it. He based his conclusion on the frequency with which McDuff associated with black crack dealers. According to Francis, McDuff spent his entire paycheck on drugs. He also remembered how McDuff slept with a butcher knife next to him at night; McDuff said he needed it for protection. Soon, their conversations turned to getting a gun for McDuff to commit robberies. Francis claims to have made clear to McDuff that he did not want anything to do with guns—he was on parole. McDuff gleefully replied that he, too, was on parole, and lucky to be out. Like he had done for Louis in Sabine Hall, McDuff placed a ski mask over his head to demonstrate how he planned to disguise himself for the crime.

That was not the only part of his past that McDuff shared with Francis. After a few beers, McDuff bragged about how good he was at killing with his bare hands. He spoke also of using a knife to kill. Francis claims to have thought that McDuff was talking about prison life, or maybe it was just liquor talking.[6]

III

Mike, Parnell, and Bill had searched for victims over large tracts of land long enough. They decided that it was time to look for McDuff. Parnell first called Tim Steglich on March 9. It was then that Tim briefed him on the status of the missing person case and his dealings with Addie. On March 17, The Boys visited Tim in Belton. Tim told them that he had already been to the McDuff house and had noticed items that led him to believe that McDuff had been there. He told them about the binoculars and a pair of boots that Addie said belonged to Kenneth. Those items were not in those places during Tim's first visit.[7]

On March 18, Mike and Parnell met Tim at the Holiday Inn in Temple. Tim showed them where Addie and J. A. McDuff lived. They parked in an area south of the house and observed for nearly three hours. They saw nothing of consequence. At about 9:00 P.M., they returned to Tim's office. Tim tried to return phone calls Addie had placed for him during the day, but there was no answer. (They later learned that Addie and J. A. had early bedtimes and turned off the phone's ringer at night.) In yet another demonstration of their irreverence for time, and sheer stubbornness, Mike and Parnell returned to keep an eye on the McDuff residence and stayed there until 1:30 the next morning.[8]

The information that Tim was able to give Mike and Parnell, however, became the basis for a fugitive warrant issued by a federal magistrate. The warrant authorizing the search of the McDuff home and property was executed the next day, March 19, 1992.

At 1:00 P.M., Mike, Parnell, Tim, Bill Miller, Bill Johnston, and ATF agents Wayne Appelt and Jeff Brzozowski descended on the McDuff homestead. They were joined by a Temple detective named Don "Mad Dog" Owens. Don Owens is cool, and moves like a cat. Parnell vividly remembers the first time he ever worked with Owens. Together they entered a store where credit card crimes were being committed. As Parnell had a suspect pinned against the store's counter, he saw a gun barrel go by his head, only to be pressed against the side of the suspect's head. "He screws his gun into this guy's ear. That really impressed me. I had never done that myself; since then I have," Parnell said with a sly smile. Mad Dog knows every thug in Temple, and they are all afraid of him. "It is like he wears war paint that every other tribe is afraid of," said Bill Johnston.[9]

The team that assembled to search the McDuff residence, however, had a more immediate problem to deal

with. The McDuffs had two very large Rottweiler dogs in
the back yard. They had been warned that the huge dogs
could kill intruders. Kenneth himself had once said that the
dogs were extremely dangerous. Even though they were
penned, the chain-link fence was only about four feet tall,
and the dogs could conceivably jump it if excited enough.
It is legal to kill such animals if they interfere with the
execution of a warrant, so when the officers arrived Mike
and Parnell observed that the dogs were viciously growling
and trying to bite through the fence to get at the officers,
Mike was "assigned" to take care of the dogs.

He walked over to their four-wheel drive Suburban and
selected his weapon of choice. Coolly and methodically, he
walked up to the dogs, who seemed to welcome his approach. Mike raised his arm to an upright position and fired,
hitting the dogs right between the eyes. He used "bear-
guard," a mace used by the park service as a defense against
bear attacks. Immediately, the dogs made a hasty retreat.
"They looked like fish out of water, flopping along a bank,"
remembered Mike. Parnell remembers how the dogs cut
flips and urinated on one another. At the back of the pen,
they fought one another in desperate attempts to dive into
a single, five-gallon bucket of water. For the rest of the
afternoon, the dogs watched Mike carefully, and stayed as
far away from him as their pen would allow. "It was almost
distracting to watch the dogs," Mike remembered. Like
McDuff, the dogs probably never appreciated how lucky
they were. As Mike pointed out, if they had ever gotten out
of the pen they would have been shot.[10]

At first, no one was home, but after a few minutes a car
drove up. Out ran Addie shouting, "Don't hurt Junior!
Don't hurt Junior!" For the first time in a long while, Addie
had little or no control over her household. Tim always
marveled at how she ran her home and everyone in it. He
noticed she always answered the door and the phone, and
always did the talking. John Moriarty, a TDCJ Investigator
and a man with vast experiences dealing with ex-cons and
their families, later stated that he had never seen a parent.

man or woman, so completely dominate a household.[11]

"Junior ain't never hurt nobody . . . the po'lice is always pickin' on Junior and trying to frame 'im and I wisht they'd just leave him alone," insisted Addie as she grabbed Parnell's shirt.

"Don't you think he has ever done *anything* wrong?" asked Parnell.

"No! Junior ain't never hurt nobody."

Inside, some of the investigators maneuvered J. A. to an area where Addie could not interfere. Soon she arrived to tell J. A. to "shut up."

"Well, Mama . . ." tried J. A.

"Shut up!" commanded Addie.

A little while later, J. A. feebly walked over to the back window. He gazed outside and looked confused. "Addie! Addie! Something's wrong with them dogs!"[12]

The experienced lawmen easily saw that Addie could not remain focused on the search and control J. A. at the same time. Tim remembers that she was so totally engrossed with the search that she never noticed that he was even there. Within days she spoke to him about the search as if she was describing something he had not seen for himself. J. A. walked slowly over to his car. He opened the door and sat. Parnell walked over to the old man. "You could tell he was fed up with the whole thing—he had been lied to and was tired," remembered Parnell.

"If you find him, you can kill him if you want to," said J. A. Resigned, the old man authorized the search of his truck. He confirmed that it was the truck that Kenneth used when he went to TSTI and was the one returned with a broken windshield. When asked if he ever asked Kenneth how the windshield got so badly broken, he said he did not because he would not have believed Kenneth's answer anyway. Mike noticed a dent on the side of the truck; he asked J. A. about that, too. "If you'd have asked him, he wouldn't have told you . . . and if he did you couldn't believe him . . . and right down to the bottom of it, I wasn't liking it very much."

Mike found two folded maps. One was of the state of Texas; the other was a city map folded to reveal a section of Austin. Lines traced roads leading to a destination near the corner of Anderson Lane and the MoPac Expressway. J. A. said the maps were not his, so they must be Kenneth's. He gave the maps to Mike.

Before Addie could regain control over J. A., the old man, as if to issue an invitation, said, "If Kenneth done what you said he done, if you find him, you ought to just go ahead and shoot him."[13]

The house seemed empty of love and tenderness common among families. Mike marveled at how a thorough search of the entire house revealed no family pictures. The men left the McDuff home at about 3:30 P.M. They regrouped at Tim's office at the Bell County Sheriff's Department.

IV

Shortly before the search of the McDuff house, Bill, Mike, and Parnell had contacted Texas Ranger John Aycock and requested more information on McDuff. They also asked Mad Dog Owens of Temple PD for whatever information he had. After the search, Tim received information that McDuff had been arrested in Temple on February 25 for public intoxication. The arrest records showed that two men, Buddy and Billy, were arrested with him. A quick background check showed Billy to have a long criminal record from 1972 to the present. Additionally, Ranger John Aycock discovered that Billy was on a probated sentence for DWI and was supposed to be doing work on the weekends, but he had not shown up for a period of two months. A young boy, believed to be Billy's son, had been delivering medical excuses showing Billy to be in the care of a physician in Galveston. This led to an outstanding warrant for his arrest for failing to appear on a misdemeanor charge. With a ready-made warrant in hand, the lawmen were able to immediately track down Billy.[14] Surely, seldom has a "failure to appear" warrant attracted such a large number of high-powered lawmen.

It did not take Tim long to locate an address for Billy; he lived on the 400 block of Boyles Street in Belton, only a few blocks from Tim's office. In minutes, Tim, Mike, Parnell, Bill, Wayne Appelt, and Jeff Brzozowski drove up to the small, white, wooden house. The neighborhood was not overrun with drugs, but it was poor and unkempt. The ditches were nearly filled with trash, and front yards looked like salvage dumps.

Bill and Mike decided to wait outside in Bigfoot while the others went into the house. Billy was not home. His wife Janice answered the door. She had been married before, and one of her ex-husbands had been Alva Hank Worley. She invited the officers into her home and was very cooperative, even after they told her that there was a warrant for Billy's arrest. She said that Billy was probably drinking at Poor Boy's Lounge, but he might be at the home of a friend named Benton. Benton's house on Eleventh Street was very near Poor Boy's. Billy, she said, would be driving her white pickup truck. (At the time, Janice was not very happy with Billy, who had the annoying habit of taking her truck from her place of employment while she was at work so he could go drinking. This often left her stranded. The habit was all the more selfish since Billy never seriously searched for a job.)

During the interview, Janice volunteered that she thought McDuff was crazy and she did not like him. When they asked her if she had ever seen McDuff with anyone else, Janice replied that Mac often ran with her ex-husband, Alva Hank Worley. She told the officers that Hank was living at Bloom's Motel, on Interstate 35 just south of Belton. She added that their fourteen-year-old daughter lived with him. When asked if Hank could be counted on to cooperate, Janice said that Hank was not mean, but that he could be counted on to lie; Hank had been taught to lie all of his life, she said. The interview ended with Janice saying that she feared for her and her children's safety. The men replied that she had a right to be scared, and consequently if she ever found out where McDuff might be, she should call the police immediately.[15]

As eventful as the interview inside of the house was the "show" outside—a display of the subculture the men would deal with for the next few weeks. Inside Bigfoot, Mike and Bill passed the time by observing the neighborhood. They saw two women in a car filled with children slowly drive by. As the driver neared her house, a young boy, about eight years old, hopped on the back of her car, intent to get a "ride." Instead of slowing down and being more careful, the mother jerked the car forward, spewing dirt and gravel behind her car and sending the little boy flying off the back. She laughed uncontrollably when she saw the boy tumbling down the gravel road. The boy staggered around the road for a few seconds, brushed himself off and wandered away. "The kid kind of limped off like you would kick a dog," remembered Parnell. The two women continued to laugh as they parked their car. As one of the children inside the car, a six- or seven-year-old girl, tried to get out, one of the women intentionally slammed the door on her head, sending her reeling back into the back seat. The woman thought that was funny too. Eventually, the little girl got out of the car and followed the others into the house. She walked through the door holding her head with both hands.[16]

Only moments later, Bill leaned forward and said, "What *is* that?" From the front porch of Janice's house Wayne Appelt saw the same thing.

After straining to see, Mike said, "That's a chicken."

On the front porch of the house directly across the street, a chicken sat on a perch. "You could see this motion. It looked like a bowling ball on a pendulum," remembered Bill. The chicken swayed and flared, but the really interesting show was the boy directly in front of the chicken doing exactly the same thing. The twosome looked like Groucho and Harpo Marx's famous "mirror" skit. Wayne thought that the boy was worshipping the chicken. Right about that time a cute little girl, about eight years old, walked up to Bigfoot as if to marvel at the size of the vehicle. "Hi, Honey, how are you doing?" asked Mike.

"Fine," said the little girl.

"Is that a chicken on that swing?"

"Uh, huh."

"Tell me, did the boy teach the chicken to do that, or did the chicken teach the boy to do that?" asked Mike.

"Well, the chicken must have taught him cause the chicken was doing it first."[17]

V

After leaving Janice, the men agreed to meet at Bobby's Hamburgers near Interstate 35 in Belton. While eating and discussing what to do next, the group agreed that Billy was a worthless louse because he made no attempts to support his family. They could not understand how anyone could be so selfish. What particularly galled the men was how Billy would take Janice's truck and leave her stranded at work so he could go out drinking while she supported him. All of a sudden Wayne Appelt broke the tension. "Billy couldn't live on Boyles Street and have a job or his friends would make fun of him." The men began to laugh. Then Wayne started talking like a teasing little girl. "Billy's got a job! Billy's got a job!" They laughed harder, providing much-needed therapy. They were heading for Benton's house and the Poor Boy's Lounge in search of Billy, and they knew no one would be laughing over there.[18]

Quite a posse had assembled. There were two Deputy U.S. Marshals, an Assistant U.S. Attorney, the head of Bell County's Criminal Investigations and one of his investigators, and two ATF agents. Soon, Mad Dog Don Owens of the Temple Police Department arrived. The group split up; one watched Poor Boy's Lounge, and the other watched Benton's house. The men could see Janice's white pickup truck parked in front of the white house, but that did not mean Billy was inside. They waited for quite a while until, finally, Billy walked past the front porch and started his truck. Just like Janice had promised, he headed for Poor Boy's only a couple of blocks away.

At the parking lot of Poor Boy's, Tim waved Billy over. Before Mike could bring Bigfoot to a complete stop, Parnell hopped out and ran for the white truck. He had a pistol in his right hand, and with his left he opened the door and grabbed Billy. Parnell then whirled Billy around the door and slammed him onto the hood of the truck. Billy did not fight, but he was not compliant either. Parnell screwed the barrel of his pistol into Billy's left ear. Moving from the right, like a cat, Mad Dog Owens removed his gun from a shoulder holster and screwed his pistol into Billy's right ear. In a tone known throughout the Temple underworld, Mad Dog admonished Billy, "If you fuck up, you gonna die in stereo!" Billy became compliant.[19]

Don, Parnell, and some of the other officers tried to talk to Billy using the native language of the subculture. It did not appear to be working; Billy seemed to relish being called foul things. It might have even enhanced his stature with the bar patrons watching the drama. In a move wholly uncharacteristic of him, Bill Johnston, a man who never curses and is always a gentleman, put his large face nose-to-nose with Billy. "You're a jerk! And your family's nothing but a bunch of scumbags, and I'm gonna put you in prison!" (Not even Billy and a hunt for Kenneth Allen McDuff could get Bill to curse.) Bill surprised his fellow officers as much as he did Billy. "Bill never talks like that," thought Tim Steglich. Anyway, Bill reminded Billy of outstanding cases involving sawed-off shotguns in which Billy was a suspect. "I am the one who is working that case!" Bill said. Parnell and Mad Dog got Billy to be compliant, but Bill got his attention.[20]

As Mike searched and handcuffed Billy, patrons in Poor Boy's began congregating inside near the door. Many of them recognized that the "feds" were arresting Billy, and wondered what he could have done to get this much attention. Surely, it was not because he had missed a work detail. One of the men asked Parnell what was going on. Several eyebrows moved upward when Parnell answered, "Child support."[21]

A Bell County deputy came over and took Billy to the jail where he was booked on outstanding warrants. At Poor Boy's, the officers remembered Janice. It dawned on them that if her white pickup was towed she might not have the money to retrieve it to go to work. They called her to pick up her truck.[22]

Near Tim's office, in the Criminal Investigations Division of the Bell County Sheriff's Office, most of the posse awaited Billy, who at first claimed to know nothing about McDuff. He was quickly told he was lying. Then the officers educated him about the Broomstick Murders of 1966. As Billy listened to the gruesome details, he slowly lowered his head and said he knew McDuff in prison, but had no idea that he had been there for killing kids. The officers reminded him that he had a wife and kids and that McDuff probably knew Billy would be in jail for the foreseeable future. Knowing they were on to something, the officers repeated the story. The Broomstick Murders seemed to matter to Billy.[23]

He insisted that he did not even like McDuff, that he was crazy and always wanted to fight someone and rob them. McDuff spoke constantly of robbing crack dealers. Billy told them how McDuff got the cut under his eye, and how he and McDuff nearly got into a fight over McDuff's treatment of Debbie. He also told them about how McDuff took an old man's bottle of whiskey, and nearly got into a fight with Jimmy. The officers wanted to know the names of everyone McDuff knew and hung around with. The first name Billy gave them was the ex-husband of his wife Janice—Alva Hank Worley.[24]

Billy admitted that he and Janice had gone to a convenience store (not the Quik Pak) to pick up Hank and McDuff and tow a Thunderbird. Billy admitted fixing

McDuff's car and that Janice should still have the receipt for the parts. He did not know it, but he provided officers with proof that McDuff was in possession of a Thunderbird during the Thanksgiving holidays of 1991.

Billy also told them that Hank lived at Bloom's Motel with his and Janice's fourteen-year-old daughter. According to Billy, he had thrown his step-daughter out of his house because she kept cussing out her mother.[25]

The Boys wanted to talk to Hank—badly. After finishing with Billy, Mike, Parnell, Bill, Wayne, and Jeff hit the road. Bill had always believed that "if you work harder than a criminal, eventually you are going to catch him."

Each of the men had families going to sleep at that very moment. They thought about their wives and children and how they had been left alone. But there was also a sense of urgency. For the next few weeks, every time darkness fell over Central Texas, they wondered if McDuff was killing another young woman. They left the Bell County Sheriff's Office looking for Alva Hank Worley.

Even for men who never wear watches and have no reverence for time, they had no idea that their evening was just beginning.

15

Searching for a Monster

"It was like playing Scrabble with a chimpanzee."
—Bill Johnston

I

ATF Special Agent Charles Meyer is a tall, lean man with an angular face and sleek, Clint Eastwood eyes. He is as good an interrogator as anyone who has ever questioned a suspect. He is so good in fact, that a frustrated Austin defense attorney once lamented in open court that "Chuck Meyer always seemed to be there when somebody needed a little interrogating."[1]

A native of San Antonio, Chuck flew helicopters for the Army in Vietnam. After earning a degree in management and marketing, he was drawn to law enforcement. He looked into different agencies and chose the ATF for a career. Chuck Meyer is an intensely disciplined investigator. It is hard to imagine him being flustered or losing his cool. He likes to work quietly. Not only does he dislike publicity of any type, he actively avoids it. Although he has been involved in some of the highest-profile cases in recent Texas history, a search through the archives of the *Austin American-Statesman* reveals a single, three-word Chuck Meyer quote: "We did great."[2]

In mid-March the ATF's initial lead investigator in the cases involving McDuff—Wayne Appelt—was temporarily relocated to El Paso to run the ATF office there. Chuck replaced him as the ATF point man in Austin. In an unrelated drug case, he had already heard of Kenneth McDuff. Chuck was already sensitive to crimes against women. At the time he was also a member of the Yogurt Shop Task Force.[3]

At the Austin Police Department another detective, Joseph Wayne "J. W." Thompson, began to get more involved in the Colleen Reed Case. At the time, he shared a cubicle with Sonya Urubek, and she often discussed elements of the case with him. Sonya suggested to the captain of the Assault Unit that J. W. would make a great addition to the Reed Case.

J. W. had grown up in the Big Thicket in a small town called Sour Lake near Beaumont, Texas. He graduated from MacArthur High School in San Antonio. Like Chuck, he is a Vietnam Veteran, but J. W. was on the ground with the U.S. Marines. He smiles and shakes his head when Chuck grins and says, "I flew over J. W." He is a patient, methodical, steady detective with little in the way of a professional ego. As the McDuff case grew, with more and more jurisdictions required to work and get along with one another, J. W. blended in with the McDuff posse quite well. He never tries to impress anyone; he does his job and is just as averse to publicity as his good friend Chuck Meyer. He, too, has been involved in some of Central Texas's most high-profile crimes. He will discuss them in public only if he is in a courtroom and under oath. Otherwise, it is "no comment."

II

While Tim Steglich stayed behind to continue talking to Billy, Mike and Parnell McNamara, Bill Johnston, Jeff Brzozowski, Wayne Appelt, Bill Miller, and Mad Dog Owens headed for Bloom's Motel, a crumbling, down-and-out motel just south of Belton along Interstate Highway 35. Wayne Appelt remembered how cold it was that night—it was freezing. He was shocked to see Hank dressed in cutoff blue jeans only: no shirt, no socks, and no shoes.

Hank claimed that he did not know McDuff. This re-

sponse reinforced what Janice had told the officers earlier
during the day; Hank is a liar and was taught to lie all his
life. They told him they knew he was lying, that they knew
he knew McDuff, and that it was a serious offense to give
false information to federal officers. "Look, I don't know
nothing about that man. I just met him one time with Billy
and I don't know nothing about that man." That was his
second lie. Finally he denied ever having worked on
McDuff's Thunderbird. That was his third lie. The men
zeroed in on Hank and reminded him again how serious it
was to lie to federal officers.

Then Mike asked Hank, "Do you know who you are
holding out for—a kid killer!" For the next few minutes,
Hank listened to how McDuff had brutally and sadistically
murdered three teenagers in 1966. The tactic, exposing
McDuff as a kid killer, worked on some of the sorriest
criminals The Boys had ever encountered; it got most of
them to talk. Only a few minutes earlier that same evening,
the tactic had worked beautifully on Billy. But in the parking lot outside of Room #5 of Bloom's Motel, when the
men finished the story, Hank Worley looked up with a
blank stare, a look of complete indifference.

"You have a daughter in that room, Hank. Think about
what McDuff would do to her," Mike pounded. "Think
about who you're holding out for, Hank," Mike said as the
men got back into their vehicles, leaving Hank Worley to
stew in his own cowardice and guilt.

If Hank thought his stoic, straight face led the investigators to conclude he had no knowledge of Kenneth
McDuff or his activities, he was sorely mistaken. The men
drove away convinced that Hank was holding out. "He
knows something. He knows a whole lot and he's not telling us," Mike told Parnell. The Boys agreed to continue
talking to Worley—whether he liked it or not.[4]

They also decided that Billy had to know more than
what he said earlier in the evening, and so they returned to
the Bell County Sheriff's Office. This time Billy told them

that McDuff hung around bars called "H&H," "He Ain't Here," and "Poor Boy's." Of more value was another name: someone else to look for. Billy told them he had introduced McDuff to a woman named Sandy, a known drug dealer in a little town between Belton and Killeen called Harker Heights. Billy did not know much else about her other than her habit of hanging out in a beer joint called Dundee's. After returning Billy to jail, Mike, Parnell, Bill, Jeff and Wayne set out for Harker Heights.[5] Dundee's was located in an area lined with smelly bars, strip clubs, and tattoo parlors. The men encountered a formidable barmaid named Nell, who told them that Sandy lived in a pink, double-wide trailer across from Highway 190. She also said Sandy drove a "sharp-looking" maroon pickup truck.

They went to the trailer but could not find her. At the time, it looked like the men would be barhopping late into the evening. After checking out a number of beer joints, they noticed a nice pickup truck in the parking lot of a place called Harv's. They approached the truck and found Sandy.

She had her child with her and was on her way to her mother's house. When she asked the men standing around her truck what this was all about, they told her that they were looking for a man named Kenneth Allen McDuff. "I don't know him," Sandy said. As each of the men took turns trying to refresh her memory, the young woman grew more insistent that she did not know who they were talking about. She was different from Hank and Billy; it looked like she was telling the truth. Even after they told her that Billy had already admitted to introducing her to him, she denied knowing anyone named Kenneth McDuff. "Are you sure?" said Mike.

"Yes," replied an exasperated Sandy.

"Hold on," said Mike.

Many other detectives would have given up and gone home; Mike decided to try one more thing. He walked over to Bigfoot and retrieved a picture of Kenneth McDuff.

"Do you know this man?" he asked.

"Oh! That's Max," Sandy said.

She followed that with a question that made an already frigid night even colder for each of the men. "Does this have to do with the girl that's missing in Austin?"[6]

They followed Sandy to her parents' home where she dropped off her child. Sandy's father approached the officers demanding to know what was going on. They showed him their badges and calmed him down by explaining the situation and telling him about Kenneth McDuff and what kind of man he was. Sandy agreed to meet them at her pink doublewide.

She promised to help in any way she could, but she was so nervous she shook. It got even worse when they pointed out to her that her size and slender figure matched the physique of McDuff's victims. "He was here," she kept saying, quickly appreciating the fact that she was still alive. At times she talked so fast, they had to tell her to slow down.

"Why did you say what you said about the missing girl in Austin?" asked one of the men. For what seemed like an eternity, she lamented, "Not Jack, he wouldn't do that."

"Who?" asked Bill.

"Jack is a nice man; he wouldn't do that," Sandy insisted.

Each of the officers sighed; the long night was getting longer, and deciphering Sandy's disjointed, stammering language was going to take a while. Finally, someone said, "One-eyed Jack?"

"Yea," Sandy replied.

After that laborious breakthrough, confirming that she was, indeed, talking about Jackie, the One-eyed Jack, was fairly easy. There aren't that many hideous looking 250-pound men completely covered with tattoos. Bill and the McNamara Boys knew Jackie from past cases involving theft from Fort Hood in Killeen.

"Not Jack, he wouldn't do that. Jack is a nice guy," Sandy insisted, as she sucked violently on one cigarette after another. She was also upset with Billy, who must have known about "Max's" past when he introduced her to him.

She said Max was crazy and always talking about robbing someone. She related a conversation she had with Jackie where he said he saw in the news that a Thunderbird was used to kidnap a girl from a car wash in Austin. The description of that car matched the car Max used on Christmas Day. He also told her that Max often drove the wrong way on one-way streets, just like the men who took the girl. Jackie told her this on the phone, Sandy said, and he told her not to spend any time around Max.

When the officers asked her where they could find Jackie, she claimed not to know. It was Sandy's first lie. She admitted only to knowing that Jackie had run from an Austin halfway house after taking a drug test he knew he would fail. He knew that there would be a warrant for him soon.[7]

Since The Boys did not get back to Waco until nearly 2:00 A.M., it was later in the same day that Bill determined that Jackie had, indeed, run away from a halfway house. He called a probation officer.

"Do we still have Jackie on supervision?" Bill asked.

"Uh, we did," said the probation officer.

"What do you mean we did?"

"Uh, he ran off from a halfway house."

"Do we have a warrant?" Bill asked.

"Uh, we'll get one."

"Well, how about getting one today?" said an exasperated Bill.

Before long, Bill had his warrant. But they still did not know where Jackie might be. Tim Steglich called and reported that he had information that Jackie had previously been seen at the home of a woman currently incarcerated in the Bell County Jail. When they visited her, she confirmed that she knew Jackie, and that they supplied one another with cocaine "so that they could all get high." Jackie, she said, was living in Austin, but he ran off to Dallas, where he currently resided with a man named Steve.[8]

Steve owned a construction company and Jackie worked

for him. Steve was one of two brothers with a very bad reputation in Dallas circles. Reportedly, Steve's brother once saw a man leisurely walking his dog on a leash—he shot the dog. The pair had also been linked to drive-by shootings in Dallas's Oak Cliff section. The Boys thought it was a good idea to make another visit to Sandy.

When confronted with what they knew about Steve, Sandy admitted that she knew where Jackie was. He was in Dallas at Steve's house. "Where in Dallas?" they asked. She could not remember the name of the street. Desperate for more information, Mike, Parnell, and Bill retrieved a Dallas city map and tried to jar her memory by asking her if the name of the street started with an "A"—then a "B," and so on. Bill vividly remembers the frustration: "It was like playing Scrabble with a chimpanzee." After a long, agonizing process, she remembered that the house was on Quinella Street near Grand Prairie. Very reluctantly, Sandy paged Steve. She told him that she needed to talk to Jack and that it was urgent. Soon, Jackie called and when she said she needed to talk to him very badly, he said he would return to Harker Heights the next day.[9]

The Boys never considered waiting. Parnell got on the phone and got authorization from Cliff Hoffman, his immediate supervisor, and Sam Williams of the Marshal's Service to go to Dallas and arrest Jackie. Then he called Deputy U.S. Marshal Larry Gunn of Dallas to coordinate the arrest. The Dallas Police Department knew exactly where Steve and his gang lived. The area was a known drug-infested neighborhood. The Dallas PD patrol sergeant on the scene immediately advised the posse that a SWAT team would be necessary. When Parnell told the sergeant that they had plenty of guns the officer replied: "If Dallas PD is going to be involved we will have to use the SWAT team because patrolmen are not trained for that type of raid." At 12:30 A.M. on March 21, the five-member team, closely followed by everyone but Bill, stormed Steve's home.

Wayne Appelt was mightily impressed with the SWAT

Team. Using it was a bright move. A fight broke out and several of the occupants had the tar beat out of them before they surrendered. One fool insisted on holding on to a 30-30 rifle. He let go only after repeated hits in the face with the butt of a SWAT member's rifle. "Where da mudder-fucker dat hit me in da moute?" asked the man, spewing blood and teeth as he spoke.

Every occupant was brought outside and made to lie face down in the grass. Jackie, an old-time con, knew better than to fight. As a matter of fact, he had warned the others of the futility of resisting: "I told you boys to keep your mouths shut."

Mike recognized Jackie right away. As Jackie lay face down in the grass, he moved over and placed a gun to the back of his head. "Look down," demanded Mike every time Jackie moved his massive head to one side or the other. "Look down, I said," Mike repeated as he pressed his gun against Jackie's long, greasy hair.

"Which one of you is Jackie?" asked a Dallas Police officer.

"I got him. He's that big, fat, stinking sweathog right here," said Mike.

"Yeah, you got it. That's me," said Jackie, with a nonchalant grin.

Bill Johnston had not taken a direct part in the raid. As a likely prosecutor of those who were being arrested, there were rules that prohibited him from becoming a witness to certain things. Bill always carefully followed those rules. As the raid developed, however, he noticed a young man hiding in a pickup. He saw the man slump down into the cab. Not willing to take a chance that the individual could be dangerous to the other officers, Bill grabbed a 10-gauge magnum and walked over to the truck. He used the gun to tap on the window. "Get out," he screamed. "Get out, now!" Looking down the barrel of the 10-gauge, the man screamed back.

The Dallas SWAT Team, dressed in their specialized garb, and the posse from Central Texas, finished up with the "slugs" lying face down in the grass. Bill Johnston, dressed in a tie and business suit, marched another suspect up the sidewalk to the house. It was quite a night; even Bill had made an arrest.[10]

Jackie was given a place of "honor" in Bigfoot for a ride to Waco. After a period of silence, just before Bigfoot left the Dallas metro area, Jackie spoke up. "What's this all about, Parnell? I know y'all didn't do all this just because I ran off from that halfway house. I know y'all better than that."

"No, Jackie, you're right," Parnell said with a piercing look from a face of stone. "We are going to charge you with capital murder."

"Wait a minute! I'll tell you what you need to know," pleaded Jackie.

"I don't want to hear any lies at this time of night. If you want to tell me the truth, then do it, but if you don't then just shut up. If you are going to continue to lie I don't want to hear your filthy voice anymore," Parnell said, keeping up his merciless face of stone.

They arrived in Waco at about 4:15 A.M. on March 21. It was a Saturday. At the McLennan County Jail, it was Mike's turn to go face-to-face with Jackie. With his own penetrating stare, Mike said, "I am going to be back on Monday. You need to do some serious thinking about what you are going to talk about." Mike turned away and went home, leaving behind the One-eyed Jack, who had been booked for running away from a halfway house.[11]

III

On the day the posse motored toward Dallas to arrest Jackie, APD Detective Don Martin called Tim Steglich and confirmed that Kenneth Allen McDuff was definitely a prime suspect in the abduction of Colleen Reed.

Since Colleen's disappearance, the Austin Police Department had approached the case by processing and clearing leads submitted by family members, friends, and anonymous sources. Lori, for example, never changed her phone number and kept it listed in the phone book. Periodically, she visited APD Headquarters to deliver whatever leads she had received. She forwarded all of them, even those from the kooks.

Both Don and Sonya worked carefully with the Goins Brothers, Stephen Marks, and Kari (Mike Goins' girlfriend). Stephen Marks, for example, readily agreed to be hypnotized in an attempt to remember more about what happened at the car wash. Don Martin took Stephen to the Police Academy Building where a DPS agent worked with him. Stephen remembered that the car used to kidnap Colleen had very long doors. Don also coordinated his efforts with Hector Polanco of the Homicide Task Force. APD made copies of all the papers in Colleen's purse, including her calendar and address book. In anticipation of needing Colleen's DNA, APD secured her latest Pap smear from her gynecologist.

On the night of March 24, during the filming of an *Unsolved Mysteries* episode at the car wash, Sonya met with Mike Goins at Kari's house. She asked him to look at a photo lineup with McDuff's picture in it. Mike Goins was able to eliminate all of the photos except McDuff. Pointing at McDuff's picture, he said he could not eliminate the picture, but he could not make a positive ID either. The photo lineup went into the APD Files as a tentative ID of Kenneth Allen McDuff.[12]

The investigation shifted into high gear when Don and Sonya returned from the ATF search of McDuff's car. They had two names to check out: a woman named Beverly from Del Valle and a parole consultant from Austin named Helen Copitka.

The day after the ATF search, Don did a background check on Beverly and found that she had been a known associate of a few men with criminal records. One of them had an outstanding warrant for theft in Travis County. With two other sergeants, Don went to the address found in McDuff's car and located Beverly's brother. He said that Beverly no longer lived there, but that she worked at a south Austin restaurant and might be at work. They went to the restaurant, but she was not there either. The manager gave them a phone number where she could be reached. When they called, they found out that it was the number to the residence they had just visited. Don asked Beverly's brother to tell her to call him the next time he saw her.

The next day Beverly paged Don. When he returned the call, she indicated that she could meet with him between 6:30 and 7:00 P.M. Don told her that he was assisting a sheriff in locating Kenneth McDuff because his car had been found abandoned and he had been reported missing. She easily recalled McDuff when Don showed her a picture. When he showed her the map taken out of the Thunderbird, she readily recognized her own handwriting. She remembered seeing McDuff only once during the summer of 1991. Her cousin, Morris, brought him to her Del Valle home to score speed. She drew the map for McDuff to return, but he never did.[13] This was the first confirmation that McDuff made trips to the Austin area.

The second confirmation that McDuff had cruised Austin came from Jackie. Chuck Meyer called Sonya and let her know that Jackie had been arrested in Dallas and was in jail in Waco. Quoting Bill Johnston, Chuck told her that McDuff had been in Austin on Christmas Day, that he stole gas, talked about taking girls, and most significantly, constantly drove the wrong way on one-way streets.[14]

When Parnell called APD after he had interviewed Jackie on March 23, he told J. W. that Jackie was in a Waco jail. Very soon, J. W. called back to say that he and Don were headed for Waco to talk to One-eyed Jack.[15]

Jackie had taken Mike's advice; he had thought long and hard over the weekend about what he would say about McDuff. He had decided to tell all.

IV

"I'm the meanest son-of-a-bitch in the jungle, but I ain't
no kid killer. Mike, I been a thief, and I used a little dope
from time to time, but I ain't never done anything like that
to a woman. I got too many girlfriends for that kind of stuff
and you can ask any of 'em if I ever done anything like
that. And I sure as hell ain't no kid killer, either, you know
that." Mike and Parnell believed Jackie. "He's a thief but
not a liar. Now that's rare," smiled Parnell.

Throughout the interview, Jackie begged to be given
truth serum or strapped to a polygraph. He wanted badly
to be cleared of any involvement in murder. When asked
why he never went to the police with his information,
Jackie replied that he was on the run himself. He told Mike
and Parnell that he heard about the abduction at the Austin
car wash on a crime stoppers' show on January 10 or 11.
He said it sounded exactly like "Max," especially the part
about going the wrong way on Fifth Street. Jackie said that
on Christmas Day, Max went down the wrong one-way
street at least three times in three hours.[16]

For Wayne Appelt of the ATF, Jackie's information
meant that Kenneth Allen McDuff abducted and killed Colleen Reed. He told Don Martin, "I guarantee you that
McDuff killed Colleen Reed."[17]

Toward the end of the day on Monday, March 23, the
day Mike and Parnell retrieved such rich information from
Jackie, a determined and courageous woman entered the
Marshal's Office in Waco. She had called earlier in the day
and wanted to talk to the McNamara brothers. She was
Barbara Carpenter, Regenia Moore's mother. She had never
given up looking for her daughter, and she wondered why
others had. She told Mike and Parnell about a man named
William, who had befriended Regenia and many other
girls on the Cut. Barbara told the McNamaras that, according to William, someone named Chester saw Regenia in

McDuff's pickup by the Chicken Shack on the Old Dallas Highway.[18] That was the last time Regenia was seen in public.

The search for the monster was now taking The Boys to the Cut. They were always heavily armed, but after the raid in Dallas, they carried an impressive arsenal. During the Dallas raid, Mike poked the back of Jackie's head with a hybrid called the "Annihilator." It was a Remington 870 12-gauge 8-shot, mounted below a fully automatic M-16 with a 90-round clip. With the Annihilator, when a user was done with one part, he could go to the other. There was also "Shorty," a double-barrel shotgun pistol Parnell wore in a shoulder harness. There was the 10-gauge magnum Bill used to capture his prisoner, two .45-caliber rifles that could fire twenty rounds per second, and a 1928 model of a Thompson Machine gun. The guns usually sat on a console in between the front seats of Bigfoot.[19] McDuff was not going to get away.

V

On March 25, a young Waco man named Terry who worked at an auto parts store decided to take his lunch in the seclusion of the heavily wooded area behind the TSTI campus. In a statement to the McLennan County Sheriff's Office, Terry wrote, "I came out here at about 12:10 P.M. [and] got me a few beers for lunch." As he walked through the woods, he came upon a mesquite patch. He heard the humming noise of hundreds of flies and something suspicious attracted him to a certain spot in the heavy brush. He came upon a pile of boards over loose dirt, looked down, and saw the eye sockets of a skull looking back at him. Spooked, Terry hurriedly left the scene and returned to the store.

At first, his friends did not believe him, but they went to the scene, saw that it was a body, and called the Bell-

mead Police Department. They, in turn, called the Mc-
Lennan County Sheriff's Department.[20]

Soon, police officers swarmed the area. Truman Simons,
Richard Stroup, Larry Abner, and Larry Abraham were
among those from the Sheriff's Office. Mike, Parnell, and
Bill arrived to watch the recovery. The body was a young
adult woman who appeared to be white. For a while, the
officers thought they might have discovered Melissa Northrup. But her hair was clearly negroid. Except for the head,
which had been exposed to the air, the body was fairly well
preserved. The dark, thick soil of the area wrapped the body
into a nearly airtight cocoon. The skull had been damaged,
probably by the hoofs of cows grazing the area. The air
smelled of death as the officers used spoons to unearth the
body, later identified by fingerprints as Valencia Kay
Joshua. She was found naked, and lying in a semi-fetal
position. In the dirt beneath her head, the officers found a
hair comb.

Near the burial site, Larry Abner found a plastic-coated
wire that appeared to have dark hairs embedded on one end
of it. It matched what McDuff's one-time friend, Chester,
called a "plastic covered rope" he had seen in McDuff's
pickup truck. The find, however, never amounted to much.
There was a lot of illegally-dumped trash in that area, and
Chester could hardly be depended on to give credible information.

Far more valuable than the plastic-coated wire was what
was found on Joshua's body. Forensic scientists in Dallas
discovered hair not belonging to the deceased. The hair
would be found to match samples later retrieved from Kenneth Allen McDuff. Her immediate cause of death could
not be determined, but because of the condition and location of her body, and the fact that she was nude, the coroner
ruled that she died as a result of homicidal violence.[21]

At the scene of Valencia Joshua's makeshift grave, Bill
Johnston wondered if McDuff could have prepared other

sites for other victims. As he roamed the area, Bill came across a freshly dug hole. He tried not to let his imagination run away with him, but he thought that it sure looked like a grave.[22]

16

Heartbreaking Stupidity

"The truth was pushing him around the parking lot."
—Tim Steglich

I

The Bell County Sheriff's Department could hardly have been more generous with Tim Steglich's time. For months he did little more than assist the many other law enforcement agencies engaged in the pursuit of Kenneth Allen McDuff. Many leads eventually led to Belton and Temple, and policemen like Tim and Mad Dog Owens provided valuable help. Officially, for Tim, it was a missing persons case filed by Addie McDuff, and as long as Kenneth was missing he had a duty to look for him. Other agencies were looking for McDuff, but for very different reasons.

On March 24, 1992, the jurisdictions with an interest in Kenneth McDuff met at Bill Johnston's office in Waco to share information. Don Martin and J. W. Thompson represented the Austin Police Department. Don briefed Tim on his interview of Beverly and mentioned that someone named Morris had directed McDuff to Beverly's house in Del Valle. Tim readily agreed to look for Morris. He found him the next day, but it was not an easy search. Although Morris was deathly afraid of McDuff, Tim successfully convinced him to give a statement, which was forwarded to the Austin Police Department. After reading the statement, Don and J. W. wanted to talk to Morris. When Tim contacted him again several days later, Morris became abusive. He said he did not want to be harassed. Very patiently, Tim worked with Morris and eventually Morris had a "change of heart." On April 7, Morris met with Don and

J. W. and repeated his statement detailing his trip to Del Valle with Billy and McDuff. He was also willing to take a polygraph to prove he had nothing to do with the abduction of Colleen Reed.[1]

Don and J. W.'s trip to Belton, however, reaped more than just an interview with Morris. Tim told them of another of McDuff's sidekicks—Alva Hank Worley. Tim agreed to find and talk to Hank. When Don asked Tim how he found out about Hank, Tim answered that it was because of Janice.

Janice was one of the more productive of Tim's contacts. Her information helped lead to the arrests and imprisonment of both her husband (Billy) and her ex-husband (Hank). Tim thought Janice was pretty intelligent compared to the people she associated with. He thought she seemed like the "savior type," a fairly decent person who married undependable men. She was always friendly and cooperative, even though Tim had a great deal to do with sending two of her husbands to prison. "It seemed to have no bearing [on Tim's relationship with her]. She just goes on to the next [husband]."[2]

Janice kept telling Tim that Hank Worley knew more than he was saying. She indicated that Hank wanted to talk to her about Kenneth McDuff, but she did not want to talk to Hank because they were engaged in a custody battle over Hank's daughter (the one living with him at Bloom's Motel). It crossed Tim's mind that Janice might be trying to exploit Hank's association with McDuff to gain an edge in the custody suit. For a few days, Tim tried unsuccessfully to locate Hank. When he called Janice about his whereabouts, she told him that Hank would be attending a child custody hearing on April 8. Tim decided to bide his time.[3]

On April 8, Tim had to find out where the custody hearing was to take place. When he got to the courtroom, he found Hank sitting with his attorney. It was the first time Tim had ever met Hank. He asked if Hank would mind walking over to his office. After assuring the attorney that the topic was completely unrelated to any civil matter involving Hank, Hank consented to an interview. From the courtroom to Tim's office, Hank and Tim engaged in small talk. Hank never asked Tim why he wanted to talk to him. "That is an almost perfect indication that they are guilty. A normal person would want to know," said Tim, who acquired that wisdom after years of experience investigating sexual assault cases.

Hank was very cooperative as he gave his first statement involving McDuff. He rode with McDuff, he said, because he did not have his own car. "The more he talked, the more jittery he got," remembered Tim. Without prompting, Hank referred to a convenience store clerk. He said McDuff spoke of a "damn good-looking girl" and that he "would like to take her." Hank readily admitted that he interpreted that to mean that McDuff would kidnap her.[4] Hank finished up his statement and left Tim's office. Tim watched him walk away, knowing Hank knew much more.

The next day, April 9, Tim drove over to the Austin Police Department and delivered a snapshot of Alva Hank Worley. At the time, Hank had a huge bushy beard he had been growing since the abduction of Colleen Reed. His investigation also took him to the S&S Trailer Park where he encountered two other McDuff acquaintances, Buddy and Jimmy. Tim saw several quarts of authentic moonshine and considered himself lucky that Buddy was sober enough to talk at all. He watched Jimmy carefully; he considered Jimmy a dangerous man, and asked him to step outside while he talked to Buddy. Both of the men maintained that they hardly knew McDuff. Tim knew better than to believe that.[5]

II

John Aycock is a decorated Texas Ranger. He wears cowboy boots, a cowboy hat, chews tobacco and spits in a cup. His office walls have pictures of John Wayne. The office

is small and horribly cluttered, wholly uncharacteristic of
his approach and success in investigations. A small closet
is stacked and filled with boxes of files. Inside, reports document just how good John Aycock is. He is one of the best
at what he does. His reports are vivid and thorough; they
reflect his eye for detail.[6]

John knew of Kenneth McDuff and the entire McDuff
clan. He was one of the first investigators on the scene of
Lonnie McDuff's murder.

As is the case with most high-profile murders, many
leads flowed in to various law enforcement offices. John
patiently and thoroughly checked out many of them. One
of his major contributions to the case was that he was able
to establish that McDuff had guns while in the H&H
Lounge. While there, McDuff was his usual, abusive self.
He tried to hit on a girl who quickly rebuffed his advances.
Frustrated, McDuff took out his anger on a patron. He
wanted the man to buy drugs. When the man declined,
McDuff displayed a gun and said: "Well, I'll just kill your
motherfucking ass."

"Man, there ain't no sense in having this kind of problem over drugs. I don't want to get killed," the frightened
man said. Luckily, McDuff walked out of the H&H.[7]

Among the law enforcement agencies, there was a
"sense of urgency," as the *Waco Tribune-Herald* reported,
"which a federal official attributed to McDuff's violent
past." On March 30, 1992, Kenneth McDuff came closer
to apprehension when two United States Marshals named
Dan Stoltz and Mike Carnevale walked into Mike and Parnell's office.

Inspector Dan Stoltz of the United States Marshals Service headed the task force that had been formed to track
down McDuff. He was based out of Houston, and because
he was an Inspector, Dan did not report to a United States
Marshal. Dan was a very capable investigator who assembled a crack team to track down McDuff. The team included undercover operatives infiltrating the Central Texas
subculture. As many as twenty people served on the task

force. Joining Stoltz was a gifted investigator named Mike Carnevale, a marshal based out of San Antonio. Carnevale had earned a reputation as being one of the nation's best fugitive hunters. Stoltz and Carnevale were fond of one another and worked very well together. From Washington, Supervising Inspector Mike Earp, a descendant of a legendary law enforcement family, provided support. During a visit to Texas, Earp said, "Until I actually got on the scene down in Texas, I didn't realize what an impact McDuff had on those small communities, that people were absolutely terrified of the man."

At the time, the U.S. Marshals were winding down Operation Gunsmoke, a nationwide program designed to apprehend fugitives. Luckily, Stoltz was able to secure the funding, manpower, and resources that were already in place and ready to be moved to Waco to be concentrated on McDuff. The resources included the "Red October," a huge trailer moved about by truck and equipped with some of the most sophisticated communications and tracking equipment available to law enforcement.[8]

Dan Stoltz established his authority fairly quickly. One of his first decisions was to refocus the investigation on the search for McDuff, rather than victims. He quickly replaced officers who did not carry their load. He had no patience with "politicians with big white cowboy hats who hung around" his headquarters. One officer from TDCJ introduced himself as "a captain." Stoltz replied, "well if you're a captain, I'm a *general*." He also pointedly instructed an area sheriff to "get out of [his] way and go on home."

Dan Stoltz struck an effective balance between being an administrator and an investigator. He personally processed each of hundreds of leads, prioritized them, and assigned them to officers.[9]

As the number of officers on the case grew, the local townspeople began seeing out-of-towners with badges. One day, Parnell received a phone call from John Aycock, who explained that he had gotten a call from a woman who worked in a bank in Temple. She was concerned because

a well-dressed stranger approached her and stated that he
worked for the United States Marshals Service and proceeded to ask questions about Kenneth Allen McDuff. (The
investigator was Larry Doreck of the Houston Police Department.) In responding to the woman's phone call, Aycock began a surveillance of Doreck. As Aycock watched
Doreck and the bank, he called Parnell in Waco. Parnell
explained that the stranger was a member of the McDuff
Task Force, and was one of Stoltz's specially deputized
marshals investigating McDuff's finances. But Doreck was
wearing shoes, John retorted; he had never heard of a
United States Marshal who did not wear boots. With fa-
cetious indignation, Aycock said that if he ever heard of
anyone else claiming to be a Marshal but not wearing boots,
he would arrest him on the spot. Parnell hung up the phone,
enjoying a much-needed laugh.[10]

In the case of Kenneth Allen McDuff, the United States
Marshals Service performed brilliantly and delivered an
amazing public service. Their agents investigated and
tracked down hundreds of leads. Carnevale later stated that
he and fifteen to twenty Marshals worked round-the-clock
for five weeks. Like The Boys, each night they quit only
after there was absolutely nothing else to do.[11] Mike Carnevale was particularly remarkable; at the time of the investigation he was battling terminal cancer. At times, Dan
Stoltz had to order him to rest.[12] Surely, in the annals of
crime, no law enforcement agency has ever expended such
time and effort to track down a suspect with a warrant for
an arrest because of one LSD tab. But then, McDuff was
special.

In looking for anyone who had any type of relationship
with Kenneth McDuff, The Boys came across the name of
Harrison. Harrison had been in jail with McDuff while the
latter was serving time for a DWI charge. After both were
released, the two men rode around together in McDuff's
truck. Harrison was dark complected and often unshaven,
and thus he matched the description of the passenger seen
in McDuff's car the night of Colleen's abduction. During

one of his trips with McDuff, Harrison had refused to have anything to do with a scheme to rob a convenience store and "take" a good-looking girl. He wisely made up his mind to have nothing whatsoever to do with McDuff. But Harrison was a strange and dangerous criminal as well, and law officers were watchful and careful whenever they were around him. That was why they all found it so odd to learn that Harrison lived with his grandmother. Shortly after reaching Harrison's grandmother's home, the men began to watch her carefully.

The Boys and a number of other officers, including Tim Steglich and Mad Dog Don Owens, arrived at the grandmother's home late into the evening. Harrison characterized his relationship with McDuff as brief. He complained that McDuff constantly talked about robbing and killing crack dealers. To Harrison, he was crazy and dangerous. So much so that he told his elderly grandmother that if McDuff ever came to the door, "don't open it or talk to him—*just shoot him.*" An incredulous silence followed. Finally, someone asked the grandmother if she had a gun. She calmly answered that she had a .357 magnum.

Afterwards, Harrison's grandmother became the object of curiosity. She told the officers that Harrison's father was a full-blooded Indian who had died of alcoholism. Harrison's mother, however, was a filthy tramp, a slut, and had been sleeping with lots of people in the Hill Country town of Kerrville. Finally, Harrison's mother had married a doctor. As she spoke, Harrison continually interrupted her, saying, "Oh, Baby," and "Oh, Sweetheart" and "Oh, Miss Suzie, dear," as he stroked the back of her head and asked her not to be upset.

Harrison's grandmother insisted that she was a good Christian woman, and that she raised Harrison in a good Christian home, and taught him to be a good Christian man. That was why, she explained, she kidnapped him from a day-care while he was still an infant. The men were enthralled as she told of how she went to the daycare and threatened "to beat the hell out of the woman" there if she ever laid another hand on Harrison. She said that Harrison had told her that the woman had hurt him. Mike McNamara, perceptive as usual, kindly asked Harrison's grandmother: "If Harrison was an infant, how could he tell you that the woman had hurt him?"

"Just the way he looked at me, Mister. He said it [with his eyes]," replied the old woman.

As the men gathered on the front porch to leave, Harrison's grandmother repeated her devotion to Christian principles, and how all she wanted to do was what was right for Harrison. It was very dark and well after midnight as the men got into their vehicles to leave. As they backed away, dogs began to bark. Looking towards the dogs, the old woman screamed at the top of her lungs, "Shut up. Shut up. You gonna wake up the whole god-damned neighborhood!"

"She's a terrorist," Tim thought.[13]

The next day, Mike, Parnell and Bill thought that it might be wise to learn more about McDuff, from an historical perspective. They called their good friend, Falls County Sheriff Larry Pamplin, who arranged for them to meet Roy Dale Green. Roy Dale still lived in the house where he and Kenneth McDuff spent the night after committing the Broomstick Murders. Only a few yards from the house was the garage where they buried the pistol used to kill Robert Brand and Marcus Dunnam. Roy Dale repeated the horrible story. He also talked about what it was like to be around McDuff. He told of how McDuff raped girls, and how the instruments of his mistreatment included a tube of Deep Heat. During the interview, Green alleged that one of McDuff's victims never recovered from her trauma and later committed suicide.[14]

Another aspect of Kenneth McDuff's past that caused an investigation was the corporation formed to market him as a victim wrongly accused and convicted of murder. On April 7, 1992, federal agents interviewed Gary and Gloria Jackson, lawyers for Justice for McDuff, Inc. Gary Jackson also indicated that he had been representing McDuff since

October of 1976. According to a report by the federal agent who conducted the interview, the couple were very certain about Kenneth's innocence and that there was no way he could have committed the crimes for which he was accused. The officer characterized both Jacksons as defensive and hostile throughout the entire interview. The report continued that the Jacksons believed in a conspiracy between the judiciary and various law enforcement agencies, an unholy alliance determined to frame Kenneth for crimes he did not commit. Gloria's last telephone conversation with Kenneth was on February 1, 1992; Gary last spoke to him on February 28, 1992, the day before McDuff kidnapped and killed Melissa Northrup. Gloria readily admitted to recent conversations with Addie. Both believed that McDuff was dead—asserting that he was very close to his mother and she had not heard from him.

The Jacksons agreed to contact law enforcement agencies if they ever heard from Kenneth. They also agreed to advise him to turn himself in. But, according to the federal officer's report, Gary Jackson also indicated that he would not be surprised to find out that Kenneth was being held somewhere by officers against his will; he might have even been killed by them. The interviewer noted that Gary Jackson voiced an intention to file a *Writ of Habeas Corpus* to get McDuff out of jail.[15] (That is an interesting anticipated legal maneuver for someone believed to be dead.)

III

In addition to the ATF warrant, the U.S. Marshals, through the tenacity of Larry Doreck, were able to make another connection between McDuff and the illegal possession of a gun. On April 4, 1992, they visited one of McDuff's sisters. In her statement she indicated that on two different occasions McDuff had taken one of her pistols, a .38-caliber Smith and Wesson revolver. McDuff claimed that he needed the weapon to kill Larry, the man who murdered

Lonnie. The sister's boyfriend had his own guns in the
same home. Wisely, he took them away and hid them at
his parents' house.

Everyone who knew him knew Kenneth was violent
whenever he took drugs. His sister's seventeen-year-old son
verified his mother's story of Kenneth taking the gun. In
an ATF affidavit, the young man confirmed that his uncle
had taken the nickel-plated revolver, placed it in his belt,
and left the home. In doing so, Kenneth violated the Gun
Control Act of 1969, which prohibits felons from possess-
ing firearms. (It also applies to persons on state or federal
probation.) By April 14, the ATF had another arrest warrant.[16]

Additionally, on April 14, Larry Doreck, the Deputized
U.S. Marshal, contacted Tim and informed him that the
Marshals intended to contact several of McDuff's known
associates. At first, Doreck wanted Tim to accompany the
group to Bloom's, but after Doreck asked Tim how to best
approach Hank, Tim suggested that he go to the motel
alone, and then bring Hank to the sheriff's office. Since
Tim had already taken a statement from Hank and managed
to communicate successfully with him, they decided to let
Tim go alone.

At Bloom's, Tim knocked on the door of room 12. Hank
answered the door and immediately became fidgety and
nervous. Tim asked him to step outside so that they could
talk in the parking lot. At that point, Tim did not know
whether Hank should be suspected of being an active par-
ticipant or a passive observer to what McDuff had done.
Thus, he did not really know how to treat him or what
questions to ask. Tim reminded Hank about that part of his
April 8 statement referring to McDuff taking a girl from a
convenience store. An already nervous Hank bristled when
Tim got to the point. "If he didn't explain it to you in detail,
then you saw it happen!" As Tim spoke, Hank began to
shift his stance; his eyes began to move back and forth,
never looking directly at the investigator zeroing in on him.
In order to keep him still, Tim placed his hands on Hank's

shoulder. "Look at me, Hank! Listen to me, Hank!" But Hank looked away. "Hank, I want you to talk to me."

"He hurt somebody real bad," Hank said as he shifted. Tim recalled that it was as if Hank was there to see it— again.

"You need to tell me about it before something else happens," insisted Tim as he kept trying to keep Hank still. The truth was pushing him around the parking lot. "Talk to me! Hank, listen to me and tell me what happened."

"I don't know and I can't tell you," pleaded Hank.

When Tim was convinced that that was as far as Hank Worley was going to go, he asked Hank to accompany him to the sheriff's office. He agreed to go and was interviewed by five members of the marshal's service. He did not add significantly to what he told Tim in the parking lot.[17] On the way back to Bloom's, Tim calmly and patiently told Hank that, "sooner or later you are going to have to tell us everything."

That was not nearly enough for The Boys. They knew Hank was holding out. For the next few days whenever they were in the area, Mike navigated Bigfoot into the parking lot of Bloom's Motel and parked it in a position Hank could not ignore. Sometimes they just sat until they could see a light go on inside room 12 and an occupant take a peek through the window. When that happened, The Boys tipped their hats and moved on. They did it every night they were in the Belton area—over and over again.

The Boys became Hank Worley's "Tell-Tale Heart". They talked to him and mercilessly reminded him about the man he was holding out on. As Bill has said, "Making someone feel guilty for what they have done is not coercion." And indeed, guilt became Hank's worst enemy; it festered each time Hank looked outside and saw three men in a huge, white Suburban.

On one evening in April, after a hard spring rain, Mike drove Bigfoot around the back of Bloom's Motel where Hank and a few other residents appeared to be barbecuing something. (Mike took a second take because he thought it

looked suspiciously like a rat.) Bigfoot motored right
through the thick mud that would have bogged down most
other vehicles, leaving huge ruts in the sticky slosh. Somehow, it made The Boys seem more unstoppable. They got
out of Bigfoot and stood, staring at Hank and the friends
around the pit. Hank's daughter stood near the door of their
room. Finally, Hank walked over to Bigfoot and asked,
"What do y'all want? I told y'all everything."

As with Edgar Allan Poe's character, for Hank, "above
all was the sense of hearing acute." Mike saw that, and he
knew what to do—he became "the beating of [a] hideous
heart."

"Hank, look at your daughter and picture her screaming.
Picture her with a broomstick across her throat. Hank, can
you hear the screams? I can hear them. Can you hear the
screams, Hank? Can you hear her say, 'Daddy help me!
Help me!' I can hear her, Hank. Can you?"

"Stop! Stop! You've got the right man! You've got the
right man! I told you, you've got the right man. Just go
and leave me alone!" Hank screamed as he placed his hands
on his ears and looked over to his daughter, as if to make
sure there was no broomstick across her throat.

"I know a lot, Hank. I know a whole lot more than you
think. I know everything," Mike said.

The men walked Hank over to Bigfoot where Mike
showed him pictures of Colleen Reed and Melissa Northrup. Silently, Hank looked at the pictures and shook. But
he regained his composure enough to give The Boys (along
with Larry Doreck) the impression that that was as far as
they were going to get—at least that night.[18] That was all
right. There would be other nights, and all they had to do
to go back to Bloom's was put more gas in Bigfoot.

Hank was terrified of McDuff and of the trouble he had
gotten himself into. But like Roy Dale Green in 1966, Hank
Worley wanted to run around with what he thought was an
impressive individual—someone like Kenneth Allen
McDuff, a big, ex-con murderer with a car and money.
Most officers associated with the McDuff murder cases be-

lieve that Hank got himself into a horrible situation and he could not back out. That is possible, but not likely. For example, during his investigation, Tim Steglich found out about an incident that occurred long before Hank helped McDuff abduct Colleen. Reportedly, Hank discovered that his daughter had gotten into a car with McDuff and ridden off. Hank was so incensed that he went over to his ex-wife's home and threatened to kill anyone who ever let her do that again. "You have to wonder what he knew or suspected before that," said Tim.

One also has to wonder how many times someone like McDuff had to talk about killing before it would occur to Hank that just maybe there was something to all of the boasting. Especially since Hank knew McDuff to be extremely dangerous. Even those in the subculture knew McDuff to be "dangerous and crazy." Billy, Harrison, the One-eyed Jack, Chester the Molester, One-Arm, T-Bone, Linda, Holly, Sandy, the whores on the Cut, any number of thieves, rapists, drug dealers and murderers, and even some of McDuff's own family, all knew him to be a violent predator. Why not Hank Worley? Until, as he asserted, it was too late. If, indeed, Hank Worley was neither a predator nor a true accomplice, then he surely suffered from heartbreaking stupidity.[19]

Or, maybe, Hank Worley knew what he was doing. At least Hank had enough common sense to fear for the safety of his family. If, indeed, guilt plagued him, it might have been because he had placed very innocent members of his own family in grave danger. He had to tell his sister, Diane, who at one time took him into her home, that "If Big Mac comes up to the house you tell him where I'm at and you call this man immediately, 'cause he might hurt you." Then he handed her Mike McNamara's card.[20]

McDuff's friends never ceased to amaze the investigators. While interrogating Billy, Dan Stoltz and Mike Carnevale got frustrated at his unwillingness to cooperate. While Carnevale kept Billy's attention, Dan took a smooth rock off the desk and asked Billy to look at it carefully.

Billy gazed at the rock as Dan moved it in a circular motion. "Billy, this is a special rock. It makes people feel real
relaxed and comfortable. See?" Dan then touched Billy's
forehead with the rock. Billy slumped into his seat and said,
"Haaaaaaaaaa!" He then shared with the investigators the
intimacies of prison life with McDuff.[21]

By April 19, Hank was at a breaking point. He called
Diane and began to cry. "I am not going to see you again,"
he said. Then he called his brother-in-law, Jerry, and asked
him to come over to Bloom's. Diane, Bess and Jerry got
there at about 2:15 P.M. As Bess and Diane sat near the
barbecue pit behind Bloom's, Jerry and Hank walked out
into the fields and played horseshoes.

Hank asked Jerry if he had ever heard about a missing
girl from Austin. Jerry answered that he had seen the story
several times on television. Then Hank rambled, almost in-
coherently, about how he could not get any rest. He mentioned how the marshals kept talking to him. Hank said,
"They are trying to pin it on me." When Jerry asked Hank
if he did it, Hank said no. "McDuff did it," he added. Hank
also denied raping the girl. He did not have to do such a
thing, he insisted, because there was "too much free stuff
out there." He added, "I'm scared but I've got to tell somebody." But he was afraid that if he said anything, he would
be killed. According to his statement and sworn testimony,
Jerry told Hank to turn himself in, ask for police protection,
and tell everything he knew: The whole conversation lasted
about fifteen to twenty minutes.[22]

The next day, Monday, April 20, 1992, Hank reported
to work. His boss walked over to him and wanted to talk.
Over the weekend, Parnell McNamara had had a conversation with the boss and suggested strongly that he help
convince Hank to tell everything he knew about McDuff.
It worked.[23]

Hank returned to Bloom's after work, and as usual,
drank a few beers. He had only one quarter to make a single
call from Bloom's pay phone. He decided to call his sister,
Diane.

Between 4:00 and 4:30 P.M., Diane was cooking supper when the phone rang. Hank asked his sister if she could do him a favor. She said she would if she could. He asked her to get a pencil and paper to take a name and number. Then he gave her Tim Steglich's name and number and asked her to give him a call and tell him to come by the motel. At the time, Diane did not know who Tim was. He also asked Diane to go by later to check on his daughter.[24]

At the Bell County Sheriff's Office, Tim Steglich had his keys in his hand and was headed out the door of his office when the phone rang. It was 5:05 P.M. and he was going home. Diane told Tim that Hank wanted to talk to him immediately and that he would be waiting at Bloom's. Tim thought that it might be a breakthrough, but he'd learned long ago not to raise his hopes. He arrived five minutes later and saw Hank standing outside of his room talking to his daughter.

Tim drove his car near where Hank stood, rolled down the window of his 1989 Chevrolet four-door sedan, and said, "Did you want to talk to me?"

"Yea," Hank said as he nervously and hurriedly walked over to the passenger side of Tim's car. Tim had to reach over and unlock the door, thinking that they must be going somewhere. Hank opened the door, bent over, and said, "McDuff is the one who took that girl from the car wash in Austin."

Tim controlled a body-wide adrenaline rush. A flurry of thoughts raced through his mind. Everything had to be done right, and it was not even his case. He had to get a statement from Hank, a statement about a case he was not familiar with. The first statement does not have to be definitive—that can come later. Hank was now a suspect and was involved in a kidnapping—at least. Hank had rights which, if violated, could have messed up the case.

"Don't say anything else. Can you go with me to the sheriff's office?" Tim would have preferred to let Hank drive himself. That way a defense attorney could hardly argue that Hank had been coerced into a statement. But Hank had no car and Tim did not want to let him go. He told Hank to go talk to his daughter and let her know where he was going. (It was a very shrewd move on Tim's part. Hank's daughter became a potential witness to Hank's voluntarily getting into a car with Tim for the purpose of making a statement.)

On the way to the sheriff's office, Tim kept telling Hank not to talk about the abduction. "I have got to get this shit straight; I am not sleeping at night."

"Wait, Hank," Tim said. Then Tim started doing most of the talking in order to keep Hank quiet until he could be read his rights.[25]

Tim knew he was going to be with Hank for a long, long time.

17

"As Nice As I Could Be"

*"Hank, what on Earth made you believe you could walk
away from this?"*
—Charles Meyer

I

The Bell County Sheriff's Office is not far from Bloom's
Motel. It just seemed like a long trip late in the afternoon
of April 20, as Tim Steglich drove Hank to make a statement. At 5:25 P.M., Tim read Hank his Miranda warning.
Tim tried to get in touch with a number of officers but
could find no one. He did not want to leave Hank alone so
he asked Deputy Ted Duffield to get in touch with Don
Martin and J. W. Thompson of the Austin Police Department as soon as possible. Getting in touch with APD was
the top priority—it was their case. Other officers could be
contacted later.

Tim had to make an immediate decision. At the time,
Hank was not a suspect or under arrest. Since he was making a voluntary statement, he could have asked for a lawyer
at any time. Tim decided to get a brief statement first; he
wanted the bottom line on paper—a girl was abducted from
a car wash and McDuff did it. And so, Tim began slowly
and carefully taking a statement for a case he was not that
familiar with. As Hank spoke of kidnapping, rape, torture,
and probable capital murder, Tim forced himself into a
mode of extraordinary concentration. It was more important
to get the statement than allow himself the luxury of normal
emotion.[1]

The statement began with a sentence that said that all of
the information in Hank's April 8 statement was true and
correct, "but I do know about something that Mac did that

I need to tell you about." Hank got very vague whenever
it came to what he did to Colleen, but throughout the evening, what he said about McDuff was consistent. After
Hank finished his first statement, Tim took it to Bill Miller,
the head of Criminal Investigations, and they witnessed it
at 7:50 P.M.

In Austin, Don Martin received a page to call the homicide detail at the Austin Police Department. He and his
family had just ordered dinner at a Red Lobster restaurant.
A sergeant at APD headquarters gave him Tim's number
and told him to call right away. Tim told Don about Hank
and what Hank was confessing to. After that, Don called
his captain and an assistant chief and advised them that he
and J. W. were going to Belton. Don then called J. W. at
home and the two men agreed to meet at APD.[2]

On the way to Belton, Don briefed J. W. about his short
telephone conversation with Tim. They also talked about
how to go about interrogating Hank. Don was the case
agent and senior officer and he stated that they needed to
take a "good-guy–bad-guy" approach. J. W. understood that
Don was to lead in the questioning.

Don and J. W. arrived at about 9:15 P.M. Mike, Parnell
and Bill were already there, and shortly afterwards, Bill
called Chuck Meyer. Hank was going to "need a little interrogating."

Don asked Tim about how Worley ended up giving a
statement. Tim described the events of the evening. Then
he handed the APD officers a copy of Hank's statement.
The men were astounded at what they read. Don looked up
from the paper and asked if Worley was under arrest. Tim
said "no." Worley had never asked for an attorney and was
still cooperating, but J. W. saw immediately how self-
serving Hank's statement really was. Don and J. W. walked
into a small office, normally used by Ranger John Aycock,
to talk to Hank.[3]

Inside the small office, Don and J. W. introduced themselves. J. W. re-read Hank his rights. Hank did not admit
to much of anything, and both men knew that Hank was

holding out. As Hank related the horrible story, J. W. thought "everything terrible that can happen to a woman has happened here." Dealing with Hank was going to be a slow process. An effective method of interrogation is to allow a suspect to minimize their role in order to move on to the whole story, then go back and fill in the holes—especially before the suspect asks for a lawyer. They were going to have to do that with Hank.

As planned, Don did most of the talking. Most of the half-hour interview was about Worley's background, beliefs, occupation and family life. Don then moved to the Reed abduction. He warned Hank that the incident could be a capital offense and that Worley could "get the needle." Quietly, J. W. began to squirm in his chair. (At the time, other officers of the Austin Police Department were coming under intense scrutiny over tactics used by officers to get confessions. The controversy endangered two previous murder convictions and eventually every detective in the homicide unit would be reassigned to other units.) Don added that it would be nice for the Reed family to be able to give Colleen a decent burial. Hank quickly stated that he did not know where Colleen was buried.

During the interview, Don's questions began to get more and more direct. At one point, Hank avoided Don's direct glare and looked at J. W. For Don this was a clear indication of lying and guilt. Don slammed his hand on the desk, making a loud, hollow sound. "You better look at me when I'm talking to you!" Don shouted.[4]

In the hallway outside of the small office, Bill Johnston was standing very, very close to the door. He could hear everything Don and Hank were saying. (Today, that small room is Tim Steglich's office, and over the years Tim has learned that even with the door closed much of what is said in a normal volume can be heard outside in the hallway.) All of a sudden Bill straightened up, looked at Tim and said, "You need to get back in there and get Don Martin out."

"I'm not going to tell anybody anything—it's their deal," replied Tim.

Bill then began talking to Mike and Parnell. Chuck decided to knock on the door. He asked to see J. W. and they spoke for a short time. J. W. reentered the room and saw that "Don was on a roll." Shortly, Chuck knocked again and spoke to J. W. "They [The Boys] don't like Don's talk about a burial." Additionally, Chuck told J. W. that other officers wanted to talk to Worley. If Don "drove him too far" he might decide to stop talking and ask for a lawyer. J. W. then reentered the room and told Don, "We need to talk." In the hallway, he told Don about how the others were upset about talk of a burial. Now, Don was angry. In nearly thirty years of police work, he had never been treated in such a way. This was an Austin Police Department case and he was the case agent. But Don decided to back off. Moreover, Worley indicated that he wanted to talk to Steglich and Don thought it might just be best to let Chuck and Tim take over. "I wanted what was best for the case," Don said years later.

The incident is more significant because of the hard feelings it caused among investigators than for its legal or investigative consequences. Bill indicated that he was concerned over Don's talk of a burial—citing the "Christian Burial Case" of *Brewer v Williams* (1977). Of course, Bill did not have his law library with him at the time. He was, quite properly, being prudent. But in *Brewer* the issue was the denial of legal representation for a suspect who was already under arrest and assigned an attorney. The attorney had instructed the accused not to answer any questions and the police officers not to engage in an interrogation. In Hank's case, he had been read his rights at least twice by the time Don spoke to him. He had also signed a statement indicating he had been told his rights and that he understood them. Don did not violate Hank's rights during his questioning because Hank knew his rights and had not asked for an attorney. Mentioning a decent or a Christian burial, *per se*, was not improper. No one ever got violent

or abusive and Hank was never deprived of anything. As
Worley later testified at one of McDuff's trials, he went to
the Bell County Sheriff's Office "freewillingly." Additionally, telling Hank that he could "get the needle" is not improper either—because it was the truth. Hank was looking
at a possible capital murder charge (and, indeed, he was
later charged with that).

Whether it was *wise* for Don to bring up the issues with
Hank in such a brusque way was another question altogether. Hank had been cooperative and informative since
Tim brought him to the sheriff's office. Now he was angry.
In his own report, Don indicated that as he and J. W.
walked out of the room, Worley said that maybe he ought
to think of getting an attorney. If Hank had asked for one,
there could have been no more questions—at all. The investigators would have had to wait for an attorney, who
would certainly have told Hank to stop talking and give no
more statements. With characteristic directness, Chuck
summed up the problem: "Look, Worley is a mouse. He
didn't want to be told, 'You sat there and let this happen.'
Everybody was thinking it but it was Don who said it. True
or not, it was not conducive to getting information." Chuck
added that things like what Don told Hank should be said
"after the last line" of a statement is firmed up.

Bill wanted Don out of that office. Don wanted what
was best for the case. It was not pretty, but both men got
what they wanted, and the incident never became a serious
issue at McDuff's trial. Except for the hard feelings, as Tim
Steglich said years later, "In the end it didn't amount to
much."[5]

After J. W. and Don left Hank for the last time, Tim
and Chuck went in and easily calmed Hank down. After
about twenty minutes, Chuck managed to get Hank to admit
that he had sexual contact with Colleen. Tim then prepared
another statement that Hank signed at 12:05 A.M. Chuck
also managed to get Hank to agree to take the officers on
a trip to the murder site. At first, Hank claimed not to know

where the murder took place. Very quickly, Chuck talked him out of that lie.

Hank rode in Tim's car with Tim and Chuck. Mike and Bill followed in Bigfoot, Parnell drove his own truck, and J. W. and Don completed the convoy to the abandoned road connecting Cedar Creek Road with Highway 317. The road looked even more remote in the dark stillness of night. They all knew that just up the road, only a few hundred yards away, slept J. A. and Addie McDuff. On the way, Hank seemed indifferent to the content of his statements. But when he got out of the car, he began to cry. At last, Hank Worley began to appreciate and come to grips with what he had done.

Every lawman at the scene later described a profound sense of sadness followed by outrage. J. W. was a member of APD's Assault Unit; this was his first in-depth murder investigation. He asked himself, "What have I gotten myself into?" Mike McNamara's eyes watered as he walked off in a futile attempt to find the remains of a young woman he never knew. "We were raised to be very respectful of women. A woman is to be revered," Mike remembered more than six years later; his lips still trembled and his eyes still showed his pain. Bill Johnston and Parnell McNamara stood silently, their sad eyes staring into the darkness. They tried mightily to keep up their faces of stone, but their hearts broke when Hank said, "Her screams were so loud they hurt my ears. And finally, she could not scream any more." Her cries made no difference; Bill could not get that out of his mind.

Chuck thought of the screams, the long ordeal, and the torture. "This was not some doper shooting another doper. How could somebody be this weak? I found myself getting madder and madder at [Hank]," Chuck remembered.[6]

The Boys from Waco left the scene in a state of anxiety. Had McDuff done this to anyone else? Was he doing it to someone at that moment? Who would be next to scream? Was there another Hank Worley out there?

For weeks Parnell had confronted "slugs" from the sub-

culture in attempts to find McDuff. In doing so, he exuded
strength and displayed his usual face of stone. But on the
way home to Waco, at about 3:30 in the morning, driving
his truck became more and more difficult as thoughts of
what happened to Colleen Reed overwhelmed him. He
drove faster. The "spiritual descendant of an unforgiving
school of lawmen" could not help but fear for the women
at home he worshipped more than life itself. And the man
of stone began to weep.

There are some things you just don't do to a woman.

II

After the field trip Hank gave another statement, which began at 3:55 A.M., to add to and clarify points in his previous
statements. At 7:00 A.M., Hank signed a "consent to search"
form for the officers to look through his Bloom's Motel
room. Hank gave Chuck the pocket knife he had in his
possession the night Colleen was abducted, but no other
items were taken from the room.[7]

Don and J. W. raced back to Austin to secure a warrant
for Hank Worley's arrest. They met with Sonya Urubek
and Travis County Assistant D.A. Marianne Powers to draft
a probable cause affidavit. Another Assistant D.A., Buddy
Meyer, signed a state's motion to seal the affidavit. Powers
and Don Martin then brought the sealed affidavit to Judge
Wil Flowers, who signed the order and sealed the papers.
Don returned to APD and faxed the arrest warrant to Tim,
who served them personally on Hank at 4:33 P.M.[8]

Hank's confession set off a flurry of attempts to locate
Colleen. The search centered on the abandoned road near
J. A. and Addie McDuff's house. On April 21, the Bell
County Sheriff's Department conducted a search of the
area. Later, the Austin Police Department organized another
massive sweep. Mounted policemen rode through vast
tracts of farmland. APD even used a class of police academy cadets to help in the search. Helicopters with special

infrared detection devices scanned the area, hoping to de-
tect decomposition gases. Colleen was not there, and Hank
Worley did not know where she was.[9]

After the search near the murder site ended, Hank was
asked if he had any ideas where McDuff might have buried
Colleen. He answered that he would not be surprised if
McDuff put her near the S&S Mobile Home Park so as to
implicate him in the murder. Immediately afterwards, a
massive search took place there.[10]

On April 22, Tim, Chuck, J. W. and another APD officer
named Mark Thompson took Worley on another "field
trip." Using a camera mounted on a tripod, and pointing
out through the front windshield, the men videotaped the
route McDuff took the night he took Colleen. The long
drive was an occasion for Tim, Chuck and J. W. to question
Hank under relaxed conditions. In many ways Hank became even more of a mystery. (It was also an occasion to
poke fun at Tim, who kept falling asleep during the trip.
He had not had any sleep for nearly three days.)

During the trip, and on several more occasions over the
next two years, officials dealing with Hank Worley were
baffled. Alternately, Hank could be perceived as repentant
or opportunistic, a victim or a predator, truthful or lying.
But that he lacked social graces and functioned on a different moral plane was never in doubt. He never understood
how ridiculous some of his statements sounded to officers,
statements including:

"I was as nice to that girl as I could be."

"I don't consider what I did as sex with her."

"I don't believe in seeing anybody get hurt. I just can't
handle that."

"The girl didn't—she didn't cry too much."

Such statements seemed normal to Alva Hank Worley.
More than a year later, during the days just before the beginning of his trial, Travis County District Attorney Investigator Alan Sanderson, who had gotten to know Hank
pretty well, asked him how he managed to get himself into

so much trouble. "It was a real bad night," Hank said. And he was serious.[11]

During the field trip of April 22, while at the murder site, Hank calmly said that when McDuff struck Colleen, it sounded like a tree limb breaking. J. W. casually asked Hank if he helped put Colleen in the trunk of McDuff's car. Enraged, Hank walked towards J. W. shouting, "I ain't never touched no dead body!"

"Don't go ballistic on me, Hank. I was just asking a question," J. W. said. He had just talked about how Colleen's death sounded like a tree limb breaking, and given the graphic, horrid statements he'd made during the previous day, why would he care if others thought he had touched a dead body? That question puzzles Tim Steglich to this day.[12]

During the same field trip, Chuck, Tim and J. W. let Hank smoke, got him drinks and fed him a hamburger. J. W. watched him eat that hamburger in seconds. He covered the burger with both hands. He exhaled as he took the first bite, so that it sounded like he was forcing the air out of the burger itself. He did it two more times and the burger was gone. J. W.'s wife remembers a phone call she got from J. W. that day. She recalls him saying, "God, you should see him eat. It's gross. He eats like a pig."

But Hank's eating habits were not the most memorable event of the day for J. W. They had stopped at a Salado convenience store to get soft drinks. While seated in the mini-van, Hank looked towards J. W.

"You know, I been cooperating."

"Yes, Hank, you have," replied J. W.

"I been giving y'all some good information, huh?"

"Yes, Hank, you have. It has been real good information."

"Do you think maybe I can get probation?" Hank asked.

J. W. looked at him carefully and concluded that he was serious. "Hank, I never lied to you before. And I'm not going to lie to you now. Probation is pretty much out of the question."[13]

Hank had a similar conversation with Chuck. Incredulous that the conversation was even taking place, Chuck said bluntly, "What on Earth made you believe that you could walk away from this?"[14]

Hank reminded Tim of the many suspects he had dealt with in child sexual assault cases. With each successive statement, Hank characterized McDuff as more brutal and heartless, and himself as braver and more heroic. So much so that he began to hint that Colleen *wanted* to have sex with him. "People who assault children say that all the time. Even people who assault a ten-year-old child, they will say, 'she wanted it.' And this was just as ridiculous."[15]

On the night of December 29, 1991, Kenneth Allen McDuff kidnapped, raped, tortured, and murdered Colleen Reed. Hank Worley was with him, and at the very best, he did nothing to stop it.

III

The arrest warrant that Tim served on Hank on April 21 resulted from a probable cause affidavit that had been carefully crafted by a number of persons. J. W. and Don returned from Belton armed with Hank's gruesome sworn statement. At 5:30 A.M., J. W. called Travis County Assistant District Attorney Marianne Powers and asked her to meet with him at APD immediately. She presented the affidavit to her supervisors at the D.A.'s office who agreed that the document needed to be sealed.

The PC affidavit needed to be sealed for three reasons. First, Colleen's family—Lori in particular—had not been told of the horrible treatment Colleen had suffered. Victims' services and counselors needed to be organized to help Lori deal with the details of the statement. Second, by that time the Marshals Service had undercover agents throughout Central Texas infiltrating McDuff's favorite haunts. Third, none of the detectives in any of the many agencies investigating McDuff wanted him to know that

Worley was in custody and that he had confessed.[16]

A number of people from APD, the Travis County District Attorney's office, and the ATF (Chuck), assembled in a meeting room on the fifth floor of the APD on the afternoon of April 22 to put together a very vague announcement of Worley's arrest. Worley's name was not even mentioned. They all knew that the affair had to be handled very carefully. There would be a 5:00 P.M. press conference at APD and the Press Office would handle it. (It would be handled by an individual who could not have given out too much information.)

What happened between 4:30 P.M. and 5:00 P.M. on April 22 is still being quietly debated by the dozens of men and women who brought McDuff to justice. At about 4:50 P.M., the First Assistant District Attorney Steve McLeery made the call to have Judge Wil Flowers unseal the affidavit and thus make it public. He did so without notifying anyone at the Austin Police Department, including two of his own assistant district attorneys. Additionally, no one from McLeery's office attempted to contact anyone from Colleen's family. McLeery's supporters argue that there was no legal basis upon which to seal the document. Every investigator from every jurisdiction investigating McDuff flatly rejects that defense. (Most of them firmly believe, with great bitterness, that McLeery buckled under pressure from the press.)[17]

At the Austin Police Department, someone walked into Don Martin's office and said, "You are not going to believe what happened. Judge Flowers unsealed the affidavit and it is being read on television right now." Some of the persons organizing the press conference (including two assistant district attorneys), were horrified when Austin news anchors read the probable cause affidavit, including details of rape, oral and anal sex, torture and murder, on live television.[18]

Don raced to victims' services and said that Lori needed to be contacted immediately and told not to watch the news. In fact, Lori had already been contacted and told that the affidavit had been sealed and they could not give her any more information. By 4:45 P.M., she was told that it had been unsealed and that the CBS affiliate was going with the story at 5:00 P.M. Lori dropped the phone. She figured she had fifteen minutes to shelter her children. After putting her boys in their room, she could not help but watch the news to see what had happened to her sister. She sat on her bed and turned on the television.[19]

Meanwhile, counselors from the APD tried desperately to reach Lori where she lived in Round Rock, but Austin's legendary 5:00 traffic slowed them down considerably. Alone in her bedroom, Lori heard the details of her sister's brutal treatment at the hands of Kenneth Allen McDuff. She gagged and ran to her bathroom to vomit. In such a condition, Lori had to make calls to her family to tell them not to watch the news—it was beyond their worst nightmare.[20]

At J. W.'s desk, the phone rang. He answered it to hear an enraged Inspector Dan Stoltz of the U.S. Marshals Service. "What the [hell] are you people doing out there? I've got some agents out and some of them don't have any cover!" For several minutes, Stoltz royally chewed out J. W., who could only sit and listen, because he agreed with every word that Stoltz had to say. "He had a right to be mad," J. W. remembered with bitterness.

Don Martin called the marshals' office in Waco. The unsealing of the affidavit, coupled with the incident involving Don and his approach to interrogating Hank Worley, were too much for the marshals to handle. "Don't you ever walk into this office again! And if you need to go to Dallas, go through Houston!"

Today, Don admits to compounding his problems. After it became evident that the name Alva Hank Worley would be made public, APD decided to have him appear at the news conference at 5:00 P.M. He forgot to thank and failed to mention other police organizations.[21]

The next day Lori Bible demanded an appointment with Ronnie Earle, District Attorney of Travis County, and Steve McLeery, his First Assistant D.A. After some haggling, her

1:00 P.M. appointment was confirmed when she threatened to show up anyway with CBS News. Lori "ripped him up one side to another." All Earle could do was sit and take it. "Ronnie understood," Lori remembered.[22]

The word was out. The name Kenneth Allen McDuff made the news all over the country, and the front pages of nearly every newspaper in Texas. "Armed, dangerous, desperate" splashed the news everywhere. Reporters spanned the Blackland Prairie for information on McDuff. At Bloom's Motel, a resident said, "We used to drink beer with [Hank]. When we saw him on T.V. we said, 'I know that guy.' " The publicity focused attention on the search for Colleen near the McDuff homestead.

All of a sudden, the name Roy Dale Green resurfaced in newsprint—big time. Roy Dale had been living quietly in Marlin and after reporters had time to look into McDuff's past, especially the Broomstick Murders, Roy Dale became the object of a great deal of curiosity. Marlin residents knew that Roy Dale still lived in the same old dilapidated house, and that he spent much of his time at his sister's beer joint. When a *Waco Tribune-Herald* reporter tried to talk to him at the bar, Roy Dale ran out through the back door. Angered, his sister asked the reporter, "He did his time. Why can't he be left alone?"[23]

Within a week, the *Rosebud News* published a headline: "How Many Rapes and Murders Has He Committed This Time?" In Alvarado, the Brand family and Louise Sullivan's survivors had to relive the horror of what Kenneth McDuff had done to their children. "I'm going to pin me on a badge and go after him, and I won't bring him back alive," threatened Jack Brand, Robert's father.[24]

The media blitz brought about a flood of McDuff tips. On April 30, the McLennan County Sheriff's Office logged four positive McDuff sightings at one time. In a two-week period, the U.S. Marshals Office received more than 500 calls. Many of the calls were a waste of time. In Bell County, a frustrated dispatcher named Judy Greenway related one incident: "A little old lady called and said there's

someone banging on her back door, and she's sure it's
McDuff. The deputies get there, and it's her Labrador Re-
triever hitting the door with his tail." The dispatcher in
Lampasas County, Theresa Holliman, marveled at how
worked up callers could get: "You'd think it was Elvis, the
way they get excited."[25]

The flood of McDuff-related stories also caught the attention of Texas Governor Ann Richards, who announced
that "McDuff must be found" and that Texas Crime Stoppers was offering a reward. Within a few weeks the Governor received a full briefing of the McDuff Affair. She
was horrified, and immediately called for an investigation
into reports that McDuff had gotten out as a result of hiring
a parole consultant. "Former board members acting on behalf of prisoners for a fee, I think, raises serious questions.
It raises questions of improper influence at the very least."
The Governor was also angered at how McDuff had been
released by the parole board staff (when Bettie Wells made
an administrative decision to reinstate McDuff's parole after being returned to prison for making a terroristic threat)
rather than by the board itself. In addition to the Governor,
Senator Ted Lyon, the Chairman of the Criminal Justice
Committee, announced that he would conduct hearings on
McDuff-related allegations.[26]

Within a year, Governor Richards accepted a suggestion
by Bill Johnston to create a special team to track down
fugitives charged with violent crimes. Through an executive
order, she formed the Governor's Fugitive Squad. "I want
these law enforcement professionals to do whatever it takes
to make sure that any Kenneth McDuff or any potential
Kenneth McDuff is brought in before he can hurt innocent
people." Immediately, the team targeted 300 parolees who
had committed violent crimes since being paroled.[27]

IV

By Sunday, April 26, the first wave of searches for Colleen
had concluded. Bell County and Austin Police Department

officers had combed vast areas around the abandoned road
Worley identified as the murder site, and in fields near the
S&S trailer park. On that day, over 200 people marched to
the Texas Capitol. They mourned the lives of loved ones
taken as a result of violent crimes. The idea was to "walk
a mile in a victim's shoes." Lori was one of the 200. She
and her two half-sisters planted three trees in an Austin park
in memory of their sister.[28]

As the marchers began to go home from the Capitol, a
fisherman named Jeffery Heard put his boat into a water-
filled gravel pit off Bois d'Arc Road near the small Dallas
County community of Combine. His uncle, Henry "Red"
Heard, leased the gravel pits from the Forge Gravel Company for fishing. The remote pits are not accessible to the
general public, but occasionally unauthorized fishermen
need to be run off the property. About three hours after he
started fishing, and approximately 100 yards from where he
put in his boat, Jeffery noticed something strange floating
in the pit. He did not recognize it at first, so he got closer.
To his horror, he saw that it was a body. Immediately,
Jeffery loaded his boat and headed for his uncle's store on
the corner of Bilingsday and Bois d'Arc Roads. A cousin
phoned the police. By dusk the Dallas County Sheriff's
Office had a crew on the scene.[29]

Melissa had been there since McDuff killed her on
March 1. She was floating in about four feet of water, about
five feet from the shore and about one and a half miles
from where her car had been discovered. Her body was in
an advanced state of decomposition. Time, water and small
animals had ravaged her. Had she not been found on April
26, or soon afterwards, she might not have been found at
all. Her hands had been tied behind her back by shoestrings,
and a jacket had been pulled down over her arms as if to
immobilize them. Her ankles had been tied together at one
time; remnants of black shoestrings were found around each
ankle. A purple shirt had been pulled over her face, and is
likely what held her head together. Deputy Tim Parker believed that she may have been weighted down for a while.

Her bra was still in place, but there was no clothing from her waist down. Nearby, someone saw a black, high-top tennis shoe floating in the water. The size 6 shoe had no laces.[30]

The officers set up floodlights to illuminate the area. By 8:40 P.M. a Dallas County Medical Examiner field agent named Charles Gaylor arrived to retrieve the body. Gaylor had to sink a body bag beneath Melissa and lift her up from behind in order to take her out of the pit.[31]

There was some initial doubt as to whether it was Melissa Northrup. She had been found wearing a shirt that was different from the one she was last seen wearing. But the next day the Dallas County Medical Examiner made a positive identification. He could not determine the immediate cause of death. Had there been injuries, they would have been hard or even impossible to see. There were no fractures in the bones of her neck, but in people her age that was common. Tissues and internal organs in her pelvic area were missing. She had been in the water far too long and ravaged far too much by the elements to determine an exact cause of death. Drowning could not be ruled out. Like Valencia Joshua, though, the manner of death was clearly homicidal violence.[32]

Brenda Solomon could never accept that Melissa was dead until she had been found.[33] At least Melissa was no longer a missing person, and her case clearly involved more than just kidnapping. There was no doubt about whether or not she had run away. Whoever took her from the Quik Pak killed her. Her family was able to bury her at Waco Memorial Cemetery along Interstate 35, only a couple of miles from the Quik Pak #8.

18

Guns and Condoms

"How much more degraded can this get?"
—Mike McNamara

I

To this day Mike and Parnell McNamara and Bill Johnston
grope for words to express how completely saddened they
were by their trip to where Colleen had been killed, and by
what they heard Hank Worley say that night. But rage
quickly replaced sadness; and their faces of stone returned.
Almost every night for the next couple of weeks, they
roamed the streets of Belton, Temple, Waco, and the hamlets of the Blackland Prairie. They did not give up until
there were no leads and there was absolutely nothing else
to do.

"Each night at about midnight the tension got almost
unbearable because you could not help but wonder if he
was killing someone else at that moment. Where is he right
now? What is he doing right now? Who is being tortured
right now? Who is choking to death?" remembered Mike.
For many nights Mike returned home during early morning
hours. Even then he could not sleep. He would sit in a chair
in the darkness, sometimes for two hours—thinking.

"We were leaving our families on their own to go on
the prowl ourselves," added Bill. Parnell remembers getting
home at ungodly hours. Some nights he ran upstairs to
make sure every member of his family was there. He
watched them sleep, and touched them.

Inside Bigfoot, The Boys depended on and protected one
another. Within the Suburban, brotherly love was no pre-
tense, there was no need for exaggerated displays of tough-

ness or the dishonesty of suppressed emotions.[1]

Their investigation took them to the McLennan County Jail where they interviewed Chester, who had been jailed for failure to appear on misdemeanor trespass, and probation violations. He admitted that he had known McDuff for about five months. They had been introduced by a prostitute called "Little Run." He repeated the story of the "plastic-covered rope" he saw under the seats of McDuff's pickup truck. Like everyone else who knew McDuff, Chester related that "Mac" always talked about robbing a convenience store. He also confirmed that at one time McDuff had a shotgun with a broken stock (the one that Chester sold to him for $40). But he did not say where McDuff got the gun. On the whole, however, it did not take The Boys long to realize Chester was a waste of time.[2]

It was also equally evident that they would have to spend a lot of time in the beer joints and trailer parks McDuff frequented. Almost every night for several weeks, assorted members of the subculture—like drug addicts, whores, thieves and degenerates lining the Cut—saw a huge, white, four-wheel-drive Suburban motor down Faulkner Lane. The dim street lighting was enough to see two big, white cowboy hats up front, and a very tall man, sometimes in a suit, in the back.

"We had a strange relationship with the whores," Parnell remembered, almost sheepishly. The girls thought McDuff was weird, dangerous, and crazy, and they wanted him caught. McDuff had stolen crack from some of the dealers and had brutalized some of the prostitutes (those he did not kill). "They didn't like him either. The hookers and thugs were on our side—for the most part," added Parnell. "McDuff was too bad even for the worst ones. One guy said if he knew where McDuff was he'd kill him for us."

While on the Cut, Mike, Parnell and Bill were appropriately cautious. After a number of visits, however, Bigfoot became a such familiar sight on Faulkner that they felt comfortable stopping and talking to the street people. Some of the prostitutes got more and more relaxed as they came to realize that The Boys were interested in getting McDuff. One of the more memorable of the girls was a bundle of nerves named Renee, whose sentences sounded like incredibly long, polysyllabic words pronounced as fast as they could be said: "Parnell-did-you-see-him-did-you-see-him?" But Renee was also memorable for two other nervous habits. She constantly picked her nose and scratched her erogenous zones. Parnell remembers the night he and Bill first encountered Renee. After talking to her, Parnell looked at Bill and asked, "God, Bill, did you see how she kept picking her nose?"

Looking straight ahead, as if to summon a reserve of dignity to disguise how completely disgusted he was, Bill replied regally, "Yes. I wondered what her interest was in that."

One evening, Mike, Parnell and Bill were in Parnell's big, extended cab pickup truck. Parnell and Bill sat on the front bucket seats; Mike sat on one of the small back "jump" seats. On the console between the bucket seat lay the huge, powerful arsenal The Boys carried with them just in case they sighted McDuff and a gunfight erupted. As Parnell turned on to the Cut, Renee and a couple of other girls came running out from behind trees and shrubs lining empty lots. "Hey-Parnell-what's-going-on?-Parnell-Parnell-did-you-see-him?" Renee asked.

"No, Renee. Have you heard anything?" asked Parnell.

Renee then looked across the front seat and saw Bill seated on the passenger side.

"Bill-Bill-I-wanna-talk-to-Bill! I-wanna-talk-to-Bill! Let-me-get-in-the-truck!"

"No, Renee, no! We got too many guns in here," pleaded Parnell.

As Renee raced around the front of the truck, Bill's head made a 180-degree turn that ended when she reached his side. He straightened up in horror when she opened the door, which illuminated the dome light inside of the truck.

"Bill-Bill!"

"Renee, what are you doing?" asked a panicked Bill.

"Bill-Bill!"

"Renee!" protested Bill.

"Bill-Bill!"

"Renee! Stop it!" pleaded Bill as she jumped into the truck and on to Bill's lap.

"Renee, get off of me!" shouted Bill as Parnell threw his arms over the guns to protect them. Seated directly behind Bill, Mike jerked backwards and started laughing.

"Renee, stop it! What's in that bag?" Bill continued.

With her right hand, Renee clutched a small, thin, plastic bag. During her efforts to get on Bill's lap, the bag tore, spilling its contents—condoms—all over Bill, Parnell's arms, and the guns. Condoms were everywhere. As Bill finally managed to get her off of him, and as Renee mercifully retreated, Bill tried to kick the condoms out of the truck and on to the street. For much of the rest of the night, Bill discovered additional condoms stuck to his shoes or wedged into the creases of his bucket seat. "Oh God, there's another one!" he exclaimed as he threw them out the window.

Mike made matters worse: "Bill, do you want to go by the Robo Car Wash? We can hose you down if you want."[3]

During another trip to the Cut, Mike asked "Little Bit" and Renee if either of them had heard anything new about McDuff's whereabouts. Little Bit said she'd had a date with McDuff only the day before. Standing nearby, Renee started shouting at Little Bit, accusing her of smoking too much crack. Little Bit replied that Renee was crazy, and the two started fighting in the middle of the street. Later, when asked if he ever thought of breaking up the battling prostitutes, Mike replied, "Oh, no. I let 'em go at it."

The subculture was Shakespearean. Dark comedy mixed with tragedy. In the midst of such a bizarre existence, Mike, Parnell, and Bill gathered leads to pursue into all hours of the night. And at times, each of the men got jolted by reminders of just how tragic these people had allowed themselves to become. For Mike, it was the night he watched Little Bit calmly walk to the intersection of Faulkner and

South Loop. While standing in the middle of the road, she leaned over and vomited. As the puke splashed on the pavement, Mike thought: "How much more degraded can this get?"[4]

It could and would get worse as a number of investigators got closer and closer to McDuff. From sources very close to and inside the family came shocking allegations of Kenneth McDuff's history of sexually assaulting members of his own family. Some of the more levelheaded of the McDuff Clan clearly understood how he needed to be returned to prison—and never released again. One of his own nephews admitted that he once "ran around" with McDuff, but now he promised to cooperate fully because he thought his uncle was a "madman" and frightening. One of McDuff's sisters spoke of how Kenneth shamelessly cared for no one but himself, grossly taking advantage of everyone who tried to help him. Not all of his sisters felt so strongly; some refused to cooperate with investigators. (They probably could not have given much in the way of information anyway.)[5]

But Mike McNamara was able to develop a reliable, confidential source close enough to the family to get good information. According to that source, Addie continued to insist to family and friends that Kenneth was innocent—and dead. The confidential source also indicated that McDuff liked to hang out in a heavily wooded area behind TSTI, and that if he had buried a body anywhere, it would be in that area in a shallow grave with debris covering it. (Only days after securing that information from the informant, the body of Valencia Kay Joshua was recovered in that area.)[6] For the next several years, Mike maintained his communication with the informant.

II

Conspicuously absent from the investigative scene was the Waco Police Department, especially when considering that the Cut is in the Waco city limits. According to their own police department reports, Barbara Carpenter, Regenia Moore's mother, contacted the Waco Police on October 21, 1991, less than one week after her daughter's disappearance. The officer did not write a report about the communication until more than seven months later, on April 28, 1992. Only the day before, the Regenia Moore case was assigned to Mike Nicoletti of the Special Crimes Unit. He and another officer worked the case, which became the "master" case for both the Moore and Brenda Thompson investigations.[7]

Nicoletti masterfully secured information from the Cut's frequent occupants. He documented McDuff's brutalization of a number of prostitutes. One unnamed girl told how McDuff once grabbed her, put a knife to her throat, and walked her over to a mirror: "Look at yourself in the mirror. You're a no-good prostitute. You're trash. I should kill you!" According to the prostitute, a few minutes later his mood changed and he put away his knife. Another prostitute, who refused to have anal sex with McDuff in his motel room, told Nicoletti of how McDuff calmly offered to take her back to her home. She foolishly accepted, only to have him take her to a secluded spot near TSTI where he told her, "We can do this the easy way, or we can do this the hard way. Anyway, I'm going to get my nut. I'll do it slow and easy." After three hours of savage sex, he offered to be "her man" and promised not to let anybody else hurt her.[8]

Desperate to find her daughter, Barbara Carpenter let the word spread that there was a $15,000 reward for information leading to Regenia's recovery. Allegedly, McDuff responded by letting it be known that he had taken Regenia, but had left her with a Mexican who raped and killed her. McDuff offered to torture the Mexican into confessing to where he buried her. McDuff then would dig her up and deliver her to her mother for a reward.[9] Of course, nothing ever resulted from the scheme.

Mike Nicoletti was able to prove, once and for all, that

Regenia Moore was not the woman seen kicking and screaming in McDuff's pickup truck on the infamous night of October 10, 1991, when McDuff drove past a WPD roadblock. Nicoletti served a subpoena on the Inn 7 to review their guest registration cards. He located a card, dated October 15, 1991, signed "Regenia Moore." (It also settled a minor dispute over whether her name was Regenia or Regina.) The signature matched several samples on file at WPD.[10]

But mixed with compelling information that McDuff had, indeed, abducted and killed Regenia Moore and Brenda Thompson, were conflicting reports that Regenia often talked of going to Houston to become a topless dancer. Another source said that she might be in Madisonville, Texas. Even more confusing was the case of Brenda Thompson, who was characterized as "much more of a loner [who] did not get picked up as often."

Like almost all other investigators looking for McDuff, Nicoletti's search led him to the ubiquitous Chester. Chester admitted that he had lied to many other investigators about McDuff. He also admitted to being a heavy crack user and dealer. To Nicoletti and APD Sergeant John Jones, "Chester the Molester" described a chilling conversation he had with McDuff. On or near the date of her disappearance, as Regenia entered a convenience store to buy candy, McDuff reputedly told Chester that he was "going to use her up, and then . . . leave her on the road."[11]

At the Austin Police Department Sonya Urubek came to the conclusion that Kenneth McDuff was "like a professor for those who would want to get away with a crime. He could teach others." She was also impressed with what ordinary people leave behind as evidence of their existence. She thought specifically of the strands of Colleen's hair she and Lori painfully removed from trash bags stuffed with Colleen's clothes, and the genetic code unique to Colleen that could be retrieved from her last Pap smear. She was also very impressed with how professional Mike Goins, one of the three witnesses to what went on at the car wash on

December 29, 1991, approached his responsibilities and instructions. After being told not to get too familiar with the
Colleen Reed Case, he made specific efforts not to do so.
It was not that hard. He lived in Houston and was a very
busy young man anyway.[12]

On March 24, the true crime show *Unsolved Mysteries*
came to Austin to tape a reenactment of the abduction of
Colleen Reed. Mike Goins and Stephen Marks played
themselves on the episode, which aired on April 24. During
the taping, Sonya, Mike, Stephen and Kari met at Kari's
house on Powell Street and this is when Mike made the
tentative identification of McDuff from Sonya's photo
lineup.[13]

On the day *Unsolved Mysteries* aired, Dan Zahara of
APD drove to Houston to show Mike Goins another photo
lineup. In a Kettle Restaurant Mike looked carefully at each
of the pictures. This one had Hank Worley's picture in it.
Mike could not make any identification.[14]

The *Unsolved Mysteries* telecast was disappointing in
that only twenty-one leads came in as a result. There were
fourteen officers at telephones ready to take calls.[15] Far
more productive was the telecast of *America's Most
Wanted*, which aired on May 1. The show generated over
fifty tips that came to a phone bank manned by the U.S.
Marshals Service. The show featured Lori and showed pictures of Colleen Reed and Kenneth McDuff. Not surprisingly, most of the tips came from Texas, although the most
valuable of them all did not, and was not phoned in to the
marshals.

III

On May 3, 1992, Kansas City Police Sergeant J. D. Johnson
received a call from an employee of the Longview Disposal
Systems. The caller was an acquaintance of Johnson who
had watched *America's Most Wanted* two nights earlier. His
friend said he believed he saw a co-worker featured on the

show. He identified the colleague as Richard Dale Fowler. That night, Johnson viewed a video tape of the program. The next day, he contacted the refuse company and obtained Fowler's birth date and Social Security number. At the police department, he did a computer search and found that a Richard Dale Fowler had been arrested for soliciting prostitution on April 10 and that fingerprints had been taken. With Fowler's fingerprints in hand, Johnson called the McLennan County Sheriff's Office and spoke to Richard Stroup. The McLennan County Sheriff's Office did not have McDuff's fingerprints on file because he had never been arrested by them. Stroup then called Bell County and spoke to Investigator Mike Elmore, who faxed McDuff's fingerprints to Johnson several times. After enlarging the faxes, Alice Dearing, a KCPD fingerprint specialist, was able to make a positive identification—Richard Dale Fowler was really Kenneth Allen McDuff.[16]

Once McDuff had been positively identified, Johnson contacted his source and determined that on Monday, May 4, McDuff would be on garbage truck number 103, and that the truck would be at Eighty-fifth Street and Hickman Mills Drive between 1:00 and 2:00 P.M. At 1:00 P.M., seven Kansas City Policemen set up an inspection station at Eighty-fifth and Prospect designed to inspect heavy-weight vehicles. They even used a specially marked car readily recognized as a weights and measures vehicle. The garbage truck rolled up at 1:32 P.M. and slowed down when an officer flagged it. As the truck came to a stop, the lawmen moved into position. McDuff, seated near the passenger side door, was readily recognized. As he started to exit the truck, two armed officers immediately pushed him to the ground and handcuffed him. (The other two bewildered trashmen hurriedly exited the driver's side door. The men told the officers that McDuff had asked them how to get a gun.)[17]

Like a crocodile with his mouth tied shut, McDuff was totally passive. Of course, as J. D. Johnson stated, "There were two officers there with shotguns; there was no oppor-

tunity for him to be argumentative." KCPD Officer Robert
Harlow loaded McDuff into a van specially fitted with a
compartment to transport prisoners. Harlow took McDuff
in for booking—alone. At the jail, he took him to the eighth
floor and placed him in a holding cell. Harlow asked him
what his name was and he replied "Richard Fowler." Harlow replied that it was no use to lie because fingerprint
cards were going to be used to make a true identification.
He then handed McDuff a piece of paper taken from his
property and pointed to the name "Kenneth McDuff." At
that point, McDuff admitted his true identity.[18]

"Let me first say, thank God that the manhunt for Kenneth Allen McDuff is over," said Mike Carnevale, as he
began a press conference in which he outlined the capture.

It was the 208th success story out of 469 re-enactments
on *America's Most Wanted*. As soon as KCPD had McDuff,
Parnell called Tim Steglich, who went to see Hank immediately. He asked Hank if he had anything to add to any of
his previous statements. He said nothing of consequence.[19]

The press scoured Kansas City for people who knew
"Richard Fowler." Barbara Harman, his landlady, seemed
stunned by the publicity. "I had no idea. I watched *America's Most Wanted* Friday, and it never sunk in. Thank God
it did with someone else." The branch manager for the temporary employment services company that got McDuff the
trash collector's job remembered him as a quiet worker.
"As far as an impression, he didn't make much [of one].
He didn't strike me as odd, he didn't strike me as overly
aggressive. In fact, he was in my office last week with a
complaint about the job. About the conditions, the people
he was working with, those things."[20]

In Texas there were many lawmen anxious to go to Kansas City to get McDuff. Dan Stoltz secured a U.S. Marshals
Service plane and asked Parnell to put together a team to
make the trip. The men, including Bobby Hogeland of the
U.S. Marshals, Joe Wylie of the Texas Rangers, and Jeff
Brzozowski of the ATF, arrived at the Hyatt Regency, an
elegant hotel next to the Hallmark Headquarters in Kan-

sas City. The posse Parnell assembled included men who
left home so fast that many of them forgot to bring basic
necessities. Mad Dog Don Owens looked at the hotel's
shiny marble floors and up at the huge open spaces and
said, "Ooo." Then he looked at Parnell and said, "I got
three bucks on me, Parnell. Can you spot me a couple of
bucks?"

McDuff had been taken to the Blue Springs Correctional
Facility in Kansas City, used to house federal prisoners.
When the posse arrived, the desk worker looked back and
forth at the cowboy hats and boots and said, "You boys
from Texas?" (Years later Parnell remembered that he saw
no one wearing boots in Kansas City. He thought that odd
for a place that had so many stockyards.) J. W. remembers
how the staff was taken by surprise at the number of officers arriving for one prisoner: "There were more of us than
was there in that police department." The guards at the
facility had to be told that they had a very dangerous serial
killer and that extra security was needed, as well as a suicide watch. The men had to decide who should question
McDuff. They decided that the master interrogator, Chuck
Meyer, and J. W., as the sole representative from the Austin
Police Department, should be there for the entire session.
A third place could be rotated among some of the other
officers.[21]

"We knew we had only one shot at him," Chuck remembered. At 2:01 A.M. McDuff was awakened and
brought to an interrogation room. The first trio to speak to
him consisted of Chuck, J. W., and Texas Ranger Joe Wylie. J. W. read him his rights from a "blue card" and asked
him to sign it. McDuff refused to sign it and so J. W. signed
his own name and noted the names of the two other officers
present.

At first, McDuff stated that he would answer any questions the men had for him. He did ask why he was being
detained, and Chuck answered truthfully that he was
wanted for distribution of narcotics and firearms possession.
While he was so agreeable, Chuck got him to agree to sign

a consent to search form for a search of his apartment. McDuff signed it and said there was nothing there but beer cans, trash and a lot of dirty clothes. This was a first meeting with McDuff for J. W. and Chuck, who both found it disgusting to have to be nice to him. J. W. remembered how filthy McDuff was. (He was still wearing the clothes he wore to collect trash.) They got him so comfortable that he joked about how one of his friends said he saw him on television on a show called "Mysterious Mysteries."

Shortly into the interview, Wylie left the room and Parnell entered. For more than two hours McDuff pontificated on his pride in being a "true" convict, a product of the old system. He was a survivor, he said, and knew more about getting by than present-day inmates. He did not belong to any particular gang, but hung around with several other inmates. In prison, McDuff developed an ability to make his own "brew" right in front of the guards—without them ever noticing. Chuck managed to get the conversation back to how McDuff got to Kansas City. McDuff stated that he really did not want to talk about it. When Chuck asked why not, McDuff answered that "there was no reason to bring anyone else into it." J. W. knew from that response that someone had to have helped this vicious killer escape from Texas.

McDuff did say that it was very hard to get a job without a picture ID, and that he would leave a business rather than explain why he did not have one. He bought the Social Security card, he explained, for $25. He had also purchased a driver's license, but the picture looked nothing like him and would likely cause more problems than what it was worth, so he threw it away.

Chuck and Parnell began to ask him about some of his former associates in the Waco and Temple area. In each case, McDuff admitted only to drinking beer with them. He claimed to prefer to run around by himself. He explained his public intoxication arrest in Temple and that he had a scar under his eye because "a nigger" had broken a bottle on his face.[22]

Chuck, J. W. and Parnell listened patiently as McDuff talked on and on about prison, whores and cars. Chuck then began to zero in. He asked McDuff about Austin, and whether McDuff had ever been there. McDuff denied that he had ever been involved in any robberies. The lawmen looked at each other; no one had mentioned robberies. McDuff admitted that he had been in Austin many times, but he insisted that he had always been alone. Parnell asked him questions related to One-eyed Jack's statement, specifically references to the young girl on rollerskates, stealing gas from a convenience store, and driving down the wrong way on a one-way street. McDuff denied it all. As the trio of lawmen began to leak out tidbits of information they had gathered from Billy, Jack and Hank, McDuff's tanned, ruddy face began to turn ash gray. As the interview continued, Chuck moved his chair closer and closer to McDuff, who responded by slowly moving back. J. W. and Parnell moved closer as well. It was as if the floor was a map in a war room and a general was moving divisions in for a kill. J. W. called it a "dance." Soon, McDuff was against a wall and could move no farther.

J. W. told McDuff that the information came from someone who claimed to have been in Austin with him. McDuff steadfastly asserted that every trip he had ever taken to Austin he had taken alone. It was J. W.'s turn to get aggressive. The source had taken a polygraph and passed it. McDuff quickly stated that he could take a polygraph and pass it too. J. W. then identified Hank Worley as the source, just to see how McDuff would react. He paused, and then denied being in Austin.[23]

Thinking about the Yogurt Shop Murders, Chuck asked McDuff if he had ever been in a shopping mall with a skating rink. (He was referring to the Northcross Mall on Anderson Lane in Austin, only a few hundred yards from the yogurt shop.) McDuff quickly answered no.

As the men hammered away, McDuff could only respond, "Wrong guy, not me." He said that a number of times. Each time he said it he became more ashen. And he

never asked what crime he was being accused of.[24] At
4:41 A.M., McDuff indicated that he would like an attorney,
abruptly ending the interview. He was returned to his cell.

The following day the ATF executed a search warrant
for McDuff's ninth-floor apartment at 350 East Armour
Boulevard. The apartment building was located in a rundown neighborhood with old houses. J. W. assisted in the
search and discovered an array of shoelaces and cotton
ropes tied in a variety of knots. Bobby Hogeland and Parnell discovered the knife McDuff slept with.[25]

Local ATF agents were able to confirm that McDuff
hung around with and once roomed with a man nicknamed
"Indian" whose real name was Francis. Francis had a serious drinking problem and had been thrown out of some
of the apartments he'd lived in. Chuck Meyer recalled, "He
kind of reminds you of that guy in *One Flew Over the
Cuckoo's Nest.*" Francis knew of McDuff's arrest; he saw
it on television at a Salvation Army station.

The officers located Francis where he worked. He agreed
to be interviewed. During the interview, Francis related
conversations he'd had with McDuff, and specifically how
McDuff talked about being good at killing with his hands,
killing with a knife, having his own graveyard, and other,
assorted horrors. Francis, like most of McDuff's associates,
thought he "talked shit." He also remembered that McDuff
had asked for shoelaces for his tennis shoes, but he picked
out black laces for white shoes. Predictably, McDuff asked
Francis about how to get a gun. He related that McDuff
nearly got a gun from a truck driver who worked with him
at Longview Disposal Service.[26]

McDuff appeared in Federal Court in Kansas City before
U.S. Magistrate Sarah Hays. She informed him of his rights
and read the charges against him. She also appointed federal public defenders to represent him. McDuff listened quietly. He was dressed in a blue golf shirt, faded jeans stained
with blotches of white paint, and tennis shoes with no laces.
When asked if he had anything to say, he replied, "I am

not even aware of where these charges are coming from, or anything."[27]

By May 6, the posse Parnell had assembled was ready to return to Texas with its prisoner. They placed McDuff in the back of the U.S. Marshals' aircraft, away from the others. No one said anything to him.[28] McDuff was heading back to Texas. There were many people waiting for him.

No one in Waco ever remembers such tight security for an individual. But the security was not to prevent McDuff from escaping, it was to protect him. "We want to keep him alive, at least for a little while," said an officer. Marshals like Dan Stoltz, Mike Carnevale, Bobby Hogeland, Ray Kondo, and Mike and Parnell McNamara now found themselves protecting the man they had hunted down. At the federal courthouse about 100 people "greeted" McDuff. Many screamed and yelled invectives and questions at him. "I hate him. I hate him. I want to see him fry," said Melissa Northrup's sister-in-law.

McDuff seemed to bring out contradictions in people. One bystander managed to mix obscenity with the Bible: "That damn fucking bastard. Vengeance is mine saith the Lord!" she screamed when she saw McDuff.[29]

In court, McDuff was charged with distribution of LSD and felon possession of a firearm—both federal charges. Waco attorney Dwight Goains was appointed to be his attorney. Goains promptly announced that McDuff would not be talking to any lawmen any time soon.[30]

Many law enforcement agencies were involved in the hunt for Kenneth McDuff. As Jeff Brzozowski of the ATF said, "it was a team effort." This investigation transcended inter-departmental rivalries. Each agency rewarded the members of the McDuff Task Force in its own way. Mike Carnevale, Mike McNamara, and Parnell McNamara received the Director's Special Achievement Award, the highest honor given by the U.S. Marshals Service, for their work. The U.S. Attorney General commended Bill Johnston for his efforts, and Texas Governor Ann Richards publicly praised them all for their service to the State of Texas.

IV

At the Austin Police Department, procedures started to transfer the Colleen Reed Case from the Assault Unit, where Don Martin was the case agent, to the Homicide Detail where Sergeant Scott Cary took over. The process began only two days after Worley's confession, and was completed two days after McDuff had been brought to Waco. Don and Scott met for over four hours reviewing what had been done. Scott also met with Travis County Assistant District Attorney David Counts. Without question, Kenneth McDuff was going to be prosecuted in Austin, even if Colleen should be found in Bell County. He had scheduled a nine-day vacation that was to begin the next day. He spent much of his time during his days off reading the case file.

When Scott Cary returned on May 19, he met with Chuck Meyer and J. W. Thompson. They agreed to return to the Temple, Belton, and Waco areas to re-interview key witnesses and McDuff associates.[31]

On May 27, Cary, Sonya Urubek and David Counts drove to Waco to do a live lineup. Lieutenant David Parkinson, the newly appointed head of the homicide detail at APD, arranged to have several officers with the same appearance and build as McDuff take part in the lineup. The procedure was complicated when McDuff arrived and refused to shave. After some discussion with McDuff's attorney, Dwight Goains, APD convinced Goains to ask McDuff to shave, but he refused. McDuff did not have much of a beard, and Goains agreed that the lineup should take place; he also agreed not to bring up questions of validity in the future.

At about 2:00 P.M. Mike Goins entered the witness room. The live lineup had already been assembled. In a sworn statement he gave only a few days later, Goins said that he recognized McDuff immediately, but he disciplined himself to look carefully at all six persons. He sat on a small chair in the center of the room and just looked carefully and methodically at every person on the stage. At one point he asked if he could move for a better look. He was told that he could, so he moved to the left and looked at the men from an angle (similar to the one he saw on the night of the abduction). Goins then signaled Sonya Urubek that he was ready. The two moved to an adjacent lounge area where she handed him an index card and a pencil. He had been told that if he could make a positive identification to write a number; if he could make a tentative identification to write a number next to a question mark; and if he did not recognize anyone to just leave the card blank. He took it and wrote #2 on it.

"Are you sure?" Sonya asked.

"You don't see a question mark on there, do you?" answered Goins, who had just identified Kenneth McDuff, and thus placed him at the corner of Sixth and Powell Streets only a minute or so before Colleen was heard screaming at the car wash.

After Goins looked at the lineup, another witness sat and looked at it. This witness had seen a suspect of the Studio M murder, which had occurred on the same day Colleen was abducted. She incorrectly identified one of the APD officers; McDuff was dropped as a suspect in that case.[32]

After the lineup, Sonya, Scott, and David drove out to the abandoned road where Worley stated that Colleen had been killed. Scott remembered the smell of death; area residents found the remote, narrow path a useful place to deposit dead animals. It made the site all the more eerie.

19

The Northrup Trial

"This was a monster that needed taking care of."
—Mike Freeman, McLennan County
Assistant District Attorney

On May 18, 1992, a Texas Department of Criminal Justice (TDCJ) Internal Affairs Investigator named John Moriarty called APD Detective Sonya Urubek at her office. Moriarty told her that he was compiling a timeline of Kenneth McDuff's known whereabouts from the time he first entered prison in 1965 to the present. Other than informal meetings among officers, this was the first serious attempt to compile data from several law enforcement jurisdictions into a central location. The synopsis Moriarty compiled became a godsend for the dozens of detectives investigating McDuff, allowing them to safely eliminate McDuff as a suspect in a number of pending murders, rapes, and abductions.[1]

John Moriarty and TDCJ had been brought into the case because McDuff was an ex-con on parole. John was originally from the South Bronx in New York, but he fit in very well with the Texas posse informally assembled to track down McDuff. John Aycock, a quintessential Texas lawman, called Moriarty "a cop's cop." The information he supplied the posse about McDuff's prison career greatly assisted in efforts to understand and profile the fugitive. He also had vast experience dealing with the families of ex-cons, and conducted masterful interviews with Addie and J. A. McDuff.

On May 15, 1993, J. A. McDuff died at Scott and White Hospital in Temple at 2:15 P.M. The hospital refused to release his cause of death, but Kenneth later said that the old man had been outside cutting grass and he got overheated. While in his house he had a heart attack and died.

As information and misinformation leaked out about the circumstances surrounding McDuff's previous releases, possible corruption on the parole board, former board members acting as "consultants" working towards the early release of prisoners, and the fact that McDuff had been released at all, political and public pressure began to mount to get to the bottom of the whole sordid mess. Moriarty had been placed in a very delicate position—investigating his own agency. Other officers began to call him the "Dancing Bear," because they were reminded of a circus bear standing on a large ball—any wrong move and the bear falls off. For the next six years, John Moriarty became more and more of a central figure in the slow process of bringing the Kenneth McDuff episode to a close.

Dwight Goains, representing McDuff, had owned a medical supply company in the Houston area before becoming an attorney. At the time he represented McDuff, ninety-five percent of his practice involved criminal law, and about seventy-five percent of that came from being a public defender. He had the reputation for liking difficult trial cases. "What everyone has to understand in my case is that I do not defend crimes, I defend a person's constitutional rights, and from that standpoint, it is easy. It doesn't matter if they jaywalked or murdered twenty people. This is still the United States of America."[2]

After advising McDuff not to speak to any law enforcement officials, he made a brief statement for his client: "He has authorized me to say that he is not guilty, and he looks forward to his day in court. My client's general feelings were that with all the media attention, they'd pressure them into indicting him. The state should not be prosecuting him in the media; that is what the courtroom is for." Goains went on to say that the federal charges were "trumped up" to allow the Marshals Service to join the manhunt.[3]

The federal charges were not "trumped up." Dealing drugs and felon possession of a firearm are serious crimes, and McDuff did much of both. Clearly, however, the size of the manhunt and the resources expended by the federal government to apprehend him had everything to do with McDuff being a serial killer. It would have been foolish to ignore his violent past and the evidence of his involvement in homicides. McDuff once stated in an interview that, "once they found my car, it was 'Get McDuff.' "[4] He was right; they wanted him very badly.

In early July, Bill Johnston went before a federal district judge and filed a motion to dismiss, without prejudice, federal charges against McDuff. He did so in order to allow the McLennan County District Attorney, John Segrest, to pursue capital murder charges. "Our posture is a safety net. It would not be prudent for us to stand in the way of the state's capital case that has a death penalty exposure that we can't offer," Bill said. He could reinstate charges within a five-year period. His motion was granted.[5]

Even in jail, McDuff managed to get into trouble and make the headlines. After several weeks in the McLennan County Jail, McDuff had been moved from isolation into the general population. He had been a "model" prisoner until September 15, 1992, when he convinced a fellow prisoner to "swap" cells with him so he would be incarcerated with an inmate who was willing to have sex with him. McDuff offered him $30 for the encounter. By the next morning, McDuff's punk was pleading for an end to the endless hours of sex. The jailers returned McDuff to isolation.[6]

The McLennan and Travis County District Attorneys Offices met and informally decided that whoever had the stronger case should prosecute McDuff first. The longer Travis County waited, the more compelling was the argument that Colleen was dead. While they had an eyewitness/accomplice to Colleen's abduction, her body had never been recovered.

In Melissa's case, there were questions about venue. Melissa's body had been found in Dallas County, and she was almost certainly murdered there. But Dallas County had "only a body floating in a gravel pit"; the advanced decomposed state of the victim made prosecuting a homicide case there problematic. In the same case, the McLennan County District Attorney started with the discovery of McDuff's car near the scene, a witness who placed him at the car near the time of the abduction, a few TSTI students willing to testify that McDuff talked about robbing the Quik Pak, a woman willing to testify that she saw a man who kind of looked like McDuff walking along Bilingsday Road, a few hairs—and Hank Worley. But there was no guarantee that Hank would be able to testify, since he had witnessed an extraneous offense.

Everyone knew Kenneth Allen McDuff to be a sadistic killer; everyone knew he had done it. It was easy for the general public and law officers to be angry at and hate McDuff, and to believe that a conviction would be a cinch. In reality, the opposite was true. Getting a conviction in a court of law outside the Central Texas area was going to be tough.

McLennan County District Attorney John Segrest is a quiet and reserved man. He could have let Dallas County take the case; he could have argued that Travis County's Reed case was stronger because they had Worley; and he could have decided that if a judge would not allow Worley's extraneous offense testimony, the risk of an acquittal for an animal like McDuff was too great. Instead, John Segrest decided to prosecute McDuff for the capital murder of Melissa Ann Northrup.[7]

John Segrest has deep roots in Waco. He was born there and graduated from University High School. After matriculating at Baylor University, he completed requirements for a law degree in three years at Baylor Law School and practiced in his hometown. In 1990, he was elected McLennan County District Attorney, and thus, the McDuff trial came towards the end of his first term. He had held no other elected office. John never discussed or considered the political implications of his decisions, but his assistants knew that mishandling the McDuff case, or even one or two adverse rulings, could have meant the end of Segrest's political career.[8]

Segrest picked First Assistant Crawford Long and another Assistant D.A. named Mike Freeman to help in the McDuff trial. Crawford Long was born in Ohio, but his father moved the family to Waco early enough for Crawford to develop a thick Texas drawl. He speaks impeccable English in the deliberate manner of a wordsmith. With ease he quotes from great pieces of literature to embellish and empower important points. Indeed, like Bill Johnston, and the McNamara Boys, he was influenced greatly by his father, the head of the Baylor University English Department. His questions, and especially his summations, have imagery normally lacking in the minutiae that often plagues complicated trials. Those oratorical skills must have had an impact on judges and juries; in every capital murder trial he has ever prosecuted, the juries have levied the death sentence.[9]

Mike Freeman grew up on a farm in the Texas Panhandle, attended Abilene Christian University and went on to law school at the University of Tulsa. Mike also served as a Russian Linguist for the United States Navy. For a time he lived in Nebraska; he had moved to Waco to report to a new job with the McLennan County District Attorney's Office on March 1, 1992—the day Melissa Northrup was kidnapped from the Quik Pak.[10] He is a big man with an easy-going manner and an infectious smile.

John Segrest, of course, took the role of lead prosecutor. He did much of the more important legal legwork, such as crafting and responding to motions and later responding to appeals. Crawford handled the scientific portions of the case such as the hair samples, and—in case it became necessary—DNA. Mike Freeman did the initial investigation.[11]

Earlier, the Valencia Joshua case had been severed because of the potential difficulty in showing a common scheme or a "continuing course of conduct." Segrest explained that "it is an area of the law which the Court of Criminal Appeals has not written upon. It would be risky at best to proceed under the multiple murders portion of the indictment." It was just easier to try the Northrup Murder alone. That there would be a change of venue for McDuff was a forgone conclusion. The trial was moved to Houston.

The presiding judge was a large, robust man named Robert N. "Bob" Burdette of the 184th District Court in Harris County. Reading the transcripts of the Northrup Trial suggests a rude and impatient judge. For example, instead of asking for the attorneys to proceed, he often glared at them and said, "Hit it." He intimidated the attorneys and witnesses as well. During jury selection he often curtly told prospective jurors, "You don't mean that!" On another occasion, instead of asking people standing in the back of the courtroom to be seated, he asked sarcastically "are those people just standing there because their legs don't bend?"

Judge Burdette's unpleasant reputation preceded the Northrup Trial. During her reporting of the capital murder trial of Theodore Goynes, a reporter named Barbara Linkin wrote that "Burdette seems to want all those involved to know he's less than pleased he's presiding over the trial. To that end he had been twirling his chair during testimony and fidgeting and sighing to express his annoyance. He also had balked at ruling on defense objections and has interrupted witnesses by asking attorneys if they are finished yet."

Judge Burdette made another annoying decision. One morning he started proceedings with information for the jurors: "Ladies and gentlemen, I have noticed that there is a puzzled look on the faces of several of you. In the evenings, to get the full service out of this courtroom, we hang meat in here." Earlier in the trial one of the prosecutors had heard Burdette tell the baliff to "hang meat." Burdette kept the courtroom so cold that at times Mike Freeman had to blow into his hands to keep them warm. On another day, a Houston reporter arrived with a furry, Russian hat.[12]

But what Judge Burdette lacked in the way of patience, social graces and common courtesy, he made up for with his grasp of the law. The Northrup Case was a hard one for everyone, and the fact that the appeals courts never overruled any of his major decisions spoke for his expertise.

Identity was the sticky issue, and since there were no witnesses to the abduction and murder, identifying McDuff as a murderer rested on the accumulation of circumstantial evidence. Segrest decided to infuse the testimony of Hank Worley, and the Colleen Reed Case, into the Northrup Trial to prove the identity issue. But as Segrest has said, "Proof of offenses other than the one on trial is disfavored by the law." Evidence and testimony of extraneous offenses is not admissible to prove that a person is of bad character, but it can be admitted for other purposes. It can be used to show proof of motive, opportunity, intent, preparation, plan, knowledge, and in this case, identity. The prosecutor is required to give a reasonable notice to the defense. Defense attorney Michael Charlton argued strenuously that "the state wants to try this Colleen Reed Case here in the Melissa Northrup Case." Getting Burdette to allow Worley's testimony was going to be a complicated legal task—yet the Judge did allow it. He may not have been pleasant while he did it, but Judge Burdette handled the issue in an expert fashion and was upheld by the Texas Court of Criminal Appeals.[13]

One of the first witnesses was Addie McDuff. For the past year, Addie felt she had been hounded as a result of the publicity surrounding her infamous son. (She certainly had been. The media reported extensively on the location Worley identified as the Colleen Reed murder site, and the fact that it was near Addie's house. Undoubtedly, the curious visited the area and probably used the McDuff driveway to turn around. She also had a listed phone number.) On the day Kenneth was arrested, a reporter from the *Waco Tribune-Herald* called her and asked for a statement. She replied, "I'm not allowed to say anything," and hung up the phone. In a series of telephone calls to Tim Steglich, she outlined a series of fears and frustrations. On one occasion she asked if charges had been filed against her and her husband. "We never broke no law. Never even got a speeding ticket."

"What?" asked a bewildered Tim.

"They spray stuff in here that chokes me. They light up my house all night long."

"Mrs. McDuff, I don't know what you are talking about. What are you telling me?" asked Tim.

She then went into a long complaint about Gary Cart-wright's *Texas Monthly* article on the McDuff Murders, but she ended her diatribe by saying she had not read the article. Even before McDuff had been found she had complained to Tim.

"They call me and tell me they are different people," she said.

"I'm sorry that happened."

"Well ain't that your deputies that are doing that?" Addie asked.

"No," Tim replied. He explained that the attention paid to her and her family would likely continue until Kenneth was found. "He has got to be located one way or another." Addie hung up.

On July 27, 1992, Tim and TDCJ Investigator John Moriarty went to the McDuffs for an interview. By that time, J. A. seemed almost unaware of his surroundings, but in a moment of fatigue, he said quietly, "You know, it is almost like an old mongrel dog. You don't know what he is doing when you are not there to watch him."[14]

Addie took the stand on February 3, 1993. She had not seen Kenneth since he disappeared on February 29, 1992. She still refused to entertain any notion that Kenneth could have done what he was being accused of. She was not called to be a character witness. Instead, she established that she paid all of the bills Kenneth rang up. More importantly, she confirmed that she had given him a credit card—the card that would be used to establish his whereabouts on the night of February 29/March 1.[15]

Addie's testimony also established the credibility of the woman McDuff spent much of his time with on that infa-

mous night—Holly. Holly's strange evening with him had
been discovered almost by accident. In early May she had
been arrested and brought to the Bell County Jail. As she
walked past Tim Steglich's office she saw a picture of
McDuff and said, "That's the man who tried to keep me in
his car." That caught Tim's attention and he spoke to her.
She kept referring to him as "Cowboy." Shortly afterwards,
she gave a very valuable statement, which was corroborated
by credit card records.

The jury clearly believed every word Holly said. "In
front of everybody she owned up to her past," remembered
Crawford Long. Tim thought Holly's attitude was "here is
who I am and if you don't like it stay away from me." He
knew Holly to be an intelligent woman. She handled the
defense attorneys very well.

Holly's testimony reminded Crawford Long of a Shakespearean play—comedy interspersed with tragedy. Her account of how she, One-Arm, T-Bone, and Darrin handled
McDuff had people sitting on the edge of their seats. When
a defense attorney tried to attack her credibility by asking
about her aliases, she replied, "I have eighteen aliases. Do
you want to know them all?" The courtroom erupted in
laughter. It continued when she described McDuff's crack-
induced tantrums in the middle of tough, black neighborhoods: "I told him to get his crazy ass back in the car."
They even laughed when she described how McDuff tried
to abduct her, and how she got away by taking off her shoe
and hitting him on the face.[16]

The prosecution team never let Melissa's husband,
Aaron, become more than a factual witness. That way, their
troubled marriage never became an issue at the trial. Her
relationship with an abusive boyfriend never became a serious issue either. Reportedly, McDuff himself nixed the
defense approach of creating reasonable doubt by casting
the boyfriend as a suspect. The prosecutors surmised that
McDuff opposed such a move because if the prosecution
could clear the boyfriend (which they could) the focus
would just return to McDuff. They were relieved that the

defense did not take such a turn. "[The boyfriend] was such a jerk that he is someone the state does not want to sponsor," Crawford Long remembered.[17]

The star witness took the stand after Judge Burdette accepted the prosecution's motion to allow evidence and testimony from the Reed case. Citing more than a dozen similarities prepared by the prosecution between the two cases, Burdette made possible the testimony of Alva Hank Worley. For the first time in court, Worley related the grisly events of December 29, 1991, and the abduction and murder of Colleen Reed. Crawford Long thought that "in order to prosecute the devil you may have to go to hell for a witness." Predictably, the defense grilled him over the inconsistencies in his five statements. When Hank testified that Colleen never fought him, Dwight Goains zeroed in on him.

"You want to tell the jury that you were just being a nice guy? You raped her, is that correct?" Goains asked with disgust.

"I was nice to her. She knew I wasn't going to hurt her," Hank lamely replied.

"So, it was a nice rape; is that what you are telling the jury?"[18]

Mike Goins followed Worley to the stand. The contrast could not have been greater. By that time Mike Goins had been an engineer for Fina Oil Company for over nine years. Without much trouble, the articulate and polished Goins identified McDuff as the driver of the tan Thunderbird he saw on Powell Street the night Colleen was abducted.[19]

Other witnesses produced memorable moments in the courtroom. When one of McDuff's friends named Mark got on the stand to testify, McDuff said aloud, "Tell 'em about the Trans Am you stole." Out of sight of the jury, Mark "flipped him the bird." Louis, the acquaintance who provided information for the first of McDuff's arrest warrants, was asked by Mike Freeman, "Why were you willing to come forward with this information since Mr. McDuff is your friend?"

"I wasn't. Y'all gave me no choice," Louis replied.[20]

Pepper Cole testified that she saw someone looking like McDuff on Bilingsday Road on the morning of March 1, but it was Shari Robinson who positively identified McDuff as the man she served a bowl of beans to on her front porch. The fact that she testified that he was dirty lent credibility to her story. She decided to come forth during the trial after she saw news coverage. Robinson "tied the knot," placing him at an area near the gravel pit.[21]

Much of the testimony involved tedious information about hair. In order to educate the jury on how hair differs from one person to another, Crawford Long systematically asked various experts to describe pigmentation, clumping, and shapes as they related to samples taken from McDuff. It turned out that McDuff's hair had Negroid characteristics, a fact that bothered the rabid racist immensely. During motion hearings McDuff got so bothered that he jumped up and blurted out his displeasure at having his hair described as Negroid—Burdette told him to sit down and control himself.

"I haven't seen that degree of clumped pigmentation in a Caucasian sample before," testified Charles Linch of the Southwest Forensics Laboratory of Dallas.

"In other words, are you telling the jury that certain of Kenneth McDuff's hair has extreme Negroid characteristics? Is that correct?" asked Long as McDuff squirmed in his chair.

"Yes, sir," answered Linch.

Some observers and lawmen could not help but be amused at how upset the testimony made the extremely egotistical McDuff. Of course, it was shallow satisfaction, but many wondered if McDuff could ever be made to feel embarrassed by what he had done. On the serious side, McDuff's hair matched that taken from the jacket removed from Melissa's body and other strands vacuumed from Melissa's Buick Regal. Pubic hairs taken from the car also matched McDuff's pubic hair samples.[22]

Each day a van dropped off McDuff at the front door

of the courthouse. Reporters asked him a flurry of questions. He reveled in the attention and may have concluded that he was a better spinmaster than he really was. As in 1966, his arrogance led him to a decision that did as much as anything the prosecution could present to lead to his conviction. He decided to speak for himself.

On February 12, 1993, in Judge Burdette's chambers, Kenneth McDuff's attorneys asked to be relieved of their duties as public defenders. Officially, they asserted that Kenneth was preventing them from presenting a viable defense. Burdette immediately denied their request. It had been difficult for McDuff's lawyers to work with him. McDuff continually interrupted the proceedings and second-guessed his attorneys. He did not understand the need to establish foundations for direct and cross examinations, and thus, got impatient with his lawyers when they did not ask the questions he wanted asked—when he wanted. Against the unanimous advice of his defense team, Kenneth insisted on testifying on his own behalf. "I am fixin' to take the stand," he said in chambers. That was probably why his attorneys asked to be relieved. They may have had reason to believe that perjury was about to be committed. Judge Burdette decided to let McDuff take the stand to make whatever statements he wanted. That was just fine with the prosecutors from McLennan County— John Segrest had a few questions in mind for Mr. McDuff.[23]

For two and a half hours, Kenneth McDuff spun a tale of drugs, prostitution, and theft. The condensed version went as follows: he wanted a job in Victoria, Texas, and had an interview with a man whose name he could not remember. When the offer was withdrawn, he despaired and decided to leave Central Texas forever. During the early morning hours of March 1, McDuff stopped at a Love's Truck Stop where he met a man named Al. Al— who never materialized to back up McDuff's story—offered to buy McDuff's car for $1,500 and a trade for Al's car, which McDuff alleged was stolen—and also was never located. From Love's Truck Stop, McDuff and Al drove to Waco. At New Road in Waco, Al said the T-Bird had broken down. While they were working on the T-Bird someone in a gray car picked up Al and said they were going to get jumper cables. They left and never returned. Poor Kenneth was stuck with two cars, one that did not run and the other one stolen. He then testified that he threw his wallet and all identifying information with the name "McDuff" on the front seat of his car, took Al's car, and drove to his dorm room and went to sleep. (He added that he slept in his clothes.)

Throughout the testimony, McDuff's lawyer, Mike Charlton, tried to keep him on topic, but it was no use. Every attempt Charlton made was met by, "Well, let me explain," and followed by endless nonsense. It was as if McDuff felt that embellishing his lies with detail somehow made them the truth.

McDuff stated that from his dorm in Waco, he went south to San Antonio. It was there he claims to have gotten the fake identification he used in Kansas City. From San Antonio he went to Austin. At that point into his testimony he launched into another long, irrelevant story. Charlton tried again. "Did you ultimately leave the Austin area?" he asked in vain.

"Well, let me describe step-by-step what occurred," McDuff answered.

Judge Burdette cut him off by calling for a recess. When everyone returned, Burdette sighed and said, "All right, Mr. Charlton, I think you were making phone calls and leaving Austin."

From Austin, McDuff said, he went to Fort Worth, then to Wichita Falls, where he hitched a ride with a black truck driver who dropped him off in Lawton, Oklahoma. He slept under a tree in Lawton, awakened and walked to a bus station, where he bought a ticket to Oklahoma City. (He added that at the bus stop he mistakenly used the women's restroom.) In Oklahoma City, he slept in an abandoned burnt-out house (just like he claimed in 1966 while Roy Dale Green murdered three teenagers).

Mike Charlton tried again: "And from Oklahoma City where did you go?"

"Let me explain what happened in Oklahoma City," McDuff said.

Seated at the prosecution table, John Segrest thought "This guy won't shut up." But he knew the state was in pretty good shape. The more McDuff talked, the more he became a star witness for the prosecution. Segrest also noticed an unusual change in the jury. The courtroom had been set up so that the witness box was very near the jury. When McDuff had been called to the stand the juror seated nearest him was a woman. When they returned after Burdette's break, all of the men had positioned themselves between McDuff and the ladies.

From Oklahoma City, he went to Tulsa where he worked in a carnival for one day. After that, he hopped a train he thought was headed for Arkansas, but he ended up in Kansas City, where a fellow train-hopper showed him how to get to the mission.

Once Charlton finally got him to Kansas City, he said, "I will pass this witness."

"Well, there's a few things I'd like to bring up, points we missed," McDuff added.

"We will go back over it later," Charlton answered as he took his seat.[24]

At the end of each day of the trial, mobs of reporters converged on the principals of the event. After McDuff's testimony, Segrest shook his head and said, "If they believe this story, then we've wasted an awful lot of time and money here." Indeed, the defense produced nothing in the way of corroboration. Segrest continued, "I think he is an absolute liar. The only thing he can do to save himself at this point is to lie, and he knows how to do that."

"You witnessed what is a personal tragedy. You saw a man determined to tell his side of the story," Mike Charlton said about testimony he had hoped would not occur.[25]

Under cross-examination, John Segrest deliberately dismantled McDuff. It was just like what Charlie Butts had done in 1966. All McDuff could do was answer, "I had nothing to do about that," over and over again.[26]

As the long trial came to a close, Crawford Long rose to begin closing arguments. He reminded the jurors of McDuff's arduous, incredible testimony. "I thought Mr. Charlton was never going to get him out of some of those towns." He also pointed out that the defense had a right to bring out witnesses supporting McDuff's character and reputation for telling the truth. "Folks, there wasn't one soul that testified in this trial that this defendant had a good reputation for truth and veracity." To McDuff's assertions that many prosecution points were "not reasonable," Long replied, "We don't have to allege he's a good criminal. We don't have to allege he's smart."

In the whole McDuff saga, it was Crawford Long who left posterity with the single most erudite description of what Kenneth McDuff was. Raising his left arm and pointing to McDuff, Long shouted, "I submit to you that the evidence shows that this defendant is every person's nightmare. The evidence shows that he's the monster that comes out of the dark and jerks innocent people off the streets and takes them out and slaughters them."[27]

Closing arguments by the defense team focused on the tight time element and how improbable it was for McDuff to choose to go to a house and ask for food. But even Skip Reaves, a defense attorney, acknowledged that McDuff represented "all that we are afraid of, crime and violence." Then he committed what was surely a tactical blunder. He referred to the weakness of Pontius Pilate and asked the jury not to repeat those mistakes.[28]

Crawford Long thought comparing McDuff to Jesus was strategically ill-advised and in bad taste. Mike Freeman could not believe what he heard. In his summation, John Segrest said simply, "I really do not want to compare this jury to Pontius Pilate and Kenneth McDuff to Jesus Christ. That is ludicrous." John went on to characterize the McDuff defense as the "ABM (Anybody But McDuff) Defense."[29]

The jury deliberated four hours and found McDuff guilty. The first vote was eleven to one for a conviction. The sole hold-out, a truck driver from Pasadena, had to be convinced by the other jurors that McDuff had time to kidnap and kill Melissa, and that the woman who testified that she fed McDuff a bowl of beans was credible. Segrest, Long and Freeman then prepared for the punishment phase. The trio became even more determined to put McDuff away—forever. "To paraphrase William Shakespeare's *Macbeth*, 'We will lay it on McDuff and cursed be he who shall first cry 'Enough!' " said Crawford Long.[30]

During the punishment phase, prosecutors called Roy Dale Green and Alva Hank Worley. Each riveted and disgusted everyone in the courtroom with their tales of horror. It took the jury sixty-five minutes to return a sentence of death for McDuff, making him the first prisoner in Texas history, and possibly in American history, to be sent back to death row after being paroled from death row. No other person had ever been given a *second* death row number— McDuff's was 999055.

"Kenneth McDuff was a kidnapper, a rapist, and a murderer and he got what he deserved," said Mike Freeman, while wearing a red and black necktie with a tie tack in the shape of a hangman's noose. For John Segrest, the most memorable moment of the trial came after the death sentence had been read. Brenda and Richard Solomon, and Melissa's brother, Clay Leger, surrounded and hugged him.[31]

As he was being led from the courthouse one last time, Kenneth McDuff tried to answer questions being shouted at him. "I guess I'm gonna die. We all do, you know."

"How many people did you kill, Kenneth?" asked one reporter.

"None. Yet," said McDuff as he got back into the police van.[32]

In 1966, Kenneth Allen McDuff had been convicted and sentenced to death for the murder of Marcus Dunnam. He had never been tried for the murders of Louise Sullivan and Robert Brand. He got out of prison in 1989. In 1993, the McLennan County District Attorney put him away again. Travis County District Attorney Ronnie Earle would not repeat the mistakes of the past. Two of his best assistants, Howard "Buddy" Meyer, and David Counts, prepared to bring McDuff back to court. McDuff was going to answer for the murder of Colleen Reed.

20

The Reed Trial

"The scary part is, those guys reproduce."
—David Counts, Travis County
Assistant District Attorney

I

Only a few days after Kenneth McDuff had been arrested in Kansas City, the Travis County District Attorney's Office began to gather circumstantial evidence to establish that Colleen Reed was dead. Under a 1974 law, such evidence could be gathered in cases where a victim's body was not found. Such laws are necessary. Without them, for example, murderers with access to the means of completely destroying bodies could never be prosecuted. "If the date or the method can be proven on circumstantial evidence, so can death," explained David Counts, the young, handsome Assistant District Attorney who became the lead prosecutor of the Colleen Reed Murder Trial.[1]

David Counts was born in the small West Texas town of Knox City, near Abilene. He graduated from Texas Tech and got a law degree from St. Mary's University Law School in San Antonio. He always wanted to try cases. At the time of the Reed abduction, David was Travis County's major crimes attorney. He had already put in so much time assisting investigators in the Reed Case that it was logical for him to go ahead and prosecute it. His supervisor, another assistant district attorney named Howard "Buddy" Meyer, asked to help. The two men were genuinely fond of one another and looked forward to working together again.[2]

Buddy Meyer was born in Taylor, Texas, a small town east of Austin. He attended a number of colleges before graduating from St. Edward's University in Austin. He earned a master's degree in Public Administration from Southwestern Texas State University in San Marcos and then went to law school. He practiced law for a short time in Louisiana, his wife's native state, where he developed a weakness for Cajun food. He is known for his massive, dust-colored mustache: Each whisker is a rugged individualist, determined to point in its own direction.

Internally at the Travis County District Attorney's office, David and Buddy faced a major challenge. The Reed Trial came at the same time the Travis County District Attorney was trying Texas's newly elected United States Senator Kay Bailey Hutchison. Over thirty people worked on that case, and it siphoned resources. But the two prosecutors and their investigator, Alan Sanderson, worked so well together that the case went "smooth and easy," as David recalled.[3]

It took less than two hours for a grand jury to return indictments of capital murder, aggravated sexual assault, and aggravated kidnapping. The case had been assigned to State District Judge Wilford Flowers. Wil Flowers could not have been more different from Bob Burdette. He had a reputation for being patient, and was well respected among judges and lawyers. Lawyers who have experience in his courtroom often describe him as "predictable." But he can be tough, especially with someone who has taken advantage of a chance he has given them. In Judge Flowers's court, there *will* be reverence for the law.[4]

The legal challenge for the Reed Case was corroboration. Of course, the cornerstone of the case against McDuff was going to be the testimony of Alva Hank Worley. But Worley was an accomplice, and under state law, "a conviction cannot be had upon the testimony of an accomplice unless corroborated by other evidence tending to connect the defendant with the offense committed; and the corroboration is not sufficient if it merely shows the commission of the offense." Hank's eyewitness testimony would not be enough for a conviction. Virtually everything he claimed in his statements and testimony needed to be supported by other testimony or evidence.[5]

The trial date had been set for January 3, 1994, but the defense asked for a continuance when they learned that David and Buddy intended to prove that McDuff was responsible for the deaths of Melissa Northrup and the three teenagers McDuff killed in 1966. Flowers granted the continuance and the trial date was reset for January 20, 1994.[6]

That there would be a change of venue was never really in doubt. "I think any lawyer would have to give some due consideration to a motion for a change of venue. I think everybody feels like he's guilty, just based on everything they've read about him and the case," said Chris Gunter, one of two lawyers appointed to represent McDuff. When representatives of the *Austin American-Statesman* revealed that they had published over 150 stories involving Colleen Reed, and producers from Austin television stations testified that they had aired over 200 stories about the car wash abduction, a change of venue was a foregone conclusion. (Nationwide, more than 1,000 TV stories appeared involving Colleen Reed or Kenneth McDuff.) Judge Flowers did not waste much time. "[This case] has gotten more coverage than anything I've ever seen in Travis County," he said, as he granted a defense motion for a change in venue. "We'll go someplace that can accommodate us."

"We're ready to try it wherever he moves us," Buddy said the same day.

Judge Flowers moved the trial to Seguin, in Guadalupe County. Seguin is a lovely and historic community just east of San Antonio. David remembers the hot tub at the Holiday Inn—it was shaped like the state of Texas—although he never got in it. The courtroom where the trial took place had high ceilings and terrible acoustics. Almost every witness had to be told to talk louder or get closer to the microphone.[7]

Just like everyone else who had ever been there, David

and Buddy both remembered the powerful sadness of their
first trip to the abandoned road Worley identified as the
murder site. Buddy recalls the day Tim Steglich took him
there: "Standing there on that old dirt road where Hank said
[McDuff] administered that final blow and feeling that she
was close . . ." Buddy could not finish the sentence. In all
of his years of putting away some very nasty people, Buddy
had never encountered anyone like McDuff.

And yet there were some, who surely did not know of
McDuff's history, who wondered why Travis County
would try someone who had already been convicted and
sentenced to death for another murder. During his preparation for trial, David Counts and J. W. Thompson encountered a jailer who asked David, "How many times can you
kill him?"

J. W. replied, "As many times as it takes."

"How lazy," an angered David thought.[8] He was right.
Kenneth McDuff had been convicted of first-degree murder
and sentenced to death in 1966. He had been convicted of
the murder of Marcus Dunnam only. He had never been
tried for his murder of Louise Sullivan, in part because of
a clerical error. McDuff's attorney filed to dismiss all pending charges against McDuff because of a denial of a speedy
trial. McDuff had been down that road before. A death
sentence is not a certainty. David and Buddy would see to
it that history was not going to repeat itself.

That he was already under a sentence of death seemed
to "liberate" McDuff to behave the way he wanted to in
the courtroom. He must have figured he had nothing left to
lose. For example, during pre-trial hearing arguments over
evidence, the owner of Big Boys Wrecker Service testified
that he had purchased McDuff's Thunderbird for $675 at
an auction. "I had that much worth in tires," shouted a
shackled and enraged killer. It was vintage McDuff, un-
moved at allegations of rape, torture and murder, but furious at the underestimated value of an old car he would
never drive again. His court-appointed attorneys, Chris
Gunter and a gifted criminal defense lawyer named Andy

Forsythe, had even more problems with him throughout the trial. Gunter and Forsythe provided an expert defense, in spite of their unruly client. A typical exchange went:

McDuff: "Let's go at it again."

Forsythe: "No, you wait. I am going to ask the questions."

McDuff: "No, wait a minute. . . . No, I insist on this."

Forsythe: "I will ask if you will wait."

Gunter: "We will ask all your questions. Promise."[9]

During the pre-trial questioning of Mike Goins, McDuff got impatient. Again, he did not understand that the purpose of the questioning was to determine the admissibility of the witness's testimony before a jury, not a determination of whether Goins was being truthful.

"I am more familiar with this witness and the testimony than my attorneys are. I would like to ask some questions. I think it is very important to clear up. May I do so?" asked McDuff.

"No!" answered Judge Flowers.

"I don't look like a thirty-year-old, five-foot-seven, 150 pounds. I am almost fifty-two, [and weigh] 255 pounds, this is stupid. I would like to clear these questions up. You ask those questions I wrote down. I would like to ask these questions."

Chris Gunter then requested, and got, a recess for a few minutes.[10]

"We have advised him to stop speaking out in court. It interrupts the flow," Gunter said in vain.

In court, even the patient Judge Flowers had had enough. Only two days later, during the testimony of Austin Police Detective Don Martin, McDuff seriously disrupted the proceedings. Andy Forsythe was finishing up the questioning about the taillights of the Thunderbird when McDuff blurted out, "Let me finish here."

"Mr. McDuff, if you want to testify in this hearing, you have that right, but you are going to have to [stop your interruptions], because we have heard too much of this," asserted a stern Judge Flowers.

"What I want to show . . ."

"You listen to what I am saying. You can whisper and talk to your lawyers. I have told you that I think your lawyers are excellent, but none of this apparently matters," continued the Judge.

McDuff would not shut up. Maybe the rabidly racist McDuff refused to take directions from the distinguished African-American Judge Flowers. Who knows? But Flowers had had enough.

"Sheriff, take him out of here," ordered Flowers.

Don Martin sat silently in the witness chair as deputies and bailiffs wrestled McDuff out of the courtroom. "You could have heard a pin drop in that courtroom it was so quiet," Don remembered. Immediately after pushing McDuff through the first door, everyone in the courtroom and in the halls heard a deputy say, "Don't you do that shit!" followed by loud thuds sounding like a body slamming into a wall. Television cameras stationed in the hallway taped McDuff's unceremonious removal. The deputies picked him up by his ankle and wrist chains and dragged him on the floor and out of the courthouse. All the television audience could see was a bald head going down the stairs.[11]

The next day McDuff addressed the court. "I would like to make a notation for the record. Yesterday after I requested my attorneys to ask questions I wanted to ask, they refused. You had me taken [out of the court]. I walked from the courtroom and your bailiffs here attacked me right out here and inflicted serious injuries to me." He wanted what is called a hybrid representation. He wanted to be able to ask the questions while his lawyers did the legal work and filed the motions. Judge Flowers told him he had no right to such representation.[12]

The next day another issue, almost as bizarre, came up in court. The defense questioned the competency of a witness named Brandon. Rule 601 of the Texas Criminal Code supports a notion that when someone takes an oath to tell the truth, the seriousness of the oath awakens, or motivates a person to be truthful. The assumption, of course, is that someone giving testimony is smart enough to appreciate the seriousness of the oath and the consequences of lying. The rule protects the very foundation of jurisprudence, that the oath assures the truth. Andy Forsythe may have inadvertently demonstrated Brandon's incompetence.

Forsythe: "Do you feel that you may have suffered some sort of brain damage from the result of drinking as much as you have been?"

Brandon: "I'm not sure what you mean by the question."[13] Brandon never became much of an issue at the trial. It did not take David and Buddy long to realize that they did not want to vouch for this guy.[14]

A similar witness was Morris, who testified about the day that he met McDuff in the H&H Lounge. He, Billy, and McDuff drove to Del Valle to try to score speed at his cousin Beverly's trailer. Tim Steglich had been assigned to drive to Davilla, Texas, to pick up Morris and take him to Seguin. He arrived in Davilla the morning after a serious ice storm hit Central Texas.

"Morris, come on, we've got to go," shouted Tim from his car.

"I'll be there in a minute after I finish prying up the chickens," Morris said.

"What?" Tim asked.

Morris had a number of fighting cocks in his yard that had been frozen to the ground. Using a flat-nosed shovel, Morris began scooping up the birds from the dirt. Tim tried to help. David remembers Tim wondering if he had pulled the legs off a couple of the roosters.[15]

For periods, the trial moved faster than most had expected, but after the testimony of yet another intellectually-challenged witness, court adjourned, and as he walked out of the courtroom, Judge Flowers looked at David Counts and said, "Boy, you guys really know how to kill that momentum."

Other witnesses included Billy, Harrison, and One-eyed Jack, chained together because they had been brought from

prison. Billy had his parole revoked for domestic violence—he had slapped Janice. While seated in the hallway
of the Guadalupe County Courthouse, Billy and Harrison
mouthed off at Tim. It did not last long—Tim got in their
faces. He made the guards very nervous.[16]

And the guilt/innocence phase of the trial had not even
started yet.

II

On February 10, 1994, opening arguments commenced in
the guilt/innocence portion of the trial. "The evidence is
going to show you the only thing that can link Colleen
Reed to Kenneth McDuff's car is five hairs," said Chris
Gunter. Later he said, "In the words of Ms. Bible, Colleen
Reed's sister, Alva Hank Worley is a worthless human being, and he implicated Kenneth McDuff after all that. The
problem with Alva Hank Worley is that he is a liar." The
defense very cleverly tried to use Lori Bible's statements
and actions—specifically, putting pressure on the Austin
Police Department—to show that APD was desperate to
solve the case.[17]

Since Mike Goins's positive identification of McDuff as
the driver of the Thunderbird at the corner of Powell and
Sixth Streets was so crucial to corroborate Hank Worley's
statements and forthcoming testimony, Gunter tried to dis-
credit the identification. He asked Goins to look directly at
McDuff.

"He's got a pretty good set of ears, doesn't he?"

"It looks like the other set of ears on your side of the
table," Goins answered.

"Now, that hurts my feelings. My ears are not as big as
Kenneth's," Gunter laughed.[18]

The big question, of course, was the testimony of Alva
Hank Worley. Hank indicated that he might not testify unless he had an approved plea agreement. The district attorneys responded with an indictment for capital murder.

Buddy Meyer pointed out to the press that even if Hank refused to testify, information he gave authorities and his testimony during the Northrup Trial could be presented to the jury. Worley's attorney, Dain Whitworth, indicated that Worley would testify for a plea bargain and a twenty-five-year sentence. For a time, however, it seemed as if Worley might be forced to testify in self-defense. McDuff's attorneys had suggested that Worley was the real killer. If so, Worley knew he had better get on the stand and tell all. He ended up testifying with the same grant of conditional immunity he had during the Northrup Trial—nothing more.[19]

As it had at the Northrup Trial, hair became a central issue. A Texas Department of Public Safety forensics expert testified that a total of five hairs found in the Thunderbird matched Colleen's hair samples. The strands of hair had been forcibly removed. And again, a great deal of time was spent arguing about the extent to which hair should be used to identify an individual. The stains and the hair did not prove, to the exclusion of all else, that Colleen had been in the Thunderbird, but they supported testimony that she was there.[20] The jury would have to decide whether that was enough.

On February 17, 1994, Alva Hank Worley arrived to testify before the jury. The grant of immunity compelled his testimony. He repeated the horrifying story of Colleen's mistreatment. "Worley described the night in chronological order, using the same grammar and street expressions of a man who said he can't remember whether he dropped out of school in the ninth or tenth grade," wrote an *Austin American-Statesman* reporter.

Predictably, Gunter went after Hank's inconsistent statements, and suggested strongly that Hank's real motivation for testifying was to save himself. Gunter's questions repeatedly suggested that a deal had been made. "Man, these people ain't done nothing for me. I can tell you that right now," Hank insisted in a quiet courtroom. Hank turned out to be a credible witness. When Gunter asked him about

prisoners who said Hank told them he had participated in
crimes against Colleen, Hank said, "That's bull. You need
to go find some more witnesses because the ones you got
ain't worth a nickel." When Gunter talked to Hank about
lies, and it could hardly be denied that Hank Worley was
a liar, Hank rose to the occasion.

Gunter: "My question is, you will lie if you think it'll
help Alva Hank Worley."

Worley: "Where have I benefited from it?"[21]

Francis, McDuff's Kansas City roommate, turned out to
be less productive for the prosecution. McDuff grinned and
waved at Francis, who testified that all of his conversations
with McDuff were more or less prison talk—not to be taken
seriously. "Hell, he was just shooting old penitentiary stories or something, you know." He claimed not to remember
other items in a statement he had given to ATF agents in
Kansas City. Francis, and a few of McDuff's former TSTI
schoolmates, ready to testify about McDuff's conversations
about disposing of bodies, were not allowed to take the
stand before the jury. Gunter and Forsythe won that battle
on grounds of relevance and hearsay.[22]

Some of the most powerful testimony came from Dr.
Hubbard Fillinger, the coroner of Montgomery County,
Pennsylvania. In a courtroom stunned into silence, he testified that Worley's statement that Kenneth McDuff had hit
Colleen so hard that she bounced off the road, could be
descriptive of the moment of her death. In a scholarly fashion, Dr. Fillinger also supported the "tree breaking" sound
Hank claimed to have heard by stating that "a blow of a
great deal of force . . . makes a cracking or snapping sound.
That tells me that something major has broken. . . . The
loud cracking noise, the fact that the person is limp
thereafter would be consistent with brain and/or spinal cord
damage." He continued, "That leads us to believe that the
neurological pathways that sent the message up, 'ouch,' are
damaged to the point where we don't have any possible
recovery. And that is an indication that life is going to be
lost very quickly."[23]

On February 23, the *Austin American-Statesman* reported that Gunter and Forsythe had persuaded McDuff not to testify on his own behalf. Surely, they did their client a great service.

Closing arguments in the Reed Trial held no surprises. Not much more could be said. The verdict came down to whether Hank Worley could be believed about what he said concerning Kenneth Allen McDuff. Wisely, Buddy and David never asserted that Worley told the truth about himself. David Counts ended the final arguments with a statement dripping with sarcasm: "If you find the defendant not guilty of this offense, you're going to be telling him, 'Okay, Kenneth McDuff, it's okay to do this. You do whatever you want to do. Go around and snatch women up at the car wash, be the opportunistic predator that you are. Whatever hunting ground you decide to hunt in, it's okay. As long as you pick somebody that's a weak coward like Hank Worley who has lied all his life, who doesn't have a sparkling record. And that's perfect for Kenneth McDuff, because look who else he hangs out with, [Billy], [One-eyed Jack], and [Harrison]. Fine, upstanding citizens, strapping young men. The scary part is, those guys reproduce."[24]

The jury deliberated two and a half hours to return guilty verdicts on all counts—capital murder, aggravated sexual assault, and aggravated kidnapping. McDuff showed no emotion or reaction until he told one of the officers to take his hand off his arm, and a minor struggle followed as he entered the elevator.[25]

While talking to reporters, McDuff lashed out at Hank Worley and accused him of confessing to the Yogurt Shop Murders. The claim horrified Worley, who agreed to take a lie detector test to clear his name. (While the Yogurt Shop investigators never officially ruled out Kenneth McDuff or Hank Worley, they were never prime suspects either.)[26] McDuff wanted to set Worley up, and it would not be the last time he would try.

The punishment phase was almost a repeat of the same phase of the Northrup Trial. There were plenty of people ready to testify to Kenneth McDuff's history of violence. Charlie Butts was there, and so was Roy Dale Green. Roy Dale had surprised David Counts when he said, "Go get 'em, David!" It was Roy Dale's rendition of the 1966 Broomstick Murders that stunned and horrified an already terror-fatigued courtroom. David Counts noticed Judge Flowers glaring at Roy Dale, as if he could not believe what he was hearing. "I thought Judge Flowers was going to jump over into the witness box at Green," David remembered.[27]

Buddy Meyer called Dr. Richard Coons, a general and forensic psychiatrist, to render an opinion. "Doctor, what I'd like to do at this point in time is to propose a hypothetical and ask you at the end of it whether or not in your opinion there is a probability that the defendant would commit criminal acts of violence that would constitute a continuing threat to society." Buddy followed with a brilliant overview of the murderous life of Kenneth Allen McDuff that took four pages of trial transcript. "Based on that hypothetical, Doctor Coons, do you have an opinion as to whether . . . there is a probability that [this man] would commit criminal acts of violence that would constitute a continuing threat to society?"

"Yes, I do," Coons answered, in what had to be the greatest understatement of the trial.

In his final argument for the punishment phase, Buddy Meyer asked the jury to make a simple promise: "And when you go into the jury room and you deliberate, don't leave your common sense out here, ladies and gentlemen." It took the jury fifty-five minutes to decide that McDuff was likely to commit similar crimes if given a chance. Judge Flowers gave Kenneth the death penalty.[28]

McDuff's court-appointed attorneys, Chris Gunter and Andy Forsythe, provided an expert defense for Kenneth Allen McDuff. The problem was that their client was guilty. Their sixty-hour weeks defending McDuff hurt their law practices. Andy recalled that "Gunter got death threats and I lost one client who felt my work on behalf of McDuff would hurt his case." For their efforts, the public defenders got about one-fourth of the going rate for a lawyer working a similar case.[29]

David Counts and Buddy Meyer accomplished something rather remarkable. Kenneth McDuff was sentenced to death in a murder case where no body or body parts had been recovered. There was no weapon and no established cause of death. These talented prosecutors got a conviction with five hairs, the testimony of an accomplice who could not remember when he dropped out of school, and a gifted engineer who saw McDuff near, not at, the car wash. David Counts and Buddy Meyer richly deserved the hugs they got from Lori Bible, who sat through every day of the trial.

III

He was more than just another serial killer. Kenneth McDuff's murderous rampage, from 1989 to his arrest in 1992, brought about large changes in the Texas criminal justice system. More significantly, he attached powerful images to the argument that helped the public overcome a conservative political tide to fund a massive expansion of state government. Arguably, the *Ruiz* lawsuit brought to the forefront the inadequacies of Texas prisons, but it was not until the Kenneth McDuff murders that Texas government, and the people, chose prison construction and increased government spending over massive paroles.

In September of 1992, The Texas Board of Criminal Justice unanimously agreed to ask the Legislature for nearly $4 billion to run the prison system for the following two-year period. Even the board members called the request "staggering" and candidly asserted that taxes and bonds were necessary. "Everybody says 'Lock 'em up and throw away the key.' If they want to do that, they're going to have to pay for it. We've got some real hard decisions for the people of Texas . . . for what will soon be the country's largest prison system," said Board Chairman Selden Hale.

Texas voters made the hard decision and approved two
bond issues for prison construction totaling more than
$2 billion. The state legislature tripled the Texas Depart-
ment of Criminal Justice's budget; the number of prison
beds tripled, and the number of prison units increased by
fifty percent.

In 1993, the revenue generator for new prisons took the
form of Proposition 14, a $1 billion bond issue. Then-
Governor Ann Richards, who had inherited a broken criminal justice system, stated publicly: "If you are going to
bring down the crime rate, you are going to have to build
prisons to lock these people up. . . . Would I rather spend
the money in another way? Absolutely! Yes. But this is a
necessity that I see no other way around." Proposition Fourteen brought about a coalition including Governor Richards, the lieutenant governor, the speaker of the house, and
associations of district attorneys, judges, and sheriffs. It
passed with a solid sixty-two percent approval from the
voters.[30]

The new prisons made possible changes in the law, especially as it related to parole. Today, those changes are
collectively referred to as the "McDuff Laws." In an article
for the Texas Criminal Defense Attorney's Association
journal, Bill Habern and Gary Cohen cautioned defense attorneys that, "If your client was sentenced in 1991 to a ten-
year term of imprisonment and you advised them that they
would be out at their first eligibility date, your advice would
most likely have been correct at the time." Afterwards, parole laws changed so drastically that the same "good faith
advice" meant little—or nothing. For example, after September 1, 1993, if a defendant received a life sentence for
capital murder, he must serve a minimum of forty calendar
years before even being considered for parole. Even then,
parole for this and certain other offenses requires a favorable vote from two-thirds of the entire eighteen-member
Board of Pardons and Paroles, not a majority of a three-
member panel like the one that released McDuff.

And long before the McDuff Laws, only two months

after McDuff had been arrested, the practice of allowing parole board staff to reinstate parole, as Bettie Wells had done for McDuff, ended. In announcing the cessation of the practice, Board Chairman Jack Kyle announced, "we are doing away with the concept of parole reinstatement altogether." He added, "This is something we had been thinking about for a long time. It is not a direct result of McDuff. However, I'd be lying to you if I said McDuff's case didn't give a lot of impetus to this policy."[31]

The forty-calendar-year minimum, or the "McDuff Rule," is nearly the functional equivalent of life without parole. If a twenty-year-old is convicted of capital murder, and not given a death sentence, he will not be released until the age of sixty, and his probability for violence is very low. Not satisfied to trust the parole board or its rules, the Legislature enacted the McDuff Rules in law; today they are called the "McDuff Laws." For convicted capital murderers, the idea that people in prison can change for the better, essential to the concept of any parole system, suffered a near-fatal blow.

It is harder to link McDuff to the intolerant atmosphere that extended to clemency, but he almost certainly contributed to what Jonathan R. Sorensen, an assistant professor at the University of Texas, Pan American, called a "sham." "I would say that clemency in Texas is a legal fiction at best," added Judge Morris Overstreet, a member of the Texas Court of Criminal Appeals, in an opinion in the Karla Faye Tucker Case (see Prologue). From 1972 to the day Tucker was executed in February, 1998, only thirty-six of 180 convicts bound for execution were approved for clemency. Not one was granted for "humanitarian" reasons. Texas has an historical attachment to the death penalty, but after McDuff, death penalty advocates had a poster boy, a visual representation of one example of the chance a state takes when it shows mercy.

"The Karla Tucker Case will become the clemency decision of this century—and how it is handled will have a lasting effect on this issue. Is it in the best interest of society to kill a reformed person, a rehabilitated person? If we decide not to give her clemency, we should not decide to give anyone clemency," said Gary Schwartz, a University of Arizona professor. Texas answered his question when the parole board voted 16–0 (with two abstaining) against clemency for Tucker. Would she have gotten clemency had McDuff not infuriated an entire state with his horror? Maybe. Who knows? But his name came up constantly during the debate as an example of how there is no such thing as a *guaranteed* sentence of life without the possibility of parole—he sure didn't help her.[32]

For the rest of his life Kenneth Allen McDuff was the most despised inmate in the entire Texas prison system, because he brought about a prison expansion so large it guaranteed that every single inmate would serve a longer sentence. On Death Row at the Ellis Unit, McDuff was placed in administrative segregation, normally saved for the most dangerous of inmates. He was placed there, however, for his own protection.

Epilogue

"FLOATING ON A CLOUD, PLAYING A HARP"

"That's a strange bird."
—J. W. Thompson, referring to Kenneth McDuff

I

"This will not be over for any of us until we find Colleen," said John Moriarty of TDCJ, seven years after she had disappeared. He spoke for every investigator involved in the Colleen Reed Case. They all tell of thinking of Colleen every time they found themselves in the Blackland Prairie, and wondering if they were near her. The Kenneth McDuff Case was not over for these men, even though they put him back on death row—twice—for good.

For years, J. W. Thompson of the Austin Police Department and ATF Special Agent Chuck Meyer painstakingly followed every lead and searched for whatever crumb of information they could uncover that might have led to the discovery of Colleen's remains. They often found themselves searching woods, ditches, and old wells. Time passed, and leads dwindled, but they never gave up. Like Dan Stoltz and Mike Carnevale, Chuck and J. W. are very good friends. Their bond strengthens with every difficult case; it is hard to imagine a circumstance where these two men would not trust each other. These men had heavy case loads and could have reasonably decided that Colleen would never be found. After more than four years the pain still showed in their eyes.

During a five-hour interview in September of 1996, McDuff volunteered justifications, excuses, and described how his life was merely a series of misunderstandings. His trouble with the law started when the people of Rosebud

got jealous of the money he made mowing lawns for old
women who loved him; as a matter of fact, the people of
Rosebud were jealous of the entire McDuff family and their
financial success; the fourteen burglaries he was convicted
of in 1965 "was just pranks"; Roy Dale Green was the one
who murdered three kids in 1966; Gary Jackson promised
him that he would be a millionaire, so he didn't look for a
job, and because he didn't become a millionaire, he fell
into a life of drugs; the black kids in Rosebud he chased
with a knife misjudged him (like everybody else); after
Furman v Georgia he should have gotten, but was denied,
a new trial; he was convicted and on death row because of
hair—"Back in 1966 hair did not exist"; when Richard
Bannister said he saw him pushing his car at the New Road
Inn, he was lying; he was convicted twice because his public defenders, all five of them, were incompetent; he often
got violent because he smoked crack, and he had to do that
because his parole officer did not let him smoke pot; "being
in a titty bar was like being in a candy store" he said as he
described why he was so promiscuous; he got drugs for
white people because they were afraid to deal with black
pushers; he nearly gouged out his dorm-mate Richard's
eyes because "he [Richard] initiated it"; he was a suspect
in Regenia Moore's disappearance because her mother
caused all the trouble; a detective [Tim Steglich] got Hank
Worley to lie in all of his statements; comments about personal graveyards he made to Francis in Kansas City were
made in jest; the One-eyed Jack told wild stories; Buddy
was "crazy as a loony"; Mark told a "bunch of bull"; Chester tried to set him up by putting a shotgun in his car; Holly
misconstrued all of what happened between him, her, One-
Arm and T-Bone; Valencia Joshua never knocked on his
window—it was another black whore who looked just like
her; Linda lied when she said that the McDuff family came
up with big money to get McDuff out of prison; Aaron
Northrup lied when he said McDuff knew Melissa Northrup; his mother, Addie, was really a quiet woman; the reason he was sent to prison in the first place was that he was

an "asshole," and lawmen should have been mature enough
to overlook that.

II

During the hunt for McDuff in 1992, the Task Force went
to as many people who knew McDuff as could be identified—from casual acquaintances to family members. Each
was thoroughly questioned as to where McDuff could be
and if they knew anyone else who should be questioned.

After weeks of sleepless nights, Mike, Parnell, and Bill
had developed a number of confidential informants. One in
particular (hereafter referred to as the CI) had been especially helpful. For example, the CI had suggested to Mike
that McDuff might have buried a victim in the woods near
TSTI, and less than two weeks later, the body of Valencia
Joshua was found there. On several occasions, The Boys
called their CI when they had no clues to follow. They
carefully cultivated, and protected the identity of, their
valuable source.

The CI had previously made occasional visits to McDuff
in prison, listening to his endless stories. Near the end of
the spring of 1998, the CI approached Mike with an idea.
Just maybe, after all those years, Kenneth might say where
he put some of the women he murdered. Regenia Moore,
Brenda Thompson, and Colleen Reed had never been recovered and returned to their families. Regenia's mother,
Barbara Carpenter, was still often seen searching fields
around Waco for her daughter, The Boys sometimes joining
in the search.

"I'm going to talk to him to see what he will tell me,"
the CI said.

"Go ahead, see what you can do," Bill answered. He
figured that nothing else had worked so far, so why not try.

At first McDuff hesitated, "If I do [say where the women
were located] they won't need me anymore." He held on
to the fiction that he had control over his destiny. The re-

ality was that no one needed him, and the highest priority for many was his execution.

After a couple more visits, the CI was stunned when Kenneth said, "I'll give you this one," then proceeded to describe where he had murdered and buried Regenia Moore. McDuff told the CI that as he dug her grave, he was so close to a road he looked up and noticed that drivers of passing cars could see him.

The CI called Mike and announced, "He told me where one of them is!" Immediately, Mike called their trusted friend Texas Ranger Matt Cawthon. The possibility always existed that McDuff was playing another of his "that would be a good place to dump a body" games. The last thing anyone needed was the birth of a rumor spun out of control. There would be enough of a stir if Regenia was found.

McDuff had identified a bridge on State Highway 6 that traversed the Tehuacana Creek. On their first trip to the site, The Boys and Ranger Cawthon could not locate the grave-site based on McDuff's directions. About a week later, the CI returned to the prison. This time, Parnell had drawn a crude map of the bridge, highway, and creek and asked the CI to have McDuff point out Regenia's exact location.[1] When told about the unsuccessful search, McDuff replied, "You idiot, it's on the Waco side [of the bridge]." Using Parnell's map, he pointed to a much more precise location and gave very specific directions: Go under and to the edge of the bridge; walk twenty paces towards the center of the bridge; turn left and go forty paces into the woods. Regenia will be under some rocks and an old carpet.

Mike and Matt Cawthon returned to the bridge, and this time, they searched on the Waco side. In the dark of night, Mike stepped off twenty paces under the bridge. He turned left and faced the woods. All he could see were trees and heavy brush, but directly in front of him a thin "cow path" stretched across the creek bottoms under the bridge and into the woods. Determined to follow the directions exactly, Mike turned left and stepped off forty paces. The weeds and brush were thick as he counted steps perpendicular to the bridge. At forty, he stopped and shined his flashlight in a semi-circular motion. Directly in front of him was an old carpet—and a pile of rocks.

Mike and Matt removed some of the rocks (actually they were large chunks of concrete) from above the carpet. They could see that the carpet had been there for quite some time. They also saw what was clearly a sinkhole. The next day, September 29, 1998, a forensics team recovered Regenia Moore.

Her hands had been tied behind her back. Her ankles had been bound with stockings and tied in such a way as to allow her to walk. McDuff apparently "marched" her to the area. The remains of her dress were wrapped around her pelvic area. He had laid her on her back and bent her legs so that they pointed to the left. After seven years, Regenia was going home to her mother.

III

While talking to McDuff about Regenia, the CI had managed to get a very vague description of where he had placed Brenda Thompson. Soon, the directions got more precise: on Gholson Road, about six or seven miles north of Waco, there are two wagon wheels at the entrance to a private driveway; just down from that at the bottom of a hill there is a dry water wash where the fence is down; go twenty paces from the fence inside the dry water wash and there is a slant. These directions were not as good as the ones McDuff provided for Regenia, but it was all they had to work with.

On October 1, only two days after Regenia had been recovered, The Boys had directions to locate Brenda. Bill wanted to go to the area right away, but Mike could not get away from his duties at the marshals' office. Late that afternoon, Bill drove out there by himself. It looked hopeless. The vast area was very heavily wooded and covered with trash and about two feet of poison ivy. Bill remem-

bered how he and others had been trained by the Smith-
sonian Institution to use probes to search for buried bodies
at the Branch Davidian Compound. He correctly surmised
that digging, whether with shovels or machinery, would be
a waste of time. The area was so undeveloped, it was hard
to walk.

So Bill got back into his truck and went to a plumbing
supply store to buy the kind of metal probes plumbers use
to locate sewer lines. The owner of the store, and a friend
of Bill's, Larry Anderson, figured out what Bill was up to
and refused to sell him any of the rods; he gave Bill three
fiberglass probes for the search. Then Bill called Parnell's
wife, Linda, and asked her if she had a shovel. Of course,
Linda knew something was up, so she told him to go over
to the stables. Bill went there and got a shovel and a crow-
bar to scratch around in the dirt.

All the while, Bill kept calling Mike, who still could not
get away. Bill told Mike about the area and how it looked
hopeless. Mike suggested that twenty paces, for one reason
or another, seemed to be important to McDuff. Why not
start with twenty paces from the fence and inside the dry
water wash. Then walk parallel to the fence and look for a
sinkhole, or something. The problem with that was that
most of the area was covered with poison ivy; Bill could
not see the ground.

He parked his truck across the street in a shallow ditch
and waited to make sure no one saw him. Newspapers all
over the country ran stories about how Regenia had been
discovered, and the last thing Bill needed was to be seen
entering a wooded area with a shovel.

When he crossed the fence he encountered so much
brush that he could not even get to the intersection of the
dry water wash and the fence. He had to mentally measure
off twenty paces. As he stood alone, ankle deep in poison
ivy, Bill looked around and said to himself, "Good God,
what am I doing here?" He would have been mortified if
anyone had seen him.

"A slant. What did McDuff mean by a slant?" Bill

thought. Maybe he meant along the side of the wash. He dropped the shovel, took the fiberglass probe and forced it into the ground. He felt an underground cavity. Only a few inches over, he did it again, and he felt the cavity again. Just to make sure he walked away and tried in another spot, but he felt no cavity. He had found something on his first attempt. He got down on his knees and scratched away in the dirt. He had to cut away a root and move a rock over before he found a bone. He knew human bones were smooth, and that most animal bones were rough. This one was smooth.

Bill hesitated. Months later he would wonder, "Why was I trying to convince myself that this was not what it must be?" But he wanted to be sure it was a human buried there. If the media coverage of Regenia's excavation was any indication of what he was in store for, he wanted to be sure he had not found a deer, so he hid the tools and sneaked out of the woods. From his truck he called Parnell's house and asked Linda McNamara if she knew where he could find Parnell. "He just came in," she said.

"Parnell, get out here now. I found her," Bill said excitedly.

Parnell met Bill in the parking lot of a nearby country store. While waiting for him, Bill paged Mike and called his good friend Robert Blossman of the Secret Service. They talked about ways to determine if the bone Bill found was really human. Parnell suggested, "How about a doctor? Let's call Gary Becker."

Dr. Gary Becker was an orthopedic surgeon and a good friend. They all met at the country store in their different trucks, but to get to the dry water wash, they piled into Bigfoot.

"Good gosh, Billy," Parnell kept repeating as Bill got on his hands and knees and moved away the dirt. He took out the bone and showed it to Becker.

"That's a human arm bone," said the doctor.

Very carefully, Bill placed the bone back where he found it, put the dirt back over it, and he and Robert Blossman piled trash over it so that animals could not get to it.

The next day, October 3, 1998, several lawmen met at
the country store on the corner of ranch roads 933 and 308.
From there a small convoy went to the site. They parked
in a shallow ditch along Gholson Road. Parnell and Mike
handed out swing blades and several men began chopping
their way through the brush and poison ivy. As they got
closer to the burial site, Parnell's wide and furious swings
sent sticks and leaves flying in all directions.

All of a sudden, Chuck pointed to the left and said,
"Look at that." It was a Coke can wedged on top of a stick.
The red can had faded to a dull, weathered orange. Some
thought McDuff might have used it as a marker, but then,
maybe it was just a can on a stick.

Once a small path had been cut, the men (and two
women on the forensics team) went farther into the woods
to where Bill had found the bone. He got down on his
hands and knees and carefully moved away loose dirt with
his fingers, exposing about four inches of the bone. The
forensics team went to work. Pretty soon J. W., Chuck,
Parnell, Mike, and Matt Cawthon put on latex gloves and
slowly assisted in the removal of dirt and compost. John
Moriarty arrived shortly afterwards.

"He was a lazy grave digger. It's deep in the middle and
the head and feet are up," Chuck said as more and more of
Brenda Thompson began to be exposed. One of the forensics persons came upon bright red polyester that showed no
decay. Other than that and a pair of socks, all of her other
clothing had rotted away.

Even more striking was a touching moment when
Brenda had been nearly completely recovered. Everyone
stood around the edge of the hole, and looked down at her
in absolute silence, as if the moment had been choreographed. Minutes later, Parnell McNamara walk out of the
woods. He stood alone along the roadway, leaning against
someone's pickup truck. He wanted to be alone.

IV

Finding Colleen was much more difficult. All they knew about where McDuff put her was that she was east of Interstate 35. At least that eliminated places like the old McDuff homestead, the abandoned road, the dams, and the area around the S&S Trailer Park.

McDuff seemed convinced that if he revealed Colleen's location he would lose certain privileges in prison. He was especially concerned about not having access to the commissary. On Monday, October 5, the CI visited McDuff for a longer time than was usually allotted to visitors. Insisting that he would not be punished if he revealed where Colleen could be found, the CI told McDuff that the U.S. Attorney was there and he could talk to him if he wanted. Of course, McDuff knew the CI had been working with officials. He said he wanted to talk to Bill.

Bill and Parnell had driven over a hundred miles an hour to get to the Ellis Unit while the CI met with McDuff. John Moriarty was already there. The CI, Bill and John met with McDuff.

"I'm Bill Johnston, Assistant United States Attorney, and this is John Moriarty of Internal Affairs here at TDCJ. We are here to do you no favor. At the same time, you should not be punished for what you tell us. That would not be fair either. I am not here to affect your case one way or another," Bill said. He chose his words carefully. Some news reports about what had been happening were pretty wild, and through coincidence, McDuff had been granted a temporary stay of execution during the same week of the recoveries. Bill continued, "John, I am asking you in front of these witnesses, can you state that if he gives us information about where to find Colleen Reed that he will be treated the same way today as he was yesterday?"

"Absolutely. We do that all the time. It would be stupid

to punish someone for giving information." Then John looked at McDuff. "If someone does something to you that is adverse, we investigate that. You call me."

McDuff stared at the threesome sitting on the other side of the Plexiglas. In a slow, bored monotone, McDuff said, "Well, there's a bridge over the Brazos River. I'll have to show y'all; you cain't find it."

Bill pressed for more details.

"There's a road that runs along the river. It's sandy. Go down that road for about 200 yards from the bridge. You cain't find it, I'm gonna have to be there with you."

Bill and John did not want to take McDuff out there, so they asked for even more details.

"It rained a lot and there was a place where I nearly got stuck. There is another road above that, and it's in between those two roads."

"Was she killed there?" Bill asked.

"I really don't like the killing part. She was killed there. Worley, he's the one that killed her. He's a liar," McDuff added.

John Moriarty and The Boys went out to the bridge across the Brazos that night. They used the probes to search for Colleen, but they could not find her; it just did not work the same way in the sand. Plus, it was dark and they could not see much.

The next day everyone's endurance would be tested. McDuff's directions about how to find Colleen had been skewed by the dark stillness of that horrible night. She was not 200 yards from the road, but given his very precise directions in the past, the search party began digging exactly where McDuff told them. Another problem was that between 1992 and 1998, the Corps of Engineers had actually changed part of the circular drive, a section called the lower road, because of frequent flooding. For hours, the men used graders to scrape dirt and sand in an area the size of a football field. Colleen was not there.

By mid-afternoon, Bill began to despair. He did not want to be seen with McDuff, and the idea of getting him out of the Ellis Unit to find Colleen was repugnant. John Moriarty was at the scene. He had a previous discussion with McDuff about just such a contingency; he knew that McDuff would cooperate if brought to the scene. Chuck Meyer and J. W. favored bringing McDuff there as well. Bill relented.

In seconds, John was on a cellular phone. He arranged for what is called a "Clandestine High Security Move." It is done on rare occasions where inmates are taken out of prison for investigative purposes. (That was why many prison officials did not know that McDuff had left the Ellis Unit. Their statement, that there was *no record* of McDuff leaving the prison, was true.)

Four investigators in two vehicles traveled with McDuff. Moriarty made arrangements to meet the cars halfway between Marlin and Huntsville. McDuff was transferred to Moriarty's car, which was equipped with heavily tinted glass. He was also "cabled" to the back seat and never allowed out of the car.

When John returned there were reporters everywhere. The word at the scene was that Austin television stations had reported that Colleen had already been found. That distressed the search team greatly. John drove through the press corps assembled on both sides of the bridge. High-powered lenses focused on the men and their work, but luckily, no one ever saw McDuff, who had been dressed up in civilian clothes and was wearing a baseball cap John had given him.

John drove the prisoner around the large circular drive. McDuff never referred to Colleen as a person, only as "it." "It may be over there," or "Move over there and you may find it," he would say.

Soon, Chuck joined McDuff on the back seat. "What's the deal, Kenneth?"

"This don't look right. Nothing looks right. It couldn't have been here because those trees were not there," McDuff said.

"You dumb son-of-a-bitch, that's a two-year-old tree," Chuck laughed.

"Well, that makes a difference," McDuff answered non-chalantly.

"What were you watching for? You didn't want anybody to see you," Chuck said, trying to get him to remember.

"It was real dark and I could see that fence line. I didn't worry about that river cause I could see it and it was roaring," McDuff remembered. He also remembered Colleen's exact position; she would be found lying partially on her right side, facing the river, and her head would be higher than her feet.

The river could not be seen where they were. Someone also figured out that there were two low-water marks that McDuff could have seen that night. The other one was much closer to the bridge. John drove him there and from the car, McDuff helped to direct officers with poles. They marked off a rectangular area. J. W. had his doubts because McDuff directed them to an area that had nothing around it for at least fifty feet.

A huge front-end loader had been brought to the scene. The men directed the earthmover into place, and in less than a half hour, Bill Johnston looked down between the bucket and the tracks and saw something that caught his eye.

"Now, that looks like a bone," he said. But he wanted a homicide detective to take a look. "J. W., you need to come look at this." Bill very carefully took his shovel and moved sand and dirt out of the way. He exposed teeth. Of course, McDuff was right, her head was higher than the rest of her, and she was found exactly as he had said.

"Those are human teeth, Bill. That's her. That's it," said J. W., before he instructed the driver of the tractor not to mix the dirt in the bucket with other piles.

Bill got on a cellular phone and called Lori, who had been prepared for just such a phone call. She knew to be patient and wait for a positive identification. J. W. tried to get in touch with Buddy Meyer at the Travis County D.A.'s

Office, but he never got through. Chuck looked at the bridge and saw the dozens of reporters rustling about. It was near deadline time, and since all of the lawmen had gathered in one spot, the reporters knew something had been discovered. "This family has been through enough already. Let's position the front-end loader between the grave and the press," he said.

"Did they find it?" McDuff asked. John Moriarty instructed TDCJ investigators to get McDuff out of there and back to death row. Again, they drove right past an unsuspecting press.

The crime scene now belonged to J. W., and after some legal wrangling, he became an authorized agent for the Travis County Medical Examiner's Office and made the call to excavate her immediately and take her to Austin. As they placed her on a sheet, Chuck noticed something in the hole. It was a white shoestring tied in a very small loop. Chuck remembered Hank's statement about how Colleen complained that her hands hurt because McDuff had tied them too tight.

They had been looking for her for so long, it seemed appropriate for Chuck and J. W. to take Colleen back to Austin. Mike McNamara does not remember any other body being treated with such reverence. When some of the other officers offered to help Chuck clear out an area of his trunk to put the body bag, he thought that there was no way in hell Colleen Reed would be placed in the trunk of any car. Instead, they cleared out the back seat and very carefully put her there. The two exhausted men drove right past the press and headed home.

It was the beginning of a journey that eventually took Colleen Reed back home to Ville Platte, Louisiana.

V

It is hard to understand what fault could possibly be found against three men who worked so diligently to find three

murdered women who had been missing for seven years.
But wild rumors circulated about McDuff being released
from prison for days. Others were convinced that only an
accomplice could have led The Boys to the graves—a sur-
reptitious deal had to have been made, the logic went. Ru-
mormongers convinced themselves that surely McDuff had
to have profited from the events of late September and early
October. After all, he had been scheduled to be executed
on October 21 but a stay had been granted. (The stay was
routine and in no way related to the recoveries.) Others
complained that McDuff was not a federal case—why were
Bill, Mike and Parnell such pivotal figures?

Central Texas newspapers carried headline stories of a
sealed motion Bill filed to reduce the sentence of one of
McDuff's nephews, who had been given fifteen years in
prison for drug charges unrelated to any crime involving
McDuff. (The sentence was reduced by five years.) Undoubtedly, these same newspapers would have carried even
larger, more scathing headlines if their reporters had found
out that The Boys had had an opportunity to find Regenia
Moore, Brenda Thompson, and Colleen Reed, and had done
nothing. These same newspapers even carried quotes from
other law officers who complained about not having enough
information to carry on an investigation into the Thompson
and Moore murders. Inexplicably, they ignored the fact that
bodies, the best evidence, were found. It was yet one more
example of how The Boys put themselves in a Rooseveltian
arena.

Whatever doubts anyone might have harbored about
whether McDuff would benefit from the information he
gave to the CI must have been settled on October 15, only
nine days after Colleen had been found. A federal judge in
Waco lifted all stays delaying McDuff's execution and re-
scheduled it for November 17, 1998.

VI

Throughout late October and early November John Moriarty spent about forty hours interviewing McDuff. He found out what many knew: if you spent time with McDuff for the purpose of getting information, you had to pay your dues by listening to long, drawn-out stories about cars, fast driving and fights. He murdered, he said, because he wanted to stay out of the pen, but he refused to explain how killing Colleen Reed and Melissa Northrup supported that objective.

"My reality is like a video game. I wouldn't pay attention to the consequences of what I do. I would just go out and get what I wanted," McDuff said, accurately describing his murderous life.

He did not like to talk about Melissa and Colleen. Maybe he harbored a small hope that he would escape the death chamber—again. He spoke candidly about Regenia and Brenda. "The first one I killed after I got out was Brenda Thompson," he said. According to McDuff, he picked her up for a date and insisted on "going around the world," which meant having all three kinds of sex. He did so, he claimed, for three hours, and by the time he brought her back to the Cut, she was fighting mad. That was why she screamed and tried to kick out the windshield when they approached the infamous roadblock on Faulkner Lane. In true McDuff fashion, he went into detail about how he outsmarted and outran Waco police officers. He took her to a field of weeds where he told her, "Bitch, you fucked up." He alleges that he had sex with her for another six hours. He said he killed her with his bare hands, put her in the back of his truck, drove to Gholson Road, and buried her.

McDuff believed that when Waco police officers visited his room he would be arrested and sent back to prison. He also told Moriarty that he checked with his mother to see if the police had been looking for him. When he found out that they had not, he decided not to skip town because "everything was O.K."

His account of his murder of Regenia Moore was much simpler. He picked her up on the Cut, smoked some rocks along the creek, and killed her there. Then he said something that sent a chill through John Moriarty. "It was just like in the movies. Did you ever see where they run off, and they fall down, and they don't get up, and they just stay there? That happened to me twice." He was talking about Regenia and Brenda. "You know, if they had just kept on running they would have just gotten away."

McDuff also spoke of how he diagnosed himself as having ADD, or Attention Deficit Disorder. But when he was a little boy, he asserted, teachers did not know about such disorders and they could not help him.

Colleen, he claimed, was the only victim he specifically targeted. He had wanted to make a statement—to get back at Austin for revoking his parole.

He also finally admitted to killing Louise Sullivan in 1966, but he claimed that Roy Dale Green was the one who shot the boys in the face. He strangled her with his hands because he did not like gore or the smell of blood.

While talking about his childhood, he admitted that his first attempt to "take" a woman was at age twelve when he and another local boy tried to rape a woman. They failed and tried again, this time wearing a mask, and the woman just laughed at him.

Incredibly, he had ill feelings towards the one person who stood by him through all of his troubles—his mother, Addie. He had no attachment to his mother or father, he said. "They turned me out like a dog," he said, apparently completely forgetting the fortune J. A. and Addie had spent on him and how they supported him until he was returned to death row.

"This life has not been good to me. I'm ready to close the door on this part of my life and ready to open the next door." One can only wonder what Kenneth Allen McDuff really expected out of this life, or the next.

On November 16, Chuck and J. W. made one last trip to the Ellis Unit to visit McDuff. At first, he was extremely cocky. "I don't know why you are here. I got nothing to say to you."

"Well, we just wanted to come by and talk to you before your big day tomorrow," J. W. replied.

McDuff talked almost continuously for the next three hours. He was convinced that he was going to get a stay, that the appeals court never executed anybody. J. W. replied, "But Mac, you're special."

Much of what he told the two lawmen from Austin he had shared with John Moriarty, but he did admit that he was "pissed" at Regenia over a dope deal or a "clipping." During this interview, he added to the dialogue he had with Brenda Thompson. This version went like: "You're in big trouble, bitch. I'm gonna kill you."

To which Brenda allegedly replied: "Yea. I know."

"I'll give this to her, she handled it well," McDuff concluded.

In the short time they had with him, Chuck and J. W. masterfully exposed some of his most important lies. They were able to establish that the "statement" that he wanted to make to Austin by abducting Colleen was absurd. When Chuck suggested that the car wash was "just around the block" from the Austin Police Department, McDuff responded with, "Yea." The APD is nowhere near that car wash. They also slipped him erroneous information about the yogurt shop. He ate it up. The next day, he fed all of the wrong information back to John Moriarty; he even got the number of girls wrong. He was willing to confess to murdering five girls when there were only four.

"God damn, they gonna kill me tomorrow!" McDuff suddenly blurted out.

"Kenneth, that is what we have been telling you all along," Chuck said.

"You know, Mac, if this thing is gonna happen tomorrow, you should prepare yourself to meet your maker," suggested J. W.

"I don't believe in God," McDuff insisted.

"Mac, you ought to think about it and hedge your bets," J. W. counseled.

"I can't see myself floating on a cloud, playing a harp," McDuff said.

"We can't either!" J. W. said, as everyone, including McDuff, started laughing.

VII

On November 17, 1998, a large group of reporters stood outside the Walls Prison in Huntsville, Texas, in an area reserved for the press. The Walls is the oldest of all of Texas's prison units. It also houses the death chamber. Unbelievably, a single, heavy, dark blue cloud hovered over the prison. Near the concrete picnic table a jungle of tripods looked like a flock of ostriches. Mercifully, the sun began to go down, and a gentle breeze flapped the yellow, "Do not cross" police tapes. No one in the press saw a single anti–death penalty protester. (They later discovered that one woman was seen with a T-shirt supporting an end to capital punishment.)

Earlier in the day, Kenneth Allen McDuff had been transported from death row to a holding cell in the Walls. Reportedly, Addie had arrived too late to see him on his last day. At 5:58 P.M., the warden received word that the Supreme Court had turned down McDuff's final request for a stay. At 6:08 P.M. a team arrived to take him to the death chamber, and one minute later he was strapped to the gurney.

Inside the witness area, Parnell McNamara gently placed his hand on the shoulder of seventy-four-year-old Jack Brand.

"I've been waiting for this for thirty-two years," said the father of Robert Brand, murdered by McDuff in 1966.

"Are you all right?" Parnell asked quietly.

"I feel like thirty-two years have been lifted from my life," the old man said.

John Moriarty stood next to the executioner behind a one-way mirror only inches from McDuff. He saw that McDuff was scared; his massive neck shook as he stared at the ceiling and a solution began flowing into his veins through an I.V. stuck into his right arm. The witnesses, including members of four different victims' families, filed into the witness room. Three of Lonnie's children represented the McDuff family. Through it all McDuff kept staring at the ceiling.

"I am ready to be released. Release me," was Kenneth Allen McDuff's last statement. To the very end, he considered himself misunderstood, oppressed, and the victim.

Notes

PROLOGUE

1. The quoted phrase was taken from a document in the personal papers of Ms. Wanda Fischer. Hereafter cited as Fischer Collection.
2. Ibid.; Ms. Wanda Fischer, in an interview with the author June 16, 1998. All interviews will be initially cited by name and date. Afterwards, each will be cited by name only; *Rosebud News*, January 9, 1986.
3. Wanda Fischer.
4. CBS News, *48 Hours* program, aired at various times and dates.
5. Ms. Ellen Roberts, in an interview with the author, June 16, 1998; *Austin American-Statesman*, April 24, 1992.
6. *Texas Monthly*, August, 1992; *Austin American-Statesman*, April 24 and May 5, 1992.
7. Ken Anderson, *Crime in Texas: Your Complete Guide to the Criminal Justice System* (Austin: University of Texas Press, 1997), pg. 1.
8. *Texas Monthly*, May, 1996.
9. Sonya Urubek, quoted in an interview with the author, June 15, 1998; *Austin American-Statesman*, April 24, 1998.
10. *Austin American-Statesman*, February 2, 1998.
11. *Waco Tribune-Herald*, May 6, 1992; Richard Stroup, quoted in an interview with the author, June 17, 1998; http://www.Lubbockonline.com/news/112496/mcduff.htm.
12. Charles Butts in an interview with the author on June 20, 1998.
13. J. W. Thompson in an interview with the author on June 15, 1998.
14. Information from F. Lee Bailey and Truman Capote is taken from Bailey's Foreword in Jack Levin and James Alan Fox, *Mass Murder: America's Growing Menace* (New York: Plenum Press, 1985), pgs. viii–ix; Charles Butts; *Texas v Kenneth Allen McDuff*, Cause #643820, Closing arguments by Crawford Long, February 16, 1993, pgs. 14–42. Note: Much of this work is taken from Kenneth McDuff's capital murder

trial transcripts. They are called *Statements of Facts [SOF]*. I have numbered the Melissa Northrup Murder Trial, Cause #643820; the Colleen Reed Murder Trial is # 93-2139.

CHAPTER I

1. *Texas Monthly*, August, 1992; Wanda Fischer; Martha Royal, interviewed by the author on July 11, 1998; Ellen Roberts.
2. *Texas Monthly*, August, 1992; Wanda Fischer; Martha Royal; Ellen Roberts. Part of the Case File of Kenneth McDuff in the Bell County Sheriff's Office is a 1992 taped telephone conversation between Addie McDuff and Investigator Tim Steglich. The quote is from that tape. This is hereafter cited as "BCSO Files: Kenneth McDuff Case File Tapes, 1992."
3. Confidential sources.
4. BCSO Files: Kenneth McDuff Case File Tapes, 1992.
5. Confidential sources.
6. *State of Texas v Kenneth Allen McDuff*, SOF in Cause #93-2139, State's Exhibit #150.
7. Confidential sources; Martha Royal; Wanda Fischer; Ellen Roberts; *Texas Monthly*, August, 1992.
8. Wanda Fischer; Ellen Roberts.
9. The following descriptions do not represent Assembly of God Churches or their members. This particular congregation disbanded some time ago.
10. Confidential sources.
11. Kenneth Allen McDuff, interviewed by the author on September 17, 1996.
12. Ibid.; *48 Hours*, broadcast of June 29, 1998; I could not locate anyone in Rosebud who remembers any such lawn care.
13. Martha Royal; Ellen Roberts.
14. Ellen Roberts.
15. Ibid.; Martha Royal.
16. Ibid.; *Texas Monthly*, August, 1992.
17. Kenneth Allen McDuff.
18. *Texas Monthly*, August, 1992; Confidential Document.
19. Charles Meyer, quote from an interview by the author on June 15, 1998.
20. Ellen Roberts; *Texas Monthly*, August, 1992.
21. Ibid.
22. Kenneth Allen McDuff.
23. Quote in Ibid.

24. *State of Texas v Kenneth Allen McDuff*, SOF in Cause #93-2139, State's Exhibit #150; Texas Department of Criminal Justice [TDCJ]: *Kenneth Allen McDuff, Synopsis*, compiled by John Moriarty, pg. 1.

25. Kenneth Allen McDuff.

26. *State of Texas v Kenneth Allen McDuff*, SOF in Cause #93-5281, Volume IA–C, pgs. 7–8; *Temple Daily Telegram*, August 9, 1966.

27. APD Files: Unidentified fax from TDCJ Pardons and Parole Division, April 23, 1992; TDCJ: *Kenneth Allen McDuff, Synopsis*, Compiled by John Moriarty, pg. 1; Bill Habern and Gary J. Cohen, *A History of Parole, Mandatory Supervision and Good Time*, Texas Criminal Defense Lawyers' Association Website; *Texas Monthly*, August, 1992.

28. *Waco Tribune-Herald*, April 29, 1992; TCSO Files: *Statement of Roy Dale Green*, August 8, 1966; Charles Butts; Confidential Document.

29. Kenneth Allen McDuff.

30. Charles Butts; *Austin American-Statesman*, February 22, 1993; *Texas Monthly*, August, 1992.

31. Tarrant County Sheriff's Office [TCSO] Files: *Statement of Roy Dale Green*, August 8, 1966; Confidential Document.

CHAPTER 2

1. For a full account of the Texas Tower shootings see Gary M. Lavergne, *A Sniper in the Tower: The Charles Whitman Murders* (Denton: University of North Texas Press, 1997).

2. *State of Texas v Kenneth Allen McDuff*, SOF in Cause #93-2139, Volume 29, pgs. 83–85; Texas DPS Files: *Report of Investigation*, by John Aycock, May 4, 1992.

3. *Temple Daily Telegram*, August 9, 1966.

4. *State of Texas v Kenneth Allen McDuff*, SOF in Cause #93-2139, Volume 29, pgs. 89–90; TCSO Files: *Statement of Roy Dale Green*, August 8, 1966; *Fort Worth Star-Telegram*, August 18 and November 11, 1966; Confidential Document.

5. *State of Texas v Kenneth Allen McDuff*, SOF in Cause #93-2139, Volume 29, pg. 90; *Fort Worth Star-Telegram*, November 10, 1966; TCSO Files: *Statement of Roy Dale Green*, August 8, 1966; Confidential Document.

6. *Fort Worth Star-Telegram*, August 8 and 11, 1966; *Waco Times-Herald*, August 9, 1966.

7. *Fort Worth Star-Telegram*, August 8 and November 11, 1966; *Temple Daily Telegram*, August 9, 1966; Bob Stewart, *No Remorse* (New York: Pinnacle), passim; Jack Brand, in an interview with the author on December 19, 1998.

8. *Fort Worth Star-Telegram*, August 8 and November 11, 1966; *Temple Daily Telegram*, August 9, 1966.

9. *Fort Worth Star-Telegram*, August 8 and November 11, 1966.

10. TCSO Files: *Statement of Roy Dale Green*, August 8, 1966; Confidential Document; *Fort Worth Star-Telegram*, November 10, 1966.

11. TCSO Files: *Statement of Roy Dale Green*, August 8, 1966; Confidential Document.

12. *Fort Worth Star-Telegram*, August 8, 1966.

13. TCSO Files: *Statement of Roy Dale Green*, August 8, 1966; Confidential Document; *Fort Worth Star-Telegram*, November 10, 1966.

14. TCSO Files: *Statement of Roy Dale Green*, August 8, 1966; *State of Texas v Kenneth Allen McDuff*, SOF in Cause #93-2139, Volume 29, pgs. 98–99; *Austin American-Statesman*, April 23, 1992 and February 18, 1993; *Texas Monthly*, August, 1992.

15. TCSO Files: *Statement of Roy Dale Green*, August 8, 1966; *State of Texas v Kenneth Allen McDuff*, SOF in Cause #93-2139, Volume 29, passim; *Austin American-Statesman*, February 18, 1993.

16. TCSO Files: *Statement of Roy Dale Green*, August 8, 1966; *State of Texas v Kenneth Allen McDuff*, SOF in Cause #93-2139, Volume 29, passim; *Fort Worth Star-Telegram*, November 10, 1966.

17. TCSO Files: *Statement of Roy Dale Green*, August 8, 1966; *State of Texas v Kenneth Allen McDuff*, SOF in Cause #93-2139, Volume 29, passim; *Texas Monthly*, August, 1992.

18. Ibid.; Confidential Document.

19. Ibid.; *Fort Worth Star-Telegram*, August 9 and November 10, 1966; Charles Butts.

20. Kenneth McDuff quoted in an unidentified newspaper article provided by Bill Johnston, United States Attorney.

21. *Fort Worth Star-Telegram*, November 10, 1966; TCSO Files: *Statement of Roy Dale Green*, August 8, 1966; *State of Texas*

v Kenneth Allen McDuff, SOF in Cause #93-2139, Volume 29, passim; Confidential Document.

22. *State of Texas v Kenneth Allen McDuff*, SOF in Cause #93-2139, Volume 29, pgs. 114–16; TCSO Files: *Statement of Roy Dale Green*, August 8, 1966.

23. *Fort Worth Star-Telegram*, August 8 and November 11, 1966.

24. *Waco News Tribune*, August 8, 1966; *Fort Worth Star-Telegram*, August 8, 1966; *Austin American-Statesman*, April 23, 1992; *Waco Times-Herald*, August 8, 1966; Jack Brand.

25. *State of Texas v Kenneth Allen McDuff*, SOF in Cause #93-2139, Volume 29, pg. 117; Richard Boyd quoted in *Fort Worth Star-Telegram*, November 12, 1966.

26. *State of Texas v Kenneth Allen McDuff*, SOF in Cause #93-2139, Volume 29, pg. 117; TCSO Files: *Statement of Roy Dale Green*, August 8, 1966; *Fort Worth Star-Telegram*, November 12, 1966.

27. Roy Dale Green quoted in *Temple Daily Telegram*, August 9, 1966.

28. Roy Dale Green quoted in *Fort Worth Star-Telegram*, August 8, 1966.

29. Roy Dale Green quoted in *Temple Daily Telegram*, August 9, 1966; *Fort Worth Star-Telegram*, August 8 and 9, 1966; *Waco Times-Herald*, August 9, 1966.

30. *Rosebud News*, August 11, 1966; *Waco News Tribune*, August 8, 1966; Brady Pamplin quoted in *Fort Worth Star-Telegram*, November 11, 1966.

31. *Fort Worth Star-Telegram*, August 9, 1966; Larry Pamplin, in an interview with the author on November 23, 1998.

32. The current Chief Deputy of the Falls County Sheriff's Office, Larry Honeycutt, confirmed that there is no mention of Kenneth McDuff in the master index at the Falls County Sheriff's Office in a telephone conversation with the author. The conclusion that there is no existing record of any arrests of Kenneth McDuff in Falls County is based on McDuff's prison record, which has a complete criminal history, and several affidavits filed on various occasions which included McDuff's prior criminal offenses.

CHAPTER 3

1. TDCJ Files: *Kenneth Allen McDuff, Synopsis*, compiled by John Moriarty, pg. 1.

2. *Rosebud News*, August 11, 1966.

3. Confidential Source; Ellen Roberts; Martha Royal.

4. The account of the hearing and the quote are from the *Rosebud News*, August 18, 1966.

5. Ibid.

6. Roy Dale Green quoted in *Temple Daily Telegram*, August 9, 1966; *Rosebud News*, August 11, 1966; *Fort Worth Star-Telegram*, August 10, 1966.

7. Lon Evans quoted in *Fort Worth Star-Telegram*, August 10, 1966.

8. Charles Butts; *Fort Worth Star-Telegram*, August 12, 1966.

9. *Fort Worth Star-Telegram*, November 8, 1966; *Journal of Texas Criminal Defense Lawyers Association*, June, 1987, pgs. 4–6; Charles Butts; *Temple Daily Telegram*, August 9, 1966; The quote describing Charles Butts is from *Fort Worth Press*, October 18, 1966.

10. Charles Butts.

11. *Fort Worth Star-Telegram*, August 18 and November 8, 1966.

12. *Rosebud News*, August 11, 1966.

13. *Texas Monthly*, August, 1992; *Fort Worth Star-Telegram*, November 8 and 9, 1966.

14. *Fort Worth Star-Telegram*, August 18, 1966.

15. Ibid., November 9 and 19, 1966; Charles Butts.

16. *Fort Worth Star-Telegram*, November 11, 1966.

17. Ibid.; Charles Butts.

18. Ibid., November 10, 1966; Charles Butts.

19. Ibid.

20. Ibid., November 13, 1966.

21. Ibid.

22. Charles Butts.

23. *Fort Worth Star-Telegram*, October 18 and November 15, 1966; Ibid.

24. *Temple Daily Telegram*, November 16, 1966; *Rosebud News*, November 17, 1966; *Fort Worth Star-Telegram*, November 16, 1966; Charles Butts quote from interview.

25. Charles Butts.

26. *Fort Worth Star-Telegram*, November 16, 1966; *State of Texas v Kenneth Allen McDuff*, SOF in Cause #93-2139, Volume 29, pgs. 121–24.

27. Ibid.; *Waco Herald-Tribune*, April 29, 1992; *Texas Monthly*, August, 1992.

28. McLennan County District Attorney's Office [MCDA] Files: Various documents related to execution dates for Kenneth Allen McDuff, passim; TDCJ Files: *Kenneth Allen McDuff, Synopsis*, compiled by John Moriarty, pg. 1.

29. Interview of Charles Meyers and Wayne Appelt, August 27, 1998.

30. I did not bother to count the number of times Kenneth McDuff made that statement in my interview with him.

31. MCDA Files: Board of Pardons and Paroles, unidentified documents, May 3, 1989.

32. *State of Texas v Kenneth Allen McDuff*, SOF in Cause #93-2139, Volume 29, Exhibit #150; The drug smuggling charge is from a confidential source in a Confidential Document.

33. *State of Texas v Kenneth Allen McDuff*, Order Dismissing Cases in Causes #20256 and 20259, in the 18th Judicial District of Johnson County, March 8, 1978.

34. *Furman v Georgia*, 408 U.S. 238, June 29, 1972, from the Villanova Center for Information and Policy, www.law.vill.edu, pgs. 35–36.

35. *Furman v Georgia*, 408 U.S. 238, June 29, 1972, from the Villanova Center for Information and Policy, www.law.vill.edu, pgs. 1, 23, 38, 93.

36. Ibid., pg. 41; *Waco Tribune-Herald*, April 27, 1992.

CHAPTER 4

1. Wayne Appelt; Charles Meyer; *Austin American-Statesman*, April 1, 1990, January 31, 1991, and December 12, 1992.

2. Ibid.

3. *Austin American-Statesman*, May 3, 1992; Bob Ozer quoted in *Austin American-Statesman*, March 2, 1989.

4. Allen Hightower quoted in *Austin American-Statesman*, June 4, 1991.

5. *Austin American-Statesman*, May 3, 1992.

6. WFAA-TV News, Dallas, Texas, investigative reports by Robert Riggs. Tapes of the reports were kindly provided to me by Lori Bible of Round Rock, Texas. Hereafter cited as WFAA-TV News.

7. APD Files: Unidentified fax from TDCJ Pardons and Paroles Division, April 23, 1992; Bill Habern and Gary J. Cohen, *A

History of Parole, Mandatory Supervision and Good Time,
Texas Criminal Defense Lawyers' Association Website.
Hereafter cited as TCDLA website followed by a page num-
ber.

8. TCDLA website, pg. 3; APD Files: Unidentified fax from
   TDCJ Pardons and Paroles Division, April 23, 1992.

9. Kenneth McDuff quoted by Glenn Heckmann in *Austin
   American-Statesman,* July 19, 1992.

10. APD Files: Unidentified fax from TDCJ Pardons and Paroles
    Division, April 23, 1992; *Austin American-Statesman,* July
    19, 1992; State of Texas v Kenneth Allen McDuff, SOF in
    Cause #93-2139, State's Exhibit #150; TDCJ Files: *Kenneth
    Allen McDuff, Synopsis,* compiled by John Moriarty, pg. 1.

11. APD Files: Unidentified fax from TDCJ Pardons and Paroles
    Division, April 23, 1992.

12. Alva Hank Worley is quoted from a taped interview with Dr.
    Matt Ferrara. The tape is part of the APD Files. The case file
    has other taped interrogations of Alva Hank Worley. They
    will be cited as "APD Files: Interview of Alva Hank Worley"
    followed by the date. This citation includes an interview of
    April 30, 1992.

13. Confidential Source; BCSO Files: *Supplementary Investiga-
    tion Report,* by W. J. Bryan, January 6, 1986.

14. Confidential Source; BCSO Files: *County Detention Admis-
    sion Record, Lonnie McDuff,* December 14, 1985; Interview
    of Bill Miller, June 17, 1998.

15. BCSO Files: *Voluntary Statement of [Doris],* and *Supple-
    mentary Investigation Report,* by C. E. Cox, January 6, 1986,
    Voluntary Statement of [Michelle], January 9, 1986 and
    [Tim], January 27, 1986; Texas DPS Files: *Report of Inves-
    tigation,* by Ranger John Aycock, January 14, 1986.

16. BCSO Files: *Voluntary Statement of [Larry],* and *[Doris],*
    January 6, 1986.

17. Ibid.; Texas DPS Files: *Report of Investigation,* by Ranger
    John Aycock, January 14, 1986.

18. BCSO Files: *Voluntary Statement of Terry Johnson,* January
    5, 1986, and *Linda Hastings,* January 16, 1986.

19. BCSO Files: *Supplementary Investigation Report,* by C. E.
    Cox, January 6, 1986; Texas DPS Files: *Report of Investi-
    gation,* by Ranger John Aycock, January 14, 1986.

20. Texas DPS Files: *Report of Investigation,* by Ranger John

Aycock, January 14, 1986; BCSO Files: *Supplementary Investigation Report*, by W. J. Bryan, January 6, 1986, C. E. Cox, January 6, 1986, and Mike Brackman, January 7, 1986.

21. BCSO Files: *Supplementary Investigation Report*, by C. E. Cox, January 6, 1986.

22. Southwestern Institute of Forensic Sciences, *Autopsy Report, Lonnie McDuff*, January 6, 1986.

23. *Texas Monthly*, August, 1992.

24. Letter from Gene R. Johnson to Gary D. Jackson, September 7, 1977.

25. *Texas Monthly*, August, 1992; *State of Texas v Kenneth Allen McDuff*, Motion to Dismiss in Causes #20256 and #20259, Court of Johnson County, September 15, 1977.

26. *Texas Monthly*, August, 1992.

27. APD Files: Unidentified fax from TDCJ Pardons and Paroles Division, April 23, 1992.

28. Texas Board of Pardons and Paroles figures cited in *Waco Tribune-Herald*, May 3, 1992.

29. TCDLA website, pgs. 3–4; *Texas Monthly*, August, 1992.

30. WFAA-TV News.

31. WFAA-TV News.

32. Granberry's memo is quoted in WFAA-TV News.

33. APD Files: Unidentified and undated document prepared by Andrew Kahan; WFAA-TV News.

34. APD Files: Unidentified Fax from TDCJ Pardons and Paroles Division, April 23, 1992; WFAA-TV News; TDCJ Files: *Kenneth Allen McDuff, Synopsis*, compiled by John Moriarty, pg. 1.

35. Confidential Document.

36. Letter of Gloria Jackson to Joseph D. Tarwater, January 28, 1991.

37. Ibid.

38. Confidential Document.

39. Letter of Gloria Jackson to Kenneth Allen McDuff, January 28, 1991.

CHAPTER 5

1. Bill Miller.

2. Texas DPS Files: *Report of Investigation*, by John Aycock, April 23, 1992; Texas Department of Criminal Justice [TDCJ] Files: *Kenneth Allen McDuff, Synopsis*, compiled by

John Moriarty, pg. 1; *Temple Daily Telegram*, October 15, 1989; *Austin American-Statesman*, April 30, 1992; Confidential Sources.

3. County of Bastrop: *Statement of [Angela]*, September 3, 1992; APD Files: *Incident Report*, by J. W. Thompson, September 12, 1992.

4. Texas Board of Pardons and Paroles: *Certificate of Parole*, Kenneth Allen McDuff, #227123, October 9, 1989; TDCJ Files: *Kenneth Allen McDuff, Synopsis*, compiled by John Moriarty, pg. 1; Confidential Document; Texas DPS Files: *Report of Investigation*, by John Aycock, March 20, 1992.

5. TDCJ Files: *Kenneth Allen McDuff, Synopsis*, compiled by John Moriarty, pg. 2; Kenneth Allen McDuff; Confidential Document.

6. BCSO Files: Kenneth McDuff Case File Tapes, 1992; *State of Texas v Kenneth Allen McDuff*, SOF in Cause #643820, Volume 2, pg. 163; Confidential Documents.

7. TDCJ Files: *Kenneth Allen McDuff, Synopsis*, compiled by John Moriarty, pg. 2.

8. Ibid., pgs. 2–3; TDCJ, Pardons and Paroles Division, Hearing Section: *Administrative Release Revocation Hearing Report*, #227,123, September 17, 1990.

9. *Texas Monthly*, August, 1992; Wanda Fischer; *Austin American-Statesman*, May 3, 1992.

10. TDCJ, Pardons and Paroles Division, Hearing Section: *Administrative Release Revocation Hearing Report*, #227,123, September 17, 1990.

11. APD Files: *Statement of [Linda]*, July 7, 1992; Kenneth Allen McDuff.

12. *State of Texas v Kenneth McDuff*, Cause of Action, #203-90, July 11, 1990; Ellen Roberts; APD Files: unidentified document prepared by Andrew Kahan, u.d.

13. TDCJ Files: *Kenneth Allen McDuff, Synopsis*, compiled by John Moriarty, pgs. 2–3; BCSO Files: *Memo*, by Major Bryan, July 18, 1990; Thomas B. Sehon to Texas Department of Criminal Justice, August 3, 1990; Larry Pamplin.

14. TDCJ Files: *Kenneth Allen McDuff, Synopsis*, compiled by John Moriarty, pg. 3.

15. TDCJ. Pardons and Paroles Division, Hearing Section: *Administrative Release Revocation Hearing Report*, #227,123, September 17, 1990; Larry Pamplin.

16. Ibid.
17. Ibid.
18. Ibid.
19. Ibid.
20. APD Files: unidentified document prepared by Andrew Kahan, u.d.; WFAA-TV News.
21. Bettie Wells quoted in *Austin American-Statesman*, September 19, 1992; *Texas Monthly*, August, 1992; APD Files: unidentified document prepared by Andrew Kahan, u.d.
22. TDCJ Pardons and Paroles Division: *Interoffice Memorandum*, December 19, 1990.

CHAPTER 6

1. APD Files: Interview of Alva Hank Worley, April 30, 1992; *State of Texas v Kenneth Allen McDuff*, SOF in Cause #93-2139, Volume 24, pg. 189; Interviews of Mike McNamara, Parnell McNamara, and Bill Johnston by the author on June 16, 1998.
2. Tim Steglich; J. W. Thompson; Charles Meyer; APD Files: *Incident Report*, by Scott James Cary, July 4, 1992.
3. Ibid.
4. Kenneth Allen McDuff; County of McLennan: *Sworn Statement of [Michael]*, June 18, 1992.
5. Kenneth Allen McDuff.
6. County of McLennan: *Sworn Statement of [Michael]*, June 18, 1992; Charles Meyer.
7. Kenneth Allen McDuff.
8. County of McLennan: *Sworn Statement of [Michael]*, June 18, 1992; APD Files: *Statement of [Linda]*, July 7, 1992.
9. County of McLennan: *Sworn Statement of [Michael]*, June 18, 1992.
10. WPD Files: *Offense Report*, by Officer Trantham, February 12, 1992, and *Supplement*, by Officer Shaw, February 13, 1992.
11. Ibid., by Officer Raup, February 25, 1992.
12. Kenneth Allen McDuff; Charles Meyer.
13. APD Files: *Statement of [Linda]*, July 7, 1992.
14. Ibid.
15. Ibid.; Kenneth Allen McDuff; County of McLennan: *Sworn Statement of [Jennifer]*, June 25, 1992.
16. Charles Meyers; J. W. Thompson; APD Files: *Transcript of*

a Taped Interview with [Mark], July 31, 1992, and Interview
of Alva Hank Worley, May 13, 1992.

17. APD Files: *Statement of [Linda]*, July 7, 1992; Texas DPS
Files: *Report of Investigation*, by John Aycock, July 10,
1992.
18. Ibid.
19. Ibid.; Texas DPS Files: *Report of Investigation*, by John Aycock, July 10, 1992.
20. Ibid., BCSO Files: *Voluntary Statement of [Glenn]*, June 25,
1992; APD Files: *Transcript of a Taped Interview with
[Mark]*, July 31, 1992; County of McLennan: *Sworn Statement of [Jennifer]*, June 25, 1992.
21. APD Files: *Statement of [Linda]*, July 7, 1992; Bill Johnston.
22. Ibid.; Texas DPS Files: *Report of Investigation*, by John Aycock, July 10, 1992.
23. APD Files: *Statement of [Linda]*, July 7, 1992; I did a criminal background search on Jimmy using the Texas Department of Public Safety Website.
24. APD Files: *Investigation of Sexually Sadistic Offenses*, by
Robert R. Hazelwood, Park E. Dietz, and Janet Warren, u.d.,
pg. 1.
25. Ibid., pg. 3.
26. Texas DPS Files: *Report of Investigation*, by John Aycock,
April 24, 1992; APD Files: *Statement of [Linda]*, July 7,
1992.
27. County of McLennan: *Sworn Statement of [Jennifer]*, June
25, 1992.
28. Texas DPS Files: *Report of Investigation*, by John Aycock,
May 14, 1992.

CHAPTER 7

1. Texas DPS Files: *Report of Investigation*, by John Aycock,
May 14, 1992; TDCJ Files: *Kenneth Allen McDuff, Synopsis*,
by John Moriarty, pg. 4–5.
2. http://amarillonet.com/stories/081297/aims.html; Ibid.
3. *State of Texas v Kenneth Allen McDuff*, SOF in Cause #93-
2139, Volume 27, pg. 8 and exhibit #150, SOF in Cause
#643820, Volume 7, pg. 184; TDCJ Files: *Kenneth Allen
McDuff, Synopsis*, by John Moriarty, pg. 9.
4. BCSO Files: *Resumé, Kenneth Allen McDuff*, u.d., and *TSTI
Transcript*, Kenneth Allen McDuff, November 26, 1991.

5. *State of Texas v Kenneth Allen McDuff*, SOF in Cause #643820, Volume 7, pg. 185; BCSO Files: *Human Relations Handbook*, Texas State Technical Institute, 1991, pgs. 0-4–0-8.

6. Every officer I interviewed who investigated McDuff's matriculation at TSTI described being frustrated with class-room attendance records kept by his teachers. APD Files: *Statement of [Linda]*, July 7, 1992.

7. BCSO Files: *Human Relations Handbook*, Texas State Technical Institute, 1991, pg. 0-4; BCSO Files: *TSTI Transcript*, Kenneth Allen McDuff, November 26, 1991.

8. BCSO Files: Human Relations coursework of Kenneth Allen McDuff, October 6, 1991. Hereafter cited as "McDuff Coursework." McDuff's writings will hereafter appear as he wrote them, without the use of [sic].

9. McDuff Coursework.

10. Ibid.

11. Ibid.; The Tim Steglich quote is from my interview with him.

12. Bill Johnston; FBI Files: *Report by Agent Freddie Vela*, March 13, 1992.

13. Confidential document.

14. Richard Stroup.

15. APD Files: *Statement of [Linda]*, July 7, 1992.

16. *State of Texas v Kenneth Allen McDuff*, SOF in Cause #643820, Volume 3, pgs. 38–43, 54, and 56; MCSO Files: *Continuation Report*, by Richard Stroup, May 15, 1992; FBI Files: *Report by Agent Freddie Vela*, March 13, 1992; Confidential Documents.

17. County of McLennan: *Sworn Statement of [Jennifer]*, June 25, 1992; Texas DPS Files; *Report of Investigation*, by John Aycock, August 1, 1992; *State of Texas v Kenneth Allen McDuff*, SOF in Cause #643820, Volume 3, pgs. 10–13.

18. APD Files: *Transcript of a Taped Interview with [Mark]*, July 31, 1992; Texas DPS Files: *Report of Investigation*, by John Aycock, August 1, 1992.

19. APD Files: *Incident Report*, by J. W. Thompson, July 27, 1992.

20. County of McLennan: *Statement of [Frankie]*, July 2, 1992.

21. Ibid.; BCSO Files: *Supplement Report*, by Tim Steglich, Incident #92-3366, dated March 3, 1992.

22. FBI Files: *Report by Agent Freddie Vela*, March 26, 1992; Richard Stroup.

23. *State of Texas v Kenneth Allen McDuff*, SOF in Cause #0935281, Volume IA-C, pgs. 88–90; *W-2 Wage and Tax Statement, 1991*, Kenneth Allen McDuff from Quik Pak Food Stores, Inc.

24. *State of Texas v Kenneth Allen McDuff*, SOF in Cause #643820, Volume 1, pgs. 89–92, 179–81.

25. Ibid., pgs. 112–13, 144–56, 182.

26. Ibid., pgs. 144, 214, and SOF in Cause # 0935281, Volume IA-C, pgs. 85 and 95.

27. Ibid. in Cause #643820, Volume 1, pg. 147, and Volume 3, pgs. 43–44, and in Cause #0935281 Volume IA-C, page 94; *W-2 Wage and Tax Statement, 1991*, Kenneth Allen McDuff from Quik Pak Food Stores, Inc.

28. *State of Texas v Kenneth Allen McDuff*, SOF in Cause #643820, Volume 3, pgs. 45–48.

29. Ibid., pgs. 15–18; APD Files: *Transcript of a Taped Interview with [Mark]*, July 31, 1992; Texas DPS Files: *Report of Investigation*, by John Aycock, August 1, 1992; BCSO Files: *Supplement Report*, by Tim Steglich, Incident #92-3366, dated March 3, 1992.

30. Kenneth Allen McDuff.

31. BCSO Files: *Statement of [Morris]*, March 25, 1992; APD Files: *Incident Report*, by Donald O. Martin, March 31, 1992, *Sworn Statement of [Billy]*, May 21, 1992; *State of Texas v Kenneth Allen McDuff*, SOF in Cause #93-2139, Volume 20, pg. 83, and Volume 20, pgs. 140–41.

32. County of Travis: *Sworn Statement of [Beverly]*, June 8, 1992.

33. BCSO Files: *Statement of [Morris]*, March 25, 1992; APD Files: *Incident Report*, by Donald O. Martin, March 31, 1992; Ibid.

CHAPTER 8

1. Interview of Lori Bible, July 14, 1998.

2. Ibid.; *Austin American-Statesman*, January 1, 1992.

3. Ibid.

4. *Austin American-Statesman*, January 1, 1992; Ibid.

5. Lori Bible.

6. Ibid.

7. Ibid.; APD Files: *Incident Report*, by Donald O. Martin, December 30, 1991; *State of Texas v Kenneth Allen McDuff*, SOF in Cause #93-2139, Volume 30, pg. 74.

8. APD Files: *Incident Report*, by Donald O. Martin, December 30, 1991; Lori Bible; *State of Texas v Kenneth Allen McDuff*, SOF in Cause #93-2139, Volume 20, pg. 196.

9. Lori Bible.

10. Lori Bible; *State of Texas v Kenneth Allen McDuff*, SOF in Cause #93-2139, Volume 20, pg. 165; *Austin American-Statesman*, December 31, 1991, and January 1, 1992.

11. Ibid.

12. Ibid.; *State of Texas v Kenneth Allen McDuff*, SOF in Cause #643820, Volume 7, pg. 100, SOF in Cause # 93-2139, Volume 20, pgs. 152–55; Heather Bailey quoted in *Austin American-Statesman*, January 1, 1992.

13. *State of Texas v Kenneth Allen McDuff*, SOF in Cause #93-2139, Volume 20, pg. 209–15; *Austin American-Statesman*, December 28, 1992.

14. *Austin American-Statesman*, January 1, 1992; Lori Bible; APD Files: *Incident Report*, by Donald O. Martin, January 7, 1992.

15. Lori Bible; APD Files: *Incident Report*, by Donald O. Martin, December 30, 1991; *Austin American-Statesman*, December 31, 1991.

16. *State of Texas v Kenneth Allen McDuff*, SOF in Cause #93-2139, Volume 22, pgs. 88, 92–95; Lori Bible; APD Files: *Incident Report*, by Donald O. Martin, January 22, 1992.

17. Richard and Brenda Solomon, interviewed by the author on June 13, 1998; *State of Texas v Kenneth Allen McDuff*, SOF in Cause #643820, Volume 1, pg. 48.

18. Brenda Solomon; Richard Solomon; MCSO Files: *Evidence Inventory, 92-1368, Melissa Northrup*, by Richard Stroup and George Foster, November 18, 1992.

19. *State of Texas v Kenneth Allen McDuff*, SOF in Cause #93-2139, Volume 29, pgs. 150–56; Brenda Solomon; Richard Solomon.

20. *State of Texas v Kenneth Allen McDuff*, SOF in Cause #93-5281, Volume IA-C, pg. 47, and Cause # 93-2139, Volume 29, pgs. 150–56.

21. Ibid., Cause #93-5281, Volume IA-C, pg. 30.

22. Brenda Solomon; Richard Solomon.

23. *State of Texas v Kenneth Allen McDuff*, SOF in Cause #93-2139, Volume 29, pg. 145, and Cause #643820, Volume 1, page 182; Brenda Solomon.

24. Brenda Solomon; *State of Texas v Kenneth Allen McDuff*, SOF in Cause #93-5281, Volume IA-C, pg. 36–37.

25. TDCJ Files: *Kenneth Allen McDuff, Synopsis*, by John Moriarty, pgs. 9, 12–17; John Moriarty; BCSO Files: *TSTI Housing Office Form*, February 11, 1992.

26. *State of Texas v Kenneth Allen McDuff*, SOF in Cause #93-2139, Volume 20, pgs. 75, 116, and 121; BCSO Files: *Statement of Alva Hank Worley*, April 4, 1992, and *Supplement Report*, by Tim Steglich, dated March 3, 1992.

27. BCSO Files: *Supplement Report*, by Tim Steglich, dated March 3, 1992; Texas DPS Files: *Report of Investigation*, by John Aycock, April 29, 1992; Confidential Document; Tim Steglich; Charles Meyer.

28. Kenneth Allen McDuff.

29. MCDA Files: *Temple Police Department Report*, by Bruce Smith, September 1, 1991; TDCJ Files: *Report of Violation*, September 30, 1991.

30. Texas DPS Files: *Report of Investigation*, by John Aycock, April 24, 1992; TDCJ Files: *Kenneth Allen McDuff, Synopsis*, by John Moriarty, pg. 16.

31. BCSO Files: *State of Texas v Kenneth Allen McDuff: Order Suspending Imposition of Sentence and Granting Adult Probation*, January 3, 1992.

32. Ibid.

33. *State of Texas v Kenneth Allen McDuff*, SOF in Cause #93-2139, Volume 24, pgs. 124 and 181, Volume 25, pgs. 19 and 124, and in Cause # 643820, Volume 7, pg. 27; Texas Department of Public Safety Website.

34. APD Files: *Taped Interview with Alva Hank Worley*, May 13, 1992.

35. BCSO Files: *Supplement Report*, by Tim Steglich, dated March 3, 1992; Tim Steglich; Bill Miller.

36. *State of Texas v Kenneth Allen McDuff*, SOF in Cause #93-2139, Volume 25, pg. 281; APD Files: *Taped Interview with Alva Hank Worley*, May 13, 1992; *Austin American-Statesman*, April 25, 1992.

37. *State of Texas v Kenneth Allen McDuff*, SOF in Cause #93-

2139, Volume 24, pgs. 84–85; APD Files: *Sworn Statement of [Billy]*, May 21, 1992.

38. *State of Texas v Kenneth Allen McDuff*, SOF in Cause #93-2139, Volume 24, pg. 182, and Volume 25, pgs. 217, 219–20; APD Files: *Incident Report*, by Scott Cary, July 4, 1992.

39. APD Files: *Taped Interview with Alva Hank Worley*, May 13, 1992 and *Incident Report*, by J. W. Thompson, July 24, 1992; BCSO Files: *Statement of Alva Hank Worley*, April 8, 1992; *Austin American-Statesman*, February 9, 1993; *State of Texas v Kenneth Allen McDuff*, SOF in Cause #93-2139, Volume 5, pg. 11.

40. BCSO Files: *Statement of Alva Hank Worley*, April 8, 1992; APD Files: *Incident Report*, by Scott Cary, July 4, 1992.

41. APD Files: *Statement of [Linda]*, July 7, 1992.

42. Ibid.

43. Ibid.

44. Ibid.

CHAPTER 9

1. Texas DPS Website; Waco Police Department [WPD] Files: *Arrest Form, #F38826*, September 6, 1991; *Waco Tribune-Herald*, October 24, 1998.

2. WPD Files: *Arrest Form, #F40130*, May 24, 1991.

3. WPD Files: *Arrest Form, #F38826*, September 6, 1991.

4. WPD Files: *Arrest Form, #F3794*, September 25, 1991, and *#F41095*, September 27, 1991; Kenneth Allen McDuff; Confidential Documents.

5. Ibid., *Offense Report, Case #91-062985*, by Officer Barrington, October 19, 1991, and by Mike Nicoletti, July 9, 1992; County of McLennan: *Sworn Statement of [Jennifer]*, June 25, 1992.

6. Ibid., *Arrest Form, #F41576*, by Officer Swanton; The times of Regenia Moore's arrest, booking, and release are from McLennan County jail logs read to the author over the phone by Deputy Ronnie Turnbough of the McLennan County Sheriff's Office on August 3, 1998.

7. WPD Files: *Offense Report, Case #91-060936*, by Officer Swanton, October 10, 1991.

8. County of McLennan: *Sworn Statement of [Michael]*, June 18, 1992.

9. WPD Files: *Offense Report, Case #91-062985*, by Officer

Barrington, October 19, 1991; Confidential Document.

10. WPD Files: *Offense Report, Case #91-062985*, by Officer Barrington, October 19, 1991.

11. Confidential Documents; County of McLennan: *Sworn Statement of [Frankie]*, July 2, 1992; *Austin American-Statesman*, April 25, 1992.

12. County of McLennan: *Statement of [Frankie]*, July 2, 1992; Charles Meyer; APD Files: *Transcript of a taped interview with [Mark]*, July 31, 1992.

13. County of McLennan: *Sworn Statement of [Jennifer]*, June 25, 1992; Confidential Documents.

14. WPD Files: *Offense Report, Case #91-062985*, by Officer Morgan, October 20, 1991, and by Officer Bradley, October 28, 1991; Confidential Document.

15. This is based on interviews of McDuff by John Moriarty of TDCJ.

16. Bill Johnston; Parnell McNamara; Mike McNamara; Confidential Documents.

17. APD Files: *Sworn Statement of [Billy]*, May 21, 1992 and *Incident Report*, by Sonya Urubek, June 22, 1992; TDCJ Files: *Kenneth Allen McDuff, Synopsis*, compiled by John Moriarty, pg. 20; *State of Texas v Kenneth Allen McDuff*, SOF in Cause #93-2139, Volume 24, pgs. 84–85, and State's Exhibit #56.

18. County of Bastrop: *Statement of [Angela]*, September 3, 1992; APD Files: *Incident Report*, by J. W. Thompson, September 12, 1992, and Sonya Urubek, June 22, 1992.

19. Lori Bible; *State of Texas v Kenneth Allen McDuff*, SOF in Cause #93-2139, Volume 20, pgs. 157–58, 160, 199, 217–18 and Volume 26, pgs. 240–41; APD Files: *Incident Report*, by Don Martin, January 7, February 10, and February 14, 1992.

20. J. W. Thompson.

21. County of Travis: *Statement of [Howard]*, February 11, 1993; Texas DPS Website; J. W. Thompson; Confidential Documents; My description of One-eyed Jack is taken from a picture provided to me by a confidential source, and another picture in the Austin Police Department Files.

22. Ibid.; Charles Meyer; Mike McNamara; Parnell McNamara; J. W. Thompson; APD Files: *Incident Report*, by Darrell Boydston, March 25, 1992.

23. Ibid.; State of Texas: *Sworn Statement of [Jackie]*, March 24, 1992; *State of Texas v Kenneth Allen McDuff*, SOF in Cause #93-2139, Volume 20, pgs. 108–13; APD Files: *Incident Report*, by Donald O. Martin, March 27, 1992.

CHAPTER 10

1. *State of Texas v Kenneth Allen McDuff*, SOF in Cause #93-2139, Volume 20, pg. 238.

2. Ibid., pg. 218; APD Files: *Incident Report*, by Donald O. Martin, December 30, 1991.

3. County of Travis: *Sworn Statement of [Oliver]*, December 31, 1991; *State of Texas v Kenneth Allen McDuff*, SOF in Cause #93-2139, Volume 20, pgs. 108–13, 218–19 and Volume 26, pg. 237; APD Files: *Incident Report*, by Donald O. Martin, January 7, 1992.

4. County of Travis: *Sworn Statement of [Oliver]*, December 31, 1991; *State of Texas v Kenneth Allen McDuff*, SOF in Cause #93-2139, Volume 20, pgs. 220–21.

5. County of Travis: *Sworn Statement of [Oliver]*, December 31, 1991; *State of Texas v Kenneth Allen McDuff*, SOF in Cause #93-2139, Volume 20, pgs. 221–22.

6. APD Files: *Incident Report*, by Donald O. Martin, January 7, 1992.

7. APD Files: Interview of Alva Hank Worley, April 30 and May 13, 1992, and *Interview of [Diane]*, May 22, 1992; *State of Texas v Kenneth Allen McDuff*, SOF in Cause #93-2139, Volume 25, pgs. 21–23; BCSO Files: *Statement of Alva Hank Worley*, 5:45 P.M., April 20, 1992. Note: Alva Hank Worley gave several statements on April 20, 1992. For this citation only I will include the time of the statement as well as the date.

8. *Texas Certificate of Title*, #33409449, December 30, 1991; APD Files: *Interview of [Diane]*, May 22, 1992; *State of Texas v Kenneth Allen McDuff*, SOF in Cause #93-2139, Volume 24, pgs. 183–88, Volume 25, pg. 22, and Volume 28, pg. 35.

9. Ibid.

10. BCSO Files: *Statement of Alva Hank Worley*, April 21, 1992, *Statement of [Doug]*, May 13, 1992, and *Supplement Report*, by Tim Steglich, March 3, 1992; APD Files: *Incident Re-*

ports, by J. W. Thompson, June 3, 1992, and Sonya Urubek, June 22, 1992.

11. BCSO Files: *Statement of Alva Hank Worley*, April 20, 1992, 5:45 P.M.; Sonya Urubek; APD Files: *Interview of Alva Hank Worley*, May 13, 1992; www.lubbockonline.com/news/112496/mcduff.htm; *State of Texas v Kenneth Allen McDuff*, SOF in Cause #643820, Volume 5, pgs. 14–15 and in Cause #93-2139, Volume 25, pgs. 23–28.

12. *State of Texas v Kenneth Allen McDuff*, SOF in Cause #93-2139, Volume 2, pgs. 30–44, Volume 3, pgs. 12–18, Volume 4, pgs. 193–95, and Volume 21, pgs. 15–19.

13 Ibid.; APD Files: *Statement of [Kari]*, December 30, 1991.

14. *State of Texas v Kenneth Allen McDuff*, SOF in Cause #93-2139, Volume 4, pgs. 196–203, Volume 21, pgs. 111–14 and 133; APD Files: *Incident Report*, by Donald O. Martin, January 9, 1992, and *Sworn Statement of [Kari]*, December 30, 1991.

15. *State of Texas v Kenneth Allen McDuff*, SOF in Cause #93-2139, Volume 2, pg. 62, Volume 3, pgs. 18–24, and 58, Volume 21, pg. 99, and Volume 22, pgs. 14–16; County of Travis: *Sworn Statement of Michael J. Goins* and *William Ray Goins, Jr.*, December 30, 1991.

16. APD Files: *Incident Report*, by Donald O. Martin, January 7, 1992, and February 3, 1992; *State of Texas v Kenneth Allen McDuff*, SOF in Cause #93-2139, Volume 20, pgs. 249–51.

17. Colleen's receipts are in the APD Files. The originals are exhibits in *State of Texas v Kenneth Allen McDuff*, SOF in Cause #93-2139; *Austin American-Statesman*, January 9 and 13, 1992.

18. APD Files: *Incident Report*, by Jeffry Adickes, January 2, 1992.

19. BCSO Files: *Statement of Alva Hank Worley*, 5:45 P.M., April 20, April 21, and April 24, 1992; APD Files: *Incident Report*, by Donald O. Martin, May 7, 1992; *State of Texas v Kenneth Allen McDuff*, SOF in Cause #93-2139, Volume 24, pgs. 189–92, Volume 25, pgs. 23–28, 137.

20. BCSO Files: *Statement of Alva Hank Worley*, 5:45 P.M., April 20, 1992, and Interview of May 13, 1992.

21. *State of Texas v Kenneth Allen McDuff*, SOF in Cause #93-2139, Volume 7, pgs. 29–32.

22. Charles Meyer; J. W. Thompson.
23. APD Files: *Interview of Alva Hank Worley*, May 13, 1998; BCSO Files: *Voluntary Statement of [Mark]*, June 25, 1992; *State of Texas v Kenneth Allen McDuff*, SOF in Cause #93-2139, Volume 25, pgs. 28–39; BCSO Files: *Statement of Alva Hank Worley*, 5:45 P.M. and 7:10 P.M., April 20, 1992, and April 21, 1992.
24. *State of Texas v Kenneth Allen McDuff*, SOF in Cause #93-2139, Volume 4, pg. 237; County of Travis: *Sworn Statement of [Kari]*, December 30, 1991; APD Files: *Incident Report*, by Sonya Urubek, July 1, 1992.
25. Ibid.; *State of Texas v Kenneth Allen McDuff*, SOF in Cause #93-2139, Volume 2, pgs. 50–61, Volume 3 pgs. 24–32, Volume 4, pgs. 203–206, Volume 20, pg. 262, Volume 21, pgs. 29, 32, 117–19; County of Travis: *Statement of Michael J. Goins* and *William Ray Goins, Jr.*, December 30, 1991.
26. *State of Texas v Kenneth Allen McDuff*, SOF in Cause #93-2139, Volume 3, pgs. 32–33, Volume 4, pg. 208, Volume 21, pgs. 120–21, Volume 22, pg. 30; County of Travis: *Sworn Statement of William Ray Goins, Jr.*, and *[Kari]*, December 30, 1991.
27. The following account of what happened to Colleen Reed at the hands of Kenneth Allen McDuff and Alva Hank Worley is taken from the many interviews, statements, and sworn testimonies of Alva Hank Worley. He has related the tragedy so many times that thorough footnoting would be heartless and pedantic. Additionally, I have interviewed all of the detectives who interviewed and conducted field trips with Worley in the course of investigating the abduction and murder of Colleen Reed. Throughout his many statements, Worley's accounts of what McDuff did to Colleen are largely consistent, but his candor relative to his own actions and complicity vary significantly. Thus, for the rest of this chapter, my reconstruction of what happened to her is based on the reasonable assumption that Worley's most complete and candid statements are the most accurate. Admittedly, his statements are self-serving, and at times, contradictory. Sadly, what follows is most likely a minimal account of what happened to Colleen Reed.

CHAPTER II

1. *Austin American-Statesman*, January 25, April 26, 1992; Charles Meyer; J.W. Thompson.

2. *Austin American-Statesman*, January 31, 1992; APD Files: *Incident Report*, by Daniel Zahara, December 29, 1991, and by Robert Bohannan and Michael Carpenter, December 30, 1991: *State of Texas v Kenneth Allen McDuff*, SOF in Cause #93-2139, Volume 7, pg. 91, Volume 21, pgs. 229–37, 270–71.

3. APD Files: *Incident Report*, by Robert Bohannan and Daniel Zahara, December 29, 1991 and by Robert Feuerbacher, January 2, 1992; Charles Meyer; J.W. Thompson; *State of Texas v Kenneth Allen McDuff*, SOF in Cause #93-2139, Volume 21, pg. 290; County of Travis: *Sworn Statement of Oliver William Guerra*, December 31, 1991.

4. *State of Texas v Kenneth Allen McDuff*, SOF in Cause #93-2139, Volume 20, pgs. 161–62 and 230–31; Lori Bible.

5. APD Files: *Incident Report*, by Don Martin, January 10, 1992; Lori Bible.

6. Don Martin.

7. Lori Bible; *State of Texas v Kenneth Allen McDuff*, SOF in Cause #93-2139, Volume 30, pg. 71.

8. *State of Texas v Kenneth Allen McDuff*, SOF in Cause #93-2139, Volume 20, pgs. 163–65, and 238–39.

9 APD Files: *Incident Report*, by Robert Feuerbacher, January 2, 1991 and by Donald O. Martin, February 14, 1992; Sonya Urubek.

10. APD Files: *Taped Interview with [Diane]*, May 22, 1992; BCSO Files: *Statement of Alva Hank Worley*, 5:45 P.M., April 20, 1992.

11. BCSO Files: *Statement of [Bess]*, and *Statement of [Jerry]*, May 7, 1992; *State of Texas v Kenneth Allen McDuff*, SOF in Cause #93-2139, Volume 24, pgs. 100, 107, Volume 25, pgs. 230, 234–35, 266–67, 280.

12. APD Files: *Incident Report*, by Sonya Urubek, June 22, 1992.

13. MCSO Files: *Statement of [Keith]*, u.d.

14. County of McLennan: *Complaint*, by Richard Stroup, May 5, 1992; Tarrant County Criminal Justice Building, Adult Probation Department, *Probationer Data Sheet*, Valencia Kay Joshua, August 29, 1991.

15 BCSO Files: *Voluntary Statement of [Debra]*, June 23, 1992; APD Files: *Sworn Statement of [Billy]*, May 21, 1992.

16 Texas DPS: *Report of Investigation*, by John Aycock, March 6, and 10, 1992; County of Bell: *Voluntary Statement*, by

David Jarveis, March 9, 1992 and William E. Llewellyn, March 10, 1992.

17. BCSO Files: *Goodyear Auto Service Center Receipt*, February 28, 1992.

18. MCDA Files: *Statement of [Wayne]* and *Statement of [Jim]*, December 9, 1992; MCSO Files: *Continuation Report*, by Richard Stroup, May 15, 1992; *State of Texas v Kenneth Allen McDuff*, SOF in Cause #643820, Volume 2, pgs. 170–78.

19. *State of Texas v Kenneth Allen McDuff*, SOF in Cause #93-2139, Volume 3, pgs. 190, 234.

20. Confidential Document.

21. BCSO Files: *Statement of [Holly]*, May 18, 1992; APD Files: *Voluntary Statement of [Bruce]*, June 2, 1992, *Interview of [Holly]*, May 21, 1992; *State of Texas v Kenneth Allen McDuff*, SOF in Cause #643820, Volume 3, pgs. 75–82, 100,159–60.

22. Ibid.; BSCO Files: *Voluntary Statement of [Nancy]*, June 3, 1992, *Supplement Report*, by Tim Steglich, March 3, 1992; APD Files: *Interview of [Holly]*, May 21, 1992, *Incident Report*, by J.W. Thompson, June 6, 1992.

23. BCSO Files: *Statement of [Holly]*, May 18, 1992; APD Files: *Voluntary Statement of [Bruce]*, June 2, 1992, *Interview of [Holly]*, May 21, 1992; *State of Texas v Kenneth Allen McDuff*, SOF in Cause #643820, Volume 3, pg. 82, 142.

24. Ibid.; APD Files: *Taped Interview with [Holly]*, May 21, 1992; BCSO Files: *Supplement Report*, by Tim Steglich, March 3, 1992; *State of Texas v Kenneth Allen McDuff*, SOF in Cause #643820, Volume 3, pg. 142–46.

25. *State of Texas v Kenneth Allen McDuff*, SOF in Cause #643820, Volume 1, pgs. 79–80, 114–15, 156–59, 185, 187–88, 191–94, and SOF in Cause # 93-2139, Volume 29, pg. 163; Texas DPS Files: *Report of Investigation*, by James Ray, March 9, 1992; Brenda Solomon; Richard Solomon.

26. MCSO Files: *Continuation Report*, by Bobby R. Hunt, March 1, 1992; *State of Texas v Kenneth Allen McDuff*, SOF in Cause #643820, Volume 1, pgs. 212–13, 226 and in Cause #93-2139, pg. 183.

CHAPTER 12

1. *State of Texas v Kenneth Allen McDuff*, SOF in Cause #643820, Volume 7, pg. 183, and Volume 9, pg. 48; TDCJ

Files: *Kenneth Allen McDuff, Synopsis*, compiled by John Moriarty, pg. 23; Confidential Documents.

2. *State of Texas v Kenneth Allen McDuff*, SOF in Cause #643820, Volume 1, pgs. 12–13, and in Cause #93-2139, Volume 29, pg. 168; Richard Stroup.

3. Aaron Northrup testified under oath that he slept in the living room of his father's house that night and could see the clock on the VCR. Thus, he is fairly certain about the times. Even so, I consider the times that follow a very good estimate, and more valuable in establishing a sequence of events. MCSO Files: *Statement of Aaron Northrup*, March 10, 1992; *State of Texas v Kenneth Allen McDuff*, SOF in Cause #643820, Volume 1, pg. 83, 161–63, and in Cause #93-2139, Volume 29, pgs. 170–73; Brenda Solomon; Richard Solomon.

4. FBI Files: Untitled reports filed by Special Agents Freddie Vela and James P. Fossum, March 27 and 30, 1992; MCSO Files: *Statement of Richard Bannister*, March 9, 1992; *State of Texas v Kenneth Allen McDuff*, SOF in Cause #93-2139, Volume 22, pgs. 112–18 and in Cause #643820, Volume 3, pgs. 203–206.

5. Ibid.

6. MCSO Files: *Statement of Louis Bailey*, March 13, 1992.

7. Ibid.; MCSO Files: *Continuation Report*, by Bobby R. Hunt, March 1, 1992.

8. *State of Texas v Kenneth Allen McDuff*, SOF in Cause #93-2139, Volume 29, pg. 148; Brenda Solomon.

9. *State of Texas v Kenneth Allen McDuff*, SOF in Cause #93-2139, Volume 29, pgs. 183 and 212 and in Cause #643820, Volume 3, pgs. 233–42; Crawford Long and Mike Freeman, interviewed by the author on June 13, 1998.

10. *State of Texas v Kenneth Allen McDuff*, SOF in Cause #643820, Volume 1, pgs. 119, 130, and 215; Richard Stroup; MCSO Files: *Continuation Report*, by Bobby R. Hunt, March 1, 1992, and Ronnie Turnbough, May 7, 1992; MCDA Files: *Statement of [Quik Pak Employee]*, u.d.

11. Of course, only Kenneth McDuff knew exactly what happened that night. He never gave a statement or testimony implicating himself. Given the evidence, timelines, and circumstantial evidence, I consider the following description of the murder of Melissa Northrup to be the best possible reconstruction.

12. Dallas County Sheriff's Department Files: *Offense/Incident Report*, by A. Jesttes, u.d., and *Supplementary Investigation Report, #92-06527*, April 30, 1992; *State of Texas v Kenneth Allen McDuff*, SOF in Cause #643820, Volume 8, pgs. 33, 36, 40–41; County of Dallas, *Affidavit*, by Pepper Cole, u.d.

13. *State of Texas v Kenneth Allen McDuff*, SOF in Cause #643820, Volume 5, pgs. 53–57 and 67–69; Crawford Long; Mike Freeman.

14. Richard Stroup; Texas DPS Files: *Report of Investigation*, by Clayton Smith, March 16, 1992; MCSO Files: *Continuation Report*, by Bobby R. Hunt, March 1, 1992, and Richard Stroup, March 19, 1992.

15. Richard Stroup.

16. Ibid.; MCSO Files: *Continuation Report*, by Richard Stroup, March 19, 1992.

17. BCSO Files: *Missing Person's Report*, by Ralph Howell, March 3, 1992.

18. Tim Steglich; Charles Meyer.

19. Tim Steglich; BCSO Files: *Supplement Report*, by Tim Steglich, March 3, 1992; TDCJ Files: *Kenneth Allen McDuff, Synopsis*, compiled by John Moriarty, pg. 24.

20. Ibid.

21. MCSO: *Continuation Report*, by Larry Abner, March 9, 1992; Richard Stroup; Tim Steglich; *State of Texas v Kenneth Allen McDuff*, SOF in Cause #93-2139, Volume 3, pgs. 88–90, 132–35, Volume 22, pgs. 128, 130, 137–44 and in Cause #643820, pg. 185.

22. *State of Texas v Kenneth Allen McDuff*, SOF in Cause #93-2139, Volume 1, pg. 236, Volume 3, pgs. 135–39, 178, Volume 4, pgs. 5–12, Volume 22, pgs. 106–108, 146.

23. Dallas County Sheriff's Department Files: *Offense/Incident Report*, by Aletha Jesttes, March 6, 1992; *State of Texas v Kenneth Allen McDuff*, SOF in Cause #93-2139, Volume 2, pgs. 53–58, Volume 30, pgs. 7, and 10, and in Cause #643820, Volume 2, pgs. 18, 20, 83–84, and 120–25.

24. *State of Texas v Kenneth Allen McDuff*, SOF in Cause #643820, Volume 2, pg. 89.

25. Parnell McNamara; Mike McNamara.

CHAPTER 13

1. *Texas Monthly*, March, 1998.

2. *Texas Monthly*, August, 1992.

3. Ibid.
4. Parnell McNamara; Mike McNamara; *Marlin Daily Democrat*, November 7, 1966.
5. Bill Johnston; Mike McNamara; Parnell McNamara; Confidential Documents.
6. FBI Files: Untitled report of Special Agents James P. Fossum and Freddie Vela, March 27 and 30, 1992; Texas DPS Files: *Report of Investigation*, by James E. Ray, Sr., March 9, 1992; Richard Stroup.
7. *Waco Tribune-Herald*, May 7, 1992; Crawford Long; Mike Freeman.
8. Bill Johnston.
9. Ibid.; United States District Court, Western District, Waco Division, *United States v. Kenneth Allen McDuff*, Warrant for Arrest, March 6, 1992 and Grand Jury Criminal Complaint, March 9, and 10, 1992; Confidential Document.
10. *State of Texas v Kenneth Allen McDuff*, SOF in Cause #93-2139, Volume 4, pg. 45, and Defendant's Pre-Trial Exhibit #13.
11. BCSO Files: *Supplement Report*, by Tim Steglich, dated March 3, 1992; Tim Steglich; Bill Miller.
12. Texas DPS Files: *Report of Investigation*, by John Aycock, March 6, 1992; BCSO Files: *List of Items Found in Kenneth McDuff's Briefcase*, u.d.
13. Mike McNamara; Parnell McNamara; Bill Johnston; Confidential Documents.
14. Ibid.
15. BCSO Files: *Supplement Report*, by Tim Steglich, dated March 3, 1992; Tim Steglich; Texas DPS Files: *Report of Investigation*, by John Aycock, March 10, 1992.
16. Ibid.
17. APD Files: Unidentified document prepared by Andrew Kahan, u.d.
18. *State of Texas v Kenneth Allen McDuff*, SOF in Cause #93-2139, Volume 20, pgs. 168, 181, 201–202, 233–34; APD Files: *Incident Reports*, by Donald O. Martin, December 30, 1991 and February 13, 1992, and Darrell Boydston, February 27, 1992, *Interview with Alva Hank Worley*, May 13, 1992; *Austin American-Statesman*, January 1, and January 13, 1992.
19. *State of Texas v Kenneth Allen McDuff*, SOF in Cause #93-2139, Volume 20, pgs. 168–71; APD Files: *Incident Reports*,

by Donald O. Martin, February 6, March 7, 19, 31, 1992.

20. Sonya Urubek; Don Martin; *State of Texas v Kenneth Allen McDuff*, SOF in Cause #93-2139, Volume 22, pg. 212.

21. Sonya Urubek; Lori Bible.

22. Don Martin.

23. *State of Texas v Kenneth Allen McDuff*, SOF in Cause #93-2139, Supp., pgs. 25–27.

24. *State of Texas v Kenneth Allen McDuff*, SOF in Cause #93-2139, Volume 3, pgs. 166–69, 178, 198–200, Volume 4, pgs. 54, 57, 61, Volume 5, pgs. 7, and 19–22.

25. *State of Texas v Kenneth Allen McDuff*, SOF in Cause #93-2139, Volume 4, pgs. 68, 84–85, and 88–89 and Volume 22, pg. 222; Don Martin.

26. APD Files: *Incident Report*, by Donald O. Martin, March 16, 1992; *State of Texas v Kenneth Allen McDuff*, SOF in Cause #93-2139, Volume 4, pg. 90.

27. BCSO Files: Taped conversation with Addie McDuff, u.d.; Tim Steglich.

28. Bill Miller; Tim Steglich.

CHAPTER 14

1. *State of Texas v Kenneth Allen McDuff*, SOF in Cause #93-2139, Volume 20, pg. 172, and Volume 22, pgs. 189, 201, 252; APD Files: *Incident Reports*, by Eleuterio Lean, January 8, by Donald O. Martin, January 7, 10, 23, and February 29, 1992.

2. Charles Meyer; TDCJ Files: *Kenneth Allen McDuff, Synopsis*, compiled by John Moriarty, u.d.

3. TDCJ Files: *Kenneth Allen McDuff, Synopsis*, compiled by John Moriarty, u.d.; *State of Texas v Kenneth Allen McDuff*, SOF in Cause #93-2139, Volume 26, pgs. 79–80, 89, 97, and 99–102, and in Cause #643820, pgs. 30–33, and 37; ATF Files: *Report of Interview*, by Robert Stumpenhaus, May 20, 1992; *Austin American-Statesman*, May 6, 1992; MCDA Files: Letter from Aubrey German to George Foster, December 17, 1992.

4. MCDA Files: Letter from Aubrey German to George Foster, December 17, 1992; *Austin American-Statesman*, May 6, 1992; *Waco Tribune-Herald*, May 6, 1992.

5. APD Files: *Incident Report*, by J. W. Thompson, June 3, 1992; *Austin American-Statesman*, May 5, and 6, 1992.

6. APD Files: *Incident Report*, by J. W. Thompson, June 6, 1992.

7. BCSO Files: *Supplement Report*, by Tim Steglich, dated March 3, 1992; Confidential Document.

8. Ibid.

9. Parnell McNamara; Bill Johnston.

10. Mike McNamara; Parnell McNamara.

11. Confidential Document; Tim Steglich; John Moriarty.

12. Parnell McNamara; Tim Steglich; Confidential Document.

13. Mike McNamara; Parnell McNamara; Confidential Documents.

14. BCSO Files: *Supplement Report*, by Tim Steglich, dated March 3, 1992; Confidential Documents; Texas DPS Files: *Report of Investigation*, by John Aycock, March 10, 1992.

15. Ibid.

16. Bill Johnston; Mike McNamara; Wayne Appelt; Parnell McNamara.

17. Ibid.

18. Mike McNamara; Parnell McNamara; Bill Johnston; Tim Steglich; Wayne Appelt.

19. Don Owens, in a conversation with the author on August 3, 1998; Ibid.; Confidential Documents; BCSO Files: *Supplement Report*, by Tim Steglich, dated March 3, 1992.

20. Mike McNamara; Parnell McNamara; Bill Johnston; Tim Steglich; Wayne Appelt; Don Owens; Confidential Documents; BCSO Files: *Supplement Report*, by Tim Steglich, dated March 3, 1992.

21. Mike McNamara; Parnell McNamara; Bill Johnston.

22. Texas DPS Files: *Report of Investigation*, by John Aycock, March 23, 1992.

23. Confidential Document.

24. Confidential Documents; BCSO Files: *Supplement Report*, by Tim Steglich, dated March 3, 1992; Mike McNamara; Parnell McNamara; Bill Johnston; Tim Steglich.

25. Ibid.

CHAPTER 15

1. *State of Texas v Kenneth Allen McDuff*, SOF in Cause #93-2139, Volume 29, pg. 50.

2. *Austin American-Statesman*, May 7, 1992.

3. Charles Meyer; Wayne Appelt.

4. Hank later testified that Mike, Parnell and Bill showed him pictures of dead bodies, presumably pictures of the teenagers McDuff killed as a result of the Broomstick Murders, but The Boys deny ever doing that; Wayne Appelt; Tim Steglich; Mike McNamara; Parnell McNamara; Bill Johnston; Confidential Documents; BCSO Files: *Supplement Report*, by Tim Steglich, dated March 3, 1992.

5. Wayne Appelt; Mike McNamara; Parnell McNamara; Bill Johnston; Confidential Documents.

6. Ibid.

7. Ibid.

8. Mike McNamara; Parnell McNamara; Bill Johnston; Tim Steglich; Confidential Documents; BCSO Files: *Supplement Report*, by Tim Steglich, dated March 3, 1992.

9. Ibid.

10. Wayne Appelt; Mike McNamara; Parnell McNamara; Bill Johnston; Confidential Documents.

11. Mike McNamara; Parnell McNamara; Confidential Documents.

12. APD Files: *Incident Report*, by Sonya Urubek, April 4, 1992.

13. APD Files: *Incident Report*, by Donald O. Martin, March 16, 1992.

14. APD Files: *Incident Report*, by Sonya Urubek, March 20, 1992. (This date is certainly incorrect; Jackie Pierce was arrested on March 21.)

15. APD Files: *Incident Report*, by Donald O. Martin, March 27, 1992.

16. Mike McNamara; Parnell McNamara; Confidential Documents.

17. Wayne Appelt; Charles Meyer.

18. Mike McNamara; Parnell McNamara; Bill Johnston; Confidential Documents.

19. Mike McNamara; Parnell McNamara.

20. MCSO Files: *Offense Report*, by Larry Abraham, March 27, 1992, and *Complaint/Witness Data Sheet*, March 25, 1992; *State of Texas v Kenneth Allen McDuff*, SOF in Cause #0935281, Volume IA-C, pgs. 809–20.

21. Ibid., and *Continuation Report*, by Richard Stroup, April 14, 1992.

22. Bill Johnston.

CHAPTER 16

1. APD Files: *Incident Report*, by Donald O. Martin, April 8, 1992; BCSO Files: *Supplement Report*, dated March 3, 1992.
2. Tim Steglich.
3. Ibid.; BCSO Files: *Supplement Report*, by Tim Steglich, dated March 3, 1992.
4. BCSO Files: *Statement of Alva Hank Worley*, April 8, 1992, and *Supplement Report*, by Tim Steglich, dated March 3, 1992.
5. APD Files: *Incident Report*, by Donald O. Martin, April 27, 1992; Tim Steglich; BCSO Files: *Supplement Report*, by Tim Steglich, dated March 3, 1992.
6. When I met Mr. Aycock I suggested that I would like to return for an interview for more complete descriptions of his investigations. I explained that official reports often lack detail and emotion. He answered that his reports were complete and detailed. He was absolutely right.
7. Texas DPS Files: *Report of Investigation*, by John Aycock, April 18, 1992.
8. Dan Stoltz; Mike McNamara; Parnell McNamara; *Austin American-Statesman*, April 30 and May 2, 1992; *Waco Tribune-Herald*, April 16, 1992.
9. Dan Stoltz; Mike McNamara; Parnell McNamara.
10. Mike McNamara; Parnell McNamara.
11. *Austin American-Statesman*, May 5, 1992.
12. Mike Carnevale died in June, 1993.
13. Mike McNamara; Parnell McNamara; Tim Steglich; Don Owens; Confidential Documents.
14. Confidential Documents.
15. Confidential Documents. Gary Jackson declined to be interviewed for this book.
16. ATF Files: *Affidavit by [McDuff nephew]*, April 8, 1992; United States District Court, Western District of Texas, *United States of America v Kenneth Allen McDuff, Warrant for Arrest*, #w-92-CR-058, April 14, 1992; MCDA Files: *Voluntary Statement of [McDuff sister]*, April 4, 1992; Dan Stoltz.
17. BCSO Files: *Supplement Report*, by Tim Steglich, dated March 3, 1992; Tim Steglich.
18. Mike McNamara; Parnell McNamara; Bill Johnston; Confidential Documents.

19. Confidential Source.
20. APD Files: *Taped interview with [Diane]*, May 22, 1992; Dan Stoltz.
21. Parnell McNamara; Dan Stoltz.
22. Ibid.; BCSO Files: *Statement of [Jerry]*, May 7, 1992; *State of Texas v Kenneth Allen McDuff*, SOF in Cause #93-2139, Volume 24, pgs. 103–104, and Volume 25, pgs. 268–77.
23. BCSO Files: *Statement of Alva Hank Worley*, 5:45 P.M., April 20, 1992; Parnell McNamara.
24. *State of Texas v Kenneth Allen McDuff*, SOF in Cause #93-2139, Volume 25, pgs. 75, 239.
25. Tim Steglich; BCSO Files: *Supplement Report*, by Tim Steglich, dated March 3, 1992; *State of Texas v Kenneth Allen McDuff*, SOF in Cause #93-2139, Volume 25, pgs. 295–96 and Volume 26, pg. 8.

CHAPTER 17

1. Tim candidly told me that he was more upset two days later with the details of Hank's statement than when he took it from Hank. For years, the sadness and horror of child abuse cases had hardened Tim. It bothers him that he did not get outraged or upset at the time of the statement. Tim Steglich; BCSO Files: *Supplement Report*, by Tim Steglich, dated March 3, 1992; *State of Texas v Kenneth Allen McDuff*, SOF in Cause #93-2139, Volume 25, pgs. 295–96.
2. Don Martin; J. W. Thompson; APD Files: *Incident Reports*, by Donald O. Martin, April 27, 1992, and J. W. Thompson, May 6, 1992. In my interview with him, Don indicated that he thought about calling J. W. instead of Sonya because he and J. W. had just been to Waco to work on the case.
3. Ibid.; Tim Steglich; BCSO Files: *Supplement Report*, by Tim Steglich, dated March 3, 1992.
4. Don Martin; J. W. Thompson; APD Files: *Incident Reports*, by Donald O. Martin, April 27, 1992, and J. W. Thompson, May 6, 1992 and January 14, 1993; *State of Texas v Kenneth Allen McDuff*, SOF in Cause #93-2139, Volume 26, pgs. 129–30, and 182; *Austin American-Statesman*, April 9 and June 11, 1992.
5. Don Martin; Charles Meyer; Tim Steglich; Bill Johnston; J. W. Thompson; APD Files: *Incident Report*, by Donald O. Martin, January 14, 1993, and J. W. Thompson, January 14,

1993; *State of Texas v Kenneth Allen McDuff,* SOF in Cause #93-2139, Volume 25, pg. 126 and Volume 26, pgs.132 and 170.

6. Charles Meyer; Tim Steglich; Bill Johnston; Mike McNamara; Parnell McNamara; J. W. Thompson; APD Files: *Incident Report,* by J. W. Thompson, May 6, 1992; BCSO Files: *Supplement Report,* by Tim Steglich, dated March 3, 1992.

7. BCSO Files: *Supplement Report,* by Tim Steglich, dated March 3, 1992 and *Permission to Search,* April 21, 1992; APD Files: *Incident Report,* by Donald O. Martin, April 27, 1992.

8. BCSO Files: *Supplement Report,* by Tim Steglich, dated March 3, 1992; APD Files: *Incident Report,* by Donald O. Martin, April 27, 1992.

9. BCSO Files: *Supplement Report,* by Tim Steglich, dated March 3, 1992.

10. Ibid.

11. APD Files: *Incident Report,* by J. W. Thompson, May 6, 1992; Alan Sanderson, interviewed by the author on June 18, 1998; APD Files: *Interview of Alva Hank Worley,* May 13, 1992; *State of Texas v Kenneth Allen McDuff,* SOF in Cause #93-2139, Volume 25, pgs. 53 and 176.

12. Tim Steglich.

13. J. W. Thompson.

14. Charles Meyer.

15. Tim Steglich.

16. Don Martin; Chuck Meyer; J. W. Thompson; APD Files: *Incident Report,* by Donald O. Martin, April 27, 1992 and J. W. Thompson, May 6, 1992.

17. Ibid.; Buddy Meyer and David Counts, interviewed by the author on June 18, 1998.

18. Ibid.

19. Lori Bible; Don Martin.

20. Lori Bible.

21. Don Martin; J. W. Thompson; Charles Meyer; APD Files: *Incident Report,* by J. W. Thompson, May 6, 1992.

22. Lori Bible.

23. *Austin American-Statesman,* April 23, 24, and May 5, 1992; *Waco Herald-Tribune,* April 29, 1992.

24. *Austin American-Statesman*, April 23, 1992; *Rosebud News*, May 7, 1992.

25. *Austin American-Statesman*, May 1, 1992.

26. Ibid., April 30, and June 25, 1992.

27. Ibid., March 10, 1993.

28. *Austin American-Statesman*, April 27, 1992.

29. *State of Texas v Kenneth Allen McDuff*, SOF in Cause #93-2139, Volume 30, pg. 25, and in Cause #643820, Volume 2, pg. 11, and Volume 5, pgs. 84–89; MCSO Files: *Continuation Report*, by Richard Stroup, April 30, 1992; Dallas County Sheriff's Department Files: *Supplementary Investigation Report*, #92-06527, April 30, 1992.

30. *State of Texas v Kenneth Allen McDuff*, SOF in Cause #935281, Volume 1A-C, pgs. 824-29, and in Cause #643820, Volume 2, pg. 104; MCSO Files: *Continuation Report*, by Richard Stroup, April 30, 1992; Dallas County Sheriff's Department Files: *Offense Report*, by R. Jacks, u.d.

31. *State of Texas v Kenneth Allen McDuff*, SOF in Cause #643820, Volume 5, pgs. 103–108 and 118.

32. Dallas County Office of the Medical Examiner Files: *Medical Investigation Report* and *Supplemental Investigation Report*, Case #1254-92-0799JG, u.d.; *Waco Tribune-Herald*, April 27, 1992.

33. Brenda Solomon.

CHAPTER 18

1. Mike McNamara; Parnell McNamara; Bill Johnston.

2. Confidential Documents; Ibid.

3. Ibid.

4. Mike McNamara.

5. Confidential Sources; Confidential Documents; *Texas Monthly*, November, 1998.

6. Ibid.; Mike McNamara.

7. WPD Files: *Offense Reports*, by Mike Nicoletti, July 9, 1992, and by Officer Bradley, May 8, 1992.

8. WPD Files: *Offense Reports*, by Mike Nicoletti, July 9, 1992.

9. Ibid.

10. Ibid., July 14, 1992.

11. Ibid.

12. APD Files: *Incident Report*, by Sonya Urubek, August 8, 1992; Sonya Urubek.

13. APD Files: *Incident Report*, by Donald O. Martin, February 10, and 29, 1992; *State of Texas v Kenneth Allen McDuff*, SOF in Cause #93-2139, Volume 2, pgs. 5–18, Volume 4, pgs. 94–101, and Volume 22, pg. 230.

14. APD Files: *Incident Report*, by Dan Zahara, April 25, 1992, and by Sonya Urubek, May 5, 1992; *State of Texas v Kenneth Allen McDuff*, SOF in Cause #93-2139, Volume 21, pg. 299.

15. *Austin American-Statesman*, April 30, 1992; APD Files: *Incident Report*, by Donald O. Martin, May 5, 1992.

16. KCPD Files: *Report and Continuation Report*, by James D. Johnson, May 4, 1992, and by Alice Dearing, May 4, 1992; BCSO Files: *Supplement Report*, by Tim Steglich, dated March 3, 1992.

17. *State of Texas v Kenneth Allen McDuff*, SOF in Cause #93-2139, Volume 26, pgs. 107–108 and in Cause #643820, Volume 4, pgs. 42–44; KCPD Files: *Report and Continuation Report*, by Thomas A. Brown, May 4, 1992.

18. *State of Texas v Kenneth Allen McDuff*, SOF in Cause #93-2139, Volume 26, pgs. 94 and 110.

19. Unidentified newspaper clipping provided by Bill Johnston; *Waco Tribune-Herald*, May 5, 1992; BCSO Files: *Supplement Report*, by Tim Steglich, dated March 3, 1992.

20. *Austin American-Statesman*, May 5, and 6, 1992.

21. J. W. Thompson; Charles Meyer; Parnell McNamara; *State of Texas v Kenneth Allen McDuff*, SOF in Cause #93-2139, Volume 26, pg. 144.

22. J. W. Thompson; Charles Meyer; Parnell McNamara; APD Files: *Incident Report*, by J. W. Thompson, May 7, 1992.

23. Ibid.

24. J. W. Thompson; Charles Meyer; APD Files: *Incident Report*, by J. W. Thompson, May 7, 1992.

25. APD Files: *Incident Report*, by J.W. Thompson, June 6, 1992; Charles Meyer; J. W. Thompson; Parnell McNamara.

26. APD Files: *Incident Report*, by J. W. Thompson, May 7 and June 3, 1992; Charles Meyer; APD Files: *Sworn Statement of [Francis]*, May 6, 1992.

27. APD Files: *Incident Report*, by Donald O. Martin, May 7, 1992; *Austin American-Statesman*, May 6, 1992.

28. *State of Texas v Kenneth Allen McDuff*, SOF in Cause #93-2139, Volume 4, pg. 30.

29. *Austin American-Statesman*, May 7, 1992; *Waco Tribune-Herald*, May 7, 1992.

30. *Austin American-Statesman*, May 7 and 8, 1992.

31. APD Files: *Incident Report*, by Scott James Cary, July 4, 1992; *State of Texas v Kenneth Allen McDuff*, SOF in Cause #93-2139, Volume 4, pgs. 254–59.

32. *State of Texas v Kenneth Allen McDuff*, SOF in Cause #93-2139, Volume 4, pgs. 101–08, 256–59, and in Volume 22, pgs. 237–41; APD Files: County of Travis, *Sworn Statement of Michael Goins*, June 5, 1992, *Incident Reports*, by Sonya Urubek, June 27, 1992, and Scott James Cary, July 4, 1992.

CHAPTER 19

1. APD Files: *Incident Report*, by Sonya Urubek, June 22, 1992; J. W. Thompson.

2. *Austin American-Statesman*, June 28, 1992 and May 16, 1993; Kenneth Allen McDuff.

3. Ibid., June 27 and July 11, 1992.

4. Kenneth Allen McDuff.

5. *Austin American-Statesman*, July 7, 1992.

6. Ibid., September 16, 1992.

7. Crawford Long; Mike Freeman.

8. John Segrest. Mr. Segrest was not available for an interview, but agreed to provide written answers to my questions. They are hereafter cited by name only; Ibid.

9. Crawford Long.

10. Mike Freeman.

11. Crawford Long; Mike Freeman.

12. Ibid.; *State of Texas v Kenneth Allen McDuff*, SOF in Cause #643820, Volume 1, pg. 3, Volume 2, pg. 178 and Volume 9, page 47; *Austin American-Statesman*, January 11, 1993.

13. Texas Court of Criminal Appeals, *Kenneth Allen McDuff v Texas*, #71,700, delivered January 29, 1998; John Segrest; Crawford Long; Mike Freeman; *Austin American-Statesman*, February 6, 1993.

14. John Moriarty; Tim Steglich; BCSO Files: *McDuff Tapes*, and *Supplement Report*, by Tim Steglich, dated March 3, 1992.

15. *State of Texas v Kenneth Allen McDuff*, SOF in Cause #643820, Volume 2, pgs. 161–63.

16. Ibid., Volume 3, pgs. 157–61; Crawford Long; Mike Free-

man; Tim Steglich; BCSO Files: *Supplement Report*, by Tim Steglich, dated March 3, 1992.

17. Crawford Long; Mike Freeman; *Waco Tribune-Herald*, February 3, 1993.

18. *State of Texas v Kenneth Allen McDuff*, SOF in Cause #643820, Volume 7, pgs. 40–63; *Austin American-Statesman*, February 11, 1993.

19. *State of Texas v Kenneth Allen McDuff*, SOF in Cause #643820, Volume 7, pg. 65; *Austin American-Statesman*, February 11, 1993.

20. *State of Texas v Kenneth Allen McDuff*, SOF in Cause #643820, Volume 3, pg. 70; Crawford Long; Mike Freeman.

21. Crawford Long; Mike Freeman; *State of Texas v Kenneth Allen McDuff*, SOF in Cause #643820, Volume 5, pg. 73.

22. *State of Texas v Kenneth Allen McDuff*, SOF in Cause #643820, Volume 5, pgs. 185–224, and Volume 6, pgs. 11–31; Crawford Long; Mike Freeman.

23. *State of Texas v Kenneth Allen McDuff*, SOF in Cause #643820, Volume 9, pgs. 29–33; Crawford Long; Mike Freeman.

24. *State of Texas v Kenneth Allen McDuff*, SOF in Cause #643820, Volume 9, pgs. 48–112; John Segrest; *Austin American-Statesman*, February 16, 1993.

25. *Waco Tribune-Herald*, February 13, 1993; *Austin American-Statesman*, February 13, 1993.

26. *Austin American-Statesman*, February 13, 1993.

27. *State of Texas v Kenneth Allen McDuff*, SOF in Cause #643820, Closing argument by Crawford Long, pgs. 20–35.

28. *State of Texas v Kenneth Allen McDuff*, SOF in Cause #643820, Closing arguments by Mr. Goains and Mr. Reaves, pgs. 56–78 and 106–29.

29. *State of Texas v Kenneth Allen McDuff*, SOF in Cause #643820, Closing arguments by Mr. Segrest, pgs. 130–62; Crawford Long; Mike Freeman.

30. *Waco Tribune-Herald*, February 17, 1993.

31. Ibid., February 19, 1993; *Austin American-Statesman*, February 19, 1993; John Segrest.

32. *Austin American-Statesman*, February 18, 19 and 22, 1993.

CHAPTER 20

1. David Counts; Buddy Meyer; *Austin American-Statesman*, July 7, 1992.

2. David Counts.

3. David Counts; Buddy Meyer; Alan Sanderson.

4. Ibid.; *Austin American-Statesman*, April 24, 1993.

5. Texas Court of Criminal Appeals, *State of Texas v Kenneth Allen McDuff*, #71,700, delivered January 29, 1998.

6. *State of Texas v Kenneth Allen McDuff*, SOF in Cause #93-2139, Volume 1A-C, pgs. 783–86.

7. *State of Texas v Kenneth Allen McDuff*, SOF in Cause #93-2139, Volume 1A-C, pgs. 221–34 and 783–86; *Austin American-Statesman*, April 24, August 12 and September 11, 1993; Buddy Meyer; David Counts.

8. David Counts; Buddy Meyer.

9. *State of Texas v Kenneth Allen McDuff*, SOF in Cause #93-2139, Volume 6, pg. 122.

10. *State of Texas v Kenneth Allen McDuff*, SOF in Cause #93-2139, Volume 2, pgs. 23–26, and Volume 3, pgs. 110–22.

11. *State of Texas v Kenneth Allen McDuff*, SOF in Cause #93-2139, Volume 4, pgs. 5–6, 119, 130–38, and Volume 6, pgs. 122 and 139; Don Martin; *Austin American-Statesman*, August 13, 1993.

12. *State of Texas v Kenneth Allen McDuff*, SOF in Cause #93-2139, Volume 7, pgs. 4–13.

13. Ibid., Volume 8, pgs. 142 and 149.

14. David Counts; Buddy Meyer.

15. David Counts; Tim Steglich.

16. Ibid.; *State of Texas v Kenneth Allen McDuff*, SOF in Cause #93-2139, Volume 20, pg. 131.

17. *State of Texas v Kenneth Allen McDuff*, SOF in Cause #93-2139, Volume 20, pgs. 64–67.

18. Ibid., Volume 22, pg. 55.

19. *Austin American-Statesman*, January 21 and February 17, 1994.

20. *State of Texas v Kenneth Allen McDuff*, SOF in Cause #93-2139, Volume 23, pgs. 161, 171, and 254, and Volume 24, pgs. 10–11.

21. Ibid., Volume 25, pgs. 4–6, 120, 131, and 210; Mr. Gunter made much of selected quotes from tape-recorded interviews of Alva Hank Worley. On one occasion, an APD Sergeant said, "We are going to take care of you, Hank." The officer was almost certainly talking about Hank's comfort. Within days of the quote in question, on May 13, 1992, J. W.

Thompson said to Hank, "Hank, we've never said what kind of sentence you were gonna get and we never said we'd try to get you anything. The only thing we ever promised you was that we would tell the judge that you cooperated with us." APD Files: *Taped Interview with Alva Hank Worley*, May 13, 1992; *Austin American-Statesman*, February 18, 1994.

22. *Austin American-Statesman*, February 19, 1994; *State of Texas v Kenneth Allen McDuff*, SOF in Cause #93-2139, Volume 26, pgs. 230–31.

23. *State of Texas v Kenneth Allen McDuff*, SOF in Cause #93-2139, Volume 26, pgs. 55–66; *Austin American-Statesman*, February 19, 1994.

24. *State of Texas v Kenneth Allen McDuff*, SOF in Cause #93-2139, Volume 28, pgs. 101–102.

25. *Austin American-Statesman*, February 24, 1994; *State of Texas v Kenneth Allen McDuff*, SOF in Cause #93-2139, Volume 28, pg. 119.

26. Confidential Source; APD Files: *Incident Report*, by Donald O. Martin, March 17, 1994.

27. David Counts; Buddy Meyer; I had the pleasure of meeting Judge Wil Flowers in April of 1998 after he set McDuff's execution date. He volunteered to me that the one thing he will never forget about the McDuff trial was the testimony of Roy Dale Green during the punishment phase.

28. *State of Texas v Kenneth Allen McDuff*, SOF in Cause #93-2139, Volume 30, pgs. 98–106, and Volume 31, pg. 7.

29. *Austin American-Statesman*, February 19, 1998.

30. Ibid., September 12, 1992, October 18 and November 3, 1993.

31. Ibid., July 10, and 25, 1992; Bill Habern and Gary J. Cohen, *A History of Parole, Mandatory Supervision and Good Time*, Texas Criminal Defense Lawyers' Website, pgs. 3–11.

32. *Austin American-Statesman*, February 1, 1998.

EPILOGUE

1. Numerous media accounts incorrectly reported that Kenneth McDuff had drawn a map or maps to assist in the recovery of victims. The only map ever used was the one Parnell hastily drew and gave to the CI to show McDuff, who could not have touched it while in the cage he had been locked in.

Notes on Sources

In the course of writing this book, I amassed approximately 19,000 pages of information and conducted dozens of interviews. It would be pedantic to list all of the sources of information already cited in the endnotes. This is to describe the largest and richest of those sources.

INTERVIEWS

Much of the content of this book chronicles relatively recent events, so I was able to easily locate and interview virtually all of the major investigators involved in bringing Kenneth Allen McDuff to justice. Investigators I interviewed or conversed with included J. W. Thompson, David Parkinson, Sonya Urubek, and Don Martin of the Austin Police Department; Tim Steglich and Bill Miller of the Bell County Sheriff's Office; Don Owens of the Temple Police Department; Jeff Brzozowski, Wayne Appelt, and Charles Meyer of the Federal Bureau of Alcohol, Tobacco, and Firearms; Truman Simons and Richard Stroup of the McLennan County Sheriff's Office; John Moriarty of the Texas Department of Criminal Justice; John Aycock of the Texas Rangers; and Parnell McNamara, Mike McNamara, and Dan Stoltz of the United States Marshals Service. Prosecutors I interviewed included former Tarrant County Assistant District Attorney Charles Butts (the only surviving member of that prosecution team); Crawford Long and Mike Freeman of McLennan County; Buddy Meyer and former Assistant District Attorney David Counts of Travis County. (David Counts is now Assistant United States Attorney in San Antonio, Texas.) McLennan County District Attorney John Segrest was not available for an interview, but instead responded in writing to questions I faxed to his office. I also interviewed Bill Johnston, Assistant United States Attorney in Waco.

Civilians I interviewed included Lori Bible, sister of Colleen Reed; Brenda Solomon and Richard Solomon, parents of Melissa Northrup; Jack Brand, the father of Robert Brand; and Larry Pamplin, the son of the late Sheriff Brady Pamplin.

Interviews with Wanda Fischer, Ellen Roberts, Martha Royal, and my brief conversation with Martha Kilgore were invaluable in describing life in Rosebud.

I interviewed Kenneth Allen McDuff on September 17, 1996. He essentially repeated his many untrue statements and testimonies asserting his innocence of the crimes for which he was convicted. During that interview, he informed me that another writer from Austin was working on a book and/or motion picture deal with certain members of the McDuff family. (This was confirmed by reliable sources in law enforcement during the week of his execution.) For that reason I decided not to contact the McDuff family. In turn, with the exception of his parents (who involved themselves in the investigation) and his late brother Lonnie, I have not mentioned McDuff's other relatives by name. I have never uncovered any evidence that surviving members of the McDuff family had anything whatever to do with Kenneth's crimes. It is my hope that his family can live in peace.

Finally, as I stated in the Author's Notes, some persons answered certain questions and/or granted interviews on the condition that they not be identified. They are cited as "Confidential Sources." They are all very reliable and knowledgeable. Even so, in almost every instance where this citation was used, I was also able to verify the information using another source.

PRIMARY SOURCES

As a matter of methodology, I depended most heavily on contemporaneous official documents. Police officers take great care with accuracy so as not to have their writings challenged in an open trial. Thus, I favored primary reports over information gathered through interviews.

Trial transcripts in Texas are called *Statements of Facts*. Without question, the statements of facts in the Melissa Northrup Murder Trial, which I cited as Cause #64820, and the Colleen Reed Murder Trial, which I cited as Cause #93-2139, were a gold mine of information. Expert and thorough direct testimony and cross-examination of witnesses under oath provided a complete story of Kenneth McDuff's depraved life and murderous spree from 1989–1992. Exhibits in those trials included sworn statements, pictures, documents, receipts, hair samples, taped interviews, videotapes of locations, and items found at crime scenes. The record is extraordinarily complete, and since much of the information provided by McDuff's associates and other members of the subculture were given under penalty of perjury, it was far more reliable than any interview I could have conducted.

Major sources from police files used in the production of this book included documents from the Bell County Sheriff's Office, the Austin Police Department, Tarrant County Sheriff's Office, the Texas Department of Public Safety, the McLennan County District Attorney's Office, the Waco Police Department, the Federal Bureau of Investigation, the McLennan County Sheriff's Office, and the Texas Department of Criminal Justice. Some of the documentation, especially from agencies not listed, was given to me on the condition that I not cite them in the endnotes. I honored that request, and as with the confidential sources, I was able to verify most of the information from other sources. There are many other sources of lesser importance; they are cited in the endnotes.

SECONDARY SOURCES

One other book has been written about Kenneth Allen McDuff; it is entitled *No Remorse* (Pinnacle, 1996) by Bob Stewart. Ken Anderson's *Crime in Texas* (University of Texas Press, 1998) is a valuable guide to criminal justice in Texas. Excellent sources of information on mass murder and serial killing can be found in the work of James Alan Fox and Jack Levin of Northeastern University in Boston. Specifically, their books *Mass Murder: America's Growing Menace* (Plenum, 1985) and *Overkill: Mass Murder and Serial Killing Exposed* (Dell, 1996), though not comprehensive, nonetheless provide a scholarly approach to the phenomenon of multiple murder.

Newspapers used in my research included: *Austin American-Statesman, Waco Tribune-Herald, Temple Daily Telegram, Fort Worth Star-Telegram, Waco Tribune* (now out of business), *Waco Times-Herald* (now out of business), *Rosebud News*, and *Marlin Daily Democrat.*

Articles in *Texas Monthly* about Kenneth Allen McDuff and The Boys from Waco by Gary Cartwright, and about Texas prisons by Robert Draper, greatly assisted me in pursuing information on those topics.

Index